INEQUALITY: STRUCTURES, DYNAMICS AND MECHANISMS

ESSAYS IN HONOR OF AAGE B. SØRENSEN

RESEARCH IN SOCIAL STRATIFICATION AND MOBILITY

Series Editor: Kevin T. Leicht

Volumes 1–3:	Edited by Donald J. Treiman and Robert V. Robinson
Volumes 4–6:	Edited by Robert V. Robinson
Volumes 7–9:	Edited by Arne L. Kalleberg
Volumes 10–13:	Edited by Robert Althauser and Michael Wallace
Volumes 14 & 15:	Edited by Michael Wallace
Volume 16:	Edited by Kevin T. Leicht
Volume 17:	The Future of Affirmative Action – Edited by Kevin T. Leicht
Volume 18:	Edited by Kevin T. Leicht
Volume 19:	The Future of Market Transition – Edited by Kevin T. Leicht
Volume 20:	Edited by Kevin T. Leicht

RESEARCH IN SOCIAL STRATIFICATION AND MOBILITY VOLUME 21

INEQUALITY: STRUCTURES, DYNAMICS AND MECHANISMS

ESSAYS IN HONOR OF AAGE B. SØRENSEN

EDITED BY

ARNE L. KALLEBERG
University of North Carolina, Department of Sociology, Chapel Hill, NC, USA

STEPHEN L. MORGAN
Cornell University, Department of Sociology, Ithaca, NY, USA

JOHN MYLES
University of Toronto, Department of Sociology, Ontario, Canada

RACHEL A. ROSENFELD
(Deceased)

2004

ELSEVIER
JAI

Amsterdam – Boston – Heidelberg – London – New York – Oxford
Paris – San Diego – San Francisco – Singapore – Sydney – Tokyo

ELSEVIER B.V.
Radarweg 29
P.O. Box 211
1000 AE Amsterdam
The Netherlands

ELSEVIER Inc.
525 B Street, Suite 1900
San Diego
CA 92101-4495
USA

ELSEVIER Ltd
The Boulevard, Langford Lane, Kidlington
Oxford OX5 1GB
UK

ELSEVIER Ltd
84 Theobalds Road
London
WC1X 8RR
UK

First edition 2004

British Library Cataloguing in Publication Data
A catalogue record is available from the British Library.

ISBN: 0-7623-1140-1
ISSN: 0276-5624 (Series)

♾ The paper used in this publication meets the requirements of ANSI/NISO Z39.48-1992 (Permanence of Paper). Printed in The Netherlands.

CONTENTS

MOBILITY AND CAREERS

STRUCTURAL INEQUALITY AND RENTS

AAGE B. SØRENSEN: 1941–2001

Arne L. Kalleberg, Stephen L. Morgan and John Myles

Aage Bøttger Sørensen died on April 18, 2001, in Cambridge, Massachusetts, less than a month before his 60th birthday (May 13). He had been in poor health since February 2000, after falling on the ice near his home in Cambridge. Aage's untimely death saddened deeply his many friends, students and colleagues throughout the world.

Before he died, the four co-editors of this volume decided to honor him with a collection of essays. We are all former students, collaborators and friends of Aage. He knew the project was in the works, and was pleased. Unfortunately, he passed away before this volume was completed. So too did one of our co-editors, Rachel A. Rosenfeld, who died on November 24, 2002, after a courageous, fourteen-year battle with breast cancer.

In this introductory essay, we provide a brief overview of Aage's professional life and his main contributions to our understanding of inequality. Aage was a creative, forceful, and opinionated scholar, and hence an influential intellectual presence who was one of the world's leading authorities on social stratification and the sociology of education. He was productive, having authored or co-authored more than 100 journal articles, book chapters and book reviews, and co-authored or co-edited five books (see Appendix A). We first briefly summarize some main events in Aage's professional life, and then turn to a discussion of the major intellectual strands that characterized his research. The latter will also serve to introduce and connect the eleven chapters of this volume.

Inequality: Structures, Dynamics and Mechanisms: Essays in Honor of Aage B. Sørensen
Research in Social Stratification and Mobility, Volume 21, 1–9

ISSN: 0276-5624/doi:10.1016/S0276-5624(04)21001-0

A SHORT BIOGRAPHY

Aage was born on May 13, 1941, in Silkeborg, Denmark. Although he lived more than half of his life in the United States, he never lost his Danish character, or his Danish accent. He received his master's degree in Sociology in 1967 from the University of Copenhagen, the first Sociology master's degree awarded there. As any student of mobility knows, starting points matter. Aage's first mentor, Kaare Svalastoga, was of course one of the more prominent students of social mobility in the postwar decades. James Coleman then invited him to continue his graduate studies at Johns Hopkins University, where he earned a Ph.D. in Social Relations in 1971. From 1971 to 1984, Aage taught at the University of Wisconsin at Madison, serving as chair of the Sociology Department from 1979 to 1982.

In 1984, he accepted an invitation to join the Sociology Department at Harvard University. As chair of that department for the next eight years, he led a substantial renewal of its faculty and programs. From 1994 until his injury, he chaired Harvard's Joint Doctoral Program in Organizational Behavior, a joint venture between the Sociology Department and the Harvard Business School. At the time of his death, Aage was a Professor of Sociology at Harvard University.

Throughout his academic career, Aage participated actively in European sociology, with extended periods of teaching, study, consulting, and research in Norway, Sweden, and Germany. Among other accomplishments, he was instrumental in restructuring the Institute of Sociology at the University of Copenhagen, and served for many years on the board of the Danish National Science Foundation.

Impressive as his scholarly and administrative contributions to sociology were, Aage also made vital pedagogical contributions to the discipline of Sociology. He was especially active as a teacher at both the University of Wisconsin-Madison and Harvard University, serving as mentor to an unusually large number of graduate students, many of whom currently hold faculty positions at universities throughout the world.

As an advisor, he pushed his students very hard, always challenging them to think better and express themselves more clearly. He held students to high standards, never willing to offer faint praise that is expedient but of little practical use. Since he also thought sociology should be fun, though, Aage's critical comments were usually spiced generously with good humor and exuberant laughter. He enjoyed giving unsolicited advice, insisting that he was "always right" – and he usually was! Because Aage gave so much time to his students, few of them languished in their doctoral studies. In regular meetings, often weekly, he methodically moved them toward completion of their dissertations, demanding chapters at regular intervals.[1] Aage's loyalty to his students did not end with the completion of the dissertation and the first job. He was well aware of the problems of *intragenerational mobility* and continued his mentoring and collaboration throughout their careers. Contrary to established sociological wisdom, we suspect he thought that "sponsored mobility" still mattered, even in the meritocratic U.S. academy. He will be sorely missed by the many that were privileged to work with him.

In the months after his accident, first while he was hospitalized and later while he was at home, crowds of current and former students (as well as colleagues and friends) from around the world wrote and visited Aage, expressing their loyalty, affection, and gratitude. In early April 2001, Aage's accomplishments in graduate education were honored by an "Excellence in Mentoring Award" presented by the Graduate School of Arts and Sciences at Harvard University (a version of the nominating letter for the competition is included as Appendix B of this volume). In his memory, the Department of Sociology at Harvard and the International Sociological Association's Research Committee 28 (Social Stratification and Mobility) have established memorial funds for graduate students. A touching memorial service for Aage was held in University Hall on the Harvard campus on May 12, 2001. Special sessions were also held at the American Sociological Association meetings in 2001 (in Anaheim) and 2002 (in Chicago) at which earlier versions of a number of the papers contained in this volume were presented.

INTELLECTUAL CURRENTS

Aage Sørensen's research sought to understand the structures, dynamics and mechanisms that underlie inequalities in industrial societies. He emphasized inequalities associated with education and schooling, class, and stratification outcomes such as income and occupational status. Within these general foci, he tackled the study of phenomena as diverse as rates of learning in elementary school reading groups and promotion patterns in large industrial corporations.

Aage's research focused on how individuals' attainments are shaped by characteristics of a society's or organization's opportunity structure, on the one hand, and individuals' education, experience and other human capital resources, on the other. In his theoretical and empirical work, he sought to develop formal models that specify how the returns to individual investments are shaped by the characteristics of the opportunity structure. These models took seriously the idea that people engage in purposive action to get ahead, but sought to understand the ways in which the results of such activities depended on social structure. He tried to demonstrate how persons' attainments reflect not only individual resources and effort, but also the opportunities and constraints of the organizational structures within which individuals act. His work made important contributions to our understanding of how individuals' educational, occupational and income achievements are enhanced or constrained by organizational and societal contexts. In this respect he remained ever the sociologist. He read avidly, and greatly admired, the contribution of economists to the questions that concerned him. Nevertheless, he took issue with the "supply-side" bias of conventional economic theory and used his talents to identify theoretically, and to locate empirically, the constraints on opportunity generated on the "demand side" of the economy.

In some of his earliest academic work, Aage showed that a person's educational and occupational achievements depend on the degree of closure in labor markets (i.e. whether individuals are subject to competition in an open market or instead protected from competitors by virtue of membership in a closed system). He demonstrated both theoretically and empirically that the economic payoff to one's education, for example, depends on characteristics of the opportunity structure, and in particular the rate at which opportunities to advance are created. This insight has important implications for judging the conditions under which certain policy interventions (such as seeking to reduce inequality by giving people more education) are likely to be effective. Individuals for whom few labor market opportunities are made available cannot use their educational training to get ahead.

The chapters of this volume address some of the main themes of Aage's research. We have divided these chapters into four main thematic sections and, in the remainder of this introduction, we summarize briefly the major issues related to these areas and the authors' main arguments.

Theoretical and Methodological Perspectives

Aage's research on stratification and inequality stressed the development of explicit dynamic models to account for observed patterns of education, career, and labor market outcomes. He drew upon both sociology and economics to develop a path-breaking set of theoretical concepts, mathematical models, and methodological techniques that he then applied to a wide array of subjects. By elaborating and promoting a foundational set of theoretical concepts, mathematical models, and methodological techniques, he developed new ways to measure and explain a wide array of empirical patterns. The two papers in this section provide an overview of Aage's theoretical and methodological orientations and summarize some of his most important contributions.

Peter Hedstrom's chapter discusses Aage's approach to theoretical explanation, and contrasts it with other views of theory. Aage sought to understand the process through which change occurs, and he represented this process by means of parsimonious mathematical models. He frowned on analysts who used linear regression equations with long lists of independent variables – the dominant approach among stratification researchers then as now – on the grounds that the implicit theories underlying them are implausible. As a result, Aage felt most regression coefficients in the sociological literature are misleading if not entirely meaningless. He felt that analytic focus should be placed on the development of theoretical mechanisms that prove meaningful because they explain the process by which change is brought about.

Aage's theoretical and methodological approaches were inextricably linked, as Trond Petersen's chapter on Aage's contributions to quantitative sociology makes clear. While Aage did not spend much time developing new methodological approaches, he was a sophisticated consumer of them. His most influential quantitative work was grounded in theory, which he specified using simple but explicit mathematical models. He then used quantitative data to estimate the size of the parameters of his mathematical models. A good example of this strategy is his "Model and a Metric for the Process of Status Attainment" (1979, *American Journal of Sociology*[2]) which illustrates how his theoretical mechanisms of the process of attainment give rise to testable empirical predictions.

Educational Inequality: School Effects and Learning Opportunities

The area of education, especially inequality in learning opportunities, was the first substantive subject of Aage's published work. He remained concerned all his life with understanding the impact of schools on learning opportunities, and his first published paper in English (in 1970 in *Sociology of Education*) examined the relationship between organizational differentiation of students and educational opportunity. Thereafter, he collaborated with Maureen Hallinan on a 1977 article in *Sociology of Education* on school effects, which became a source of debate with his Wisconsin colleague Robert Hauser (e.g. 1978 *Sociology of Education*). After work on ability grouping in the 1980s (again, with Maureen Hallinan), he turned toward a closer consideration of the work of his mentor, James Coleman, in the 1990s. He began to teach a popular undergraduate course at Harvard entitled "Schooling and Society," and he assembled an "Ed Group" of graduate students, with whom he met on Friday afternoons from 1995 until his injury. He collaborated on education-related papers with several of his last students, and he was at work on a group paper revisiting the main findings of the Coleman Report (but this time with his learning opportunities model!) the week he fell.

Three chapters of this volume deal with issues related to Aage's interest in topics related to schools, school effects, and educational achievement. Robert Hauser's chapter assesses the implications of relaxing a key assumption of Aage's models of school effects and learning opportunities, namely that there is a uniform cohort progression of all students through schools. Hauser argues that this is an unrealistic assumption in modern society. A complete understanding of how learning opportunities affect student achievement must be built on an account of variation in these opportunities across time and place. Hauser focuses on the complications introduced by grade retention in American schools, arguing that it should be considered along with the classroom and intra-school differences in learning opportunities that Aage emphasized in much of his work.

Maureen Hallinan summarizes and elaborates Aage's learning opportunities model. Aage used this mathematical model to explain inequalities in educational outcomes on the basis of interactions between structures (such as schools and learning opportunities) and individuals, much in the same way as his theory of stratification sought to explain inequality in jobs that people held (see the discussion in Trond Petersen's paper). Hallinan first derives and explicates Aage's model and then tests it using data that were not available to him. She then develops a broad conceptual foundation for the model, which builds on his brief remarks about learning theory. In conclusion, she discusses extensions of the model that would increase its validity as a description of the learning process.

Warren Kubitschek also elaborates on Aage's learning opportunities model of school effects. He first discusses Aage's theoretical model and then presents a simple alternative. He develops alternative indicators of school effects and new methods to estimate them. He concludes by considering some of the implications of his estimates for Sørensen's theory of school effects and for research on the consequences of schooling in general.

Mobility and Careers: The Structure of Inequality and the Process of Attainment

Aage also used his mathematical model of attainment to explain the timing of career mobility. He focused primarily on the process of intragenerational mobility, and sought to explicate the ways in which achieved charcteristics of individuals, especially education, combined with features of labor markets to influence the attainment of income and occupational status. He also considered the process of intergenerational mobility, however, especially when he sought to explain the extent to which educational attainment and other individual attributes are rooted in one's family background. The two papers in this section address intergenerational as well as intragenerational mobility.

Gosta Esping-Andersen discusses the relationship between class origins and subsequent educational inequalities, seeking to understand how inequality is perpetuated from one generation to the next. He analyzes how cross-national differences in cognitive inequalities are related to the strength of social inheritance, and he finds that levels of cognitive inequality are systematically and powerfully related to the strength of class inheritance. At the same time, he argues that there is considerable evidence that public policy can loosen the link (which he describes using the metaphor of the "Gordian Knot") between class origins and cognitive and educational inequalities.

Sonja Drobnic and Hans-Peter Blossfeld discuss the careers of couples in contemporary capitalism. They draw on several concepts that are central to Aage's work: career mobility as process, open and closed positions as structure, social class and social stratification, the life course perspective, cross-national comparative institutional analysis, and event history analysis. They further develop these concepts and apply them to the analysis of coupled careers, arguing that it is necessary to acknowledge that employment histories are intimately related to family processes. They use the principle of interdependent or linked lives to examine the careers of couples in various types of societies. Drobnic and Blossfeld argue that cross-national differences in institutions, social policies and cultural traditions influence the prevailing model that characterizes families (i.e. whether the prevailing male breadwinner model as opposed to the dual-earner family model); this underscores the need to study careers as they are embedded in social institutions and contexts.

Structural Inequality and Rents

Aage's work consistently sought to understand the structure of inequality and its impact on individuals (e.g. his 1974 paper in the *American Journal of Sociology* and his 1975 paper on the "structure of intergenerational mobility" in the *American Sociological Review*). In his last major works (e.g. his 1996 *AJS* paper, on "The Structural Basis of Social Inequality" and his 2000 *AJS* paper on "Toward a Sounder Basis for Class Analysis"), he ambitiously sought to re-formulate all of class analysis, grounding the concept of exploitation in what he considered to be an economically acceptable theory of rent-based inequality. He tried to use this framework to explain recent changes in social inequalities, including rising wage differences between white-collar and blue-collar workers. His research demonstrated clearly that changes in individual endowments need not alter inequality in the social distribution of outcomes. For example, policies to decrease income inequality by expanding educational opportunities will fail if the prevailing structure of opportunity within a labor market remains unchanged. Three papers in this section draw upon Aage's ideas regarding rents to explain various kinds of inequalities; all four papers show how structures affect individual outcomes.

One of these key ideas is the notion of closure in labor markets, a concept derived from Max Weber. Processes of social closure operate to prevent "outsiders" from competing with insiders in labor markets. As a result, the competitive market processes posited by neoclassical economic theory (wage competition) did not operate and alternative mechanisms (vacancy competition) were more appropriate. The contrast between open and closed employment relationships was initially presented in an article Aage co-authored with John Myles in 1975 in the *Canadian Journal of Sociology*.

Rakesh Khurana and Mikolaj Jan Piskorski discuss the importance of social closure in understanding managerial labor markets. They argue that actors are able to obtain unearned advantages in labor markets through two kinds of mechanisms: (1) social closure that, under certain cultural conditions, may arise through mechanisms that restrict access to a position to those who conform to certain socially defined criteria; and (2) composite rents between productive assets. They illustrate these models using data from the executive labor market.

Michèle Ollivier uses the concept of rent to develop a structural theory of inequality that seeks to understand status in contemporary social life. She argues that status structures (consisting of mutually-sustaining sets of cultural schemas and resources) provide advantages similar to those that Aage conceptualized as rents (i.e. returns obtained from positions in social structure rather than from individual talent and effort). She illustrates the usefulness of this framework by means of a study of prestige among popular music artists in Quebec and an exploratory study of tastes. She argues that conspicuous openness to diversity may be emerging as "one of the master cultural schemas of our times."

Stephen L. Morgan and Mark W. McKerrow analyze recent changes in earnings inequality, focusing on the black-white gap in the earnings of men (as did Aage in some of his work from the 1970s). Although they rely on a social class schema that Aage criticized effectively in his 2000 *AJS* article, Morgan and McKerrow make the case that traditional modes of class analysis remain useful for analyzing inequality in post-industrial societies, especially when combined with the rent-based perspective Aage proposed.

In the final paper in this section, Trond Petersen and Vemund Snartland examine the consequences of payment systems based on commissions, piece rates and production bonuses. This analysis responds to Aage's observation that there are relatively few empirical studies of the distributional consequences of incentive systems, and it builds on Aage's 1994 chapter in the *Handbook of Economic Sociology* on "Firms, Wages, and Incentives." Petersen and Snartland find that structure matters for individual attainment: for example, there are both productivity gains for employers and wage benefits for workers associated with such output-related incentive systems.

Taken as a whole, then, the chapters of this volume illustrate some of the major themes that characterized Aage's research. They also illustrate topics that are likely to constitute important themes for future efforts to understand the nature, dynamics and consequences of structured social inequality in society.

NOTES

1. There is some dispute over this point among Aage's former students. One faction, claiming to be more mature and competent, remember Aage intervening only at "critical junctures" when he thought he had something to offer to seriously advance the project. All, however, agree that he loved a good argument and students who took pleasure from such exchange.

2. This was one of Aage's favorite papers, and he was disappointed and often complained about its lack of influence and citations. It was therefore a great pleasure for him that Guillermina Jasso found his model very helpful for her work on status processes. The last sociology paper that Aage read was a preprint version of her paper on "Studying Status: An Integrated Framework," published in the February 2001 issue of the *American Sociological Review*.

THEORY AND METHODS

GENERATIVE MODELS AND EXPLANATORY RESEARCH: ON THE SOCIOLOGY OF AAGE B. SØRENSEN

Peter Hedström

INTRODUCTION

Aage Sørensen's most important intellectual contributions are to be found in the areas of social stratification and labor market sociology. He contributed to these fields throughout his career; from his very first article published in Denmark in 1969 (Sørensen, 1969) to his most recent publications (e.g. Sørensen, 2001). These field-specific contributions are also of importance for sociology in general because they illustrate how one can achieve a tight coupling between sociological theory and empirical research – a problem that has plagued much of sociological research. In explaining labor market outcomes (or any other type of outcome, for that matter) we make use of empirical data and relevant theories. The specific ways in which theory and data are used to explain an observed outcome differ considerably among different sociological traditions. Sørensen's work is a representative example of one important approach to using theory and data for explanatory purposes, and it is this approach that I will focus on in this article. Much of my discussion will center on Sørensen's so-called vacancy competition model because, in addition to being an excellent scholarly accomplishment in itself, it illustrates well the logic of his general approach.[1]

Inequality: Structures, Dynamics and Mechanisms: Essays in Honor of Aage B. Sørensen
Research in Social Stratification and Mobility, Volume 21, 13–25

ISSN: 0276-5624/doi:10.1016/S0276-5624(04)21002-2

TRADITIONS OF CAUSAL ANALYSIS

The core of Sørensen's approach can be characterized as an approach using non-experimental data to empirically calibrate theory-based explanations. It differs from most mainstream approaches in being concerned with explanations rather than descriptions and with aiming at theoretical calibration rather than hypothesis testing (see Fig. 1).

As the terms description and explanation are used here, they differ in that they denote research that seeks to answer different types of questions. A description tells us *how* something is constituted, or how something varies over time, or between different groups or social settings, while an explanation tells us *why* something looks, changes, or varies as it does.[2] Producing accurate and relevant descriptions clearly is what sociologists are best at, and it is also what most sociologists are engaged in. Sørensen's research was almost exclusively concerned with explaining social processes, however. Documenting facts or describing social trends was never a primary concern of his, although it clearly was something he valued in the work of others.

The second major difference between Sørensen's type of approach and that of most other quantitatively oriented sociologists engaged in causal analysis concerns the primary aim of the empirical analysis. While most quantitative sociologists seek to explain phenomena by isolating causally relevant factors using a quasi-experimental setup, Sørensen always insisted that explanations must be based on theoretical models that explicate the mechanisms assumed to bring about an outcome. The role of empirical analysis is not to test these theories in the experimental meaning of the term, but rather to calibrate the theoretical model to reality by finding the parameter values that fit best. On the surface the differences

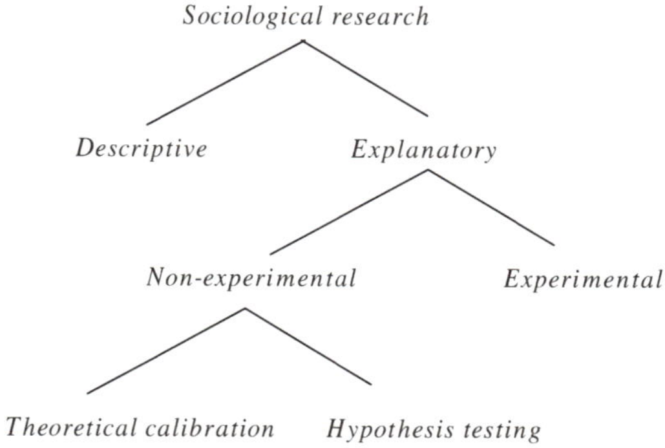

Fig. 1. Traditions of Empirical Research.

between these two approaches may not appear to be particularly important. After all, they often use the same non-experimental data and similar types of methods to estimate the parameters of the models. These similarities are deceptive, however. As will be detailed below, the two approaches represent rather fundamental differences in how to use theory and data to explain social phenomena.

We can use Goldthorpe's (2000) typology of different traditions of causal analysis in sociology and statistics to highlight some of the differences between these two types of approaches (see Table 1). The first two traditions identified by Goldthorpe – causation as robust dependence and causation as consequential manipulation – are the main traditions within the hypothesis-testing branch of empirical research referred to in Fig. 1. Both traditions are concerned with testing hypothesized effects using quasi-experimental statistical techniques. They differ mainly in terms of how they conceptualize the problem, and how they go about testing the hypotheses.

Most of us are familiar with the robust-dependence tradition from textbooks in quantitative methods. In this tradition, causality is established by partialling out the effects of confounding variables. If a relationship between two variables persists even after controlling for likely confounders, the relationship is interpreted as a "causal effect." In the words of Lazarsfeld (1955, pp. 124–125): "If we have a relationship between *x* and *y*; and if for any antecedent test factor the partial relationships between *x* and *y* do not disappear, then the original relationship should be called a causal one."

The consequential-manipulation tradition has a long history in statistics and dates back to the works of Ronald Fisher and Jerzy Neyman (see Freedman, 1999).

Table 1. Traditions of Causal Analysis.

Tradition	Key People[a]	Key Focus of the Explanation
Causation as robust dependence	Lazarsfeld, Blalock, Duncan	Causal relations as displayed by robust dependence between variables
Causation as consequential manipulation	Fisher, Neyman, Rubin	Causal effects as displayed by comparing outcomes with and without "treatment"
Causation as generative process	Sørensen, Coleman	Causal processes as expressed in models of how outcomes are brought about

[a] For representative work by these "key people," see Lazarsfeld (1955), Blalock (1964), Duncan (1975), Rubin (1974), Coleman (1964), and Sørensen (1998). See Freedman (1999) on the contributions of Fisher and Neyman.

It now seems to be entering sociology through the work of Rubin and others (e.g. Holland, 1986; Rosenbaum, 1984; Rubin, 1974). Using the vocabulary of experimentation – as most of those who work in this tradition do – the core idea is that a causal effect can best be assessed by comparing the outcomes for individuals (or other relevant units) when they are "treated" and when they are not. An obvious difficulty with such an approach is that individuals are normally observed only in the treatment *or* in the control group, but that the causal effect can only be revealed by comparing their outcomes in both groups. The methods that have been developed by Rubin and others try to estimate a counterfactual effect, i.e. what the outcome would have been for those in the treatment group had they been in the control group, and vice versa for those in the control group (see Winship & Morgan, 1999 for a useful overview of this literature).

The third tradition – causation as generative process – is the one of which Sørensen, together with Coleman, was a leading proponent. The basic difference between this tradition and the other two centers on what one considers to be an acceptable explanation, and this has repercussions for the type of analyses deemed to be necessary.

As previously mentioned, analysts in the consequential-manipulation and robust-dependence traditions aim to establish the causal effects of one (or several) variables upon another. The causal explanation then typically consists in pointing to the existence of factors that seem to make a systematic difference for the probability of the outcome being observed. Sørensen's approach was different. He conceived of explanatory theory as a conceptualization of what goes into a social process, and he meant that adequate explanations require that we specify plausible processes through which outcomes are brought about. These causal accounts are not based exclusively on the information contained in the data being analyzed, but draw on many other sources of knowledge, not least of all the existing theories of relevance for the problem at hand.[3]

These differences in explanatory schemas also influence the types of models being estimated. In the consequential-manipulation and robust-dependence traditions the role of sociological theory is typically limited to suggesting relevant variables. Once this has been decided, the model being estimated tends to be a generic statistical model, and the choice between different statistical models (e.g. logistic regression model, OLS regression model, or some form of event-history model) is dictated exclusively by the characteristics of the data to be analyzed.

In the tradition represented by Sørensen the main focus in not on generic statistical models but on *substantive* models of the processes believed to have brought about the outcome. Coleman described the core of the approach as follows:

> The general approach will be: (1) to begin with the idea of a process; (2) to attempt to lay out the mathematical model that mirrors this process; and then (3) given particular kinds of data, to transform the mathematical model into a statistical model for estimating parameters of the process. In general the goal will not be one of testing hypotheses but rather one of estimating parameters in a mathematical model designed to mirror a substantive process. . . . There is a distinct difference between the way I am proceeding and a more common way of proceeding in the analysis of data in the social sciences. The more common way can be termed *statistical data analysis*, in which the method of statistical analysis is designed for a particular form of data, and, in effect, determined by that data form (Coleman, 1981, p. 5).

If one agrees with Sørensen and Coleman, as I think one should, that if we are to explain something, we need to specify the process through which it was brought about, then it seems to follow that the foundation of the empirical analysis should be a model of this process and not some ad hoc statistical model. Otherwise, a wedge is introduced between the theory and the empirical analysis which will reduce the explanatory relevance of the empirical analysis.[4] As often emphasized by David Freedman (e.g. 1987), estimating parameters of models that do not mirror substantive causal processes can only rarely be expected to yield valuable insights into causal process. This point was also emphasized by Sørensen in his critique of the "gas station approach" to theorizing (to be discussed below), and by Coleman in his *Introduction to Mathematical Sociology*[5]:

> Note, however, that there is nowhere the proposal simply to engage in curve-fitting, without an underlying model which expresses a social process. If the data happen to fit a simple curve, this may provide an economical statement of the data [. . .] But if there is no underlying model with a reasonable substantive interpretation, little has been gained by such curve fitting (Coleman, 1964, p. 518).

Basing the empirical analysis on substantive models of social processes brings to the foreground an important question about the role or primary aim of the empirical analysis. The outcomes we observe in society are doubtless the result of a multitude of different processes. A useful theoretical model typically explicates the core mechanisms of one or some of these processes. By choice and necessity much of the complexity of social life is abstracted away and the resulting model will provide a highly stylized account of what goes into the process. As emphasized by Coleman (1981), when we estimate parameters of such models it does not seem reasonable to refer to the activity as one of testing causal hypotheses. What we are doing, rather, is to calibrate the theoretical model to reality by trying to find realistic values of the parameters of the theoretical model. Once these parameter values are arrived at we can engage in counterfactual what-if analysis, and if the substantive model is plausible, these counterfactual analyses can provide important insights into the real-world processes. But the empirical analysis as such is best described as theoretical calibration rather than hypothesis testing.

THE VACANCY-COMPETITION MODEL

The focus of Sørensen's approach is thus on the *process* that generates observed outcomes. In 1977 he published "The structure of inequality and the process of attainment," in the *American Sociological Review*. In it he developed a generative model suggesting a process through which the observed relationship between time in the labor force and earnings could be explained. This article, in my view, is Sørensen's single most important publication, and it illustrates well the logic of his general approach.

Economists like Mincer (1974) had argued that the observed relationship between labor-force experience and earnings was due to a causal relationship between accumulated experience, individual productivity, and earnings. The longer people had been in the labor force, Mincer argued, the more skills they had acquired, and the more productive they were therefore likely to be. The relationship between labor-force experience and earnings, Mincer suggested, was therefore simply due to the "fact" that people's earnings reflected their productivity.

Sørensen believed that this model did not mirror what we know about the functioning of labor markets, and hence he was skeptical about the explanation offered by Mincer. He set himself the task of developing an alternative model that better corresponded to existing sociological ideas about the process. Unlike Mincer, Sørensen did not think that the observed relationship was primarily due to changes in individual attributes, i.e. to their becoming increasingly more productive. His view was that earnings are primarily tied to jobs, and that individuals attain higher earnings by getting access to better-paid jobs. Individuals' attributes are important, not because of the productivity mechanism suggested by Mincer, but because they influence individuals' chances of getting access to vacant jobs. Time enters into the picture because it takes time to move up the job ladder.

This is not the place to describe the vacancy-competition model in any detail – the interested reader should read Sørensen's article instead – but by way of summary it can be said to consist of three interrelated components[6]:

(1) A model of a hierarchical job structure.
(2) A model of how vacancies are generated and move in this structure.
(3) A model of how people move between these vacancies, and thereby change their earnings.

These three components were part of the model for substantive reasons; they were formal representations of Sørensen's ideas about the core mechanisms governing the process. Through well-chosen simplifications he then arrived at the following model of the process of attainments:

$$y(t) = \frac{z}{b}(e^{bt} - 1) + y(0)e^{bt}$$

where $y(t)$ = earnings (or attainments) at time t, z = a comprehensive measure of an individual's labor-market-relevant resources, and b = a parameter that describes the rate at which vacancies arrive (which in turn is a function of the "shape" of the job structure and the rate at which jobs become vacant as people leave the system).

This model generates concave career lines with respect to the time axis that are similar to empirically observed career lines, and similar to those predicted by human capital theory. Thus the mechanisms proposed by Sørensen provided a plausible alternative to the human capital model and an alternative explanation of this frequently observed pattern.

In the article, Sørensen also related his model to results obtained from more traditional studies in the robust-dependence tradition, and provided interesting reinterpretations of their findings in light of his own model. For example, he showed that a regression coefficient in a traditional attainment model (e.g. the regression coefficient obtained when regressing earnings on education) is a function of: (1) the amount of time individuals have spent in the labor force; (2) "structural" opportunities for advancement (which are in turn influenced by the rate at which vacancies are created and by the shape of the job hierarchy); and (3) the contribution of the independent variable in question to the individual's overall labor-market-relevant resources. Since the size of a specific regression coefficient will reflect all these different types of factors, it will not tell us much of value about the causal process at work. In order to understand the causal process we must focus directly on the generative mechanisms, and this is what Sørensen did in his vacancy competition model.

In later work (e.g. Sørensen, 1979) he showed how the parameters of the model could be estimated with longitudinal data, and he produced results that were interesting as well as suggestive.[7] In these empirically estimated models, unlike so many other regression models estimated by sociologists, the claim to causality did not rest exclusively on the size and significance of the regression coefficients. They were simply one piece in a much larger causal puzzle.

So why do I find the approach represented by this article to be of such importance for explanatory sociology? First and foremost, I think it is a textbook example of middle-range theorizing at its very best. It takes a well-documented empirical observation and proposes a novel and precise explanation for it. Second, the model is formulated in such a way that it is possible to link it directly with empirical data, thereby avoiding the "theory gap" (Granovetter, 1979) that has been so detrimental to much of sociological research (see also Bäckman & Edling, 1999). Third, and possibly less important, the theory is beautiful. The clean mathematical representation of the theory, which arrives at powerful results with a minimum of irrelevancies, has esthetic qualities rarely found in this line of research. Finally, the focus on generative processes directs attention away from the type of variable-based theorizing that has come to dominate so much of sociology during last few decades.

THE "GAS STATION" APPROACH TO THEORIZING

The widespread use and knowledge of survey analysis, and the statistical techniques needed for analyzing such data, have clearly improved our ability to describe various aspects of social life. The increasing use of these techniques has also fostered the development of a variable-centered type of theorizing that has not been equally favorable for the advancement of the discipline (see Abbott, 1998; Coleman, 1986; Goldthorpe, 2000; Hedström & Swedberg, 1998). As Sørensen emphasized in his chapter "Theoretical mechanisms and the study of social processes" (1998), much of sociological theorizing has degenerated into eclectic storytelling about the potential importance of different variables.

The traditional approach of most quantitative labor market sociologists in the 1970s and the 1980s was to elaborate on the traditional attainment model[8] by including variables or groups of variables believed to measure aspects of the social structure in which individuals were embedded. Some of these studies included variables measuring individuals' class position of (e.g. Wright & Perrone, 1977), while others included variables describing their labor market sector (e.g. Beck et al., 1978). The importance of the theories represented by these variables would supposedly be indexed by the magnitude of the regression coefficients associated with the variables, particularly whether or not the regression coefficients were significantly different from zero.

For the results of a regression analysis to be indicative of causal relations, the regression model must represent reasonably well the process through which the outcome was generated (e.g. Freedman, 1987). In his 1998 chapter, Sørensen raised the question of whether anyone really believes in the "gas station" theory of earnings that these regression models imply:

> This model, in fact, proposes a theory where each person receives x dollars from education, y dollars from family background, q dollars from gender, and z dollars from class. All of it adds up to the person's yearly earnings. We can imagine people walking around among pumps in a large gas station getting something from each of the pumps. The picture should be complemented by specifying hypotheses about how many dollars each pump provides, and this would give us

> some idea of the relative importance of the pumps that we could teach in courses on getting ahead in society (Sørensen, 1998, p. 248).

Obviously, no one seriously believes in such a theory. Yet many quantitatively-oriented sociologists continue to estimate such models. As Sørensen noted later in the same chapter, "We learn very little from such research."

The gap between sociological theories and the empirical models used to test theories are particularly striking as far as the role of social interaction is concerned (Åberg, 2003). Most sociological theorists – Weber, Simmel, Mead, Goffman, Park, and Burgess to name a few – strongly emphasized how important social action and social interaction are for understanding and explaining social processes and social change. Similarly, sociologists often criticize economists for assuming individuals to be social atoms not much influenced by the social structure in which they are embedded (e.g. Granovetter, 1985). Yet, to judge from the statistical models estimated by most quantitative sociologists, much of this appears to be lip service. Social interaction and social influence play as little role in most sociologists' statistical analyses as they do in the economists' analyses.[9] Sørensen did not subscribe to this gas station approach to theorizing, however. He took social interaction seriously and developed a model in which the movement of vacancies in a social structure created social interdependencies between individuals, and these interdependencies played a major role in explaining the outcome of the process.

CONCLUDING REMARKS

Many sociologists mistakenly thought of Sørensen as a quantitative *methodologist*. In reality, he was a mathematically-oriented *sociologist* serious about sociological theorizing and research. In my view, the publications focused upon here – the 1977 *ASR* article and the meta-theoretical chapter from 1998 – should be required reading in *theory* classes in sociology. The *ASR* article is an example of middle-range theorizing at its very best, and the meta-theoretical chapter develops a most convincing and lucid argument for the importance of theoretically informed empirical research.

The core of Sørensen's approach may be summarized as follows:

(1) To use statistical models with elaborate control variables to simulate an experimental situation is inappropriate and misleading.
(2) Causal understanding is achieved by understanding the process through which change is brought about.
(3) A mathematical model should be specified that contains the abstract analogies to the mechanisms governing this process.

(4) Quantitative data should be used to estimate the size of the parameters of the mathematical model.

Sørensen thus proposed a different division of labor between sociologists and statisticians than the one that currently predominates among quantitatively-oriented sociologists. The proper division should be one in which sociological theory suggests a mathematical model of a social process and statistics provides the tools to estimate the model, not, as is common today, that statistics provides models that sociologists use as ad hoc models of social processes.

My own position on these matters largely overlaps with that of Sørensen, except that I would place greater emphasis on the importance of action-based explanations, i.e. that explanations in the social sciences should refer directly to the causes and consequences of individual actions (see Hedström & Swedberg, 1998). In one of the last papers that Sørensen wrote, we may discern a slight reorientation toward action-based explanations: "[T]he appropriate causal language to be used in empirical work should be one of causal narrative, accounts of how the causal linkages are created. . . . [A] model focusing either on change over time or change in utility, is indeed the proper basis for empirical work" (Sørensen, 1999, p. 10). The core element of Sørensen's approach remained constant throughout his career, however, and this was his insistence on the importance of explicitly modeling the mechanisms at work. Explanatory models should be abstract analogies to the processes believed to have generated observed outcomes, not summaries of statistical relationships between variables.

In his aforementioned book, Goldthorpe concluded that, "an understanding of causation simply as robust dependence would seem best regarded more as a feature of sociology's past than of its future" (Goldthorpe, 2000, p. 142). In this respect, the future is Sørensen's.

NOTES

1. Another possibility would have been to use Sørensen's research on school effects, which also illustrates well the logic of his approach. See Sørensen and Hallinan (1977), as well as the exchange between Sørensen (1978) and Hauser (1978) on the utility of his approach.

2. Obviously these definitions are not particularly precise, but they are sufficiently precise for the purpose at hand. As noted by Sen (1980), we can say a great deal about explanations and descriptions without necessarily having to define their exact boundaries, just as we can say a great deal about India and China without knowing the details of their borders.

3. Some writers in the more statistically oriented traditions downplay the importance of such subject-specific knowledge. The most extreme position in this respect is the one taken by Clark Glymour and his associates, who seek to develop computer algorithms that, with little or no subject-specific input, automatically should detect causal structures and relations. See Glymour (1997). As Stephen Morgan pointed out when reading a draft of this article, this certainly was not the position of O. D. Duncan. In his text book on structural equation modeling (Duncan, 1975), he argued that the variables to be used in the analysis must reflect the core elements of one's theory, and the models must have a substantive depth if they are to be regarded as structural models.

4. In his applied research (e.g., his educational research), Coleman often did not follow his own principles, but estimated simple regression models that did not reflect any plausible substantive process. This somewhat puzzling behavior was interpreted by Sørensen (1996) as an expression of the hegemony of the statistical mode of data analysis. Had Coleman not used this form of analysis, his results would not have had the same impact as they now had.

5. Boudon is another leading representative of this tradition. In his well-known debate with Robert Hauser about the importance of theoretical models in sociology, Boudon similarly argued that causal understanding is normally achieved not by means of statistical models, but through theoretical models that show the mechanisms behind the process being analyzed. Statistical analyses produce descriptive accounts of data, and in order to achieve causal knowledge, Boudon argued, "we must go beyond the statistical relationships to explore the generative mechanism responsible for them" (Boudon, 1976, p. 117). See also Cox (1992).

6. The vacancy-competition model took its point of departure from the work of White (1970), but it represented a major development of White's work in that it also took into consideration how individuals compete for the vacant jobs being generated.

7. Sørensen and Coleman rarely engaged in collecting data better suited for testing and/or calibrating their theoretical models (the school data collected by Coleman were not collected for this purpose). Instead they devised clever ways of using existing survey data for this purpose. I believe this was an unfortunate decision on their part. With more appropriate data at their disposal their empirical research would have been more authoritative and their scholarly impact even greater.

8. These models usually related an individual's status or earnings to his or her own education, and to the status of the family of origin. See Blau and Duncan (1967).

9. Notable exceptions to this rule are to be found in the literatures on social networks and on diffusion processes.

ACKNOWLEDGMENTS

An earlier version was presented at the meetings of the American Sociological Association in Anaheim, August 2001. I wish to thank Yvonne Åberg, Magnus Bygren, Christofer Edling, David Freedman, John Goldthorpe, Arne Kalleberg, Fredrik Liljeros, Stephen Morgan, and Richard Swedberg for their useful comments.

REFERENCES

Abbott, A. (1998). The causal devolution. *Sociological Methods and Research*, *27*, 148–181.

Åberg, Y. (2003). *Social interactions: Studies of contextual effects and endogenous processes.* Department of Sociology, Stockholm University.

Bäckman, O., & Edling, C. (1999). Mathematics matter: On the absence of mathematical models in quantitative sociology. *Acta Sociologica*, *42*, 69–78.

Beck, E. M., Horan, P. M., & Tolbert, C. M. (1978). Stratification in a dual economy: A sectoral model of earnings determination. *American Sociological Review*, *43*, 704–720.

Blalock, H. M. (1964). *Causal inferences in non-experimental research.* Chapel Hill: University of North Carolina Press.

Blau, P. M., & Duncan, O. D. (1967). *The American occupational structure*. New York: Wiley.

Boudon, R. (1976). Comment on Hauser's review of *Education, Opportunity, and Social Inequality. American Journal of Sociology*, *81*, 1175–1187.

Coleman, J. S. (1964). *Introduction to mathematical sociology*. New York: Free Press.

Coleman, J. S. (1981). *Longitudinal data analysis*. New York: Basic Books.

Coleman, J. S. (1986). Social theory, social research, and a theory of action. *American Journal of Sociology*, *91*, 1309–1335.

Cox, D. R. (1992). Causality: Some statistical aspects. *Journal of the Royal Statistics Society, Series A*, *155*, 291–301.

Duncan, O. D. (1975). *Introduction to structural equation models*. New York: Academic Press.

Freedman, D. (1987). As others see us: A case study in path analysis. *Journal of Educational Statistics*, *12*, 101–128.

Freedman, D. (1999). From association to causation: Some remarks on the history of statistics. *Statistical Science*, *14*(3), 243–258.

Glymour, C. (1997). A review of recent work on the foundations of causal inference. In: V. R. McKim & S. P. Turner (Eds), *Causality in Crisis? Statistical Methods and the Search for Causal Knowledge in the Social Sciences* (pp. 201–248). Notre Dame: University of Notre Dame Press.

Goldthorpe, J. H. (2000). *On sociology: Numbers, narratives, and the integration of research and theory*. Oxford: Oxford University Press.

Granovetter, M. (1979). The theory-gap in social network analysis. In: P. Holland & S. Leinhardt (Eds), *Perspectives on Social Network Research* (pp. 501–518). New York: Academic Press.

Granovetter, M. (1985). Economic action and social structure: The problem of embeddedness. *American Journal of Sociology*, *91*, 481–510.

Hauser, R. (1978). On 'A reconceptualization of school effects'. *Sociology of Education*, *51*(1), 68–72.

Hedström, P., & Swedberg, R. (1998). Social mechanisms: An introductory essay. In: P. Hedström & R. Swedberg (Eds), *Social Mechanisms: An Analytical Approach to Social Theory* (pp. 1–31). Cambridge: Cambridge University Press.

Holland, P. (1986). Statistics and causal inference. *Journal of the American Statistical Association*, *81*, 968–970.

Lazarsfeld, P. F. (1955). Interpretation of statistical relations as a research operation. In: P. F. Lazarsfeld & M. Rosenberg (Eds), *The Language of Social Research* (pp. 115–125). New York: Free Press.

Mincer, J. (1974). *Schooling, experience, and earnings*. New York: Columbia University Press.

Rosenbaum, P. R. (1984). From association to causation in observational studies: The role of tests of strongly ignorable treatment assignment. *Journal of the American Statistical Association*, *79*, 41–45.

Rubin, D. B. (1974). Estimating causal effects of treatments in randomized and nonrandomized studies. *Journal of Educational Psychology*, *66*, 688–701.

Sen, A. (1980). Description as choice. *Oxford Economic Papers*, *32*, 353–369.

Sørensen, A. B. (1969). Social ulighed i fordelningen af uddannelse i et uddannelsesystem i vaekst. [Social inequality in the distribution of education in an expanding educational system]. *Sociologiske Meddeleser*, *13*, 5–22.

Sørensen, A. B. (1977). The structure of inequality and the process of attainment. *American Sociological Review*, *42*, 965–978.

Sørensen, A. B. (1978). Reconceptualizing school effects. *Sociology of Education*, *51*, 230–233.

Sørensen, A. B. (1979). A model and a metric for the analysis of the intragenerational status attainment process. *American Journal of Sociology*, *85*, 361–384.

Sørensen, A. B. (1996). Educational opportunities and school effects. In: J. Clark (Ed.), *James S. Coleman* (pp. 207–226). London: Falmer Press.

Sørensen, A. B. (1998). Theoretical mechanisms and the empirical study of social processes. In: P. Hedström & R. Swedberg (Eds), *Social Mechanisms: An Analytical Approach to Social Theory* (pp. 238–266). Cambridge: Cambridge University Press.

Sørensen, A. B. (1999). Statistical models and mechanisms of social processes. Paper presented at the Annual meeting of the Swedish Sociological Association in Stockholm.

Sørensen, A. B. (2001). Careers, wealth and employment relations. In: A. L. Kalleberg & I. Berg (Eds), *Source Book on Labor Markets: Evolving Structures and Processes*. Plenum Press.

Sørensen, A. B., & Hallinan, M. T. (1977). A reconceptualization of school effects. *Sociology of Education*, *50*, 273–289.

White, H. C. (1970). *Chains of opportunity: System models of mobility in organizations*. Cambridge: Harvard University Press.

Winship, C., & Morgan, S. L. (1999). The estimation of causal effects from observational data. *Annual Review of Sociology*, *25*, 659–706.

Wright, E. O., & Perrone, L. (1977). Marxist class categories and income inequality. *American Sociological Review*, *42*, 32–55.

AAGE BØTTGER SØRENSEN'S CONTRIBUTIONS TO QUANTITATIVE SOCIOLOGY: FROM STUDYING PROCESSES TO STUDYING STRUCTURE

Trond Petersen

ABSTRACT

This article discusses Aage Bøttger Sørensen's contributions to quantitative sociology and mathematical modeling of social processes, with an emphasis on the published works in social stratification in the 1974–1979 period. It draws three lessons from his modeling approach: (1) The frequent use of a reduced-form equation for estimation; (2) the use of few variables in the regression equation; and (3) the emphasis on dynamic models. The article ends by discussing the character of Sørensen's empirical work and its place in quantitative sociological research.

INTRODUCTION

Aage Bøttger Sørensen published on a wide array of topics. But his main area was social stratification and labor markets. I shall focus on his key contributions in this area in the period 1974–1979. This body of scholarship demonstrates a particular

---

Inequality: Structures, Dynamics and Mechanisms: Essays in Honor of Aage B. Sørensen
Research in Social Stratification and Mobility, Volume 21, 27–44

ISSN: 0276-5624/doi:10.1016/S0276-5624(04)21003-4

approach and research style that was characteristic of much of Sørensen's work. It is also a style for which it is difficult to find parallels, both then and even more so now, and it is a style that continues to be worth emulating.

His contributions were varied: many to mathematical modeling of social processes, most of which included empirical assessments of the models, a handful to quantitative methods proper, some primarily empirical contributions, and finally a number of articles that were purely conceptual and theoretical, a type of work that became more important in later years.

As a summary assessment one can without hesitation state that Sørensen was a quantitative researcher with a very fine eye for theory. He was not a quantitative methodologist. He found such methods important and used them, but valued careful and formal thinking about how social processes operate even more.

Below I first outline the central features of Sørensen's work on inequality. I then proceed with discussing modeling lessons to be drawn from it, and end with a discussion of some of Sørensen's views on the practice of quantitative sociology.

THE STYLE OF RESEARCH

The Conceptual Work

Trying to characterize someone's style of research is rarely easy, especially when the scholar published in many areas using different kinds of approaches. But there is I think a core approach that permeates much of Sørensen's research and which separates it from what others do in social stratification and quantitative sociology more broadly.

First, Sørensen had very strong theoretical ideas. These were usually built on a solid intuition about real world social processes. He then proceeded to formalizing the ideas in mathematical models. These were almost always models that could, in some way, be estimated with data.

Second, he was never very interested in trying to test whether his models could be said to be correct. He hoped his assumptions were reasonable and his arguments persuasive. The empirical work then illustrated the usefulness of the approach, how it gave sensible results. The interpretations of the results could not have been obtained in the absence of his strong conceptual ideas. In one sense, he rarely let the data speak. He formulated forceful ways of looking at data, and then the data spoke accordingly.

Third, his approach was not the one favored in social stratification at the time, where theorizing occurred in the context of so-called statistical path models, and often in a manner that Sørensen would have called ad hoc. Nor is Sørensen's a style of research common today. And even though path models are hardly with us any more, what Sørensen would call ad hoc reasoning still is, especially in quantitative empirical research.

Below I shall give an example of where Sørensen's mode of doing sociology was most effective, namely in two articles from 1977 to 1979, which grew out of two prior articles from 1974 to 1975 (Sørensen, 1974, 1975a, 1977a, b, 1979). In these articles Sørensen clearly contributed toward empirical knowledge, as well as to quantitative methods. But the central contributions were to theory and modeling of social processes.

Contributions to Quantitative Methods

While Sørensen's main contributions were in theory and formal modeling, he also contributed to quantitative methods. The most important was an article in *Sociological Methodology* (1977) on estimating rates. Here he drew on Feller's (1966) two-volume treatise, which is not a statistics book, but a book that applies probability theory to various processes, including social processes. It addresses one particularly difficult question in estimating rates, namely problems that arise when one samples from the stock of people who are in a given state at a particular point in time, rather than sampling all entrants into a state. The part of the article addressing right-censored observations was made superfluous soon, through the work of Nancy B. Tuma and Michael T. Hannan on event history analysis (e.g. Tuma & Hannan, 1984), but the other issues raised still lack attractive solutions. Sørensen immediately saw the promise of event history analysis, and published an early application (Sørensen & Tuma, 1981).

He later wrote several expository pieces on event history analysis, including one with Alberto Palloni (Palloni & Sørensen, 1990). But these would often stress the process aspect rather than the statistics.

He wrote one major expository piece, a book coauthored with Annemette Sørensen on mathematical sociology, in *Current Sociology* in 1977, but this was more on theory and less on methods (Sørensen & Sørensen, 1977). It also included discussions of purposive action models and game theory.

THE VACANCY COMPETITION MODEL

In 1974–1979 Sørensen did some very important work on careers. A prelude was a paper taken from his Ph.D. thesis that was published in the *American Journal of Sociology* (Sørensen, 1974). The ideas were then further refined in a series of papers (Sørensen, 1975a, b, 1976), published in the *American Sociological Review* (1975a), *Social Science Research* (1975b), and *Social Science Information* (1976). This research stream culminated in two papers being published in the *American Sociological Review* (1977) and the *American Journal of Sociology* (1979), where the latter built closely on the former. I will focus on the 1977 and 1979 articles.

The Central Building Blocks

These two articles address how people get ahead in the occupational structure. The five central building blocks first developed in the 1977 article were these:

(1) There is a fixed occupational structure, characterized by a distribution of jobs;
(2) Opportunities to get ahead will be determined by the rate at which vacancies in the occupational structure open up, through turnover, job creation, and more;
(3) People differ in the job-relevant resources they possess (e.g. human capital, experience), which help them compete for positions in the occupational structure;
(4) People want to get ahead in the structure (the action part);
(5) The rate at which opportunities to get ahead in the occupational structure opens up varies systematically between demographic groups.

From these five features characterizing a stratification system, his analysis focuses on the immediate implication that individual success depends not only on (3) individual resources, but also on the (1) distribution of positions, (2) the rate at which positions open up, and (5) which group one is in and when one entered the labor market.

Sørensen referred to this particular conceptualization of inequality as the *vacancy competition model*. Several features are noteworthy, but two call for further comments. First, wages and rewards in a job are not determined by the incumbent's individual resources and productivities. They are determined by the job, being attached to titles or positions. Individuals get access to jobs by competing for these, and then their amount of individual resources are relevant. This is a common conception in the stratification literature. Second, and more important, with respect to modeling the role of personal resources, Sørensen pointed out that it is not the absolute amount a person possesses that is decisive. What matters is the person's resources relative to those possessed by others who compete for the same vacant positions. The relevance of this view is most easily seen in an historical perspective, as Sørensen (1979, p. 371) did. A bachelor degree in 1930 meant something very different from one in 1970, because the percent of say 25-year-olds with bachelor degrees increased strongly between the two years, making this particular educational credential potentially less valuable in 1970 than 1930. In 1930, it may have given access to rather privileged positions. In 1970, it may have given access to routine middle-class positions and perhaps prevented one from ending up in the low-wage economy that started to become important. It follows that when education is to be measured in empirical analyses, it should first be standardized in a way that reflects a person's relative standing in an educational distribution in their comparison group, say, those born in or who entered the labor force in the same five-year period.

This work was in part developed as a criticism of human capital theory in economics, which posited that individual resources were the sole sources of success. Sørensen (1979, p. 383) states: "The model also provides a plausible alternative to the human-capital/marginal productivity theory of attainments developed in economics." As Sørensen (1977b, p. 974) notes, his approach predicts the same career lines as human capital theory in economics, but derived from opposite assumptions. It was also a critique of status attainment research in sociology (e.g. Blau & Duncan, 1967), criticizing in part the metric for the dependent variable, in part the lack of dynamic analysis with only scant documentation of the movement of people between positions. The 1977 article was entirely theoretical, with no empirical results, though it derived empirical implications.

Sørensen was not alone in arguing for a more structural approach in social stratification research around 1980 (Beck, Horan & Tolbert II, 1980). And while there were points of agreement between Sørensen and other writers, his was nevertheless a very different approach. It was unusually careful in the theorizing. He never engaged in what may be seen as ad hoc empiricism in some other approaches.

This then was a central conceptual contribution. It has shaped much thinking in stratification research. It was based on verbal and mathematical theorizing. He implemented the ideas in quantitative analyses. In my view this is the most important theoretical work coming out of the stratification tradition in this period. As a conceptualization it stands independently of the mathematical theorizing, the latter in one sense being a dressing-up of the ideas, an implementation of intuition on these issues.

In this conceptualization, the structure of inequality is rigid. There is a fixed set of positions to which people are allocated and to each position there is a fixed reward.

How well does this conceptualization capture reality? In a stable economy, with little growth and innovation, this is the correct conceptualization. The same holds for many stable organizations. As Sørensen (1979, p. 383, also p. 365) writes: "...the vacancy competition model might offer a more plausible theory of the earnings attainment process in the large sectors of the economy where earnings are attributes of jobs and not of persons." But for a more dynamic economy, this is only a partial characterization. It can take account of the fact that some positions disappear and others are created, so that the number and mix of jobs in an economy change. But it does not reflect how individuals sometimes create their own jobs, either through self-employment or through initiatives vis-à-vis their employers, as in many professional jobs. An important characteristic of contemporary labor markets is that many people do not sit around and wait for opportunities to arise. They actively create them. The imagery of individuals competing for open vacancies need to be supplemented with one where individuals create positions, and where in the end, part of the occupational distribution reflects the distribution of initiatives of individuals. Using Sørensen's (1983a) later terminology, there has been a shift from so-called closed to more open positions. The occupational structure has probably become less rigid, and the relative role of individual qualifications may have become more important for success and the role of vacancies less so. But as of 2003, Sørensen's conceptualization of vacancy competition is probably more correct for the years ahead of us than for the preceding ten years of the U.S. economy. With more people looking for fewer jobs, competition for vacancies will likely increase.

The Extension to New Measures of Status and Educational Attainment

The 1979 article took as its point of departure the 1977 article. The main novelty was to develop a new scale for socioeconomic status or prestige. Sørensen had noted already in 1977 (p. 969) that socioeconomic status or prestige really has an arbitrary metric. He then went on to argue that such scores rather should have a metric corresponding to a conceptualization of the distribution of inequality in society. This conception comes from building block (1) in the ASR 1977 article. But in the 1979 article this gets carefully developed. It led to a transformation of standard socioeconomic status or prestige scores. That transformation resulted in a metric with a very clear and theoretically meaningful interpretation. Unlike what is common in quantitative sociology, there is no argument here for transformation of a variable in order to obtain symmetry, normality, or homoskedasticity. The transformation is all about substance, only substance. At one point Sørensen (1979, p. 375) comments that the "extreme skewness" of the two central variables in his empirical analysis implies heteroskedastic error terms which may lead to inefficient estimates. But he then remarks, "However, the sample sizes are so large that it seems unnecessary to use weighted least-squares procedure to correct for the inefficiency of the OLS." Sørensen always focused on the sensibility of the theoretical model, and its implementation in equations to be estimated, but rarely on tangential concerns such as heteroskedasticity and efficiency of estimators.

Sørensen also proposed a new metric for educational attainment. The central idea, as stated above, is that in terms of the role of education in getting access to jobs, it is not its absolute amount that matters, but the education a person has relative to others, namely its competitive advantage. The new educational metric thus measures such competitive advantage. It was derived from the person's standing in the cumulative percentile educational distribution in his or her cohort.

The 1979 article also contains several empirical analyses, presented in four tables and 10 pages of text. The first table gives correlations between the six variables in the analysis. A second table compares results from standard measures of socioeconomic status and educational attainment to the new measures proposed in the article. He shows that the new metrics produce higher explained variances, "... the criterion of performance conventional among sociologists ..." (1979, p. 375). But more important, the new metrics yield substantively more meaningful results. Using the standard metrics for socioeconomic status and education attainment, Treiman and Terrell (1975, p. 182) found similar returns to education for white men and women, thereby refuting the "... feminists claim that women must present higher qualifications than men to compete for equivalent jobs ...." Using the new metrics, Sørensen concludes that the feminist claim is correct (1979, pp. 375–376): "Hence the feminists alluded to by Treiman and Terrell seem to have a valid complaint: white women have lower status returns to education than any other group."

Having demonstrated the relevance of the new metrics, by comparing results to those obtained using conventional measures and models, Sørensen goes on to use the new metrics in assessing the vacancy competition model. In a third table he reports estimates of the reduced form coefficients from the model, to use a term from econometrics. In this, each coefficient consists of several coefficients from the underlying system of equations, the structural form of the model, another term from econometrics. One of the coefficients has the interpretation of measuring the opportunities for upward movement. As in the previous table, Sørensen's new measures show that women have lower opportunities for upward movement, and similarly that blacks have lower opportunities than whites. Sørensen (1979, p. 380) argues for the new metric that it "clearly produces the most meaningful results."

Sørensen concludes the analysis by recovering the structural parameters in his vacancy competition model. From the results for the reduced form coefficients in Table 3, it is possible to calculate, by simple algebraic manipulations, the underlying coefficients in his vacancy competition model. Again, this gives substantively meaningful results. Sørensen (1979, p. 381) writes: "This combines to produce the most unfavorable opportunities for status attainment for black women and the most favorable for white males."

In these regression analyses, Sørensen includes only two independent variables. In the first analysis (Table 2), where the new measures are validated, he includes education and labor force experience, while in the second analysis (Table 3), where the vacancy competition model is estimated, he includes the lagged value of the dependent variable plus educational attainment. The analyses are done separately for four groups, white males, white females, black males, and black females. The rationale is that these groups differ in the opportunity structures they face. This is also what he finds using the new metric.

This approach is just very different from much research in social stratification. It was and is common to include an extensive array of independent variables, and then to provide separate but brief justification for each variable. Sørensen in contrast discusses only two variables, and provides a careful derivation and justification for their relevance. In the context of the mathematical model, the coefficient for each variable has a specific and conceptually deeper interpretation than in a more regular regression analysis.

Even though the regressions included very few variables, the results, once presented and discussed in text, appear to be quite rich. Sørensen shows that the attainment process in fact differs in conceptually meaningful ways between demographic groups. As he writes (p. 382): "Plausible results regarding differences by sex and by race in opportunities for status gains and in resources are established," and further that, "In particular, it establishes that the attainment process for women indeed differs from the process for men, despite the impression created by status attainment research carried out in the conventional metric."

At one point, results appear to counter good intuition and other evidence. Sørensen (p. 381) argues: "Although it should surprise no one that white males have a more favorable position than any other group, it may seem surprising that black women are suffering the most severe employment discrimination. Black women are generally observed (including here; see Table 2) to have higher attainments than black men and higher observed returns to their education. The reason for their higher achievements can be seen from Table 4 to reside in their higher levels of resources, which compensates for less favorable opportunities." Sørensen here provides a different interpretation of the attainment advantage of black women over black men. It is not due to black women facing less discrimination. According to his results, the opposite is the case. It is due to black women possessing more personal resources that they can translate into more gains, even in presence of a less favorable opportunity structure than among black men.

In summary, Sørensen's empirical analysis is subtle and impressive. And it makes full sense. But it requires the carefully delineated model to reach these conclusions. As Sørensen (1979, p. 363) writes: "The main task of this paper is therefore to show that the model of the status attainment process generates plausible results using the new metric and that the new metric is necessary to obtain these results." One can only imagine the excitement he must have felt when first producing these forceful empirical results.

Discussion

This then was a very major work. It influenced several later writers. I always thought of it as important, as a model for formal theorizing, which proceeds by capturing essential features of a social process in an elegant way, and at the same time addressing important societal questions.

In discussing a piece of formal modeling such as Sørensen's, one can always find some aspect that could have been done better, for example, by pointing to alternative and more realistic assumptions. But for this kind of research, it is the broader vision that matters, not any specific assumption made in developing the mathematical model. His broader vision was both important and subtle. There is however one issue in connection with the empirical analysis that I would like to discuss, the solution to which may have resulted in even more powerful empirical results.

Sørensen provides a transformation of socioeconomic status scores that conforms to a particular vision of inequality in society, where rewards follow a pyramidal distribution. This is defensible since traditional scores are measured on an ordinal scale (e.g. 1979, pp. 361–362). An order-preserving transformation such a Sørensen's retains all the information in the scale. He writes (1979, p. 363): "Empirical support for it can be expected only if the assumptions of the model are approximated to a reasonable degree. This is impossible if the traditional status metric is used, since the assumption about the distribution of attainments will then not be valid. A new metric is necessary for ascertaining the usefulness of the model." He then demonstrates the usefulness of his vision by using this new metric in the empirical analysis. That Sørensen used the new metric for socioeconomic status in the research makes sense given the importance of such measures in stratification research at the time (see Hauser & Warren, 1997; Wegener, 1992). In that manner he engaged maximally the status attainment literature he was challenging.

But for assessing the usefulness of his model, and its relevance vis-à-vis human capital theory in economics, another literature he challenged, using earnings as the dependent variable may have made more sense. For one, it is not a constructed variable as socioeconomic status scores are, which often are derived from a regression analysis of income and education. Sørensen's new score, transformed from socioeconomic status scores, is then a construction upon a construction, far removed from anything directly observable. Using earnings would also have given larger transparency to the results. They correspond to the actual distribution of inequality in society as well as to the phenomenology of people's life; employees experience and know what their earnings are. No transformation is needed, there is no arbitrariness in the metric. Or one could, as Sørensen perhaps would have argued, transform earnings to its percentage distribution, so that each person gets a score determined by their placement or rank in the cumulative distribution of earnings, from lowest to highest. Earnings data from occupied jobs are thus unmediated observations in a way that socio-economic status scores are not.

Turning then to other aspects of these articles, in rereading them I was struck by three things: (a) how creative and intelligent they were; (b) how they had a forceful vision and were at the same time subtle, contradictory features difficult to combine; and (c) how effortlessly they read. But they must have taken much effort to write.

Especially the 1979 article may not have received the attention it merited. I think I have an appreciation of why: It is too subtle, exceptionally intelligent, and it requires too much work to master and expand on. One may also speculate whether it too forcefully challenged part of the conceptual thinking at the time, as well as widespread styles of doing research, and may, at least among some sociologists, have appeared combative and controversial, with the result that the subtle and rather measured and above all sensible argument it put forth may have had less impact than deserved.

Later Elaborations

Sørensen returned to many of the themes in the 1977–1979 articles later in his career. He implemented some of the ideas in empirical research. But in terms of the kinds of theorizing these exemplified, he did less to expand on them. But around 1981 he broadened his theoretical agenda considerably. He moved into some more verbal and expansive lines of theorizing. Here he addressed the concerns of stratification and labor market research more broadly, in Sørensen and Kalleberg (1981), and in several other conceptual pieces (1983a, b), including the work on open and closed positions.

In this new line of research there was an added emphasis on understanding aspects of the social structure, not only people's movements between positions in this structure, as had characterized much of the research on vacancy competition. Sørensen (1983a) did however make one important extension of the ideas in the vacancy competition model. From Weber (1978 [1922–1923], pp. 43–46, 341–343), he made the observation that some positions in society are open to competition, whereas other positions are less so. In the part of the labor market with so-called open positions, the opportunities for upward movement in the occupational structure should also be more favorable. In terms of the empirical analyses flowing from the vacancy competition model, a distinction should then be made between positions that are open vs. closed, with separate estimation done for the two, not only separate estimation by sex and race.

In one respect there is a strong continuity between the earlier and later work. In the human capital model of inequality, the rewards that actors receive are "deserved" in the sense that no one receives any unearned advantages, which Sørensen later described as rents. In Sørensen's vacancy chain model, in contrast, as people progress through the occupational structure, they may be held up because there are no opportunities for them to advance. They may possess the skills needed for advancement to higher positions, but when these are already occupied, they cannot progress, and hence suffer a structural disadvantage. Their disadvantage is offset exactly by the structural advantage held by the sometimes less accomplished actors currently occupying the positions.

These themes are taken up again in Sørensen's (1996, 2000) later work on structural inequality, rents, and class. In an economy with open positions, the distribution of inequality will closely mirror the distribution of individual resources. But with many closed positions, the fit is less tight, and individuals and groups earn rents, unrelated to their resources and merits, as a function of structural advantages gained at fortuitous earlier points in historical time.

His original vacancy competition model connected very closely to key concerns in the social stratification literature, perhaps most important, to the question of how open a society is. The central parameter in his model measures the degree of openness. The added distinction between open and closed positions strengthens the ties to concerns in classical sociology, by pointing out that various positions in the labor market vary in how open they are, and that rents may be earned in closed positions.

THREE METHODOLOGICAL LESSONS FROM THE VACANCY COMPETITION MODEL

The theoretical contribution was the central one in these articles. But here I want to discuss some methodological lessons to be drawn from the work. I now need to go beyond the written record and extrapolate. I don't know whether this is the way Sørensen viewed these matters. But I would like to think that he would agree with what I say. Sørensen himself (1998, pp. 257–263) draws some general methodological lessons from his vacancy competition model, but then stressing a different aspect than I do, namely the need for formulating mathematical models specifying the mechanisms at work in various social spheres.

Lesson 1: The Mathematical Modeling Approach

For the models in Sørensen (1977a, b, 1979) there were three or four central equations: describing the opportunity structure, the rate at which opportunities arise, and the individual resources. The equations made up what one could call the structural form of the model.

Sørensen then usually combined all the equations into one final equation, a so-called reduced form, which would consist of elements from each of the original equations. Each parameter in the final equation would then be a mongrel of the fixed opportunity structure, the rate at which opportunities arrive, and individual resources. Then a verbal argument was put forth: Usually that different groups, for example, blacks versus white, women versus men, differed in the rate at which opportunities arrive. This would lead to estimation separately by group, and then comparison of coefficients across groups. There was rarely an attempt at estimating an entire system of equations. Mostly a single, usually simple, reduced form was estimated. But each parameter in the reduced form was interpreted relative to the underlying system of equations. And from the reduced form he could by algebraic manipulation recover the parameters in the structural form.

In my view, this is a fruitful and sometimes even the right way to proceed in formal modeling leading to quantitative empirical analysis. It is so for two reasons. One is that the reduced form is easier to estimate. It does not involve estimation of several non-linear equations, which can make one nervous about the extent to which results reflect what the world looks like vs. reflecting possibly dubious assumptions needed for the estimation. Another is that estimates from the reduced form often are very interpretable, even without the theory. They have some descriptive immediacy beyond the interpretation that can be given in connection with the stated theory.

Lesson 2: Most Equations Estimated Had Very Few Variables

Why was this? There are often compelling statistical reasons to have only a few control variables in a regression equation. The reason is that with many controls, the estimated parameters might ride on the results in small subgroups in the data, describing marginal parts of the population, and thus missing entirely the broad patterns of what goes on. But that was not Sørensen's reason.

I don't think one can satisfactorily understand why Sørensen included few variables by looking at his written work. He comments on the virtue of simplicity several places (Sørensen, 1977b, p. 969; 1979, p. 363), but he clearly has in mind the simplicity of the mathematical formulation, not of the resulting regression equation. One needs rather to turn to his legacy as a teacher and colleague, from interactions as an advisor, in colloquia, and so forth. And in these roles he could be quite different from how he comes across in his written work, equally interesting and stimulating, but different.

In teaching, while arguing for simplicity, he once stated: "You need to believe God created the world simple." Whether he believed this as a correct statement about the world, I doubt. But I think he took it as a guideline when doing research. I remember one incident, around 1995, when he told me of a dinner he went to with two distinguished chemists at I believe a Max Planck Institute in Germany. They were discussing a particularly difficult problem in contemporary chemistry. At some point in the discussion one of the chemists declared, "The problem is unsolvable. It has too many variables: Three." Sørensen was very pleased with this story. He favored simplicity.

Sørensen may on this account have placed too much faith in God; there is little in the social world that suggests great simplicity. But the lesson Sørensen took from this was still on target: Social science analysis should try to be simple, not necessarily because the world is simple, but because that is the only way we can make sense of it. Sørensen (1998, p. 242) later wrote as much: "Social processes are complicated phenomena. The task of theory is to simplify them and characterize them in terms of their essential elements."

Lesson 3: The Need for Dynamic Analysis

In several of these articles, Sørensen (esp. 1975b, 1976) stressed the need for over-time data and dynamic analysis. He showed how a cross-sectional regression equation really could been seen as a snap-shot taken at one point in time of a dynamic process. As such it could be misleading of what went on.

This lesson is now widely accepted. There has been a revolution in dynamic models for data analysis and in longitudinal data collection. Sørensen (1977b, p. 976) writes: "A test of the proposed model for the dependency of the rate of job shifts on time in labor force can be obtained using life-history data that give information on the completed durations of each job." Sørensen provided some rudimentary methods (pp. 375–377). It was however Tuma, Hannan, and others that developed the needed statistical methodology.

Summary

In summary, the combined forces of Lessons 1 and 2 result in a reduced-form equation to be estimated, usually by simple procedures, least squares, logit, hazard rate, and very few variables included in the estimated equation. This approach of low-fat statistics is healthy for data and for science. But it is not an approach that is much heeded in current quantitative sociology. The most important exception is in some of the research in population ecology (e.g. Carroll & Hannan, 2000). The third lesson, the need for dynamic models and longitudinal data, is now fully accepted. Sørensen was among the earlier proponents of such approaches, and here his views have prevailed.

DISCUSSION AND CHARACTERIZATION OF THE QUANTITATIVE WORK

I have already given a main characterization of Sørensen's quantitative work: It was deeply informed by theory, carefully so. He rarely reported large regression models, he was always to the point, using a rather slim menu of variables. This work will be remembered less for the actual findings, more for the conceptualization leading up to the empirical work.

There are obviously many ways of doing empirical quantitative research, but one contrasts clearly to Sørensen's style and is especially important, namely that which uses interesting and new data to document social trends or facts.

In this the role of theory is less important. James Coleman was a regular contributor. Sørensen was however critical of such endeavors. He wrote (Sørensen, 1999, p. 31) that there was a disjuncture in Coleman's oevre, between his theorizing and his empirical work. The theorizing was careful, specifying the processes at work, exemplified in Coleman (1964). But the large-scale empirical work used "ad hoc statistic models for the estimation of relationships among variables." Sørensen (1999, p. 33) attributed this to Coleman's desire to influence policy. As he wrote in 1998 (pp. 264–265): "I believe the reason was that, for policy research, he thought that the presentation of sociological theory in mathematical models would make the research unacceptable to everyone but a few sociologists."

I have much sympathy for Sørensen's criticism of less formal and more ad hoc empirical work. But it is in my view not always correct. For some social processes, useful documentation can be made without being particularly explicit when it comes to theory. It requires an approach from Sherlock Holmes: "It is a capital mistake to theorize before one has data. Insensibly one begins to twist facts to suit theories, instead of theories to suit facts" (Doyle, 1986, Vol. 1, p. 212). And perhaps even stronger, "The temptation to form premature theories upon insufficient data is the bane of our profession" (Doyle, 1986, Vol. 2, pp. 163–164). When little is known in a field, when massive and informative data have been assembled, a more descriptive approach is sometimes what is needed. And that is in fact one of the ways Coleman (1970) defended his at times "ad hoc" statistical analyses. Sørensen, in contrast, worked in what may be described as a mature area of sociology. Within this he charted new conceptions and ways of thinking about the phenomena. He also used new types of data, event histories, and with it new types of methods. But the central goal was to derive novel ways of thinking about processes around which much thinking had already been done, as opposed to generating new empirical facts.

On balance, despite the criticisms he often raised, I don't think Sørensen was against the kind of empirical research that emphasizes findings more than conceptualizations. He just favored a more deeply informed theoretical approach. He even did some work which documented broad empirical patterns. One of his last papers was with Susan Dumais and Stephen Morgan analyzing educational data, "Schools, Learning, and Educational Opportunity" (Sørensen et al., 1999). It gave several interesting and broad findings. But it also interpreted many of these within a carefully delineated theory. Even when he perhaps tried to, he could in the end not let his strong theoretical vision go.

That said, there is one thing he unquestionably was against, namely the practice in much quantitative research "to consider too many variables simultaneously . . ." (1998, p. 241), that is, of using a large array of explanatory variables. Such regression-type models would clearly not correspond to a meaningful theory of the processes in question. But they would not even give useful but more theory-free empirical findings. As Sørensen (1998, p. 243) states: "The result is a conceptually meaningless list of variables preventing any kind of substantive conclusion. . . ." And he continues (p. 243): "While the wish to control by introducing additional variables is taken over directly from tabular analysis, there is an important, but largely unnoticed, difference between the two modes of analyzing data. In tabular analysis, there are no restrictions on the form of relationships among the variables. In regression analysis, the relationship is assumed to be additive."

The research style Sørensen exemplified is unquestionably important for the discipline. But even within quantitative work, it cannot be the only style, and probably not the most important. The reason is that there is a significant role for sociologists and social scientists for merely finding out about the empirical world. And such discovery and documentation of facts must occur primarily using simple procedures, ones that do not rely on complex functional forms, derivations and transformations of central variables. These are situations where the data ought to speak in a rather unmediated form. Without routinely establishing new facts our roles as social scientists would furthermore soon be in peril. And with this I think Sørensen also agreed. It was just not a type of sociology he often practiced.

But for this kind of research, which attempts to establish facts, Sørensen clearly thought regression models with many variables would not be a fruitful way for proceeding. It requires instead an approach closer to cross-tabular analysis, which has the advantage of being non-parametric with respect to functional form, but also of being accessible to a larger readership. And with the large data sets that increasingly have become available, there is also more scope for tabular analyses, even when many variables are to be taken into account. This extends to regression analysis with few independent variables but done separately for many subgroups defined by say race and sex and other variables, an approach close in spirit to tabular analysis. As Sørensen (1998, p. 239) wrote: "Simple cross-tabulations and percentages are, in fact, often better able to express sociologists' simple theoretical ideas than the ad hoc models suggested by statistical techniques." Or as he wrote in the conclusion to the same chapter (p. 264): "Simple tabular analysis, as was done before the advent of high-speed computing, is often not a bad idea."

So I would say in conclusion about Sørensen's empirical work that it is not at all ostentatious, exercising considerable restraint, seldom letting out all the stops. It was rarely work that would stand primarily on the empirical findings, although those were important too. It was work where the conceptualization was as important as the results. It shaped the ways we think about social processes in the area of inequality. As my colleague Michael Hout said: "You would ignore it at your own peril."

ACKNOWLEDGMENTS

I thank Mike Hout, Arne Kalleberg, Stephen Morgan, Mikolaj Piskorski, and Bernd Wegener for comments. The article is based on a presentation given at the Annual Meetings of the American Sociological Association in 2001 at a session on "Aage Sørensen's Contribution to Quantitative Methodology," Anaheim California, August 19, 2001.

REFERENCES

Beck, E. M., Horan, P. M., & Tolbert, C. M., II (1980). Stratification in a dual economy: A sectoral model of earnings determination. *American Sociological Review*, *43*, 704–720.

Blau, P. M., & Duncan, O. D. (1967). *The American occupational structure*. New York: Wiley.

Carroll, G. R., & Hannan, M. T. (2000). *The demography of corporations and industries*. Princeton, NJ: Princeton University Press.

Coleman, J. S. (1964). *Introduction to mathematical sociology*. Glencoe, IL: Free Press.

Coleman, J. S. (1970). Reply to Cain and Watts. *American Sociological Review*, *35*(2), 242–249.

Doyle, Sir A. C. (1986). *Sherlock Holmes: The complete novels and stories* (Vols 1 and 2). New York: Bantam Books.

Feller, W. (1966). *An introduction to probability theory and its applications* (2nd ed.). New York: Wiley.

Hauser, R. M., & Warren, J. R. (1997). Socioeconomic indexes for occupations: A review, update, and critique. In: A. E. Raftery (Ed.), *Sociological Methodology* (Vol. 27, pp. 177–298).

Palloni, A., & Sørensen, A. B. (1990). Methods for the analysis of event history data: A didactic overview. In: P. B. Baltes, D. L. Featherman & R. M. Lerner (Eds), *Life-Span Development and Behavior* (Vol. 10, pp. 291–323). Hillsdale, NJ: Lawrence Earlbaum.

Sørensen, A. B. (1974). A model for occupational careers. *American Journal of Sociology*, *80*(1), 44–57.

Sørensen, A. B. (1975a). The structure of intragenerational mobility. *American Sociological Review*, *40*(4), 456–471.

Sørensen, A. B. (1975b). Models of social mobility. *Social Science Research*, *4*(2), 65–92.

Sørensen, A. B. (1976). Models and strategies in research on attainment and opportunity. *Social Science Information*, *15*(1), 71–91.

Sørensen, A. B. (1977a). Estimating rates from retrospective questions. In: D. Heise (Ed.), *Sociological Methodology* (pp. 209–223). San Francisco: Jossey-Bass.

Sørensen, A. B. (1977b). The structure of inequality and the process of attainment. *American Sociological Review*, *42*(6), 965–978.

Sørensen, A. B. (1979). A model and a metric for the process of status attainment. *American Journal of Sociology*, *85*(2), 361–384.

Sørensen, A. B. (1983a). Processes of allocation to open and closed positions in social structure. *Zeitschrift für Soziologie*, *12*, 203–224.

Sørensen, A. B. (1983b). Conceptual and methodological issues in sociological research on the labor market. *Work and Occupations*, *10*, 261–287.

Sørensen, A. B. (1996). The structural basis of social inequality. *American Journal of Sociology*, *101*(5), 1333–1365.

Sørensen, A. B. (1998). Theoretical mechanisms and the empirical study of social processes. In: P. Hedström & R. Swedberg (Eds), *Social Mechanisms* (pp. 238–266). New York: Cambridge University Press.

Sørensen, A. B. (1999, January 27). *Statistical models and mechanisms of social processes*. Manuscript. Department of Sociology, Harvard University, Cambridge, MA.

Sørensen, A. B. (2000). Toward a sounder basis for class analysis. *American Journal of Sociology*, *105*(6), 1523–1558.

Sørensen, A. B., Dumais, S. A., & Morgan, S. L. (1999, August 27). *Schools, learning and educational opportunity: A replication of the main conclusions of the equality of educational opportunity report*. Manuscript. Department of Sociology, Harvard University, Cambridge, MA.

Sørensen, A. B., & Kalleberg, A. L. (1981). An outline of a theory of the matching of persons to jobs. In: I. Berg (Ed.), *Sociological Perspectives on the Labor Market* (pp. 49–74). New York: Academic Press.

Sørensen, A. B., & Sørensen, A. (1977). *Mathematical sociology: A trend report and an annotated bibliography* (Vol. 23, No. 2 of *Current Sociology*). The Hague: Mouton.

Sørensen, A. B., & Tuma, N. B. (1981). Labor market structures and rates of job shifts. In: D. Treiman (Ed.), *Research in Social Stratification and Mobility* (Vol. 1, pp. 67–97).

Treiman, D. M., & Terrell, K. (1975). Sex and the process of status attainment: A comparison of working women and men. *American Sociological Review*, *42*, 184–200.

Weber, M. (1978 [1922–1923]). *Economy and society*. Berkeley and Los Angeles, CA: University of California Press.

Wegener, B. (1992). Concepts and measurement of prestige. *Annual Review of Sociology*, *18*, 253–280.

EDUCATIONAL INEQUALITY

SCHOOLING AND ACADEMIC ACHIEVEMENT IN TIME AND PLACE

Robert M. Hauser

> Much as age-grading changed the definition of a quality school system from one with high rates of failure to one with high rates of promotion, so in the 1940s, educators began to adopt the idea that automatic promotion, or as it would later be called 'social promotion,' of virtually all students was the sign of true educational quality (Angus et al., 1988, p. 227).

Aage B. Sørensen was a wonderful friend and a stimulating and generous colleague. We had many common interests, especially in the areas of education and of social stratification. We also never hesitated to disagree with one another – indeed we both loved to disagree with one another, often and with passion. I especially recall a research conference in Hawaii in December 1980, at which scholars from Japanese and American universities were equally represented. Aage and I – among others – went at it hammer and tongs, much to the dismay of our Japanese colleagues, who were unaccustomed to such heated academic exchange. I can recall the two of us having a great laugh afterwards about the manifest distress that we had created. In this essay I seek to honor Aage's important scientific contributions by taking them seriously enough to disagree-in hopes of extending and redirecting future research. I wish that Aage were still around to hassle me at every turn.

Aage B. Sørensen's research on schooling and academic achievement – like the vast share of research on the effects of education – is predicated on an ideal-typical conception of the process of schooling. The implicit idea is that students progress in lock step from grade to grade within a school, or within a set of schools in which progression from grade to grade is the norm. To be sure, schools are differentiated internally, e.g. by systems of academic tracking and other mechanisms of classroom

Inequality: Structures, Dynamics and Mechanisms: Essays in Honor of Aage B. Sørensen
Research in Social Stratification and Mobility, Volume 21, 47–65

ISSN: 0276-5624/doi:10.1016/S0276-5624(04)21004-6

assignment (Sørensen, 1970), and schools and school systems are differentiated from one another, e.g. by their auspices (public or private), by geographic location, and by modes and degrees of integration between family and school organization (Sørensen & Morgan, 2000). Thus, as demonstrated in much of Sørensen's work on education, the important theoretical and methodological task is to specify a mathematical model of learning and the implications of the model for estimation of the effects on current achievement – *at a specific grade level* – of prior learning, opportunities for learning, and student background factors. This is well illustrated in a number of Sørensen's papers across a span of about 25 years (Hallinan & Sørensen, 1987; Sørensen, 1970, 1978; Sørensen & Hallinan, 1977; Sørensen & Morgan, 2000), of which many are collaborations with Maureen Hallinan, Stephen Morgan, and others.

Sørensen's theoretical and methodological innovation in this work is his steadfast emphasis on the importance of opportunities to learn (Sørensen, 1978; Sørensen & Hallinan, 1977; Sørensen & Morgan, 2000). He argues consistently that opportunity to learn increases learning by those who are best prepared to learn more than among those less well prepared. Thus, in the absence of strong countervailing organizational forces, greater opportunity to learn tends to increase inequality in educational outcomes. This is a powerful and persuasive idea, one that is cautionary, say, to analysts and policymakers who focus on opportunity to learn as a key variable in the equalization of educational outcomes. By virtue of its implication that learning will occur differentially, it also calls attention to the possibility that levels and rates of learning will interact with student background characteristics and with their prior academic preparation.

Time enters Sørensen's educational models in one – but only one – important way. Academic achievement is measured at two (or more) points in time. This permits analyses of differential growth in achievement, or of differences in the level of achievement at a later time that depend on prior achievement and other relevant variables. School effects, in this setup, differentiate growth in achievement among students from one time of year to another or one grade level to the next. The structure of data typically available in studies of academic achievement virtually dictates this research design and this way of thinking about differential growth in academic achievement.

In his recent essay with Stephen Morgan (Sørensen & Morgan, 2000), Sørensen notes the importance of assessing the effects of schooling per se – a process that occurs across time-in addition to comparing the effects of teaching methods and curricula:

> . . . it is important to recognize that the absence of associations between school differences and learning does not support the conclusion that schools are unimportant. For example, if all schools successfully produce the same level of achievement among students on some

> outcome, no impact will be inferred from an examination of variation across schools with different characteristics. Nonetheless, the effect of schooling may still be powerful, especially if uniform achievement across schools compensates for inequality in outcomes that would otherwise arise from individual differences in family background and genetic endowments. The possible existence of such a research finding justifies a distinction between the effects of schools (i.e. the effect of variation among schools on outcomes) and the effect of schooling (i.e. the overall effect of the schooling process) (p. 138).

There is a great deal to be said in favor of studying the effects of schooling, rather than school effects, not least among which is that we have good reason to think that the latter effects are large, while the former remain problematic more than three decades after the publication of the largest and most influential study in the field (Coleman et al., 1966). However, Sørensen and Morgan had been commissioned to write about school effects,[1] and thus they turned immediately from that astute observation to an exposition of models and methods for studying the effects of school-to-school differences.

Even in a world of lockstep grade progression, a focus on changes in academic achievement across time would create measurement problems in Sørensen's analytic approach. That is, the assumption is that, if y_1 and y_2 are measurements of academic achievement at times t_1 and t_2, it is appropriate to analyze the difference variable, $y_2 - y_1$. However, this analysis is appropriate only if y_1 and y_2 are on the same vertical scale. This is a serious problem in test construction – and one that has led to erroneous inferences in at least one sociological analysis of school learning. Alexander, Entwisle and Dauber (1994) compared growth in achievement on a scale that was compressed at the low end and stretched out at the high end on the supposition that early learning occurs faster than later learning. Thus, weak students – those whose scores were initially low – gained more scale points and appeared to learn more across time than strong students as a direct and inevitable consequence of the way in which the achievement scale had been constructed (Alexander, 1998; Alexander et al., 1994; Shepard et al., 1996, 1998). In the absence of metric equivalence, it is of course possible to analyze y_2 in a model that includes y_1, among other explanatory variables.

There are other serious theoretical and methodological problems in the straightforward, repeated measurement research design. I shall focus on the pervasive violation of its simplifying assumptions about the progress of students through school. That is, a great deal of variation in educational opportunities and in opportunities to learn arises by dint of the movement of students from school to school and of the failure of students to progress from grade to grade. To be sure, for methodological and operational reasons, it is difficult to follow students from school to school, to cope with the variable pace of progress through the grades, and to ascertain comparable measures of academic achievement and of opportunities to learn across different educational settings. Thus, the conventional model of change in academic achievement unfortunately rests on the conflation of an idealized conception of the educational process with a relatively simple design for data collection and analysis. This is convenient, but it misses unknown – but probably very large components of inequality in opportunities to learn.

Student mobility from school to school is well-known to be a common and highly disruptive occurrence in elementary and secondary schooling-and especially among poor and minority students. Such movement is to some degree correlated with and similar to movement across academic tracks or streams – structures that are clearly recognized in Sørensen's accounts of the schooling process. However, student mobility frequently occurs for reasons that are exogenous to the schooling process and entirely outside the control of school personnel. For example, Rumberger and Larson (1998, pp. 1–2) report:

> A national longitudinal survey of U.S. eighth graders in 1988 found that 31% had changed schools two, or more times between the first and eighth grades and 10% changed schools two more times between the eighth and twelfth grades, not counting regular promotions between elementary, middle, and high schools [(National Center for Education Statistics, 1995, Indicator 46)]. A more recent national study found that more than 40% of all third graders had changed schools at least once since first grade and 17% had changed schools two or more times [(United States and General Accounting Office, 1994)]. In both studies student mobility was higher among Latino, black, Native American, and poor children than among white, Asian, and middle – and high – income children.

I have not studied rates or consequences of student mobility, and I will say no more about them, except that they ought to be taken into account in analyses of school achievement and completion (Rumberger & Larson, 1998).

In the remainder of this essay, I review recent research on the extent and consequences of grade retention in American schools. Grade retention – along with student mobility – looms large as a limitation of opportunity to learn. It is thus a mechanism that complements and amplifies the classroom and intra-school differences in learning opportunities on which much of Sørensen's work focuses. Note, for example, the emphasis on tracking and curricula in Sørensen (1970) and the references to teacher behavior, teaching methods, curricula, and time on task in Sørensen and Hallinan (1977, p. 276). Indeed, Sørensen (1970, p. 360) prefaces his analysis of organizational differentiation in schools with the provision, "Because of its near universality, age-grade grouping is taken for granted in the following discussion." Thus, the movement of students from place to place and in violation of age-grade norms is absent from these accounts of the organization of learning, and they are incomplete on that account.

Students are rarely pushed ahead – or "double-promoted" – in school, but they are very often retained in grade. Until President Clinton called for "an end to social promotion" in 1998 (Clinton, 1998), retention in grade had long been ignored as an educational practice. However, by extending the length of elementary and secondary schooling – or reducing it through early dropout – retention practices have large effects on academic achievement and ultimate educational attainment (Shepard & Smith, 1989).

RATES OF GRADE RETENTION IN THE UNITED STATES

To support its analyses of high-stakes testing for promotion and retention, the National Research Council's Committee on Appropriate Test Use assembled and analyzed data on rates, trends, and differentials in grade retention (National Research Council, Committee on Appropriate Test Use 1999, Table 6–1).[2] Perhaps the most striking fact from this effort to bring together existing data is that – despite the prominence of social promotion as an issue of educational policy – very little information about it is available.

No federal or independent agency monitors social promotion and grade retention. Occasional data on retention are available for some states and localities, but coverage is sparse, and little is known about the comparability of these data (Shepard & Smith, 1989). For example, the denominators of retention rates may be based on beginning-of-year or end-of-year enrollment figures. The numerators may include retention as of the end of an academic year or as of the end of the following summer session. Some states include special education students in the data; others exclude them. In the primary grades, retention is usually an all-or-nothing matter; in high school, retention may imply that a student has completed some requirements but has too few credits to be promoted.

Some states do not collect retention data at all or collect very limited data. For example, the NRC study found that 13 states – Colorado, Connecticut, Illinois, Kansas, Montana, Nebraska, Nevada, New Hampshire, New Jersey, North Dakota, Pennsylvania, Utah, and Wyoming – collect no statewide data on grade retention. Twenty-two states, plus the District of Columbia, provided data on retention at some grade levels, but in some cases the data were very limited. For example, New York State collects such data only at the 8th grade.

Retention rates are highly variable across states. They are unusually high in the District of Columbia, whose students are largely black. Rates are relatively low in some states, like Ohio, including states with relatively large minority populations, like South Carolina and Georgia. Retention rates tend to be relatively high in the early primary grades – though not in kindergarten – and in the early high school years.

The main federal source of information about education, The National Center for Education Statistics, provides essentially no statistics about grade retention or social promotion. For example, there are no data on this subject in current editions of its two major statistical compendia, the Digest of Education Statistics (National Center for Education Statistics, 2002b) and the Condition of Education (National Center for Education Statistics, 2002a).

One egregious exception to the lack of federal information about grade retention and promotion is an Education Department publication, *Taking Responsibility for Ending Social Promotion: A Guide for Educators and State and Local Leaders* (U.S. Department of Education, 1999). While it also cites more reputable estimates of grade retention, the *Guide* features a "conservative" estimate from "1996 Current Population Statistics" that "only about 3% of students are two or more years over age for their grade (an indication that they have been retained at least once)" (p. 6). This estimate is indefensibly low for three reasons. First, it covers only currently enrolled students, ignoring persons of normal school age who have fallen behind and dropped out. Second, by referring to K-12 students at all grade levels, it aggregates data for children in the primary grades, who have had few years at risk of retention, with data for children in higher grades, who have had many years at risk of retention. Third, by counting as "retained" only those students who are two or more years above the modal age for their grade, the Guide fails to include a large number of retained students. I cannot think of any rationale for this statistic, other than an effort to mislead the public about the true extent of grade retention.

The most uniform, current source of information on levels, trends, and differentials in grade retention is the Current Population Survey (CPS) of the U.S. Bureau of the Census. Using published data from the annual October School Enrollment Supplement of the CPS, it is possible to track the distribution of school enrollment by age and grade each year for groups defined by sex and race/ethnicity. These data have the advantage of comparable national coverage from year to year, but they say nothing directly about educational transitions (or about the role of high-stakes testing in grade retention). We can only infer the minimum rate of grade retention by observing changes in the enrollment of children below the modal grade level for their age from one calendar year to the next. Suppose, for example, that 10% of six-year-old children were enrolled below the 1st grade in October of 1994. If 15% of those children were enrolled below the 2nd grade in October of 1995, when they were seven years old, we would infer that at least 5% had been held back in the 1st grade between 1994 and 1995. Using this approach, the CPS data, and other data collected by the National Research Council's Committee on Appropriate Test Use, I review below trends in retention and social differentiation in retention.

Extended Kindergarten Attendance

Historically, there has been great variation in age at school entry in the United States. This variation had more to do with the labor demands of a farm economy and the availability of schooling to disadvantaged groups than with readiness for school. The variability declined as school enrollment completed its diffusion from middle childhood into younger and older ages (Duncan, 1968; National Research Council, 1989).

The age at entry into graded school has gradually crept upward since the early 1970s, reversing one of the major historic trends contributing to the growth of schooling in the United States. The Census Bureau's statistics on grade enrollment by age show that, from the early 1970s to the late 1980s, entry into 1st grade gradually came later in the development of many children. However, for the past decade there has been little change in age at school entry. Figure 1 shows percentages of 6-year-old children who had not yet entered the 1st grade as of October of the given year.[3] Among six-year-old boys, only 8% had not yet entered the 1st grade in 1971,[4] but 22% were not yet in the 1st grade in 1987, and 20% were not yet in the 1st grade in 2000. Among six-year-old girls, only 4% had not yet entered the 1st grade in 1971, but 16% were not yet in the 1st grade in 1987 or in 2000. While boys are consistently more likely than girls to enter 1st grade after age six there are only small differences between blacks and whites in age at entry into graded school, and these differences consistently favor black children. That is, six-year-old black children are slightly less likely than white children of

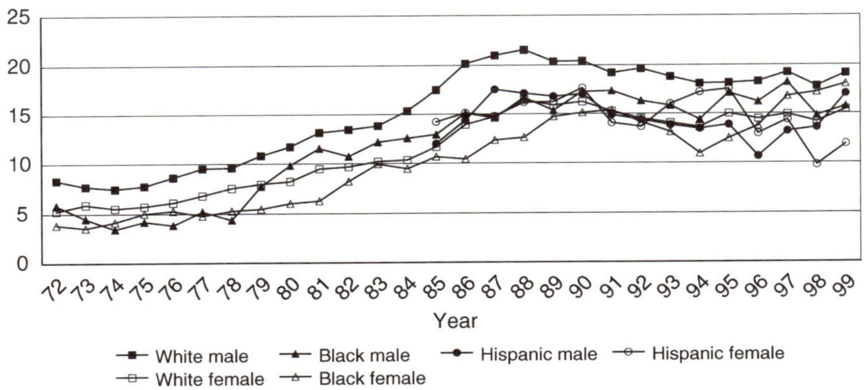

Fig. 1. Percentage of Six Year Old Children Who Have Not Entered First Grade, 1972–1999. *Source:* U.S. Bureau of the Census, Current Population Reports, Series P-20. Entries are three-year moving averages.

the same age and sex to be enrolled below the 1st grade or not enrolled in school. Also, six-year-old Hispanic boys are consistently more likely than white boys to have entered the 1st grade. However, six-year-old Hispanic girls are less likely than white girls to have entered the 1st grade.

It is not clear why age at school entry has increased. One contributing factor has been the influence of state laws on minimum age at school entry. Another – suggested by the initially slow school entry of white boys – is that some parents "red shirt" their children at an early age in order to give them an advantage in athletic competition later on (Graue, 2000). Early school retention is yet a third potential explanation of the trend.

Over the past two decades, attendance in kindergarten has been extended to two years for many children in American schools. There is no single name for this phenomenon. As Shepard (1991) reports, the names for such extended kindergarten classrooms include "junior-first," "prefirst," "transition," and "readiness room." There are also no distinct categories for the first and second years of kindergarten in Census enrollment data. Fragmentary reports suggest that, in some places, kindergarten retention may have been as high as 50% in the late 1980s (Shepard, 1991; Shepard & Smith, 1989). There are also reports of inappropriate use of cognitive tests in such decisions (Shepard, 1991, p. 287; Shepard et al., 1998). The degree to which early retention decisions originate with parents, e.g. to increase their children's chances for success in athletics, rather than with teachers or other school personnel is not known. Moreover, there are no regular national estimates of the prevalence of kindergarten retention, and none of the available state data indicate exceptionally high kindergarten retention rates. From occasional national surveys, Karweit (1999) suggests that, "by first grade between 7 and 11% of children have been retained."

Excepting the ubiquitous tendency for girls to enter (and complete) primary and secondary school at earlier ages than boys, there is little sign of social differentiation in age at school entry. Instead, socially differentiated patterns of grade retention begin to develop after entry into graded school, and they persist through secondary school.

Retention in the Primary and Secondary Grades

Age-grade retardation refers to enrollment below the modal grade level for a child's age (and no broader meaning is either intended or implied). I have examined national rates of age-grade retardation by age, sex, and race ethnicity for three-year age groups at ages 6–17 from 1971 to 1996 and, also, at parallel tabulations for young children by single years of age, 1971–1996. In each case, I have organized

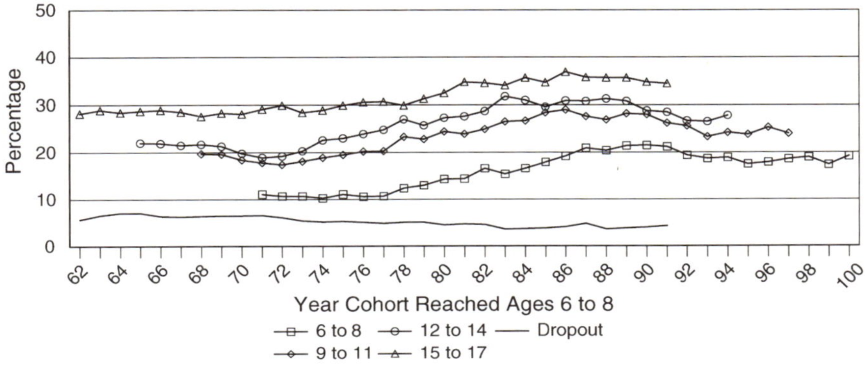

Fig. 2. Percentage of Children Enrolled Beiow Modal Grade for Age by Age Group and Year in Which Cohort was 6–8 Years Old. *Source:* U.S. Bureau of the Census, Historical Statistics, Table A-3, persons 6–17 years old. Dropouts are included in the series at ages 15–17.

the data by birth cohort (year of birth), rather than by calendar year, so it is possible to see the evolution of age-grade retardation throughout the schooling of a birth cohort, as well as changes in age-grade retardation rates from year to year.

The recent history of age-grade retardation is summarized in Fig. 2. It shows age-grade retardation at ages six to eight, nine to 11, 12–14, and 15–17 among children who reached ages six to eight between 1962 and 2000. The horizontal axis shows the year in which an age group reached ages six to eight, so vertical comparisons among the trend lines at a given year show how age-grade retardation cumulated as a birth cohort grew older.

For example, consider children who were six to eight years old in 1991 – the most recent cohort whose history can be traced all the way from ages six to eight up through ages 15–17. At ages six to eight, 21.2% were enrolled below the modal grade for their age. By 1994, when this cohort reached ages nine to 11, age-grade retardation grew to 26.2%, and it was 28.5% in 1997, when the cohort reached ages 12–14. By 2000, when the cohort reached ages 15–17, the percentage who were either below the modal grade level or had left school was 34.5%. Almost all of the growth in retardation after ages 12–14, however, was due to dropout (4.3%), rather than grade retention among the enrolled.

One could read the rate of enrollment below the modal grade at ages six to eight as a baseline measure, that is, as if it did not necessarily indicate that grade retention had taken place. Relative to that baseline, increases in enrollment below the modal grade at older ages clearly show the net effects of retention in grade.

This reading of the data would suggest that, in most birth cohorts, retention occurs mainly between ages to six to eight and nine to 11 or between ages 12–14 and 15–17.[5] This way of looking at the data surely understates the prevalence of grade retention, for much of it occurs within ages six to eight and ages 15–17, that is, early in elementary school or during the high school years.

The series for ages 15–17 includes early school dropout, which is also shown as a separate series along the bottom of the figure. Dropout, rather than retention, evidently accounts for a substantial, but declining component of the increase in age-grade retardation between ages 12–14 and ages 15–17.

The trend in age-grade retardation at ages 6–8, 9–11, 12–14, and 15–17 can be read across Fig. 2 from left to right. Age-grade retardation increased in every age group from cohorts of the early 1970s through those of the middle to late 1980s. Age-grade retardation increased at ages 15–17 after the mid-1970s, despite the slow decline in the early school dropout component throughout the period. That is, grade retention increased while dropout decreased. Peak rates occurred earlier at older than at younger ages, suggesting that policy changes occurred in specific calendar years, rather than consistently throughout the life of successive birth cohorts. Among cohorts entering school after 1970, the percentage enrolled below the modal grade level was never less than 10% at ages six to eight, and it exceeded 20% for cohorts of the late 1980s. The trend-lines suggest that age-grade retardation has declined slightly for cohorts entering school after the mid-1980s, but rates have not approached the much lower levels of the early 1970s.

Overall, a large share of each birth cohort now experiences grade retention during elementary school. Among children aged six to eight from 1982 to 1997, age-grade retardation has reached 24–29% by ages 9–11. There is also great geographic variability in age-grade retardation across the United States. For example, Figs 3–5 show my tabulations of October CPS data, parallel in structure to Fig. 2, for the states of Texas, New York, and Utah. Obviously, retention is far more prevalent in Texas than in New York, while there is scarcely any age-grade retardation in Utah.

In summary, grade retention is pervasive in American schools. No national data are available to tell us the cumulative risk of grade retention across grades 1–12, but some states provide enough data to make such estimates (National Research Council, Committee on Appropriate Test Use, 1999, Table 6–1). For example, Texas has regularly reported the percentages of students who are retained at each grade level, and the rates are reported separately by race/ethnicity. Retention rates have been stable and high from 1990 onward, well before the new initiatives to "end social promotion." For example, if all Texas students were subject to the failure rates of 1996–1997, 17% would fail at least once between the 1st and 8th grades, and 32% would fail at least once between the 9th grade and high school

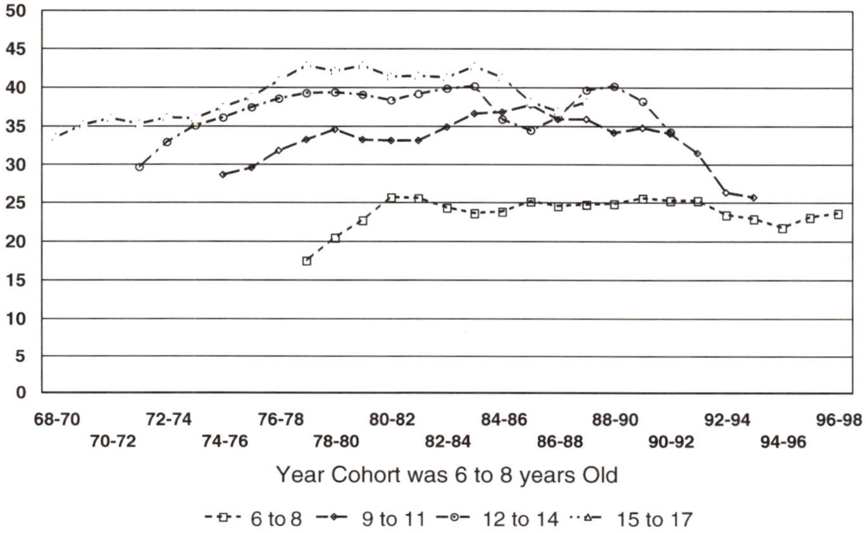

Fig. 3. Percentage Below Modal Grade for Age, Texas: 1968–1970 to 1996–1998.

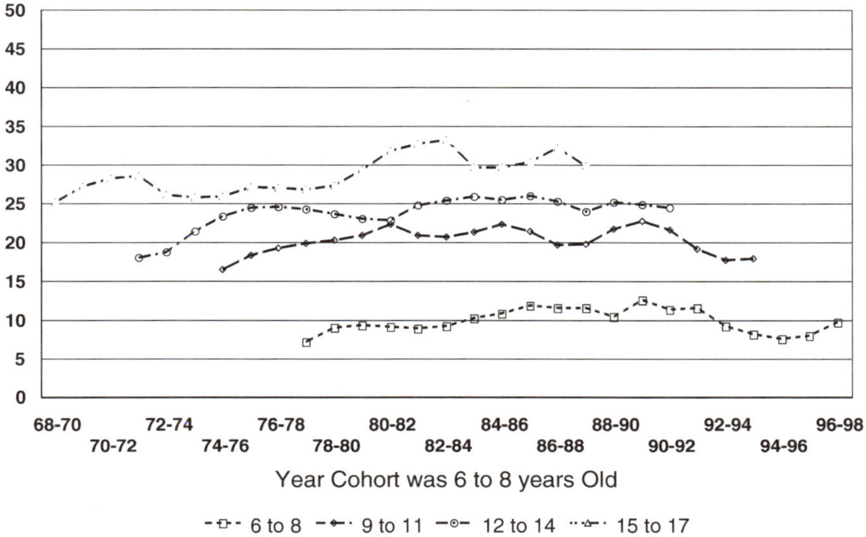

Fig. 4. Percentage Below Modal Grade for Age, New York: 1968–1970 to 1996–1998.

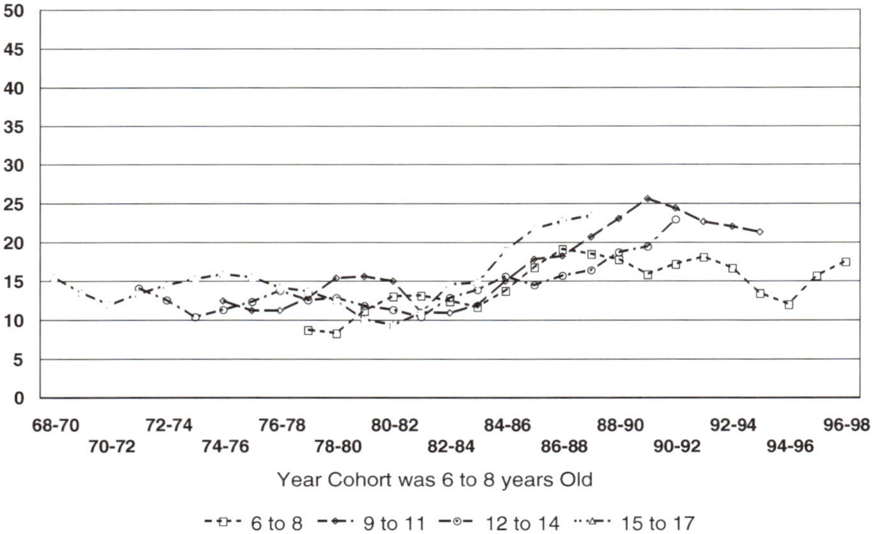

Fig. 5. Percentage Below Modal Grade for Age, Utah: 1968–1970 to 1996–1998.

completion (Texas Education Agency, 1998). Among African American students, the corresponding rates are 20 and 42%, and among Hispanic students they are 21 and 44%.

Social Differences in Retention

While there are similarities in the age pattern of grade retardation among major population groups – boys and girls and majority and minority groups – there are also substantial differences in rates of grade retardation among them, many of which develop well after school entry. Figure 6 shows rates of age-grade retardation of boys and girls at ages six to eight and ages 15–17. Overall, the gender differential gradually increases with age from five percentage points at ages six to eight to 10 percentage points at ages 15–17. That is, boys are initially more likely than girls to be placed below the modal grade for their age, and they fall further behind girls as they pass through childhood and adolescence.

The differentiation of age-grade relationships by race and ethnicity is even more striking than that by gender. Figures 7 and 8 show the development of age-grade retardation by race/ethnicity for children and youth aged six to eight years old and 15–17 years old. Unlike the case of gender differentiation, at ages six to

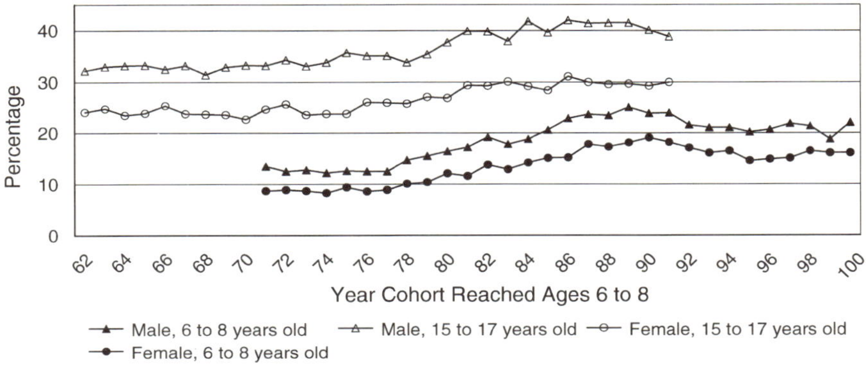

Fig. 6. Percentage Enrolled Below Modal Grade at Ages 6–8 and at Ages 15–17 by Sex and Year Cohort Reached Ages 6–8. *Source:* U.S. Bureau of the Census, Historical Statistics, Table A-3, persons 6–8 and 15–17. Dropout is counted as age-grade retardation at ages 15–17.

eight the rates of age-grade retardation are very similar among whites, blacks, and Hispanics. As early as ages 9–11, the percentages enrolled below modal grade levels have typically been five to 10 percentage points higher among blacks or Hispanics than among whites. The differentials continue to grow with age, and at ages 15–17, rates of grade retardation range from 40 to 50% among blacks and Hispanics, while they have gradually drifted up from 25 to 35% among whites. By ages 15–17, there is a differential between Hispanics and blacks, favoring

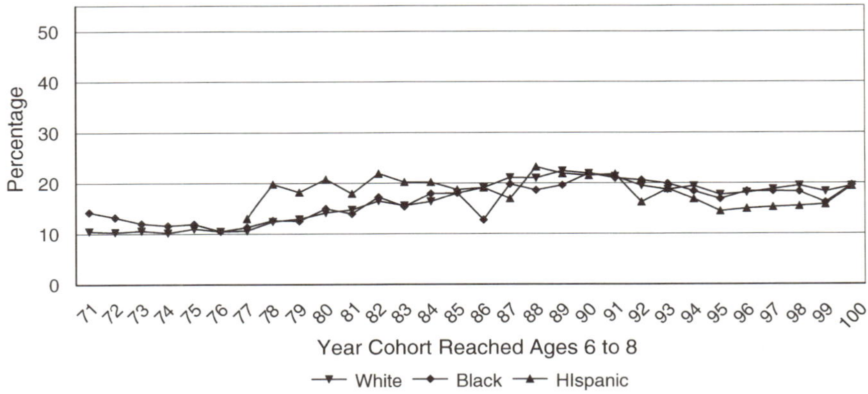

Fig. 7. Percentage Enrolled Below Modal Grade at Ages 6–8 by Race-Ethnicity and Year. *Source:* U.S. Bureau of the Census, Historical Statistics, Table A-3, persons 6–8.

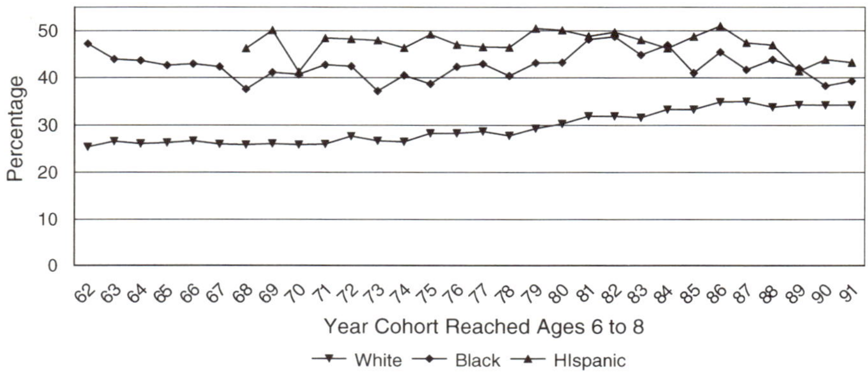

Fig. 8. Percentage Enrolled Below Modal Grade or Dropping Out by Ages 15–17 By Year Cohort Reached Ages 6–8 by Race-Ethnicity. *Source:* U.S. Bureau of the Census, Historical Statistics, Table A-3, persons 15–17. Dropout is counted as age-grade retardation at ages 15–17.

the latter, and this appears to follow from high rates of early school dropout among Hispanics.

In recent years, gender and race-ethnic differentials in age-grade retardation, even at young ages, develop with school experience and are not primarily consequences of differentials in age at school entry. Social differentials in age-grade relationships are vague at school entry, but a hierarchy is clearly established by age 9, and it persists and grows through the end of secondary schooling. This growth can only be explained by selective grade-retention. By age nine, there are sharp social differentials in age-grade retardation, favoring whites and girls relative to blacks or Hispanics and boys. By ages 15–17, close to 50% of black males have fallen behind in school – 30 percentage points more than at ages six to eight – but age-grade retardation has never exceeded 30% among white girls of the same age. These rates and differentials in age-grade retardation are characteristic of a schooling regime in which social promotion is perceived to be the norm. Both the rates and differentials could become much larger as new policies of achievement testing and accountability are put in place.

There is much more to be said about social and economic differentials in grade retention. For example, Hauser et al. (2000) find that socioeconomic background and family structure account for virtually all of the race-ethnic differentials in grade retention over the period from 1972 to 1999. However, their findings, like those reported above, are characteristic of a schooling regime in which social promotion is perceived to be the norm. Both the rates and differentials could become much larger as new policies of achievement testing and accountability are put in place.

EFFECTS OF GRADE RETENTION

Retention in grade is not a negative outcome if it benefits students. But are there positive consequences of being held back in school? Do students do better after repeating a grade, or would they have fared just as well or better if promoted with their peers? Research data indicate that simply repeating a grade does not generally improve achievement (Holmes, 1989; House, 1989; Jimerson, 2001). Furthermore, there is overwhelming evidence that retention increases school dropout (Anderson, 1994; Darling-Hammond & Falk, 1995; Gampert & Opperman, 1988; Grissom & Shepard, 1989; Hauser et al., 2000; Luppescu et al., 1995; Reardon, 1996). Indeed, the latter findings might be traced back to Ayres' seminal observations about the link between promotion, age, and school-leaving (Ayres, 1909, pp. 139–140).[6]

Grade retention is not merely ubiquitous, but it has great consequences for subsequent academic achievement and school continuation. This is the reason that non-movement from grade to grade-along with movement from school to school-should be included in research on academic achievement and opportunities for learning.

CONCLUSION

As time passes, students who begin school at a given time and place are typically dispersed widely across schools and grade levels. Modes and rates of dispersion are variable. They tend to vary with student preparation and background characteristics-precisely the characteristics that – as Aage Sørensen noted – are likely to affect rates of learning and opportunities to learn. There is, to be sure, real scientific value in studies of student achievement that adopt the stylized assumptions of uniform cohort progression through schools. However, uniform progression of school cohorts is to the progress of all students through schools as the "Ozzie and Harriet" family is to all American families (Hernandez, 1993). Thus, a full account of variations in student learning in relation to opportunities must take account of the realities of dispersion in time and place.

Where does this leave the work of Aage Sørensen, and that of others who will continue to study the determinants of levels and changes in academic achievement? The realities of dispersion of the schooling process across time and place challenge educational researchers to adopt new research strategies. In my opinion, research designs should be elaborated to cover the departure of students from the ideal-typical window of observation.[7] Student moves, and student failure, should not be regarded as unfortunate losses of longitudinal data, but as essential opportunities to study some of the most important features of the process and organization of schooling as it actually occurs. This is very difficult to accomplish, both for operational reasons-the cost and difficulty of spreading the process of measurement across multiple venues-and for technical reasons-the problem of assuring comparable measurement across grade levels. One partially successful example is Alexander and Entwisle's (Alexander et al., 1994, 2001) study of a cohort of Baltimore school entrants-which followed all students across time-but not across the boundaries of the Baltimore school system. Another is the recent study of grade retention in Texas (Lorence et al., 2002), in which student records were followed across time within the state-but, again, with coverage loss due to geographic mobility. It is no accident that studies of the effects of school retention have come closest to representing the realities of the schooling process in American society.

In the context of the new, national educational policies, such research designs will be all the more necessary. These policies – those engendered by the *No Child Left Behind Act* as well as those already implicit in the oligopoly of textbook publishing and distribution – will include increased testing of students and increased use of state-mandated standardized tests to make educational decisions about students, e.g. graduation, grade retention, and tracking. Another corollary of increased reliance on tests developed at the state level to make educational decisions will be increased standardization of curricula and teaching methods. That is, the micro-social processes of schooling are becoming increasingly homogeneous. Amidst standardized curricula and instructional processes, the distribution of schooling in time and space is likely to become a more important determinant of learning opportunities and educational outcomes.

NOTES

1. Personal communication from Stephen Morgan.
2. This section of the text draws upon, but updates and expands selected sections of Hauser (2001).
3. U.S. Bureau of the Census, *Current Population Reports*, "School Enrollment: Social and Economic Characteristics of Students" for various years. Percentages shown in Fig. 1 are three-year moving averages and do not agree exactly with the annual estimates reported in the text.
4. The percentages include those enrolled below 1st grade level and a small share of six-year-olds who were not enrolled in school. The data are virtually unchanged if non-enrolled children are eliminated from the analysis: Neither the trends nor the differences by race-ethnicity and gender are affected.
5. We ignore the logical possibility that age-retardation at younger ages could be counter-balanced by double-promotion at older ages.
6. See Hauser (2001) for a detailed review of the effects of grade retention.

7. To an increasing degree, this is being done in the major national longitudinal studies sponsored by the National Center for Education Statistics.

ACKNOWLEDGMENTS

Prepared for a Festschrift in memory of Aage B. Sørensen. This research was supported by The Russell Sage Foundation, through its program of research on social dimensions of inequality and its visiting scholar program, and by the Vilas Estate Trust at the University of Wisconsin-Madison. The opinions expressed herein are those of the author.

REFERENCES

Alexander, K. L. (1998). Letter to the editor. *Psychology in the Schools, 35*(4), 402–404.

Alexander, K. L., Entwisle, D., & Kabbani, N. (2001). The dropout process in life course perspective: Early risk factors at home and school. *Teachers College Record, 103*(5), 760–822.

Alexander, K. L., Entwisle, D. R., & Dauber, S. L. (1994). *On the success of failure: A reassessment of the effects of retention in the primary grades*. Cambridge: Cambridge University Press.

Anderson, D. K. (1994). *Paths through secondary education: Race/ethnic and gender differences*. Unpublished Doctoral Dissertation, Department of Sociology, University of Wisconsin, Madison, Wisconsin.

Angus, D. L., Mirel, J. E., & Vinovskis, M. A. (1988). Historical development of age stratification in schooling. *Teachers College Record, 90*(2), 211–236.

Ayres, L. P. (1909). *Laggards in our schools a study of retardation and elimination in city school systems*. New York: Charities Publication Committee.

Clinton, W. J. (1998). *Memorandum to the secretary of education*. Washington, DC: White House Press Release.

Coleman, J. S., Campbell, E. Q., Hobson, C. J., McPartland, J., Mood, A. M., Weinfeld, F. D., & York, R. L. (1966). *Equality of educational opportunity*. Washington, DC: Government Printing Office.

Darling-Hammond, L., & Falk, B. (1995). Using standards and assessments to support student learning: Alternatives to grade retention. In: *Report to the Chancellor's Committee on Grade Transition Standards. National Center for Restructuring Education, Schools and Teaching*. New York: Teachers College Columbia University.

Duncan, B. (1968). Trends in output and distribution of schooling. In: E. B. Sheldon & W. E. Moore (Eds), *Indicators of Social Change: Concepts and Measurements* (pp. 601–672). New York: Russell Sage.

Gampert, R., & Opperman, P. (1988). Longitudinal study of the 1982–1983 promotional gates students. Paper Presented at the Annual Meeting of the American Educational Research Association, New Orleans, LA.

Graue, M. E. , & D. J. C. (2000). Academic reasserting and early retention. *American Educational Research Journal, 37*(2), 509–534.

Grissom, J. B., & Shepard, L. A. (1989). Repeating and dropping out of school. In: L. A. Sheperd & M. L. Smith (Eds), *Flunking Grades: Research and Policies on Retention* (pp. 34–63). London: Falmer Press.

Hallinan, M. T., & Sørensen, A. B. (1987). Ability grouping and sex differences in mathematics achievement. *Sociology of Education*, *60*(2), 63–72.

Hauser, R. M. (2001). Should we end social promotion? Truth and consequences. In: G. Orfield & M. L. Kornhaber (Eds), *Raising Standards or Raising Barriers? Inequality and High-Stakes Testing in Public Education* (pp. 151–178). New York: Century Foundation Press.

Hauser, R. M., Pager, D. I., & Simmons, S. J. (2000). Race-ethnicity, social background, and grade retention. CDE Working Papers. 2000–08. Madison, Wisconsin: Center for Demography and Ecology, The University of Wisconsin-Madison.

Hernandez, D. J. (1993). *America's children resources from family, government, and the economy.* New York: Russell Sage.

Holmes, C. T. (1989). Grade level retention effects: A meta-analysis of research studies. In: L. A. Sheperd & M. L. Smith (Eds), *Flunking Grades: Research and Policies on Retention* (pp. 16–33). London: Falmer Press.

House, E. R. (1989). Policy implications of retention research. In: L. A. Sheperd & M. L. Smith (Eds), *Flunking Grades: Research and Policies on Retention* (pp. 202–213). London: Falmer Press.

Jimerson, S. R. (2001). Meta-analysis of grade retention research: Implications for practice in the 21st century. *School Psychology Review*, *30*(3), 420–437.

Karweit, N. L. (1999). Grade retention: Prevalence, timing, and effects. In: *CRESPAR Report*. 33. Baltimore, Maryland: Center for Social Organization of Schools.

Lorence, J., Dworkin, A. G., Toenjes, L. A., & Hill, A. N. (2002). Grade retention and social promotion in Texas: Academic achievement among elementary school students. In: D. Ravitch (Ed.), *Brookings Papers on Educational Policy 2002* (pp. 13–52). Washington, DC: Brookings Institution.

Luppescu, S., Bryk, A. S., Deabster, P., Easton, J. Q., & Thum, Y. M. (1995). *School reform, retention policy, and student achievement gains*. Chicago, IL: Consortium on Chicago School Research.

National Center for Education Statistics (1995). *The condition of education 1995*. Washington, DC: Government Printing Office.

National Center for Education Statistics (2002a). *The condition of education 2002*. NCES 2002–025. Washington, DC: Government Printing Office.

National Center for Education Statistics (2002b). *Digest of education statistics 2001*. NCES 2002–130. Washington, DC: Government Printing Office.

National Research Council (1989). In: G. D. Jaynes & R. M. Williams, Jr. (Eds), *A Common Destiny: Blacks and American Society*. Committee on the Status of Black Americans, Commission on Behavioral and Social Sciences. Washington, DC: National Academy Press.

National Research Council, Committee on Appropriate Test Use (1999). In: J. Heubert & R. M. Hauser (Eds), *High stakes: Testing for Tracking, Promotion, and Graduation*. Washington, DC: National Academy Press.

Reardon, S. (1996). Eighth-grade minimum competency testing and early high school dropout patterns. Paper Presented at the Annual Meeting of the American Educational Research Association New York, NY.

Rumberger, R. W., & Larson, K. A. (1998). Student mobility and the increased risk of high school dropout. *American Journal of Education*, *107*(1), 1–35.

Shepard, L. A. (1991). Negative policies for dealing with diversity: When does assessment and diagnosis turn into sorting and segregation? In: E. Hiebert (Ed.), *Literacy for a Diverse Society: Perspectives, Practices, and Policies* (pp. 279–298). New York: Teachers College Press.

Shepard, L. A., Kagan, S. L., & Wurtz, E. (1998). *Principles and recommendations for early childhood assessments*. Washington, DC: Government Printing Office.

Shepard, L. A., & Smith, M. L. (1989). *Flunking grades: Research and policies on retention*. London: Falmer Press.

Shepard, L. A., Smith, M. L., & Marion, S. F. (1996). Failed evidence on grade retention. *Psychology in the Schools*, *33*(3), 251–261.

Shepard, L. A., Smith, M. L., & Marion, S. D. (1998). On the success of failure: A rejoinder to Alexander. *Psychology in the Schools*, *35*(4), 404–407.

Sørensen, A. B. (1970). Organizational differentiation of students and educational opportunity. *Sociology of Education*, *43*(4, Autumn), 355–376.

Sørensen, A. B. (1978). Reconceptualizing school effects. *Sociology of Education*, *51*, 230–233.

Sørensen, A. B., & Hallinan, M. T. (1977). A reconceptualization of school effects. *Sociology of Education*, *50*, 273–289.

Sørensen, A. B., & Morgan, S. L. (2000). School effects: Theoretical and methodological issues. In: M. T. Hallinan (Ed.), *Handbook of the Sociology of Education* (pp. 137–160). New York: Kluwer Academic/Plenum Publishers.

Texas Education Agency (1998). *1998 comprehensive Biennial report on Texas schools: A report to the 76th Texas legislature*. Austin, TX: TEA.

U.S. Department of Education (1999). *Taking responsibility for ending social promotion: A guide for educators and state and local leaders*. Washington, DC: U.S. Department of Education.

United States and General Accounting Office (1994). *Elementary school children many change schools frequently, harming their education: Report to the honorable Marcy Kaptur, House of Representatives*. Washington, DC, Gaithersburg, MD (P. O. Box 6015, Gaithersburg 20884–6015): The Office. Office distributor.

SØRENSEN'S LEARNING OPPORTUNITIES MODEL: THEORETICAL FOUNDATIONS, MATHEMATICAL FORMALIZATION, AND EMPIRICAL ANALYSES

Maureen T. Hallinan

INTRODUCTION

Inequality has long been a central concern in sociology. Typically, sociologists have studied inequality either by focusing on social stratification processes or by analyzing educational opportunities. Stratification researchers have examined how individual characteristics, such as class, race, ethnicity, and gender, and structural factors, such as the structure of job opportunities, affect occupational status and income. Sociologists of education have shown how background and school characteristics affect academic achievement and educational attainment.

In their effort to understand social inequality, many sociologists have tried to link stratification processes and educational processes. Beginning with the Wisconsin study of social stratification, several sociologists have examined the structural and social psychological mechanisms that relate education and occupational mobility and have studied how educational attainment affects occupation and income. Others investigate how schooling influences life outcomes and study ways

Inequality: Structures, Dynamics and Mechanisms: Essays in Honor of Aage B. Sørensen
Research in Social Stratification and Mobility, Volume 21, 67–89

ISSN: 0276-5624/doi:10.1016/S0276-5624(04)21005-8

that education either perpetuates a social order built on privilege, or creates a more meritocractic society where achieved characteristics determine occupational opportunity.

While Aage Sørensen's research interests encompassed both stratification and education, his approach to the study of social inequality differed from that of researchers who attempt to link these two bodies of research. Sørensen's aim was to determine whether similar social patterns could be detected in the generation of both labor market inequalities and educational inequalities. Interested in the way structure shapes opportunity, Sørensen was predisposed to see similarities in how structure affects different social outcomes.

Sørensen conceptualized the labor market as a hierarchy of positions or jobs filled by individuals. Jobs are associated with status and income. The distribution of jobs based on these properties forms the structure of inequality. When a person vacates a position or job, the vacancy generates mobility. Individual characteristics influence the likelihood that a person will utilize a vacancy to move to a higher status position in the occupational hierarchy.

Sørensen assumed an exponential distribution to depict the structure of inequality. He then hypothesized a simple differential equation model to represent the probability of change in an individual's status attainment over time as a function of the structure of vacancies in the job market. Empirical data provided support for his model, referred to as the vacancy competition model.

Sørensen proposed a similar mathematical model to explain the effects of the structure of educational opportunities on student achievement. He argued that school characteristics account, at least in part, for inequalities in student outcomes. Between school effects on student achievement are generated by differences in learning opportunities across schools. Within school differences in student achievement are created by differences in learning opportunities across tracks and ability groups in school. Sørensen formulated a differential equation model to represent the likelihood of change in a student's achievement over time as a function of the structure of opportunities presented to the student. In effect, Sørensen was suggesting that the structural effects of the organizational differentiation of instruction in schools on growth in student learning are similar to the structural effects of the labor market on change in job status.

This chapter focuses on Sørensen's learning opportunities model. First, Sørensen's model will be derived and explicated. Second, the model will be tested on data that were not available to Sørensen. Third, a conceptual foundation for the model, which builds on Sørensen's brief remarks about learning theory, will be presented. Finally, modifications of the model that would increase its validity as a description of the learning process will be discussed.

SØRENSEN'S LEARNING OPPORTUNITIES MODEL

Sørensen was convinced that the models typically used in the 1960s and 1970s to estimate between or within school effects were inadequate. These models depict student achievement as a linear, additive function of student and school characteristics. Challenging this assumption, Sørensen argued that even if students had considerable ability and exerted maximum effort to succeed, they would still fail if they had no opportunities to learn. Consequently, rather than depicting learning as an additive function of ability, effort, and opportunities to learn, Sørensen claimed that these determinants of learning are in a multiplicative relationship with each other.

Sørensen (Sørensen & Hallinan, 1977) theorized that student achievement is a product of opportunities to learn and student ability and effort. He argued that organizational characteristics of schools create differences in learning opportunities for students. These between and within school differences in learning opportunities, he claimed, account for the structure of inequality in student achievement.

Sørensen formulated a differential equation model to describe the impact of learning opportunities, ability, and effort on student achievement. In the model, achievement at time, t, is designated as $y(t)$ and measured as a continuous variable. The rate of change in achievement, or rate of learning, can be depicted as $dy(t)/dt$. This is the quantity which is to be explained in terms of the opportunities to learn provided by a school and student ability and effort.

Opportunities to learn is the key concept in the model. How to operationalize this concept is not obvious. Sørensen focused on the amount of instruction a student receives as the central component of opportunities to learn. He depicted instruction as consisting of the presentation of new material and the review of previously taught material. He assumed that as a semester progressed, the amount of material a teacher reviews would increase, and the amount of new material presented to the students would decrease.

Sørensen designated the amount of new material a student receives at time, t, as $v(t)$. The rate of change in $v(t)$ is $dv(t)/dt$. Since the amount a student learns is proportional to the amount of material presented, the rate of change in achievement, $dy(t)/dt$, is proportional to the rate of change in the amount of material presented, $dv(t)/dt$. The constant of proportionality is determined by the ability and effort of the student and designated as s. Hence,

$$\frac{dy(t)}{dt} = s\,\frac{dv(t)}{dt} \tag{1}$$

This equation states that the rate of change in achievement is dependent on a combination of student ability and effort, s, and the rate of change in the amount of new material presented.

Sørensen's aim in formulating the model was to depict change in achievement as a simple linear differential equation with a negative feedback mechanism of achievement on itself. To achieve this goal, two assumptions are necessary. The first assumption is that as time goes on, less new instructional material is presented to students. The second assumption is that the proportional decline in new material presented is the same for all units of time.

These assumptions imply that the rate of change in amount of material presented, $dv(t)/dt$, declines as t increases, and is related to time as an exponential function. Time can be defined so that $t = 0$ at the start of the period of interest. At the end of the period of interest, $dv(t)/dt = 0$, that is, all new material has been covered, and instruction consists only of repetition. This can be expressed as

$$\frac{dv(t)}{dt} = ke^{-b't} \tag{2}$$

where $b' > 0$ and k is the amount of material presented in the first unit of time. Without loss of generality, one can set $k = 1$. This yields

$$\frac{dv(t)}{dt} = e^{-b't} \tag{3}$$

The solution to Eq. (3) is:

$$v(t) = \left(\frac{1}{b'}\right)(1 - e^{-b't}) \tag{4}$$

When $t = \infty$, $v(t)$ becomes the total amount of opportunities for learning, which Sørensen called v^*. Equation (4) shows that $v^* = (1/b')$ so, $b' = (1/v^*)$. Thus, b' is the inverse of the total amount of instructional material covered. More material provides more opportunities for learning and a greater v^*, but the more material to be covered, the lower the rate of decrease in new material presented, a lower b'. Note that this implies that $b' > 0$.

If one assumes that $y(0) = 0$, that is, nothing has been learned at time 0 because nothing has been taught, Eq. (1) has the simple solution:

$$y(t) = s\, v(t) \tag{5}$$

For notational convenience, let $b = -b'$. Thus, $b < 0$. Substituting Eq. (4) into Eq. (5) gives:

$$y(t) = \left(\frac{s}{b}\right)(e^{bt} - 1) \tag{6}$$

That is, a student's level of achievement at any time, $y(t)$, is determined by the student's ability and effort, s, and the opportunities to learn that are provided by the school over time, indicated by b.

Equation (6) is one mathematical representation of Sørensen's learning opportunities model. This model clearly describes a process in which student achievement is a multiplicative function of individual characteristics and a structure of opportunity. This distinguishes the model from more traditional linear, additive models of achievement, especially those models typically relied on in educational research at the time Sørensen first proposed this model.

Differentiating Eq. (6) with respect to t yields a simple linear differential equation:

$$\frac{dy(t)}{dt} = s + by(t) \tag{7}$$

Equation (7) is the more usual representation of Sørensen's learning opportunities model. Consistent with the theory, the model shows that it is change in achievement, not achievement itself, that occurs in a linear additive fashion.

Two other features of the model are noteworthy. First, the model portrays a negative feedback of achievement on itself. Since $b < 0$, the level of student achievement will have a negative impact on the growth of student achievement. Because b characterizes learning opportunities, the model indicates that this negative feedback mechanism is governed by the rate at which schools and teachers present opportunities to learn to their students.

Second, and most important, the model provides an explicit measure of learning opportunities, b. The scale of this parameter is unknown, and to some extent arbitrarily fixed by certain assumptions. However, this parameter could be investigated across schools, tracks, teachers, and classrooms, allowing a comparison of the differences in learning opportunities for these groups.

Due to the linearity of Eq. (7), the solution does not depend on a specific t, or on the assumption that $y(0) = 0$. If one has observations at two time points, t_1 and t_2, then:

$$y(t_2) = e^{b\Delta t}y(t_1) + \left(\frac{s}{b}\right)(e^{b\Delta t} - 1) \tag{8}$$

where $\Delta t = t_2 - t_1$. If one sets $b^* = e^{b\Delta t}$ then the model becomes:

$$y(t_2) = b^* y(t_1) + s\left[\frac{b^* - 1}{b}\right]. \tag{9}$$

Mathematically, Eq. (9) is a lagged linear model that is commonly used in studies of achievement. However, Sørensen's derivation of this model gives it an explicit interpretation of the coefficients, one which is not common (Sørensen & Morgan,

2000, p. 150). The estimate of b^* is an estimate of learning opportunities and is the key parameter of interest in Sørensen's discussions. Values of b^* vary between 0 and 1, and higher values indicate greater learning opportunities.

Since precise measures of ability and effort, s, are not available, Eq. (9) cannot be estimated. However, indicators of ability and effort are available. These indicators can include many different factors such as family background, prior school performance, grades, and previous track placement. All these factors reflect both students' ability and the effort they have made in school. These indicators also can be thought of as measuring antecedents to students' intellectual resources. Thus, various demographic and geographic factors such as race or region that are not typically conceived of as indicating individual student ability and effort can be included in the model.

Sørensen assumes that these indicators are linearly related to ability and effort. Thus, with M indicators, one has:

$$s = a_0 + a_1x_1 + a_2x_2 + \cdots + a_Mx_M. \tag{10}$$

Achievement, ability, effort, and other individual level characteristics vary from student to student. To make this explicit in the model, the appropriate subscript is added. Substituting Eq. (10) into Eq. (9), yields:

$$y_i(t_2) = b^*y_i(t_1) + a_0^* + a_1^*x_{i1} + a_2^*x_{i2} + \cdots + a_M^*x_{iM} \tag{11}$$

where $a_0^* = a_0[(b^* - 1)/b]$, $a_1^* = a_1[(b^* - 1)/b]$ and so on. The estimates of a are given little attention in Sørensen's empirical analyses using this model.

Note that this parameterization of the model provides only one estimate of learning opportunities, effectively the average learning opportunities across all students. However, learning opportunities vary by schools, by tracks within schools, and possibly even by classrooms within tracks. A separate estimate of learning opportunities for each appropriate unit can be calculated. If there are j schools, k tracks within each school, and l classrooms within each track, one could theoretically estimate the model:

$$y_i(t_2) = b_{jkl}^*y_i(t_1) + a_0^* + a_1^*x_{i1} + a_2^*x_{i2} + \cdots + a_M^*x_{iM} \tag{12}$$

which would provide a separate estimate of learning opportunities for each classroom within each track within each school.

Theoretical interests may lead to different parameterizations of the model. For example, one may wish to estimate the average track effect across all schools in a sample, with or without school effects; or one may wish to compare the track effect within schools or the classroom effect within tracks. While these comparisons are possible by estimating the parameters of Eq. (12), they may be unwieldy in practice. For instance, even in a small data set, the number of classrooms may be too large for classroom learning opportunities to be readily estimated. In a large data set, the number of schools may be too large for the practical estimation of individual school effects. Also, depending on the way the sample is selected, the number of sampled students in a classroom or even in a school may be too small to allow estimation of learning opportunities for that unit, regardless of overall sample size.

Careful selection of a research design can limit the difficulties of estimating opportunity effects across various units, such as schools, tracks, or classrooms. Strategic choice of a sample can allow for efficient tests of the model. However, even if rigorous empirical tests of the model are conducted and show support for the model, this is not the main goal. The outstanding feature of the learning opportunities model is its formalization of a theory of learning. Further theoretical work is needed to better understand the learning process. The primary contribution of empirical work, at this stage of the research on the learning opportunities model, is to inform the theoretical formulation of learning in order to give the model greater comprehensiveness and depth.

EMPIRICAL TEST OF SØRENSEN'S LEARNING OPPORTUNITIES MODEL

In Sørensen's basic model, ability and effort are assumed to be relatively constant, at least during the period under investigation. Day-to-day fluctuations may occur, but there is no general trend of increase or decline in ability and effort during this time. In Sørensen's analyses of the High School and Beyond data (HSB), the duration of the study was two years and he assumed that ability and effort did not change in that length of time. If ability and effort do change in some discernable pattern during this period, however, then the theory is inaccurate and model estimates are biased.

Since the data analyzed in this chapter are for periods of one or two years, Sørensen's assumption will be followed as a reasonable first approximation. Despite limitations of the model represented in Eq. (12), the analysis should provide some insight into whether differences in learning opportunities exist across schools, tracks and ability groups, especially since the data are more appropriate than those available to Sørensen.

Sample

The analyses are conducted on two data sets. The first is the National Educational Longitudinal Study of 1988 (NELS) (National Center for Education Statistics,

1994). NELS is a nationally representative survey of approximately 25,000 8th graders in public and private schools in 1988, with follow-up surveys conducted at two-year intervals for several subsequent years. For these analyses, the 8th and 10th grade data are used.

The second data set is the Ability Group Project (AGP), a survey of over 4,000 students in two cohorts. All students in five public high schools in one school district, one public high school in a neighboring school district, and one Catholic high school in a moderate-size, Midwestern city, were followed from 7th grade through 12th grade. The first cohort began 7th grade in the fall of 1986, and the second cohort began 7th grade the following year. Thus, these data are contemporaneous with the NELS data. The 8th and 9th grade information is used in these analyses.

Dependent Variable: Student Achievement

The NELS survey developed its own standardized test. Each student was provided with a subsample of the items on the test, and an overall score was calculated for the student using Item Response Theory (IRT) methods. These analyses use the composite IRT Theta score, a combination of the reading and mathematics subtests. The dependent variable is the 10th grade test score.

The AGP test scores are percentile scores from a standardized test given to all students in the state in which the study was conducted. The test was designed by a national testing company and normed against a national reference group. All students in the sample took the test in the spring of 8th and 9th grades. Separate analyses were conducted using the Language and Mathematics scores from this test.

Independent Variables: Learning Opportunities, Ability, and Effort

The key independent variable is previous test score, which provides an estimate of learning opportunities. For the NELS analyses, the 8th grade composite IRT Theta score is used. For the AGP analyses, the Language and Mathematics percentile scores from 8th grade are used.

As discussed above, separate estimates of learning opportunities are desirable to examine the effects of schools, tracks, or classrooms. Interactions of previous test score and the appropriate school, track, or ability group generate these estimates of learning opportunities. In practice, the NELS data contain too many schools to provide separate estimates of school effects, but do allow separate estimates of learning opportunities by school sector and track. The school sector analysis includes public and Catholic schools; other private schools are excluded from the analysis. The term track refers to the assignment of students to a program of study by ability. A tracking structure, once characteristic of comprehensive high schools, is seen less frequently today. The track analysis presented here relies on students' self-reported assignment to the Academic, General, or Vocational track.

In the AGP data, learning opportunities are estimated by school sector, school, and ability group. The term ability group refers to the organization of middle and high school students into separate classrooms by ability for each academic subject. Ability group placement in English and Mathematics was taken from school records and coded from course descriptions and discussion with teachers and counselors. Classes are designated as Basic, Regular, Honors, or Advanced, in both English and Mathematics. In addition, a Very Basic ability group is found in Mathematics. The number of ability groups varies slightly from school to school.

Analyses of both the NELS and the AGP data control for demographic factors. Dichotomous variables are included for sex (male = 0, female = 1) and race (nonblack = 0, black = 1). Age is included as a continuous variable, measured in years. For the NELS analyses, a set of dichotomous variables is included for region (using Northeast as the comparison group) and for urbanicity (using Suburban as the comparison group). For the AGP analysis, a dichotomous variable is included for cohort (Cohort 1 = 0, Cohort 2 = 1). In the NELS analyses, socioeconomic status is controlled for using a composite SES measure calculated as a function of education, status, and income. In the AGP analyses, the measure of SES is a dichotomous variable indicating whether the student is receiving a free or reduced lunch (coded "1") or not (coded "0").

The analysis controls for previous achievement, which is an indicator of ability and effort. In the NELS data, previous achievement is measured by a student's self-reported, average grades. In the AGP data, the final grades for the student's previous English and Mathematics class are used. Letter grades are converted to the usual four-point scale (A = 4.0, B = 3.0, and so forth). In addition, the AGP analyses include previous standardized test scores. For the Mathematics analysis, previous English test score is controlled, while in the English analysis, previous Mathematics test score is controlled. Attendance is included in the AGP analyses, but not used in the NELS analysis.

Other indicators of ability and effort include previous track in the NELS analysis and previous ability group placement in the AGP analysis. The NELS analyses include two dummy variables indicating whether the student reported ever having participated in an accelerated or gifted English or Mathematics program, on the one hand, or in a remedial English or Mathematics program, on the other. In the AGP data, dummy variables are added for ability group placement with the categories including Basic, Regular, Honors, and Advanced in English and Mathematics.

Eighth grade ability group placements include additional categories, such as participation in a gifted or remedial program or attending a school that did not track or ability group students for instruction.

Missing Data

Missing data were handled in two ways. Because the dependent variable is test score and the key independent variable is lagged test score, cases with missing data on test scores were excluded from the analyses. Also excluded from the analyses were cases having missing data that are usually available, such as sex and race. For other independent variables where many cases were missing data (such as grades), the mean value of the variable (or, for categorical variables, the median or modal value) was imputed. For each independent variable in which this was done, a dichotomous variable indicating this imputation is included in the models.

Data Limitations

The HSB survey which Sørensen analyzes and the NELS data analyzed in this paper are actually of limited value as measures of what is learned in school and, therefore, less than ideal indicators of opportunities for learning. In the NELS survey, student learning is measured by using a general standardized test, which is a composite of reading and mathematics knowledge. What is needed, but is unavailable, is a test that measures how much a student learned of the material that was presented in class. In addition, the self-reported track placement in NELS and HSB is prone to error. Finally, in NELS, the test measures reading and mathematics knowledge, while students may assess their track placement based upon social studies, science, or other classes in addition to their English and Mathematics classes.

The AGP data allow for somewhat more accurate estimates of learning opportunities than do NELS or HSB. The measure of ability group placement is more exact in the AGP survey: learning opportunities are assessed specifically by subject, and the achievement test was constructed to be administered statewide, based on the curriculum recommended by the state education department. The test is still more general than would be ideal, however.

Statistical Model

In the NELS data, the IRT test scores are theoretically unbounded, justifying the use of ordinary least squares regression to estimate the models. In the AGP data, the percentile scores have an upper bound of 99 and a lower bound of 1. Previous research indicates that regression analyses on these data would be affected by ceiling effects, though not by floor effects. Thus, a tobit model with an upper bound is used for these analyses. It should be noted that Sørensen also used a tobit model for his HSB analysis since that test too has an upper and lower bound.

RESULTS

Table 1a–c shows results from Sørensen's own research, taken from his published estimates. Table 1a reports results of an analysis based on a sample of elementary school classes. The results for high school shown in Table 1b and c are based on the HSB survey. The models Sørensen estimates are similar to the statistical model described in Eq. (12), but with the effects of the ability and effort variables allowed to vary by group. They do not, however, vary by student within group. Where necessary, summed estimates of main effects and interaction effects have been used to arrive at b^* for the indicated group.

Sørensen's results for ability groups in elementary school and tracks in high school are consistent with his expectations. Elementary school students in low-ability groups have the fewest learning opportunities ($b^* = 0.69$), those in middle-ability groups have more learning opportunities ($b^* = 0.76$), and those in the highest-ability group have the most learning opportunities ($b^* = 0.83$) (Table 1a). In high school, students in the Academic track have more learning opportunities than students in other tracks, regardless of the subject matter in question (Table 1b, col. 1 and 2).

Sørensen's initial results for school sector are inconclusive (Table 1b, col. 3 and 4). Students in Catholic schools appear to have more opportunities to learn reading and advanced Mathematics, but fewer opportunities to improve their vocabulary and to learn elementary Mathematics than students in public schools. Sørensen argued that despite his use of a tobit model, the inconsistencies in the results may still be due to not properly controlling for ceiling effects. He claimed that a preferable way to insure unbiased coefficients would be to remove the upper bound altogether. To achieve this end, he repeated the tobit analysis using only the students in the lower half of the achievement distribution since the scores of these students are unlikely to approach the upper bound of the test. The results of this analysis are presented in Table 1c. As Sørensen expected, the parameter estimates from this analysis indicate greater learning opportunities in Catholic schools on all four subject areas (Sørensen, 1996).

In the following analyses, Sørensen's learning opportunities model is estimated on the NELS data and the AGP data, and the results are compared to those Sørensen

Table 1.

(a) OLS Estimates (b^*) for Sørensen's Learning Opportunities Model by Ability Group for a Sample of Elementary School Students ($N = 384$)

School Sector	Ability Group		
	Low	Middle	High
Public	0.69	0.76	0.83

Source: Sørensen and Hallinan (1986, p. 538), Table IV, Model 4.4.

(b) Tobit Estimates (b^*) for Sørensen's Learning Opportunities Model by Track and School Sector for HSB ($N = 18{,}650$)

Standardized Test	Track		School Sector	
	General & Vocational	Academic	Public	Catholic
Vocabulary	0.74	0.76	0.77	0.74
Reading	0.68	0.72	0.72	0.75
Mathematics (Elementary)	0.80	0.82	0.84	0.83
Mathematics (Advanced)	0.51	0.64	0.59	0.62
Sørensen (1996, p. 217)	Table 14.3		Table 14.4	

Source: Sørensen (1996, p. 217), Tables 14.3 and 14.4.

(c) Tobit Estimates (b^*) for Sørensen's Learning Opportunities Model by Track and School Sector for HSB Students Scoring Below the Median as Sophomores ($N = 9{,}207$)

Standardized Test	School Sector	
	Public	Catholic
Vocabulary	0.71	0.79
Reading	0.58	0.65
Mathematics (Elementary)	0.72	0.79
Mathematics (Advanced)	0.32	0.38
Sørensen (1996, p. 218)	Table 14.5	

Source: Sørensen (1996, p. 218), Table 14.5.

obtained from an elementary school sample and the HSB survey. Table 2 shows that, for the most part, the model estimates for the NELS and AGP data are consistent with previous research and with Sørensen's results.

The NELS results shown in Table 2a reveal the expected differences in learning opportunities across track in the public and Catholic schools. In the public schools, students in the Vocational track have the fewest learning opportunities ($b^* = 0.73$), those in the General track have more learning opportunities ($b^* = 0.75$), and those

Table 2.

(a) OLS Estimates (b^*) for Sørensen's Learning Opportunities Model by Track and School Sector for NELS ($N = 12{,}279$)

School Sector	Track		
	Vocational	General	Academic
Public	0.73	0.75	0.76
Catholic	0.69	0.76	0.76

(b) Tobit Estimates (b^*) for Sørensen's Learning Opportunities Model by Ability Group and School Sector for 9th Grade Students in Ability Group Project

School Sector	Ability Group				
	Very Basic	Basic	Regular	Honors	Advanced
English ($N = 2809$)					
Public					
1.1		0.69	0.72	0.81	0.83
1.2		0.65	0.76	0.79	0.80
1.3		0.71	0.75	0.79	0.85
1.4		0.77	0.77	0.77	0.77
1.5		0.62	0.76	0.80	
2.1		0.63	0.78	0.82	0.82
Catholic					
3.1		0.75	0.80	0.82	
Mathematics ($N = 2802$)					
Public					
1.1	0.52	0.44	0.57	0.65	0.62
1.2	0.62	0.50	0.57	0.62	0.61
1.3	0.57	0.58	0.59	0.68	0.60
1.4	0.41	0.42	0.42	0.58	0.61
1.5	0.50	0.50	0.49	0.58	0.61
2.1	0.28	0.56	0.60	0.62	0.62
Catholic					
3.1	0.49	0.56	0.58	0.64	0.59

in the Advanced track have, by a trivial amount, the most opportunities ($b^* = 0.76$). In the Catholic schools, those in the Vocational track have the fewest learning opportunities ($b^* = 0.69$), while those in the General and Academic tracks have more opportunities than the Vocational track, but the same learning opportunities as each other ($b^* = 0.76$).

The expected sector effect on opportunities to learn is less obvious. In the NELS data, public and Catholic school students have essentially the same learning opportunities in the Academic track and in the General track. Further, within each sector, the differences between learning opportunities in these two tracks is trivial. Students in the Vocational track have fewer, rather than more, learning opportunities in Catholic schools than in public schools.

Table 2b presents the results for 9th grade learning opportunities in English and Mathematics in the AGP data. The data reveal the expected pattern of learning opportunities by ability group in both subjects. In general, lower-ability groups have fewer learning opportunities than higher-ability groups. Very few exceptions to this pattern occur. The more precise measurement of the variables in the AGP data may explain the greater differences in learning opportunities across ability groups observed in these data than in the NELS data.

A few exceptions to this pattern should be noted. In 9th grade English, while the expected pattern of the fewest learning opportunities being available in the Basic ability group holds in six of the seven schools, the learning opportunities are the same in all ability groups in School 1.4. Another exception occurs in 9th grade Mathematics. Students in the Very Basic ability group appear to have as many or more learning opportunities than students in the Basic group in most schools. Further, students in School 1.2 and 1.5 have slightly more learning opportunities in the Very Basic group than in the Regular group. These findings may be due to the small number of students in the Very Basic classes or to the nature of the subject matter taught at this level. Another exception to the expected pattern is found for students in the Advanced Mathematics group who frequently have fewer learning opportunities than students in the Honors Mathematics group.

Examining the effects of school sector in the AGP data for English shows a distinct Catholic school advantage. The Catholic school generally has more learning opportunities in English than the public schools. Students in the Basic English group in the Catholic school have more learning opportunities than those in the Basic group in all but one public school, while students in the Regular and Honors groups in the Catholic school have as many or more learning opportunities than students in the same groups in the public schools.

In contrast to the English results, the Catholic school in the study is not exceptional in providing opportunities to learn Mathematics. It offers more learning opportunities in some ability groups than in some public schools, but fewer opportunities in others. However, two factors raise questions about the Mathematics results. First, the Catholic school in the study is a relatively elite school academically, with the average Mathematics test score about 20 percentile points higher than in any of the public high schools. Given the higher achievement of the Catholic school students, it may be that the Mathematics curriculum at each ability group level in the Catholic school is more advanced than at the same ability group level in the public schools. This lack of comparability may make sector comparisons misleading. This situation is less likely in English, given the fairly standard English curriculum found at each grade level in most Catholic and public high schools. The second factor is that the estimates for learning opportunities in the Advanced ability group in the Catholic school are based on a sample of only nine students, compared to 20 or more students in the public schools. The large standard error of the Catholic school estimate makes close comparisons in the magnitude of the learning opportunities coefficient unwise.

In general, the estimation of Sørensen's learning opportunities model on the NELS data and the AGP data reveal the same pattern of learning opportunities that Sørensen detected earlier in an elementary school sample and in the HSB survey. In general, students assigned to higher tracks or ability groups are given more opportunities to learn than those assigned to lower groups. In terms of sector effects, the NELS data reveal little evidence of a Catholic school advantage in terms of greater learning opportunities. However, the AGP data, which are more appropriate for this analysis, do show some evidence of a Catholic school advantage. Students have greater opportunities to learn English in Catholic schools than in public schools in almost all track levels and ability groups. Catholic school students may or may not have learning advantages in Mathematics.

The analysis also shows a number of deviations from this pattern of greater learning opportunities in higher tracks and ability groups and a Catholic school advantage in terms of learning opportunities. The inconsistency of these findings, as well as noted limitations of the learning model itself, demonstrate the need to develop further the theoretical foundation of the model as well as its mathematical formulation.

THEORETICAL CONSIDERATIONS

While Sørensen estimated the learning opportunities model on several occasions (for example, Sørensen & Hallinan, 1977, 1986), he stated more than once that the model is both misspecified and preliminary. Sørensen understood that ability, effort, and opportunities to learn can vary over time and noted this in his work. He also recognized that these variables could be interdependent (Sørensen & Hallinan, 1977, p. 286). But apart from recommending the estimation of a fully interactive model in which the values of the a^* terms can vary by classroom, ability group, track, and school, Sørensen did not pursue these ideas himself.

In an attempt to extend Sørensen's basic conceptual model of learning, this section describes the learning process as an interactive function of learning opportunities, ability, and effort. The considerations presented here will suggest how these three variables are linked. By providing a more complex understanding of learning, the theoretical model will suggest the conditions under which students learn. The theoretical model then can be used to derive more realistic assumptions about learning as the basis for the mathematical formulation of the learning opportunities model.

Opportunities for Learning

The key concept in the theoretical model is learning opportunities. By relating learning opportunities to school characteristics, Sørensen located the model in an extensive body of literature on school effects beginning with the first Coleman Report. This landmark study, *Equality of Educational Opportunity* (Coleman et al., 1966), was commissioned by Congress to determine whether black and white students were receiving equal educational opportunities. Coleman found that, contrary to the popular belief of the time, school differences in resources had only a small effect on student achievement compared to the fairly powerful influence of family background characteristics. The Coleman Report was followed by several cross-sectional and longitudinal studies that showed, at best, modest school effects of school racial composition, climate, size, organizational characteristics, and resources on student achievement.

Research on school effects waned during the eighties and nineties. However, recent interest in school choice policies, and specifically in voucher plans, has drawn attention again to the question of whether school characteristics affect student achievement. In particular, researchers have been interested in the effects of school sector on student outcomes. Using comprehensive longitudinal surveys, Coleman, Hoffer, and Kilgore (1982), Bryk et al. (1993), and others have demonstrated statistically significant differences in achievement between Catholic and public school students. Coleman found a Catholic school advantage in the HSB survey while Bryk et al. found similar results in other surveys and in their reanalysis of the HSB data. To explain these results, researchers point to the rigorous academic program, strict discipline, and close community in Catholic schools that support student efforts to learn. These studies suggest that Catholic schools may provide greater learning opportunities to students than public schools.

School effects may occur within a school sector as well as across sectors. Moreover, opportunities for learning may vary across students within the same school. For example, student learning is dependent, to a considerable degree, on the quality of instruction a teacher provides. Quality of instruction varies by teachers who differ in characteristics such as educational background and experience, professionalism, expectations, and commitment to student learning. Given the organizational differentiation of students for instruction in most contemporary schools, learning opportunities provided by teachers vary across grades and across classes within grades. More subtle school factors, such as an interaction between teacher and student characteristics, and the academic, social, and cultural climate of a school, also may create an unequal distribution of learning opportunities for students.

The way students are assigned to groups for instruction in a school also creates unequal learning opportunities. A general principle is that student learning increases with the quantity and quality of instruction. Research is consistent in documenting that the quantity and quality of instruction vary across ability group or track. In higher-level groups, teachers spend less time on administrative matters and discipline, and more time on instruction. Also, in higher groups, the curriculum and instructional materials tend to be more interesting and challenging, the pace of instruction is faster, and pedagogical techniques, such as interaction style and student involvement, are more rewarding. These findings suggest that students have more learning opportunities in higher-ability groups and in the academic track, compared to lower-ability groups or the general or vocational track.

The various ways schools channel learning opportunities to students indicate that the b parameter in the learning opportunities model is likely to vary across and within schools. Initially, Sørensen concentrated on between school differences in his discussion of the model. Later, he also focused on within school differences. In doing so, he suggested that careful selection of categories, based on theoretical insights, would allow for a comparison of learning opportunities across different environments and under different conditions. These categories may include sector, school, track, ability group, and classroom.

Student Ability

The first of the two individual level constructs on which the learning opportunities model is built is student ability. The meaning of ability has evolved in social science literature. Scholars initially defined the term narrowly as an individual's mental capacity or general intelligence (Binet & Simon, 1905; Terman, 1916; Thorndike, 1926). The trait was measured by an intelligence quotient or IQ test. Mental ability or IQ was assumed to be genetically inherited and fixed over an individual's lifetime.

Over time, social scientists' understanding of mental ability evolved. While continuing to view intelligence as mental capacity, they began to define it more broadly. For example, Gardner (1993) identified multiple intelligences, such as kinesthetic, athletic, and musical ability. Sternberg and Wagner (1986) defined "practical intelligence" to cover the ability to function well in a social situation.

Piaget (1960, 1970) brought a new dimension to the understanding of ability. Rather than focusing on a limited set of cognitive traits or mental skills, Piaget claimed that individuals develop deductive structures that serve as tools for learning. His main insight was that the development of these mental structures occurs through interactive engagement with the world. Vygotsky (1978) went further than Piaget and emphasized the role of social interaction in cognitive development. He argued that individuals learn interpretive frameworks during social participation. In addition, they learn a common value system and commit to an acceptable set of behaviors. He viewed intelligence as useful knowledge, as ways of representing knowledge, and ways of thinking and reasoning.

More recently, researchers extended the concept of mental ability beyond cognitive skills, structures for reasoning, and knowledge of cultural practices developed through social interaction. Many social scientists began to view the ability to absorb cultural practices appropriate in a particular society as a dimension of intelligence. Recognizing that society rewards different kinds of learning, researchers (Goodnow, 1992; Pellegrino & Glaser, 1982; Reed, 1993) attempted to teach U.S. children the kinds of learning rewarded in this society. They conducted experimental studies in which mental skills measured by standardized aptitude tests were taught. The results showed that while individuals can learn certain practices, these skills disappear when the situation changes and the practices are no longer relevant. This research led to the realization that a learned skill must become a habit, by being continually reinforced by contextual factors, in order to become internalized and a part of a person's mental ability.

Other social scientists have developed a different perspective on mental ability, that of intelligence as a social construction. They focus more on people's consistent thought patterns and less on thinking processes or knowledge structures. Resnick and Nelson-Le Gall (1997, p. 149) describe "people who are intelligent-in-practice," that is, people whose habits of the mind are influenced by their beliefs about intelligence. They claim that being intelligent in practice means believing that one has the right to understand one's environment and make it work. Intelligence is based on the conviction that one can analyze and solve problems, has the skills and intuitions needed to solve problems, knows how to obtain help in solving problems, and has habits of mind that lead them to actively use their skills to acquire and use information.

Building on several decades of theoretical and empirical work on mental ability, contemporary social scientists are attempting to integrate these various perspectives on intelligence. They conceptualize mental ability as a combination of thinking processes, knowledge structures, higher order thinking skills, metacognitive strategies, and habits of thinking formed in a culture that rewards these intellectual processes. Further, they believe that at least some of these dimensions of intelligence are responsive to external stimuli leading to change in one's mental ability. Empirical research supports these propositions. Based on this theoretical and empirical work, current thinking is that ability is not a fixed trait, but one that can be modified by contextual factors.

An understanding of mental ability as a variable trait affected by context suggests that school characteristics are apt to affect change in a student's ability. Organizational characteristics of schools that distribute learning opportunities unequally across students are likely to influence a student's capacity to learn. For example, if tracking or ability grouping provides different learning experiences for students, their ability is likely to expand by a different amount. Moreover, the effect of differences in learning opportunities is cumulative. Students who have fewer opportunities to learn over their school careers are likely to have considerably lower ability than students with more learning opportunities.

For the sake of simplicity, only one or a few variables were used to measure a student's ability in prior estimations of Sørensen's learning opportunities model. Moreover, ability was assumed to be constant over the estimation period. These simplifications are inconsistent with contemporary understanding of how ability evolves and affects learning over time. Recognized scholarship now indicates that ability should be treated as a variable, not as a constant, in examining the effects of ability on student learning.

Student Effort

The second individual level concept in the learning opportunities model is student effort. Effort refers to how hard a student tries to learn. The concept has two dimensions: time and intensity. Terms such as perseverance or time on task reflect the time dimension of effort, while concentration and attention refer to its intensity. Researchers have pointed to motivation and need for achievement as two important determinants of effort. Motivation increases with intrinsic and extrinsic rewards while need for achievement is influenced by contextual factors.

Individuals who view ability as a fixed trait are likely to see effort as a fixed trait as well. If no amount of effort can affect innate ability, an individual has no motivation to exert more or less effort to learn, regardless of variation in learning opportunities. Researchers demonstrate that individuals who believe ability is fixed tend to approach problems by relying on skills they have already developed, and avoid new learning situations that might call for new skills and hence require additional effort to learn. In other words, fixed ability leads to little change in effort, regardless of learning opportunities.

A belief in the fixed nature of ability has a second effect on effort. If intelligence is unchangeable, then a person with high ability does not need to exert great effort in order to be successful, while a low-ability person must work hard to achieve. This belief leads to the assumption that ability is negatively related to effort. A person who exerts little effort to learn is believed to have high ability while a person who exerts considerable effort is seen as having low ability.

Most social scientists reject the view that ability is fixed or that it is negatively correlated with effort. Instead, they argue that ability can change over time, and that effort varies in response to ability as well as to opportunities to learn. Student motivation and need for achievement are influenced by the learning opportunities that a school provides. The greater the instructional challenge, other things constant, the more effort a student will exert in trying to learn. In the absence of a challenging learning environment, students will show little effort to learn. Moreover, since effort can produce change in ability, these two variables interact with each other as they change over time. Finally, both ability and effort interact with opportunities to learn. A student's ability and effort increase in response to opportunities to learn and decrease in the absence of learning opportunities.

SUMMARY AND CONCLUSIONS

As a theoretical formulation, Sørensen's model of learning opportunities incorporates a crucial concept: learning opportunities provided by schools interact with a student's ability and effort to produce student achievement. Sørensen is explicit in stating that with few or no opportunities to learn, even the most able student will learn little or nothing. The model also makes clear that increased learning opportunities can compensate for lower-student ability and effort, but that the amount of compensation is limited.

As an analytical tool, Sørensen's differential equation model provides a way to estimate the learning opportunities provided by any school or instructional unit, without having to specify precise measures of those learning opportunities. Considerable research has been conducted on what contributes to effective teaching, and what are the best practices to use in classrooms. This research has identified some, but likely not all, of the factors that contribute to increased learning opportunities. Sørensen's model does not require that all factors be specified. For example, it could be used simply as a way to assess whether a particular pedagogical practice improves learning opportunities.

In addition to highlighting the theoretical contribution and practical application of Sørensen's learning opportunities model, this chapter discusses some of the model's limitations and oversimplifications. Ability and effort, treated as one factor in the model, are more appropriately thought of as separate. Ability and effort, which are assumed to be constant over time in the model, are more appropriately treated as varying. It is also likely that there is feedback among ability, effort and learning opportunities. Other simplifications in the model have not been discussed, but deserve consideration because they rely on unrealistic assumptions. For example, even within a classroom, a learning opportunity for one student is not necessarily a learning opportunity for all students. Moreover, review of material previously presented is not a learning opportunity for those students that learned it the first time, but is a learning opportunity for those that did not.

Despite the simplifications, results generated from Sørensen's learning opportunities model prove interesting. Some results are consistent with expectations and with other research. Paramount among these is that lower tracks and ability groups generally have fewer learning opportunities than higher tracks and ability groups. Differences in learning opportunities across tracks is small, when tracks are conceived of and measured as discrete educational entities in which each student belongs to only one track. However, this form of tracking is seldom practiced in U.S. schools today. The difference in learning opportunities across ability groups is larger, especially when ability groups are measured by specific subject.

A few results are not consistent with expectations or with arguments made by some researchers. The findings that low tracks or ability groups do not always have fewer learning opportunities than high tracks or ability groups is unexpected, but not surprising. Likely some schools make special efforts to assist students who have difficulty learning. Another unexpected finding is that Catholic schools do not consistently have more learning opportunities than public schools. Further research is needed to better understand this finding. Of course, any of the findings obtained by estimating Sørensen's differential equation model may be affected by oversimplifications in the assumptions of the model. Unexpected findings also may be an indication of theoretical inaccuracies or of misspecification of the model by failing to incorporate certain interactions between school and student.

The theory of learning that underlies Sørensen's learning opportunities model has been developed further since he formulated the model. Researchers now have a better understanding of how ability and effort interact with learning opportunities. Much of this understanding has come from extensive research on ability grouping and tracking. Researchers also have a better understanding of how to motivate students to increase their effort to learn. These theoretical developments suggest modifications in the assumptions of the learning model that would increase its relevance and its specification.

Two ways the mathematical model can be improved are immediately evident. First, the implications of changing ability and effort can be explored analytically.

Examining the effects of feedback among ability, effort, and learning opportunities should generate a better specification of the model, as well as better assessments of learning opportunities. Second, new statistical techniques can improve the estimation of the model. For example, a hierarchical linear modeling structure, allowing one to assess the contribution of various school or classroom factors to learning opportunities, would yield better estimations. Given the significant theoretical and empirical contribution of Sørensen's simplified model, each of these developments and extensions should greatly improve the study of school effects on student learning and achievement.

ACKNOWLEDGMENTS

The author gratefully acknowledges support for this research from the Institute for Educational Initiatives at the University of Notre Dame and from the U.S. Department of Education, Grant # ED R215K010011. I also am grateful to Warren Kubitschek for his significant contribution to the analysis.

REFERENCES

Binet, A., & Simon, T. (1905). New methods for the diagnosis of the intellectual level of subnormals. *L'Année Psychologique*, *12*, 191–244.

Bryk, A., Lee, V., & Holland, P. (1993). *Catholic schools and the common good*. Cambridge: Harvard University Press.

Coleman, J. S., Campbell, E. Q., Hobson, C. J., McPartland, J., Mood, A. M., Weinfeld, F. D., & York, R. L. (1966). *Equality of educational opportunity*. Washington, DC: U.S. Department of Education.

Coleman, J. S., Hoffer, T., & Kilgore, S. (1982). *High school achievement: Public, Catholic, and private schools compared*. New York: Basic Books.

Gardner, H. (1993). *Multiple intelligences: The theory in practice*. New York: Basic Books.

Goodnow, J. J. (1992). *Parental belief systems: The psychological consequences for children*. Hillsdale, NJ: Lawrence Erlbaum.

Pellegrino, J. W., & Glaser, R. (1982). Improving the skills of learning. In: D. K. Detterman & R. J. Sternberg (Eds), *How Much and How Can Intelligence Be Increased* (pp. 197–212). Norwood, NJ: Ablex.

Piaget, J. (1960). *The child's conception of the world*. Totowa, NJ: Littlefield, Adams.

Piaget, J. (1970). *Science of education and the psychology of the child*. New York: Orion Press.

Reed, S. K. (1993). Imagery and discovery. In: B. Roskos-Ewoldson, M. J. Peterson & R. E. Anderson (Eds), *Imagery, Creativity, and Discovery: A Cognitive Perspective* (pp. 287–312). Amsterdam: Elsevier.

Resnick, P., & Nelson-Le Gall, S. (1997). Socializing intelligence. In: L. Smith, J. Dockrell & P. Tomlinson (Eds), *Piaget, Vygotsky and Beyond* (pp. 145–158). London: Routledge.

Sørensen, A. B. (1996). Educational opportunities and school effects. In: J. Clark (Ed.), *James S. Coleman* (Chap. 14). London: Falmer Press.

Sørensen, A. B., & Hallinan, M. T. (1977). A reconceptualization of school effects. *Sociology of Education*, *50*(4), 273–289.

Sørensen, A. B., & Hallinan, M. T. (1986). Effects of ability grouping on growth in academic achievement. *American Educational Research Journal*, *23*(4), 519–542.

Sørensen, A. B., & Morgan, S. L. (2000). School effects: Theoretical and methodological issues. In: M. T. Hallinan (Ed.), *The Handbook of the Sociology of Education* (pp. 137–160). New York: Kluwer/Plenum.

Sternberg, R., & Wagner, R. K. (1986). *Practical intelligence: Nature and origins of competence in the everyday world*. Cambridge: Cambridge University Press.

Terman, L. M. (1916). *Measuring intelligence: An explanation of and a complete guide for the use of the Stanford revision and extension of the Binet-Simon intelligence scale*. New York: Houghton Mifflin.

Thorndike, E. L. (1926). *The measurement of intelligence*. New York: Bureau of Publications, Teacher's College, Columbia University.

Vygotsky, L. S. (1978). *Mind in society: The development of higher psychological processes*. Cambridge: Harvard University Press.

SCHOOL EFFECTS AND SØRENSEN'S THEORIES OF LEARNING OPPORTUNITIES AND ACHIEVEMENT

Warren N. Kubitschek

INTRODUCTION

The modern study of school effects originated with the publication of Coleman et al.'s *Equality of Educational Opportunity* (1966). A popular though somewhat incorrect summation of this work was that schools had "no effect" on academic achievement. This finding was both unexpected and not accepted. Since then, many sociologists of education have sought to uncover the effects schools have on academic achievement.

Aage Sørensen argued that there is a basic flaw in almost all of this research. That flaw is an inappropriate conception of how schools and students interact in the learning process. As a result, any measures and models based on this flawed conception would be inappropriate and any meaning they had would be limited.

Sørensen presented an alternative conception of student learning and school effects in a series of articles (primarily Sørensen, 1996; Sørensen & Hallinan, 1977, 1986; Sørensen & Morgan, 2000). He proposed a theory of the process through which schools affect student learning. Based on this theory, he derived an indicator of school effects, and advocated one method for estimating this indictor. He also presented empirical results for illustrative purposes.

In the first two sections of this paper, I discuss Sørensen's theoretical model and present a simple alternative for illustrative purposes. Next, I present indicators of

Inequality: Structures, Dynamics and Mechanisms: Essays in Honor of Aage B. Sørensen
Research in Social Stratification and Mobility, Volume 21, 91–112

ISSN: 0276-5624/doi:10.1016/S0276-5624(04)21006-X

school effects based on these models. I then show ways to estimate these indicators of school effects, and will argue that the estimators Sørensen provided should be revised. I use these various estimators in an empirical example. I conclude by considering some of the implications of these estimates for Sørensen's theory and for school effects research.

THEORIES AND MODELS OF LEARNING OPPORTUNITIES

Sørensen's work on school effects is sometimes presented as a theory of learning opportunities and sometimes presented as a theory of student achievement. In actuality, it is two theories. One theory describes the rate at which schools present learning opportunities to students. The other theory proposes a particular relationship between learning opportunities, student ability and effort, and student achievement. One could use Sørensen's theory of learning opportunities without using his theory of achievement, or use his theory of achievement with a different theory of learning opportunities.

Learning Opportunities

Schools provide many opportunities for student learning. Learning opportunities are intentionally provided by the school, through policies and practices that encourage achievement. These would include such factors as the pace of instruction and the academic press of the school or classroom. Learning opportunities are also provided unintentionally or coincidentally in association with the school. Students learn from their interactions with fellow students, a non-random assortment of individuals organized by geography, school tracking practices, chance classroom assignments, and other factors. Students may also learn from the larger school community, including parents, informal encounters with teachers, and so on.

Many studies of learning opportunities attempt to separate these types of learning opportunities, and study only the learning opportunities intentionally provided by the school (e.g. Carbonaro & Gamoran, 2002). This type of learning opportunity may be amenable to improvement through changing policy and practice. Sørensen's discussion of learning opportunities also focuses on "students' exposure to . . . classrooms, teachers and textbooks" (Sørensen & Hallinan, 1977, p. 275). He correctly notes that, if opportunities to learn academic material are available outside of school, our results may be confounded. However, this is frequently true in such research, and does not prevent us from using Sørensen's model to study and identify policies and practices which improve intentional school learning opportunities.

Learning opportunities may also be viewed in terms of presented opportunities and realized opportunities. In any classroom, there are moments during which the teacher is lecturing on instructional material, leading discussions, and so forth, presenting material for the students to learn. Whether a student learns anything during those moments is another question. Sørensen's definition of learning opportunities requires that a student actually learn, that a moment of learning opportunities presented by a teacher be realized by a student (Sørensen & Hallinan, 1986, p. 524).

Sørensen's conception is most easily considered at the classroom level. Essentially, if there is a moment in the classroom where any student learns any new academic material, not previously known to himself or to any other student in the classroom, Sørensen would consider that a learning opportunity. If no student learns anything new, regardless of the teacher's intentions, Sørensen would not consider that a learning opportunity.

Clearly, Sørensen's definition subsumes a host of psychological and classroom processes. Was any student motivated? Was any student paying attention? Was the teacher presenting new material, rather than reviewing material the students already knew? Was the teacher presenting material that was not too difficult for the students? Was the teacher presenting material effectively, so the students were able to learn it? These are important and interesting questions, but Sørensen took an ultimately practical view of the matter. Only if all the conditions for learning are met, only if some student in the classroom actually learns something, would there be a learning opportunity.

Learning opportunities will vary from day to day and from teacher to teacher, but in terms of school quality, the most important quantity is the total learning opportunities to which a student is exposed over time. Some students will have had more learning opportunities, while other students will have had fewer. This is the basis of Sørensen's indicator of school effects: Schools have effects on student achievement insofar as they provide learning opportunities. This is also the basis of Sørensen's indicator of school quality: Good schools provide students with more learning opportunities.

Rate of Change

Sørensen used the letter v to indicate learning opportunities. This quantity is indexed over time, thus $v(t)$ represents the total learning opportunities to which a student has been exposed by time t, starting from time 0. As noted above, this quantity will be different for every student, and thus is most explicitly written as $v_i(t)$. However, for studying the effects of schools, we will not examine individual student learning opportunities per se. Instead, we are interested in the typical or average number of learning opportunities for students in each school. Using j to indicate schools, this quantity can be written as $v_j(t)$.

For a measure of school effects, we will be interested in a particular period of time. If we study the effects of high schools, we must examine the learning opportunities in high schools and exclude any learning opportunities the student had in elementary school. The beginning of the period of interest can be arbitrarily set to time t_1 and the end of the period to time t_2. The total learning opportunities in the school by time t_2 is $v_j(t_2)$, the learning opportunities before the period of interest is $v_j(t_1)$, and thus, we are interested in the change in learning opportunities, $v_j(t_2) - v_j(t_1)$.

Theoretically, the length of the time period can vary. We might study learning opportunities in a day or over several years. Obviously, we would expect more learning opportunities to occur in a year than in a day, so we must adjust the indicator according to the length of time. Since we have set the beginning of the time period to t_1 and the end of the period to t_2, we would adjust the change in learning opportunities by the quantity $t_2 - t_1$.

This leads us to Sørensen's specific conception of school quality, which can be represented in a simple mathematical form familiar to sociologists. I find it a useful beginning for linking the sociology and the mathematics. I will represent school quality with the letter B. Thus, for each school, j:

$$B_j(t_2, t_1) = \frac{v_j(t_2) - v_j(t_1)}{t_2 - t_1} \tag{1}$$

If we could measure learning opportunities, this could be Sørensen's measure of school quality. Good schools, those with a higher $B_j(t_2, t_1)$, would provide more learning opportunities $v_j(t_2) - v_j(t_1)$ during some period of time $t_2 - t_1$. Good schools provide more average learning opportunities, calculating the average over the length of the time period.

Note that this quantity is indexed by time. The total learning opportunities to which a student has been exposed during some period will depend on the starting and ending points we select. Some schools may provide many learning opportunities one year, but few learning opportunities the next year.

Using learning opportunities as an indicator of school quality is not unusual. Most discussions of school effects include this as a part of their conception of quality, either explicitly or implicitly. Because Sørensen's conception of learning opportunities is broadly defined, his definition of quality can be seen as simple: Good schools are schools where students learn, for whatever reason. On the other hand, because Sørensen's conception of learning opportunities is broadly defined, his definition of quality can also be seen as quite complicated. It includes a broad range of factors such as teacher effectiveness, curricular quality, classroom management, the academic press of the school, social capital, and more.

Sørensen's model is also complicated because he is not interested in B_j as an average but as a rate. Equation (1) is a formula for a slope, as in a regression. A slope is a rate, and here specifies that v_j changes by a constant amount per change in t.

This is a subtle change of focus in the conception of learning opportunities. Sørensen was not thinking about average learning opportunities. Rather, he was thinking about how fast schools provide learning opportunities. If we think in those terms, we can imagine shrinking the time period of interest from years or semesters down to minutes or seconds, and theoretically, down to an infinitesimal instant. We are asking "What is the rate at which the school is providing learning opportunities this instant?"

Mathematically, differential equations are required to capture the concept of instantaneous rate of change. Thus, Sørensen's conception of school quality is better defined as:

$$B_j(t) = \frac{\mathrm{d}v_j(t)}{\mathrm{d}t} \tag{2}$$

At any instant, time t, we define an indicator of better schools, $B_j(t)$, by the rate at which the school is providing learning opportunities in that instant, $\mathrm{d}v_j(t)/\mathrm{d}t$.

We can think of $B_j(t_2, t_1)$ as the average of the $B_j(t)$ from t_1 to t_2. To better understand Sørensen's conception, though, consider the following. We expect the rate of learning opportunities to vary from instant to instant: Classes get disrupted, teachers switch from review to new material and back, and so forth. In the unlikely event that there is some period of time, t_1 to t_2, during which the rate of learning opportunities never varies, then throughout that period, $B_j(t) = B_j(t_2, t_1)$. If the rate of learning opportunities is constant, the instantaneous rate of learning opportunities provided is always the same as the average rate.

Equations (1) and (2) illustrate Sørensen's concepts of learning opportunities, school quality, and the means by which quality should be measured. If learning opportunities, $v_j(t)$, could be measured, the $B_j(t)$ could be calculated. One would obtain Sørensen's index of school effects and school quality. Unfortunately, measuring learning opportunities as defined by Sørensen is impossible in practice. One would have to identify each and every moment when any student learned any academic material, in school and out.

Because we cannot measure the $v_j(t)$, we cannot calculate the $B_j(t)$. We must somehow estimate them. Sørensen demonstrated that it was possible to do so, provided we make several assumptions. The most important assumption we make is how the $B_j(t)$ vary over time.

Two Models of the Rate of Change in Learning Opportunities

We must assume some mathematical function accurately models any changes in the rate at which the school provides learning opportunities. There are many functions we could use, and so this is, in part, a mathematical assumption. More importantly, it is a theoretical assumption. The function we use is a theoretical model of how schools present learning opportunities. Here, I present two possible functions. The first function is the simplest function we could use, while the second is the function Sørensen used.

The simplest model assumes that the rate of change in learning opportunities does not change over time. The rate of change in total learning opportunities is constant in the school, at all time points. Different schools may provide learning opportunities at different rates, of course. This model is:

$$\frac{\mathrm{d}v_j(t)}{\mathrm{d}t} = b_{Cj} \tag{3}$$

The subscript C reminds us that this indicator assumes a constant rate of learning opportunities.

The assumption that learning opportunities occur at a constant rate, regardless of the time point, is a very strong one. Clearly, it is too simple an assumption. We know that learning opportunities vary within a single class period, during the week, and over the semester. But while too simple a theoretical model, it may be that this model of learning opportunities is useful as an empirical indicator of the average learning opportunities for some period of interest. If we are interested in differences in school quality in one school year, for example, this model may provide sufficient indication of variation by school. On the other hand, this model may be too gross a simplification to reveal important differences in school learning opportunities.

Sørensen used a more complicated model for the rate of learning opportunities. He assumed that the rate of learning opportunities followed an exponential function:

$$\frac{\mathrm{d}v_j(t)}{\mathrm{d}t} = ke^{b_j t} \quad \text{where } b_j < 0 \tag{4}$$

(1996, p. 212 or see Hallinan, 2004, Eq. (2)). Without loss of generality, one may assume $k = 1$. Thus, k will be excluded henceforth.

I will discuss the implications of this model at more length in the next section of the paper, but note that time is an explicit part of this model. Time was not a factor in the first model. There, we assume learning opportunities are provided at a constant rate, so there is no change over time in that rate. In Sørensen's model, the rate at which learning opportunities are presented changes over time. Because Eq. (4) is an exponential function and we assume $b_j < 0$, the rate at which schools provide learning opportunities will decline over time.

Two Models of Change in Total Learning Opportunities over Time

I find it easier to understand these models sociologically if I examine what they imply about total learning opportunities over time. Each function that specifies how the rate of change in learning opportunities changes over time is also a function that specifies how total learning opportunities change over time. An illustration of these two models is shown in Fig. 1. For purposes of this illustration, a different and arbitrary b was chosen for each model, so that both models would fit conveniently on the same graph.

The first model specifies that learning opportunities are provided at a constant rate. This results in a constant, linear increase in total learning opportunities over time, hence I sometimes refer to this as the linear model. Sørensen's model of learning opportunities implies a nonlinear increase in total learning opportunities over time. Initially, total learning opportunities increase rapidly. However, the rate of this increase slows continuously. Eventually, total learning opportunities are

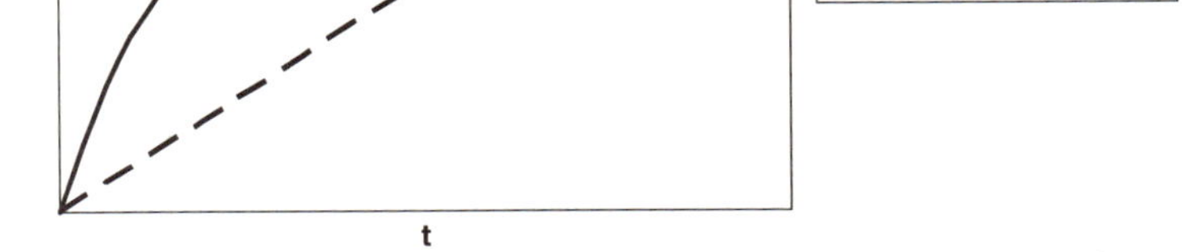

Fig. 1. Total Learning Opportunities and Achievement over Time for Two Models of the Rate of Change in Learning Opportunities.

increasing extremely slowly. The increase in learning opportunities never ends, but will become infinitesimal as total learning opportunities approach a limit.

Compared to what we know about teaching during any time period, both functions are obvious simplifications. Consider a school year. We know that teachers spend the first few weeks of the year on review of material from the previous year. If most students already know this material, there will be few learning opportunities. We know that teachers typically spend more time on review at other times of the year, as well, and so there will be fewer learning opportunities at those times. Neither of the two models presented captures this ebb and flow of in the rate of learning opportunities.

Sørensen's model may seem particularly problematic, in that it indicates a large number of learning opportunities at the beginning of the year, just when we know teachers spend the most time in review. Yet as an empirical simplification, Sørensen's model is not necessarily more problematic than a linear model. We know both models are simplifications. Linear models, such as the one used here, are common simplifications in the literature but have a number of well known problems. For example, the linear model here suggests that learning opportunities will continue, unabated, even to the end of the school year and by extension, through the summer. Sørensen's model should be seen as a different simplification than the one we are used to, not necessarily a more problematic one.

More importantly, Sørensen's model is superior in terms of theory, in that it is based on a particular concept of learning. His model is a diffusion model of teaching and learning, which incorporates a feedback mechanism which controls for student learning during the year. We can think of this model as follows. At the beginning of the year, the teacher has a body of material that she will present over the course of the year. When she first presents this material, it is entirely new to the students, and thus students have a great many learning opportunities. Over time, the students learn some of the material, and so, as she presents it, less of it is new. Therefore, there are declining learning opportunities. By the end of the year, the students have learned almost all of this material, and there are few or no learning opportunities. The linear model, by contrast, is not based on any particular conception of learning, nor does it have any built-in feedback mechanism (Sørensen & Hallinan, 1986, p. 524).

Many other functions could be specified, each representing some different theoretical model of the rate at which schools provide learning opportunities to students. One might, for example, use a spline or piecewise linear function, to model an initial period of few learning opportunities, a middle period of greater learning opportunities, and a final period of few learning opportunities. A similar but more smoothly continuous model might use a logistic function. Examination of such models is beyond the scope of this paper.

THEORIES AND MODELS OF ACHIEVEMENT

Sørensen's Model of Achievement

Sørensen realized that by linking learning opportunities to student achievement, one can use measures of student achievement to estimate the number of learning opportunities to which the student had been exposed. Sørensen proposed a simple theory of achievement. Following my discussion above, it would be expressed as:

$$\frac{\mathrm{d}y_i(t)}{\mathrm{d}t} = s_i \frac{\mathrm{d}v_j(t)}{\mathrm{d}t} \tag{5}$$

where $y_i(t)$ is student achievement at time t, $v_j(t)$ is of course the learning opportunities provided through time t, and s_i is student ability and effort (Sørensen & Hallinan, 1977, p. 277 or see Hallinan, 2004, Eq. (1)). With this model, and some mathematical derivation, it is possible to estimate the rate at which schools provide learning opportunities, if we can measure student achievement and student ability and effort.

Again, this model is expressed as a differential equation. That is, the model specifies, not student achievement per se, but the rate of change in achievement. The rate of change in a student's achievement is the product of that student's ability and effort multiplied by the rate of change in the learning opportunities provided by the school. Better schools will provide learning opportunities at a faster rate, and thus their students will learn at a greater rate. Student ability and effort is included in the model, and the formula indicates that students of higher ability and effort will learn faster than students of lower ability and effort, all else constant.

In his discussions of this model, Sørensen paid little attention to ability and effort, concentrating on learning opportunities and on the mathematical model itself. In other research, sociologists have used various measures of ability and effort, and such measures could be used here. However, Sørensen stated that it would be sufficient to model s_i with a linear equation and the usual control variables in our models of student achievement: sex, race, socioeconomic status, family structure, and so forth (1996, p. 214). Thus, if we select K such variables:

$$s_i = a_0 + a_1 x_{i1} + a_2 x_{i2} + \cdots + a_K x_{iK} = \sum_{k=0}^{K} a_k x_{ik} \tag{6}$$

Note that the indicators of student ability and effort, and thus ability and effort itself, are not indexed by time. In addition, the effects of ability and effort are not indexed by school. That is, for this model Sørensen assumed that ability and effort do not change during the period studied, and that the effects of ability and effort would be the same in all schools (Sørensen & Hallinan, 1977, pp. 278–279).

These are crucial assumptions for simplifying the model. Sørensen noted that a more accurate model would incorporate changes in ability and effort. Indeed, he stated that changes in ability and effort would be caused both by changing student achievement and by differences in school learning opportunities (Sørensen & Morgan, 2000, p. 150). It is clear that Sørensen hoped to develop more complicated models, which would explicitly include such processes (Sørensen & Hallinan, 1977, pp. 285–287). However, he did not do so, and thus his model of achievement remains a model based on the simplifying assumptions of constant ability and effort and constant effects for these factors.

Two Models of Learning Opportunities and Sørensen's Model of Achievement

Any theoretical model of learning opportunities that can be expressed mathematically can be incorporated into Sørensen's model of achievement. Above, I presented two different functions that might be a useful summary of the rate at which learning opportunities are presented in schools. Substituting Eqs (3) and (6) into Eq. (5), we see that the first, linear model of student achievement is:

$$\frac{\mathrm{d}y_i(t)}{\mathrm{d}t} = s_i \frac{\mathrm{d}v_j(t)}{\mathrm{d}t} = s_i b_{Cj} = \left(\sum_{k=0}^{K} a_k x_{ik} \right) b_{Cj} \tag{7}$$

Substituting Eqs (4) and (6) into Eq. (5) gives us the second model of student achievement:

$$\frac{\mathrm{d}y_i(t)}{\mathrm{d}t} = s_i \frac{\mathrm{d}v_j(t)}{\mathrm{d}t} = s_i(e^{b_j t}) = \left(\sum_{k=0}^{K} a_k x_{ik} \right) (e^{b_j t}) \tag{8}$$

This second model is Sørensen's model of learning opportunities in Sørensen's model of achievement.

Because student ability and effort, s_i, is assumed to be constant, these models specify that the growth of student achievement follows exactly the same pattern as the growth in learning opportunities. Thus, Fig. 1, which shows the increase in total learning opportunities over time, also shows the increase in student achievement over time. The linear model of growth in learning opportunities implies student achievement will grow in a constant, linear fashion. Sørensen's model implies student achievement will grow rapidly initially but then ever more slowly, as achievement approaches some upper bound. For each model, the shape of the curve would be the same for all students, although the actual height and slope will vary depending on the school's learning opportunities and the student's ability and effort.

ESTIMATORS OF LEARNING OPPORTUNITIES

Sørensen proposed a model of the rate of change in learning opportunities in schools, and incorporated that into a model of achievement. I have shown one way this can be generalized, by presenting an alternative model of the rate of change in learning opportunities and incorporating it into Sørensen's model of achievement. The result, in both cases, is a model of achievement which includes a parameter which is explicitly an indicator of school quality and school effects. How can this parameter be estimated?

Theoretical Estimators

Integrating the differential Eqs (7) and (8) is a necessary first step. Space does not permit this to be shown here. The results of these integrations show that we can obtain estimates of the two indicators of learning opportunities by using Eqs (9) and (10), below.

Using Sørensen's notation, let $y_{1i} = y_i(t_1)$ and $y_{2i} = y_i(t_2)$. To obtain the indicator of learning opportunities for the simple linear model of learning opportunities (Eq. (7)), one must estimate:

$$y_{2i} = y_{1i} + b_{Cj} \left(\sum_{k=0}^{K} a_k x_{ik} \right) \tag{9}$$

This is a lagged regression equation, predicting current achievement based on previous achievement and the set of indicators of ability and effort, with the effect of previous achievement fixed to be 1. This model could also be estimated using a gain score, $y_{2i} - y_{1i}$, as the dependent variable.

All variables are measured at the individual level. There is a separate estimate of learning opportunities for each school, the b_{Cj}. For each variable indicating student ability and effort, the model includes a single estimate for the effect of that variable, an a_k. Recall that a simplifying assumption was that the true effects of student ability and effort were the same across schools. Of course, these true effects of ability and effort are modified by the learning opportunities available in the school, since the a_k are multiplied by the b_{Cj}.

To obtain the indicator of learning opportunities for the Sørensen's model of learning opportunities (Eq. (8)) one must estimate:

$$y_{2i} = b_j^* y_{1i} + \left(\frac{b_j^* - 1}{b_j}\right)\left(\sum_{k=0}^{K} a_k x_{ik}\right) \tag{10}$$

where $b_j^* = e^{b_j \Delta t}$ and $\Delta t = t_2 - t_1$. Since $b_j < 0$, $0 < b_j^* < 1$. The b_j^* are Sørensen's indicator of learning opportunities. As in the previous model, there is a single estimate for the effect of each indicator of student ability and effort, an a_k, which is then modified by a function of b_j.

Sørensen's Estimation

Unfortunately, Eqs (9) and (10) are not identified, and so are not directly estimable. In his own analyses, Sørensen used two different equations to obtain estimates for his model. These are equations which are estimable and include an indicator of learning opportunities.

The simpler of these two equations is:

$$y_{2i} = b_j^* y_{1i} + \left(\sum_{k=0}^{K} a'_k x_{ik}\right) \tag{11}$$

This is a lagged regression equation with a separate estimated effect of previous achievement for each school. It includes a single estimated effect for each of the variables indicating student ability and effort. In most research, this type of model would be estimated by including a set of dummy variables for schools, and interacting that set of dummies with previous achievement.

Sørensen demonstrated that the estimates of the a_k in Eq. (10) can be calculated from the a'_k and the b'_j in Eq. (11). To do so, one must assume $\Delta t = t_2 - t_1 = 1$. For Sørensen's purposes and my purpose here, this assumption can be made without loss of generality. However, such calculations do not produce an entirely satisfactory result. Because there are J estimates of b^*, there will be J different calculated estimates for each a_k.

Sørensen rarely used Eq. (11) (e.g. Sørensen & Hallinan, 1986, Tables 1 and 2). From the first (1977, p. 286), he argued that this model was misspecified. Instead, he advocated estimating:

$$y_{2i} = b_j^* y_{1i} + \left(\sum_{k=0}^{K} a_{jk}^* x_{ik}\right) \tag{12}$$

The difference between Eq. (12) and Eq. (11) is that in Eq. (12), the a explicitly have a j subscript. This model contains J separate true a coefficients for each x in the estimation equation. In Eq. (11), there is only one true a coefficient for each x, although there are J separate calculated estimates of that true a.

Equation (12) is identical to a fully interactive model, often used in school effects research. Effectively, one is estimating a separate equation "for each school (or classroom)" (Sørensen & Hallinan, 1977, p. 278). The effect of every variable is allowed to vary from one school to the next.

While this estimated model may be used in other research, the interpretation of the estimates is quite different under Sørensen's theories. Typically, researchers ignore the effects of previous achievement, treating it as a control variable. For Sørensen, the effect of previous achievement is precisely the effect of interest. Typically, researchers discuss the a^*_{jk} coefficients as the effect of the x_k variable on achievement in the jth school. For Sørensen, those estimated effects are modifications of the true effect of the variables: They are the contribution of that variable multiplied by the indicator of learning opportunities available in the school.

Sørensen argued (e.g. 1977, p. 286) that Eq. (12) is a better model than Eq. (11) because there is likely to be an interdependence of achievement and student ability and effort, with the latter being affected by the former. As achievement depends on learning opportunities, which vary by school, student ability and effort will also vary by school. Sociologically, then, this is a better model for studying schooling and learning.

Unfortunately, Eq. (12) is not consistent with the mathematical derivation of the school effects indicator based on Sørensen's theoretical model, shown in Eq. (10). In advocating Eq. (12), Sørensen explicitly argues that ability and effort will vary with student achievement. Since achievement varies over time in the model, this implies ability and effort will change over time. To obtain Eq. (10), however, we made the simplifying assumption that ability and effort will not change over time.

As written, Eq. (10) cannot be estimated because it is not identified. Fortunately, Sørensen was willing to make an assumption that will identify Eq. (10). That assumption is $\Delta t = t_2 - t_1 = 1$, which he makes in order to calculate the a_k from the a^*_k. As a result of this assumption, $b_j = \ln(b^*_j)$, and Sørensen's theoretical model can be estimated without changing the assumption that ability and effort do not change over time.

A Multilevel Approach

In a brief aside in his last paper on this model (Sørensen & Morgan, 2000, pp. 150–151), Sørensen noted that multilevel models would be more appropriate for estimating the b_j^*, because learning opportunities are a characteristic of the school. This was not a new idea for him. In his first paper on the model (Sørensen & Hallinan, 1977, Table 2), he provided a form of multilevel estimates, examining the effects of school characteristics on learning opportunities.

A multilevel model uses two (or more) equations that are estimated simultaneously. Here, one equation, usually called the Level 1 equation, would predict student achievement using student characteristics. Another equation, the Level 2 equation, would use school characteristics to predict some of the coefficients of the Level 1 equation. In these models of achievement, the key coefficients we would predict with the second equation are the indicators of school effects, the b_j^*, in the first equation. This enables us to explicitly estimate the effects of any school factor on school quality.

For this model, we begin with Eq. (10) as the Level 1 equation, modified by assuming $\Delta t = 1$. For the Level 2 equation, we could use any school characteristics as predictor variables. We might use a full set of dummy variables for schools, to assess the quality of each school. More sociologically, we might use factors that are thought to affect school quality, such as teacher experience or the socioeconomic composition of the school.

Thus, we would have the multilevel model:

$$y_{2i} = b_j^* y_{1i} + \left[\frac{b_j^* - 1}{\ln(b_j^*)}\right]\left(\sum_{k=0}^{K} a_k x_{ik}\right) \tag{13.1}$$

$$b_j^* = \sum_{l=0}^{L} g_l z_{jl} \tag{13.2}$$

The z_{jl} are L measures of school characteristics for the J schools.

Equation (13.1), by itself, is consistent with Sørensen's theories and mathematical assumptions. It allows us to estimate the b_j^*, Sørensen's indicator of learning opportunities and school quality, based on Sørensen's theories of learning opportunities and achievement. Estimating the combined Eq. (13) provides us with estimates of the g, the effects of various school factors on learning opportunities. This allows us to test which specific policies and practices increase learning opportunities.

Simplified Estimation of Sorensen's Multilevel Model

I have not yet been able to properly estimate Sørensen's multilevel model with any software commonly used by sociologists. There are two methods to simplify the procedure, both of which provide an approximation of the model. Both methods should provide reasonably accurate estimates. Ultimately, of course, one would wish to estimate the model properly.

The first simplifying method is to estimate the model as a single equation, ignoring the hierarchical structure. By substituting Eq. (13.2) into Eq. (13.1), we see that the single equation version of this multilevel model is:

$$y_{2i} = \left(\sum_{l=0}^{L} g_l z_{jl}\right) y_{1i} + \left[\frac{\left(\sum_{l=0}^{L} g_l z_{jl}\right) - 1}{\ln\left(\sum_{l=0}^{L} g_l z_{jl}\right)}\right]\left(\sum_{k=0}^{K} a_k x_{ik}\right) \tag{14}$$

Because this equation does not properly partition the variance between individuals and schools, the resulting coefficients will be biased if the hierarchical specification is the true model.

The second method of simplifying the estimation maintains the hierarchical structure of the model. The key problem in estimating the combined Eq. (13) is the nonlinear function of b_j^*, the $(b_j^* - 1)/\ln(b_j^*)$ term. However, Sørensen's published estimates of b^* typically range from 0.5 to 0.9. In a fortunate numeric coincidence, there is an almost linear relationship between a number in that range and that particular nonlinear function of the number. It turns out that, for any $0.5 \leq x \leq 0.9$:

$$\frac{x - 1}{\ln(x)} = 0.4418 + 0.5677x + u, \quad \text{where the error } u \text{ is small} : |u| < 0.0045 \tag{15}$$

By substituting this approximation into Eq. (13.1), we see we could estimate:

$$y_{2i} = b_j^* y_{1i} + [0.4418 + 0.5677(b_j^*)]\left(\sum_{k=0}^{K} a_k x_{ik}\right) \tag{16.1}$$

$$b_j^* = \sum_{l=0}^{L} g_l z_{jl} \tag{16.2}$$

Of course, this method of estimation will be increasingly less accurate, the further the true b_j^* are outside the range (0.5, 0.9).

ANALYSES

While the various models and different indicators discussed above are theoretically and mathematically interesting, it remains to be seen whether they are useful. I will examine estimated values of these indicators of school quality to see whether they produce results consistent with findings from previous research. This is a weak but informative test of the utility of these indicators.

Methods

The data used in these analyses are the NELS data, using composite IRT test score as the measure of achievement and 8th and 10th grade as t_1 and t_2. The sample and the indicators of student ability and effort used in these models are the same as those used for the analyses in Hallinan's chapter in this volume (2004, see that chapter for details). The only difference is that I drop somewhat more cases due to missing data.

I have been discussing these models in terms of school differences and individual school quality. However, these models can be used for any organizationally defined grouping of students. For these analyses, I will not divide students by the hundreds of schools available in NELS. Rather, I divide students into six groups defined by self-reported track placement (Vocational, General, Academic) and school sector (public, Catholic: students in other types of schools were dropped from the sample).

I calculate estimates for four different models. Even though some of these models are linear, I estimate all of them using Stata's nl routine.

Three of the four models provide different estimates of Sørensen's indicator of school quality. I include both models suggested by Sørensen, the first approximation model (Eq. (11)) and the model he advocated (Eq. (12)). I also estimate the single equation simplification of the multilevel version of Sørensen's model (Eq. (14)).

The fourth model uses the linear specification for rate of learning opportunities (Eq. (9)). This equation is not identified. However, there are various common ways of estimating such models. A simple technique, which I use here, is to fix the value of one of the b_{Cj} at some arbitrary but reasonable constant. I set the effect for the public school General track coefficient, $b_{C2} = 0.75$.

Results

Table 1 presents the results for the first set of analyses. Each model includes an effect of previous achievement for each of the six groups. I present these estimates, which are the estimates of the b for that model. I also present the coefficient estimates for the effect of SES, as a single example of the estimated effects of the other variables in the equation. Coefficient estimates for the remaining variables in the model are not shown. For Sørensen's own models, I present the adjusted

Table 1. Estimated Effects of Previous Achievement and SES using Four Methods ($N = 12053$).

School Sector	Track					
	Effect of Previous Achievement b			Effect of SES A		
	Vocational	General	Academic	Vocational	General	Academic
Sørensen's first approximation model (Eq. (12))						
Public	0.73	0.75	0.76	0.67	0.66	0.65
Catholic	0.69	0.76	0.76	0.68	0.65	0.65
Sørensen's suggested model (Eq. (13))						
Public	0.83	0.79	0.69	0.37	0.44	0.75
Catholic	0.69	0.71	0.61	0.84	1.89	1.53
Linear learning opportunities, single equation hierarchical model (Eq. (17))						
Public	1.64	0.75	0.90		−0.13	
Catholic	3.42	−2.64	−0.04			
Sørensen's learning opportunities, single equation hierarchical model (Eq. (15))						
Public	0.77	0.77	0.78		0.18	
Catholic	0.73	0.78	0.78			

coefficients for SES, that is, the result of the appropriate calculation using the estimated SES coefficient modified by the appropriate function of the b for the group.

Based on previous research, we expect to see that learning opportunities increase with track. Vocational track students are expected to have the fewest learning opportunities and Academic track students are expected to have the most. Catholic school students are expected to have more learning opportunities than public school students. Previous research also indicates that the effect of SES on student achievement should be positive, and somewhat weaker in Catholic than in public schools.

The first estimates in Table 1 are from the model Sørensen proposed as a first approximation for his indicators of school quality, the b_j^* from Eq. (11). These results are mostly consistent with our expectations in terms of track placement. Students in higher tracks generally are exposed to learning opportunities at a faster rate than students in lower tracks. The only exception is in Catholic schools, where students in both the General and Academic tracks are exposed to learning opportunities at an equal rate.

The results for sector are not as expected, however. Compared to their public school counterparts, Catholic school students have fewer learning opportunities in the Vocational track, slightly more learning opportunities in the General track, and the same learning opportunities in the Academic track. These results do not show a clear Catholic school advantage.

Estimates for the effect of SES are in the proper direction. Students with higher SES have higher achievement scores. Overall, then, the estimates from this model, while not completely consistent with previous research, are not clearly inconsistent with previous research.

The next estimates are from the model Sørensen advocated, Eq. (12). Here, the b_j^* are inconsistent with previous research. These estimates suggest that lower tracks typically are exposed to more learning opportunities than higher tracks. They suggest that Catholic schools provide fewer learning opportunities than public schools. The results for SES are also inconsistent with previous research. They indicate that the effect of SES on student achievement is stronger in the Catholic schools than in public schools. All in all, these estimates suggest that this estimator is not a useful tool for evaluating school quality.

The same is true for the next set of estimates, which show the results for the linear model of learning opportunities. I remind the reader that these estimates are for the b_{Cj}, which have different numeric properties than the other three estimates, which are estimates of the b_j^*. These results suggest that learning opportunities are greatest in the lowest track, and that learning opportunities are fewest in the Catholic school General track. The results also suggest that the effect of SES is negative. Clearly, this is not a useful indicator of school effects.

The final results in Table 1 are for the multilevel version of Sørensen's model, estimated as a single equation (Eq. (14)). As with the first set of estimates, these are not completely consistent with previous research, but are not clearly inconsistent. There is some slight indication that learning opportunities are greater in higher tracks. There is little difference in learning opportunities between public and Catholic schools. The effect of SES is positive.

Of these four methods of estimating learning opportunities in schools, only the first and last seem potentially useful. The first, though, is hampered because it provides many different estimated effects for the other variables in the model. In this example, I showed the separate effect of SES for each group. In these results, the six empirical estimates of the SES effects are little different from each other. However, since the theoretical model is based on the assumption that there is only a single effect of SES, we should not allow them to differ at all.

This leaves only the last model, the multilevel estimation of Sørensen's model of learning opportunities. Perhaps the key objection at this point to the utility of this model is that it shows so few differences in learning opportunities by track and sector. Previous research indicates greater differences between these groups.

However, one should not make too much of these specific numeric results. There are a host of methodological issues I have not addressed, all of which imply these specific estimates are not very accurate indicators of learning opportunities. First, the models were not properly estimated as hierarchical models. Second, the NELS test scores are theoretically unbounded but in practice may exhibit some ceiling effects: No controls for ceiling effects were used here. Third, studying learning opportunities using a general composite test score is an inherently inaccurate way of doing so. To discover how much the students have learned in a class, one should test them on the material that was taught in the class. Fourth, the broad, self-reported measure of track placement used here will act to minimize between track differences in estimates of learning opportunities.

Space does not permit a full examination of these issues. However, the reader should examine the results for the AGP data in Hallinan's chapter (2004). There, she uses better, more subject-specific test scores, a better measure of track placement, and controls for ceiling effects. Those results indicate considerably larger differences in learning opportunities between schools and tracks than are shown in these NELS analyses, while still being generally consistent with our expectations about the pattern of learning opportunities by track and sector.

Thus, there are reasonable explanations for the small differences in school effects in the results here. Yet an indicator of school quality and school effects that is not particularly useful in data sets such as NELS is of limited use in current sociological research. Fortunately, the limitations of this indicator are perhaps not as great as they appear in Table 1.

Table 2 shows a different set of estimates for the multilevel model based on Sørensen's theory of learning opportunities. For these results, rather than estimating a separate indicator of school quality for each group, I use two dummy variables to capture the effects of track placement (comparing Vocational and Academic tracks to General) and one dummy variable to capture the effect of school sector (comparing Catholic to public schools). The main effect of previous achievement is the effect for the comparison group, students in the General track in public schools. The other effects are estimated as the differences in learning opportunities, by track and sector, from this comparison group.

Table 2. Estimated Effects of Previous Achievement.

	B
Public school General track	0.749
Vocational track	−0.022
Academic track	0.006
Catholic school	0.003

Note: Using Sørensen's Learning Opportunities Model and a Single Equation Version of a Hierarchical Model ($N = 12053$).

Such a model is more likely to be useful for sociological research purposes than the model of Table 1. We are rarely interested in identifying the quality of individual schools or other groupings, except perhaps as a first, descriptive effort. Rather, we seek to determine the factors that increase or decrease school effectiveness. Under Sørensen's model, the effects of the Level 2 variables on the b_j^* are the effects of those variables on school effects and school quality.

The results in Table 2 show a pattern of effects that conforms to our expectations. Vocational track students have fewer learning opportunities than General track students. Academic track students have more learning opportunities than General track students. Catholic school students have more learning opportunities than public school students. Also, the difference in learning opportunities between school sectors is less than the difference in learning opportunities between tracks. The differences in learning opportunities by track and sector still appear to be too small, but they are otherwise consistent with previous research findings.

The results in Table 2 may appear to be inconsistent with the results in Table 1. Adding the terms in Table 2, to obtain predicted school quality for each combination of track and sector, yields rather different values than those in Table 1. This is due to the nonlinearity of the model. Changes in the parameterization of a nonlinear model will affect the numeric values of the estimates rather differently than our experience leads us to expect, as our experience is based on changes in the parameterizations of linear models.

Summary and Conclusions

Sørensen's theory of learning opportunities specifies a function which models the rate of change in learning opportunities provided by a school. As an example of an alternative theory of the rate of change in learning opportunities, I use a simple, constant rate model. Sørensen specified a theory of achievement, and incorporated his theory of learning opportunities into it. I show how this could be done using the constant rate model of learning opportunities.

This provides two theoretical models of achievement, both of which allow us to estimate the rate at which schools provide learning opportunities to their students. Such a rate is Sørensen's indicator or index of school effects and school quality. Better schools provide learning opportunities to students at a faster rate. School factors which affect the rate of learning opportunities are those factors which affect school quality.

Sørensen presented two equations by which to estimate the rate of learning opportunities under his model. I argue that neither equation is consistent with the mathematical specifications and assumptions of his theory, and present a model that is consistent with those assumptions. This model can be expanded to a multilevel specification, which allows us to explicitly test school and classroom factors that may affect learning opportunities. The necessary software may not yet be available to calculate true estimates for this multilevel model (or I may not be aware of it), but I suggest two approximations of this model which can be estimated at present.

I examine results from some simple analyses using both theoretical models and, in the case of Sørensen's model of learning opportunities, several different estimators. In the initial analyses, none of these estimators provided results that were completely consistent with our expectations of the differences in learning opportunities in different tracks and different school sectors. Although one of Sørensen's estimators provided results that were not inconsistent with our expectations, this method of estimating school quality has the drawback of providing a multiplicity of estimates of the effects of all control variables in the model.

A multilevel estimator for Sørensen's indicator provided initial results that were not inconsistent with our expectations. A subsequent analysis, using a more sociological approach to the research question, provided estimates which are more consistent with our expectations. This multilevel method also provides only a single estimate of the effects of other variables in the model, eliminating that drawback of other estimators.

To say that a theory and model provide estimates that are generally consistent with our expectations is not a sign of strong support. Yet in this instance, I think it is a crucial step. Sørensen's model has been little used in the literature. I see a number of reasons for that. In part, the theoretical model can be seen as too simple: It does not allow for changing student ability and effort, and it subsumes a host of processes under a broad conception of learning opportunities. Another reason for its lack of use may be that the mathematical model is complicated by sociological standards. But perhaps the primary reason it has not been generally used is because of empirical findings. Estimates from the model Sørensen advocated, when interpreted according to Sørensen's theories of learning opportunities and achievement, often contradict the knowledge we have of, and the expectations we have about, learning opportunities. Sørensen's model of learning opportunities and achievement is, apparently, falsified.

However, the alternative estimator of Sørensen's indicator of school quality that I present provides results that are consistent with our expectations. It remains to be seen whether such results continue to be consistent with previous research and our understanding of schools and learning. However, this first, critical empirical disadvantage of the model may be gone.

The theoretical advantages of the model remain. Sørensen's theories and mathematical models provide a simple but powerful theoretical statement. It is a statement about the rate at which schools generate learning opportunities. It is a statement about how those opportunities and individual students interact to produce student achievement. Sørensen himself suggested ways in which the theory underlying the model can be elaborated. In Hallinan's chapter in this volume, she suggests additional ways in which the model can be expanded theoretically. Any theoretical additions which can be incorporated into the mathematics of the model will only add to its strength. In the meantime, I have shown that Sørensen's model can be used in a multilevel modeling context, which broadens its current utility. It gives us an indicator of the learning opportunities which a student has experienced, and a method by which to test the effects of school characteristics on school quality.

ACKNOWLEDGMENTS

A previous version of this paper was presented at the Sixth Annual Conference of the Center for Research on Educational Opportunity at the University of Notre Dame, Notre Dame, Indiana. I thank Maureen Hallinan and the attendees of the conference for their comments and questions, Rob Plunkett for his assistance with the mathematics, and Stephen Lich-Tyler and G. Mitchell Sanders for their instruction in performing the crucial statistical estimation. I thank Steve Morgan, Stephanie Arnett, Bill Carbonaro, and an anonymous reviewer for their comments on an earlier version of this paper.

REFERENCES

Coleman, J. S., Campbell, E. Q., Hobson, C. J., McPartland, J., Mood, A. M., Weinfeld, F. D., & York, R. L. (1966). *Equality of educational opportunity*. Washington, DC: U.S. Department of Education.

Carbonaro, W. J., & Gamoran, A. (2002). The production of achievement inequality in high school English. *American Educational Research Journal, 39*, 801–827.

Hallinan, M. T. (2004). Sørensen's learning opportunities model: Theoretical foundations, mathematical formalization, and empirical analyses. In: A. L. Kalleberg, S. L. Morgan, J. Myles & R. A. Rosenfeld (Eds), *Inequality: Structures, Dynamics and Mechanisms: Essays in Honor of Aage B. Sørensen*. Research in Social Stratification and Mobility (Vol. 21, pp. 67–89). Oxford, England: Elsevier.

Sørensen, A. B. (1996). Educational opportunities and school effects. In: J. Clark (Ed.), *James S. Coleman* (Chap. 14). Bristol, PA: Falmer Press, Taylor and Francis.

Sørensen, A. B., & Hallinan, M. T. (1977). A reconceptualization of school effects. *Sociology of Education, 50*(4), 273–289.

Sørensen, A. B., & Hallinan, M. T. (1986). Effects of ability grouping on growth in academic achievement. *American Educational Research Journal, 23*(4), 519–542.

Sørensen, A. B., & Morgan, S. L. (2000). School effects: Theoretical and methodological issues. In: M. T. Hallinan (Ed.), *The Handbook of the Sociology of Education* (pp. 137–160). New York: Kluwer/Plenum.

MOBILITY AND CAREERS

UNTYING THE GORDIAN KNOT OF SOCIAL INHERITANCE

Gøsta Esping-Andersen

SUMMARY

Post-war sociologists painted an optimistic portrait of our stratification systems, suggesting a future of heightened mobility, due to industrialism, and of more meritocracy, due to the rise of professional-technical occupations. Their predictions, alas, have not been born out by research. The link between social origins and educational, occupational or income attainment appears as strong as ever and, hence, life chances continue to be powerfully dependent on the luck of birth.

We are now in the midst of a major social transformation that may decisively influence life chances. There are in particular two facets of the post-industrial economy that push up the levels of human capital required to ensure a good life. On one hand, production is increasingly knowledge-intensive and demands ever stronger skills. On the other hand, many of the growing service jobs may not necessarily require strong skills, but they are likely to become low-wage career traps for those who do not possess the kinds of skills needed for mobility. In short, the "ante" for good life chances, so to speak, is rising across-the-board. It follows that inequalities in life chances may actually intensify unless social inheritance diminishes.

The problem can be likened to a Gordian Knot. The *constant flux* of inter-generational mobility that research identifies is, in many ways, puzzling considering the spate of educational reforms, and the growth of welfare state

Inequality: Structures, Dynamics and Mechanisms: Essays in Honor of Aage B. Sørensen
Research in Social Stratification and Mobility, Volume 21, 115–138

ISSN: 0276-5624/doi:10.1016/S0276-5624(04)21007-1

redistribution. Are, indeed, the mechanisms of social inheritance thoroughly immune to policy? Is the pursuit of equal opportunities bound to be fruitless? This paper takes its lead from scattered, but mounting, evidence that suggests that the Gordian Knot is not necessarily unbreakable. Some countries do exhibit signs of less ascription and greater equality of life chances. This study follows up on these clues and employs therefore nation comparisons in order to get closer to the mechanisms that reproduce or de-couple life chances from class origins.

We break the issue into two questions. Firstly, how unequal is the distribution of human capital? I construct Gini coefficients for cognitive inequalities and examine how these, cross-nationally, are related to the strength of social inheritance. Second, and most importantly, I turn to a more conventional analysis of the extent to which social origins continue to influence cognitive skill development and educational attainment. Like our sociological forbears I, too, conclude on an optimistic note. If we can agree that early cognitive development is key to later success, then there is considerable, albeit circumstantial, evidence that public policy can loosen the Gordian Knot.

DILEMMAS OF POST-INDUSTRIAL LIFE CHANCES

The permanency of social inheritance has become something of a basic sociological fact. There is strong and consistent evidence that social origins affect life chances as much today as in the past, be it in terms of occupational class mobility or in terms of educational attainment (Erikson & Goldthorpe, 1992; Shavit & Blossfeld, 1993).[1]

This constant flux, to use Erikson and Goldthorpe's expression, may seem counter-intuitive when we consider the phenomenal institutional and structural changes that have swept across the advanced democracies over the past half century. For one, as the optimistic post-war theories stressed, the occupational mix is increasingly biased in favour of professional jobs and this ought to place a premium on merit rather than origins in hiring decisions (Bell, 1976). Also, welfare state redistribution combined with educational expansion ought to have helped level the playing field. Basic want and insecurity has been sharply limited, and this should reduce the inherent disadvantage that children from poor families start with.

Of course, it is well-known that advanced welfare societies differ substantially in the incidence of poverty and need, with the U.S. notoriously occupying one extreme, and Scandinavia famously the other. Indeed, post-transfer/tax child poverty is close to non-existent in Scandinavia but remains stubbornly around 20% in the U.S. (Vleminckx & Smeeding, 2001). There is in fact a case, albeit a speculative one, to be made that very egalitarian welfare states may have succeeded in softening the impact of social origins. Both Erikson and Goldthorpe, and also Shavit and Blossfeld show that Sweden (followed by the Netherlands) *does* exhibit a declining impact of social origins on class mobility as well as on educational attainment. Similarly, economists show that inter-generational income mobility is far greater in Sweden than elsewhere (Bjorklund & Jantti, 1997; Corak, forthcoming; Solon, 1999). The precise mechanisms at play remain pretty murky, but the reigning hypothesis is that it must be welfare state induced.[2]

A note of caution is warranted in terms of the professionalization of the occupational mix. Contemporary employment dynamics depend heavily on growth in *personal* and *social* services, and this suggests two alternative evils. On one hand, since both types of services include a sizable share of low-skilled, routine, and often precarious jobs, a dynamic job growth scenario will produce many low-end jobs. The main problem with low-end service jobs is that they easily become "low-skill traps," considering the scarcity of training and skill improvements that is typical of such jobs. On the other hand, where job growth is sluggish the result will be less job polarity but instead more widespread exclusion from the employment relationship. This could nurture the kind of insider-outsider cleavage, depicted by Van Parijs (1986), in which the possession of a job per se constitutes a scarce asset.

The point here is that no matter which employment scenario will prevail, the importance of human capital will strengthen. What is more, the skills needed for accessing good jobs are also changing. If the acquisition of any bundle of qualifications remains as powerfully linked to class origins as ever then, clearly, the repercussions of ascription will become increasingly powerful. Put differently, it is possible that class inheritance will matter much more in the emerging post-industrial order than it ever did before.

We can imagine two kinds of knowledge-economy scenarios. One characterized by "islands of excellence in a sea of ignorance," a society with a highly polarized cognitive and skill structure. Another scenario might look more like a calm pond with modest ripples. As we shall see shortly, the United States come close to the former; Scandinavia exemplifies the latter.

CLASS INHERITANCE AND LIFE CHANCES

In contemporary society the problem of life chances is quite different from how sociologists and economists analysed social stratification in the past. Traditional stratification research believed that industrialism raised total social mobility rates (Featherman et al., 1975; Lipset & Bendix, 1959), if primarily for reasons of structural change. Sons of farmers and workers were quite likely to attain more education and superior (white collar) positions than their fathers. This shift towards a "middle class" society was, of course, compositional; an artifact of the marginals in mobility tables. Education levels and white collar jobs rose throughout society, and this helped improve the well-being of workers. As Levy (1998) shows, the post war era was unique in that it seemed to guarantee that each new cohort would do better than its parents. White collar or not, the basic skills needed in order to make a decent living were by and large modest. In most industrialized countries the standard production worker could count on wages sufficient to permit automobile and even homeownership, and also to allow wives to be full-time home workers.

Post industrial life chances are unlikely to be so blessed. For one, it is widely believed that a novel array of skills and resources has come to play a decisive role. Social skills, personality traits, and "cultural capital" may be as important as educational certificates in hiring and promotion decisions or, more broadly in getting ahead (Bourdieu, 1983; Bowles et al., 2001; De Graaf et al., 1998; DiMaggio, 1982; DiMaggio & Mohr, 1985; Jencks, 1979). But also education and skills in the more conventional sense appear to matter more and more (see below). This has clearly been widely recognized among policy makers, too, and hence the call for life-long learning, activation and retraining programmes. Sadly, it is quite firmly established that remedial training later in life is ineffective if people do not already possess adequate cognitive and motivational resources to begin with (Heckman, 1999). In other words, it all begins in (early) childhood, and this is exactly why it is so difficult to disentangle the impact of social origins on schooling and career achievement from related key resources, such as cognitive abilities, motivation to learn or for that matter social capital.

It is possible that the influence of social origins on life chances embraces two kinds of mechanisms at once. There is, firstly, the impact of family conditions and parental stimulation which are especially concentrated in early childhood. And there is, secondly, the decision process that operates later on when youth make educational transition choices. As Mare (1993) argues, the real impact of class origins concerns transitions from one educational level to another. Once the transition has been made, say to secondary education, class differences in attainment or performance weaken. Class matters primarily in terms of selecting those who do jump the first major hurdles, and later transitions, such as to tertiary level, should be less awesome. The selection effect is probably a drawn-out, self-reinforcing process which begins in early childhood and culminates with youths' transition choices. Following Breen and Goldthorpe (1997), it is likely that "lower class" youth will shy away from embarking on higher education out of a rational risk and cost calculus. They will set their educational aspirations lower than their "upper class" peers, and they will more likely also assess their risk of failing as being higher.[3]

But rational educational choices are themselves likely to co-vary with the mechanisms that link social origins to educational attainment and cognitive development. A rational risk calculus of the probability of failure or of the opportunity cost of continued studies will be affected by nebulous factors such as cultural and social capital. A working class youth with substantial cultural or social network resources is probably more likely to discount the risk of failure. Erikson and Jonsson (1996), for example, place considerable emphasis on families' ability to "navigate" the education system in the best interests of their children. If culture and social ties matter importantly, education transitions will be mediated by mechanisms which we normally cannot observe. Yet, we can offer hypotheses. Hence, the neighbourhood and school milieu will have an effect (Brooks-Gunn et al., 1993). The more that schools and neighbourhoods are class-mixed, the more likely it is that lower class children may possess resources that reduce the perceived risk of failure. In fact, pre-school child centres, if class-mixed and of high pedagogical standards, may have a very powerful ability to neutralize unequal cognitive or cultural capital in the parental home since it is during the first 5–6 years that the cognitive foundations of children are laid (Currie, 2001; Duncan & Brooks-Gunn, 1997; Haveman & Wolfe, 1995; Mayer, 1997; Waldvogel, 2002).

This study explores these questions by utilizing two data sets: the International Adult Literacy Survey (IALS) and OECD's PISA study of the cognitive performance of 15-year olds.[4] I deliberately select countries that stand as prototypical examples of world-wide varieties of post-industrialism and, of course, also of types of welfare state. The latter is potentially crucial if, indeed, observed changes in inter-generational inheritance are linked to social policies. We shall therefore compare representative nations of three ideal-typical groupings: the U.K. and the U.S. (un-regulated economies with residual welfare states); Denmark, Norway, and Sweden (the World's most comprehensive welfare states); and Germany. The Netherlands is a key country to include because, with Sweden, it is cited as an exception to the "constant flux" thesis. Unfortunately, coding problems in the Dutch file of the IALS data prohibit its inclusion in educational attainment comparisons. Germany represents the core Continental welfare model, with a strong accent on familialism, huge gaps in male and female employment, and a highly transfer-biased social policy. It is an economy in which official educational and skill certification plays an unusually powerful role. In terms of educational systems, there are important group-crossovers. The classical "dual-system" of vocational training in Germany is in great part shared also by Denmark (and by the Netherlands). Sweden stands out with its very comprehensive schooling system, while the U.K. boasts an unusually undeveloped vocational training system.[5]

Compared to existing research, my analyses offer three novelties. One, the IALS data, collected in the mid-late 1990s, allows us to estimate inter-generational correlations of educational attainment for very recent cohorts (born in the 1970s). This is decisive, precisely because any potential welfare state effect on educational equality ought to become really manifest towards the 1980s. Two, the IALS data permit us to control for off-springs' cognitive abilities. In this way, we are somewhat better able to identify the relative influence of ascriptive and meritocratic processes. Three, the PISA data, albeit limited to youth still in school age, allows us to separate economic from cultural resources in the family of origin.

Is the Ante Rising?

Most agree that skills matter more and more for life chances, but there is little clarity about exactly how. Rising wage inequalities are no doubt related to changing skill demand, but this could be for two different reasons. It may be that more skills are needed in order to ensure a good career – whether or not the jobs actually require such – or it may simply be that the lack of adequate skills will increasingly condemn individuals to a life of precarious employment. The OECD (2000) shows, for example, that those with less than secondary level schooling (and those with low cognitive resources) are twice as likely to be unemployed as the average. In any case, whichever way it works, the inescapable result is that the "skills premium" is rising.[6]

Still, studies of the impact of education fail to explain most of the variance in earnings (Blau & Kahn, 2000; Bowles et al., 2001; Card, 1998). Hence the growing attention to usually unmeasured variables, such as personality traits, motivation, or cognitive abilities. It is especially the latter which merit attention. For one, cognitive skills are *sine qua non* for successful schooling in the first place. It is also clear that they are fundamental for later adult training and life long learning. And, thirdly, inherent to the "knowledge economy" is the capacity to understand and productively manipulate information – the very essence of cognitive skills.

There is also substantial evidence that cognitive abilities affect life chances *independently* of educational attainment (Jencks & Phillips, 1996; Warren et al., 2000). In fact, the two probably tap quite different dimensions of human capital – as is evident when we note that the simple correlation between years of education and cognitive performance scores is a modest 0.4.[7] We also know that cognitive skills are, to a great extent, developed *prior to* normal school age. The ages 0–6 constitute the critical phase and, as a rule of thumb, a person's cognitive abilities have matured more or less at age 16 (Duncan & Brooks-Gunn, 1996). Bowles et al.'s (2001, p. 1154) review of econometric evidence from 24 studies suggests that "a standard deviation difference in cognitive performance is associated with something less than a 10% increase in wages, and is in this respect roughly equivalent to a year of schooling." A few studies do suggest that the "ante" is rising over time (Bowles et al., 2001; Gangl, 2002). Nonetheless, solid evidence is lacking simply because we need a long time-frame in order to gauge real shifts, and such data simply do not exist. One exception here is Jonsson's (1996) study of Sweden which spans the years 1968–1991 but, alas, he is able to measure solely the impact of formal education, not of cognitive skills. As rates of formal school attainment begin to reach saturation point, the less tangible skills – like cognitive performance – ought to rise in importance.

INTERNATIONAL DIFFERENCES IN COGNITIVE INEQUALITIES

The IALS permits us to estimate the distribution of skills across a large number of advanced countries. Its three measures of cognitive performance (quantitative, document and prose literacy) can be utilized to compute standard decile distributions and summary "inequality" indicies, like the Gini coefficient. Earlier studies (such as OECD, 2000) demonstrate huge international differences in cognitive distributions.[8] The proportion of adults (aged 16+) falling into the lowest quintile ranges from 28% in the U.S. to 6% in Denmark. These discrepancies remain even when immigrants are excluded. That formal education may not guarantee adequate cognitive capacities is evident in the U.S. data which show that almost 15% of Americans with completed high school fall into the lowest quintile.[9] Or, if we use the combined prose, document and quantitative literacy scores, we again find huge cognitive differences between populations with at least upper secondary education, ranging from a mean score of 259 in the U.S. (followed by Italy and the U.K. with 280) to a mean score of 305 in Sweden (followed closely by Denmark, the Netherlands and Germany).[10]

As illustrated in Table 1, cognitive inequalities are generally much lower than are income inequalities. But nation differences are quite massive. Italy, the U.K. and the U.S. have four times as many citizens in the bottom (quantitative) cognitive quintile as does Denmark, the single most egalitarian cognitive performer. Or if we compare Ginis, the U.S. is exactly twice as unequal as is Denmark. Of course, it is to be expected that such inequalities reflect population compositions, in particular a large residue of rural populations. Indeed, the Gini does decline in some countries when we narrow in on urban or youth only – not surprisingly, the decline is very marked in Italy.

How might we account for such different cognitive dispersions? One tempting answer is, simply, that inegalitarian societies produce inegalitarian outcomes, more or less across-the-board. There is, for example, a very strong correlation between

Table 1. Cognitive Inequalities.[a]

	% in Lowest Cogn. Quintile	Gini all	Gini 16–25	Gini Urban Only
Denmark	5.9	0.079	0.072	0.079
Finland	10.4	0.094	0.071	0.087
Norway	7.7	0.089	0.081	0.088
Sweden	9.3	0.101	0.081	0.099
Germany	7.3	0.089	0.083	0.090
Italy	26.7	0.131	0.097	0.121
Holland	10.8	0.091	0.076	0.090
U.K.	23.8	0.130	0.121	0.135
USA	28.1	0.158	0.133	0.132

[a] The cognitive dimension used here is quantitative literacy.

cognitive and income inequalities. Certainly, the causal direction is wholly unclear. Is, for example, the American income distribution more unequal than elsewhere simply because the U.S. distribution of skills is more unequal? Or is it vice-versa? If we can get at the mechanisms, we might be better placed to hypothesize causal chains. For example, if cognitive performance is more powerfully related to social origins in inegalitarian societies, this would suggest that cognitive inequalities stem from broader ascriptive social inequalities (rather than vice-versa). A simple cross-national regression of cognitive Ginis on the *net* impact of class origin on cognitive performance shows in fact a very strong statistical relationship (see Fig. 1).

Nations' level of cognitive inequality appears quite strongly related to the force of parental inheritance. And since we control for immigrant status, we can rule out the possibility that the more inegalitarian profiles of some countries are driven by greater immigration. The social origin Betas are systematically weaker in the cognitively egalitarian countries, such as Denmark, Germany and Norway. And they are systematically stronger in the cognitively unequal group of nations, such as Poland, the U.S. and Italy.[11]

Certainly, these correlations do not help much establish the true causal chain. If severe cognitive inequalities are what produce huge income inequalities, the twain in unison are likely to mutually reinforce class inequalities from generation to generation. What we probably can conclude is that cognitive inequalities go hand in hand with a host of social inequalities. In unison, this is what most likely consolidates and maybe reproduces a society marked by inequality and equality, respectively. The really central question is whether, and how, such consolidation and reproduction might be broken. How might we diminish inequalities of life chances? To get at such questions, we need to move from macro-level nation comparisons to micro-analyses.

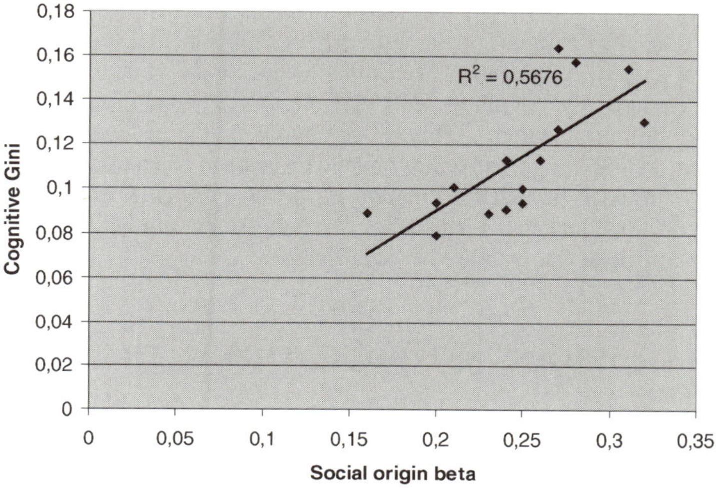

Fig. 1. The Relationship between Cognitive Inequalities and the Relative Importance of Social Origins on Cognitive Performance. *Note:* The social origin Beta derives from a regression of child's cognitive score on father's educational attainment, controlling for child's educational attainment, adult education participation, age, and being immigrant. Regression based on 15 countries listed in Appendix Table 1. *Source:* IALS Microdata.

SOCIAL ORIGINS AND LIFE CHANCES

Most research on inter-generational mobility focuses on either educational attainment, social prestige, on occupational class mobility, or on income mobility. The core inheritance model that economists and sociologists adopt is surprisingly similar and can be summarized as follows: Parents' income (or social status) affects children's destinations via their investment in their offspring's education. A standard income mobility model typically takes the following form:

$$\ln Y_{i,c} = (1 + r)\ln Y_{i,p} + \varepsilon_{i,c} + \mu_{i,c}$$

where child's income Y (in family i) is correlated with parental income because parents invest in their offspring's education. The r-term takes into account prevailing rates of return to human capital and can thus be seen as capturing also the rising "ante." In addition, the child's income will depend on its endowments (ε), and on "luck" (μ). The latter is assumed to be normally distributed. A simple model of educational or occupational mobility would look quite similar.

One principal problem in such models is that endowments, like cognitive skills, are also related to parents' resources, such as their income, level of education or cultural capital. Hence, when we estimate educational attainment models, we need to "cleanse" the cognitive skills variable of the parental influence so as to eliminate multi-co-linearity.[12] This is done by taking the residuals from an OLS regression of child's cognitive scores on father's years of education. Unfortunately, the IALS provides limited information on social origins. Data on father's or mother's occupational status is lacking, and father's and mother's education will therefore constitute our measure of social origins.[13]

SOCIAL ORIGINS AND EDUCATIONAL TRANSITIONS

We turn now to educational attainment and focus, as does most recent research, on transitions.[14] In part, this will facilitate comparison; in part, it has now become quite established that inter-generational social transmission is primarily related to the hurdles constructed within educational systems. It is, for example, the decision to move from one level to another that underpins Breen's and Goldthorpe's rational choice-based thesis of how social origins influence schooling. The rationale is straightforward: moving from one level to another implies a fairly long and possibly strenuous commitment, and hence both uncertainty and the opportunity costs mount. Moving from one year to the next in, say, secondary education will, comparatively speaking, involve far fewer dilemmas and trade-offs.[15] Tables 2 and 3 present analyses for the transition to upper secondary and tertiary level education, respectively. I follow, as far as possible, the modelling procedure used in the country studies in Shavit and Blossfeld (1993). But unlike most comparative studies, I am able to control also for offsprings' cognitive abilities.[16]

Table 2. The Impact of Fathers' Education on Transitions to Upper Secondary Education Across 4 Cohorts (Logistic Odds-Ratios).

	USA	U.K.	Denmark	Norway	Sweden	Germany
Cohort born: 1970–1980	2.49***	1.66***	1.22*	1.40***	1.74***	2.04***
Cohort born: 1960–1970	2.53***	1.83***	1.80***	1.37*	1.97***	2.46***
Cohort born: 1950–1960	2.11**	1.52***	1.64***	1.46**	1.57***	7.57
Cohort born: 1940–1950	2.28***	1.76***	2.22***	2.43***	2.67***	2.00***

Note: Estimates derive from repeated cohort-specific models with controls for gender, immigrant status, and cognitive scores.

Source: IALS.

Table 3. The Impact of Fathers' Education on Transitions to Tertiary Level Education (Logistic Odds Ratios for Four Cohorts).

	USA	U.K.	Denmark	Norway	Sweden	Germany
Cohort born: 1965–1975	1.96***	1.65***	1.33***	1.63***	1.26***	2.01***
Cohort born: 1955–1965	1.63***	1.60***	1.42***	1.89***	1.43***	2.08***
Cohort born: 1945–1955	1.89***	1.68***	1.82***	1.42***	1.67***	2.35***
Cohort born: 1935–1945	1.58***	2.10***	1.67***	2.58***	2.20***	2.23***

Note: Estimates derive from repeated cohort-specific models with controls for gender, immigrant status, and cognitive scores.
Source: IALS.

For reasons of space, the tables present, for four cohorts, only the log odds ratios of father's education on child's probability of making the educational transition. The estimates derive from repeated cohort-specific models that include controls for gender, immigrant status, cognitive test scores, and mothers' educational attainment. I choose to estimate for each cohort separately so as to overcome multi-co-linearity problems when a variable for age is included. The key question we address here is whether or not the inheritance effect is stable or has declined across the cohorts.

Examining the transition to upper-level secondary education in Table 2, one is first of all struck by the broad convergence in the countries' point of departure. There are few differences in the parental effect for the oldest cohorts. International divergence begins to unfold with the baby-boom generations of the 1950s. It is clear that Germany, the U.S. and U.K. all conform to the *constant flux* scenario – although we should note that the parental effect is consistently weaker in the U.K. Indeed, the social origins effect appears to be strengthening in the U.S. In contrast, and far more interesting, we find that the earlier mentioned Swedish success story is equally, if not more, shared by the two other Scandinavian countries. Denmark is clearly the star performer on two counts: the decline is unusually strong, and for the youngest cohort the origin effect almost disappears. These results appear quite robust when we consider that basically the exact same pattern emerges when, instead of fathers', we compare the odds for mothers' education.[17]

An alternative way of assessing the possible equalization of opportunities is to compute a "meritocracy ratio" for each cohort-country combination. This I calculate by taking the log-odds estimate for the cognitive score variable (from the full table, not shown) over the father education variable. To illustrate, for Denmark the meritocracy ratio increases from 1.6 for the oldest cohort to 4.8 for the youngest. In the case of Sweden, it rises from 1.0 to 1.6, while in the U.S. the ratio actually falls from 2.6 to 1.4.

Practically the same kinds of patterns emerge for transitions to tertiary level education (in Table 3). Again, the U.S. and Germany are clear cases of the constant flux, and the three Scandinavian countries all portray a substantial weakening of the social origins effect. The U.K., however, is now a mixed case, with a noticeable drop from the oldest to the second-oldest cohort only to be followed by a stabilized parental effect. Also here we can compare meritocracy ratios. Like before, the U.S. seems to become more ascriptive. The ratio for the oldest cohort is 2.2 and for the youngest, 1.6. Notwithstanding the weaker origins effect in the U.K., there the meritocracy ratio also worsens (from 2.1 for the oldest to 1.7 for the youngest cohort). Similarly, notwithstanding their ability to reduce social inheritance, the meritocracy ratio for both Denmark and Sweden is quite stable between the cohorts. This implies that these countries may very well have progressed in terms of abolishing social inheritance, but that recruitment to higher education has, simultaneously, become less contingent on cognitive abilities.

This suggests a troublesome alternative hypothesis, namely that the Nordic success story may really lie in an overall lowering of the intellectual requirements of their education systems. But there are two reasons why this is doubtful. Firstly, the Nordic countries out-perform most other countries in terms of mean cognitive test scores. Secondly and, I believe, more decisively the Nordic countries' ability to reduce social inheritance is especially pronounced when we focus more narrowly on educational transitions among children with *very low educated parents*. The latter constitutes the equivalent of an acid test since one would expect that mobility opportunities – especially to tertiary education – are especially constricted among children who come from very under-privileged or very low educated milieux. Indeed, much comparative research suggests that upward mobility from the bottom is typically far less likely – as is downward mobility from the very top (Corak, forthcoming). Tables 4 and 5 repeat the same kind of analyses as before, but now focusing only on children of fathers with very low education (ISCED 0–2, which means less than secondary level schooling).

Table 4. Transitions to Secondary Education for Children of Low Educated Fathers (Logistic Odds Ratios).

	USA	U.K.	Denmark	Norway	Sweden	Germany
Cohort 1	0.115***	0.185***	0.449**	0.661	0.320**	0.094***
Cohort 2	0.097***	0.153***	0.248***	0.447**	0.164***	0.067***
Cohort 3	0.116***	0.359**	0.428***	0.445**	0.237***	0.053***
Cohort 4	0.133***	0.162***	0.213***	0.205***	0.091***	0.098***

Table 5. Transitions to Tertiary Education for Children of Low Educated Fathers (Logistic Odds ratios).

	USA	U.K.	Denmark	Norway	Sweden	Germany
Cohort 1	0.071***	0.185***	0.387***	0.351***	0.365***	0.143***
Cohort 2	0.285***	0.177***	0.700*	0.226***	0.287***	0.228***
Cohort 3	0.219***	0.196***	0.280***	0.331***	0.189***	0.106***
Cohort 4	0.347***	0.071***	0.313***	0.175***	0.091***	0.124***

The patterns we find when focusing exclusively on children of very low educated fathers are consistent with the previous results. There is a pervasive constant flux in Germany, the U.K. and in the U.S. and, moreover, in these three countries the likelihood of a child making the transitions is extraordinarily small. Once again, the situation seems actually to be deteriorating in the U.S., especially with regard to transitions to tertiary education. In contrast, all three Scandinavian countries reaffirm their earlier status as equalizers, roughly doubling the probability that a child from low educated origins will attain secondary level schooling. There is, for the Nordic countries, a similarly evident decline in the father-effect on transitions to tertiary education, although the odds here are somewhat lower than for secondary level (except for Sweden). It is also informative to compare the odds among the youngest cohorts. In the U.S. and Germany, the odds are as low as one-tenth compared to Sweden (one-third), and Denmark (almost half). In other words, it would appear that the Nordic countries' success in equalizing opportunities has been especially concentrated among the socially least privileged children.

SEARCHING FOR THE CAUSAL MECHANISMS

Our analyses confirm the prevalence of a constant flux, but they also suggest that there exists a common Scandinavian record of diminishing social inheritance.[18] Basically, the challenge is to identify what the Nordic countries have jointly accomplished and which deviates systematically from other countries.

The list of Scandinavian commonalities is potentially endless, but the literature can guide us to a more manageable set of variables. Firstly, it is well established that economic conditions during childhood matter greatly. American research shows that childhood poverty is associated with two years less of schooling, substantially lower earnings as an adult, and a far greater likelihood of becoming a poor parent, thus perpetuating the problem from one generation to the next (Mayer, 1997). European studies come to parallel, if less dramatic, conclusions (Machin, 1998). Secondly, and now taking the lead from developmental psychology, there seems to be little doubt that one crucial link between social origins and educational success lies in the transmission of cognitive skills – and this implies that the years *prior to* formal schooling are decisive. Once cognitive inequalities are in place, they are largely reproduced rather than corrected in the school system (Duncan & Brooks-Gunn, 1996; OECD, 2000, 2001).

We already know that Scandinavia's generous family support plays an important role in limiting child poverty, but it is undoubtedly the fact that virtually all mothers work which is decisive (Erikson & Jonsson, 1996; Esping-Andersen, 2002). Yet, this may very well cut both ways since one problematic side-effect of mothers' employment is that parents will have far less intense interaction with their children and may accordingly prejudice their cognitive or motivational maturation (Duncan & Brooks-Gunn, 1996; Ermisch & Francesconi, 2002). This remains a hotly disputed question which I shall address below.

The issue can be posed as a dilemma inherent to advanced societies. We must now take for granted women's life long attachment to paid employment. This may have the salutable effect of diminishing poverty risks but may, in turn, jeopardize children's skill development. There certainly exist compensatory mechanisms, among which high quality child care is the most important (Waldvogel, 2002). If this is the case, we should perhaps begin a radical rethinking of Becker's (1964) and Becker and Tomes' (1986) classical human capital theory, according to which parental advantages are transmitted to their children via educational investments. No doubt, parents may boost their children's life chances if they can finance twelve years in elite schools, followed by four years at Harvard or Princeton. But perhaps the key investment lies in pre-school institutions. The question, then, turns to the distribution of pre-school age cognitive stimulus.

The recent PISA data set offers us an excellent opportunity to identify the mechanisms that operate in the development of children's cognitive skills. Like the IALS data it provides us with cognitive test score information, but in this case for 15-year-olds, and it also includes fairly good data on the family conditions during childhood – including information on both the economic and the cultural standards.[19] We turn therefore to the PISA data and examine how children's cognitive performance is related to social origins.

Below, I present (robust) OLS regressions for the same countries examined earlier, now with the inclusion of the Netherlands as well. The analysis aims to gauge the relative importance of cultural and economic effects. It also includes basic controls for gender (girls routinely perform better on cognitive tests), and immigrant status (children of immigrants are disadvantaged in cognitive tests). It is crucial to identify the relative impact of mothers', as opposed to fathers', educational level since early childhood development is far more related to mothers' stimulus. Because of marital selection, the two are inevitably highly correlated and

I therefore measure fathers' education in years and mothers' in levels (less than secondary being the reference group). Hence, the estimated models do not suffer from multi-co-linearity problems. The PISA data do not provide direct information on household incomes, but there are two variables that indirectly capture their economic resources. One is a measure of household amenities and the size and standard of the dwelling. This variable yields systematically very low correlations and has been ignored. The other is an index of the family's socio-economic status, a weighted measure of the parents' occupational and income status, utilizing the index developed by Ganzeboom et al. (1992). The culture variable is also a weighted measure (using factor analysis) that includes three items: the number of books in the home, the frequency of reported familial communication concerning "cultural" issues, and an item that captures familial consumption of "high culture," such as theatre, opera, concerts, and the like. In practice, the 'number of books' item is by far the most important of the three. Finally, our analysis must address the potentially adverse effect on children's cognitive development that motherly employment may cause. I include therefore two dummy variables for whether the mother is employed either part-time or full-time (the reference category is not employed). Table 6 presents the results.

Table 6 confirms the widely recognized superior cognitive development of girls, compared to boys, as well as the predictable circumstance that immigrant children perform less well than native speakers. It is, however, remarkable that the immigrant disadvantage is far greater in non-English speaking countries. The immigrant penalty is on the order of −18 in the U.K. and the U.S., while three or even four times greater in Germany, the Netherlands and Scandinavia.[20]

Predictably, parents' educational level has a powerful influence on children's performance. By and large it is the mother-effect which is all-dominant. But to this we should add two important observations. One, there are no real cognitive gains from mothers having tertiary, as opposed to secondary, level schooling. What appears decisive is that she has more than basic education. Two, when we run the same models separately for girls and boys (not shown) there emerges a clear sex-specific parental influence. Fathers' education matters more among boys, and mothers' education is far more decisive for girls.

When we compare the relative importance of "money" and "culture" in determining children's cognitive skills there is little doubt that the latter is, by some distance, the key. Converting the estimates into standardized Beta coefficients, the cultural capital coefficient is between 50 and 100% larger than the socio-economic status variable. Surprisingly, the two variables are only weakly correlated (strongest in the U.S with a correlation of 0.36, weakest in Sweden with 0.13). This suggests that the rich do not necessarily have an edge on culture, or that cultured citizens rarely make much money. This finding casts serious doubt on conventional

Table 6. Family Characteristics and Cognitive Performance Among 15-year Olds (OLS Regressions).

	USA	U.K.	Germany	Netherlands	Denmark	Norway	Sweden
Constant	421.34***	444.86***	375.97***	465.29***	388.85***	406.06***	433.92***
Gender	18.68***	15.53***	25.57***	10.04***	20.24***	27.51***	27.51***
Immigrant	−15.98*	−14.01**	−40.92***	−30.87***	−25.48***	−35.25***	−35.66***
Father education	3.57*	0.76	7.52***	0.58	8.19***	2.98*	−0.27
Mother educ: Secondary	13.79*	10.31	43.61***	27.24***	37.87***	30.83***	20.59*
Mother educ: Tertiary	13.88*	15.42*	50.01***	22.34***	52.72***	20.44**	17.07*
Socio-economic level	1.10***	1.17***	0.90***	0.92***	0.50***	1.01***	1.06***
Cultural capital	34.21***	40.65***	36.39***	35.82***	34.17***	38.73***	30.84***
Mother part-time	16.84**	12.92***	5.00	9.55**	8.24	4.76	5.05
Mother full-time	−8.91*	5.99**	−3.09	−10.66*	−0.77	2.91	7.41
R^2	0.182	0.200	0.247	0.230	0.199	0.170	0.170
N	2571	7458	3933	2169	3933	3470	3836

Notes: Reference for mothers' education is less than secondary (ISCED 0–2). Reference for mothers' part-time/full-time employment is not employed. To improve upon comparability of education systems, for the United States we include "some college" (usually two years) with upper secondary education.

Data Source: OECD PISA study.

human capital investment theory, as represented by Becker and Tomes (1986) and Solon (1999). Of course, the finding that cultural capital overshadows economic variables does not mean that "money" does not matter, nor that parents do not invest in their children's opportunities. Rather, the results point to a very different investment logic than the one assumed by economists, namely the passing of cultural knowledge and appreciation from parents to children. We should also not forget that the cultural capital variable is potentially ambiguous. As here measured, it should reflect the levels of cultural consumption and communication within the family, but this may arguably also capture aspects related to "nurturing," i.e. that the parents care more for their children. To exclude this potential ambiguity I have rerun the regressions in Table 6, including a control for "intensity of social interaction" in the family (frequency of talking and eating together). The results (not shown) indicate that the coefficients for cultural capital are not affected. In other words, the cultural capital variable appears to be reliable and robust.[21]

If parents' education and cultural standards emerge as a key mechanism that links social origins to children's opportunities, via cognitive development, then we are better placed to account for the convergent Scandinavian success in reducing social inheritance. The key lies, most probably, buried in the far greater cognitive equalization that affects Scandinavian children *precisely because* virtually all mothers work. In the Nordic countries this implies that practically all children participate in high-quality day care and pre-school institutions. What is especially telling is the historical coincidence between the timing of day care expansion in the Nordic countries, and the cohort-specific decline in social inheritance effects we identified earlier. There is a noticeable drop in the inheritance coefficients for the youngest cohort which is exactly the cohort that came to benefit most abundantly from universal child care.

In the United States, too, the vast majority of mothers work, but here access to day care is a direct function of parental income and affordability. Only a minority of American children benefit from quality care, and the vast majority are either placed in some informal care (the lady down the street) or even remain wholly unsupervised (Blau, 2001; Waldvogel, 2002). Indeed, as Waldvogel's review of the evidence shows, quality child care has generally very positive effects on children's cognitive development. If such care is universally provided, the overall consequence must be a substantial equalization of cognitive stimulus since it helps compensate for weaker cultural and educational resources within the family of origin. As a result, children will arrive at the first year of school far more homogeneously prepared.[22] If, on the other hand, the quality of child care mirrors parents' ability to pay, then it is likely to simply reproduce existing inequalities.

This brings us to the hotly disputed effects of mothers' employment. Some research has demonstrated quite negative effects of motherly employment on a range of factors relevant to child well-being, such as emotional security, cognitive development, and school performance; other studies find no such effects and some even identify positive effects.[23] The results depicted in Table 6 suggest that part-time employment has positive or, at least neutral effects. Moving to full-time employment, we begin to detect a negative influence, statistically significant in the U.S. and in Germany. In the U.K., surprisingly, the effect is positive for children's cognitive performance which contradicts the recent findings of Ermisch and Francesconi (2002).[24]

We should, nonetheless, interpret with care because, parallel to the sex-specific impact of mothers' education, also here the impact is almost orthogonally different for boys and girls. If we re-estimate the model in Table 6 for boys and girls separately we find, firstly, that the effect of part-time employment is nowhere negative for either boys or girls. In fact, the effect is systematically positive – but far more positive for girls. Turning, secondly, to full-time employment this is where orthogonal effects appear: in the U.S., Germany, and the Netherlands, the effect is powerfully negative for boys but not for girls.[25] The Nordic countries, on the other hand, show absolutely no significant effects whatsoever for either boys or girls. This, again, provides indirect support for the thesis that high quality care can fully compensate for parental stimulus and, at the same time, help equalize such stimulus across families.

SOME SPECULATIVE CONCLUSIONS

Indisputably, inequalities in human capital persist. But there is clearly no inherent rule that stipulates *how much* inequality. Such inequalities appear also to be systematically linked to other inequality indicators, such as income or to the strength of social inheritance.

This study, like its many forbears, has not advanced much in identifying the precise mechanisms that link class origins and life chances. On the positive side, our results can be read as confirmatory. They confirm that the constant flux is, and remains, a dominant characteristic among advanced nations. It is also on the positive side that our findings correct contemporary received wisdom. We have learned that Sweden may not after all be the real vanguard of democratising life chances. In fact, Denmark is now the clear front-runner, both in terms of weakening inheritance and in terms of promoting equality of outcomes.

In terms of identifying the precise mechanisms that underpin social inheritance, this study has, at best, mounted some circumstantial evidence in favour of a cultural capital explanation. Certainly I do not dismiss monetary arguments, but we might fruitfully distinguish the relative importance of the two. It is tempting to argue that income is a necessary but not sufficient variable. It is well established that poverty and insecurity in childhood has potentially devastating consequences for children's later opportunities and attainment. No doubt, poverty and economic insecurity co-vary with low parental education or cultural capital. Reducing financial deprivation and installing a measure of long-term security should reduce the negative effects of poor, lower class origins. But what if, as Mayer (1997) and also Corak (2001) argue, the real problem is not so much income poverty as cultural poverty, i.e. that low educated (and often poor) parents fail to transmit sufficient cultural capital to their children via, for example, reading or censuring TV consumption?[26]

The equalization of cultural capital is unlikely to occur simply through welfare state redistribution. But social policy, such as securing universal, high-quality early childhood institutions, may. In Denmark and Sweden, pre-school centres began to grow rapidly since the late 1960s and came close to universal coverage already in the 1980s. In addition, organized after-school activities are equally near-universal, especially during elementary and lower-secondary education. Also, policy deliberately favours children from at-risk homes, such as single mother or low-wage families. This should all help compensate for poor cultural capital transmission in the least privileged families: on one side, children depend less on their parents for cognitive development; on the other side, they profit from professionalized cognitive stimulus at middle class standards, possibly *together with* middle class children.

One clear message does emerge from the data, namely that social scientists and policy makers may have erred throughout the post-war era in believing, too myopically, in educational reform and expansion as the great social leveller. The standard causal model that underpins most research, namely the *origins → education → destiny* sequence is, if not mis-specified, at least seriously under-specified. If the race is already halfway run even before children begin school, then we clearly need to examine what happens in the earliest years. This is why parents' cultural capital matters so much, and this is why the goal of equalizing opportunities must include measures of redistributing cognitive stimulus across families. Social research has, so far, been highly sceptical of the rise in married women's employment insofar as this may jeopardize children's development. We may very well revise this view since the very same rise in mothers' employment offers societies a golden opportunity which, if taken, may effectively help us untie the Gordian Knot of social inheritance.

A POSTSCRIPT

A paper driven by lifeless correlations does little justice to the vivid memory of Aage Sorensen. Happily, the correlations make Denmark into the hero of my study. Now, Aage was not one to harbour nationalistic sentiments but he was truly enamoured by two core principles that lie deeply entrenched in the Danish psyche. He loved to belt out the refrain that is sung at all soccer matches: "we are red, we are white, we are Danish dynamite." He loved even more "Svantes Viser," a collection of songs that echo the true philosophy of being Danish, namely "no one can be better than anyone else." Now, you may ask, how does one reconcile these two principles? I shall provide three answers, the first, of course, drawn from soccer: the Danish team is truly dynamite, routinely victorious even against the strongest nations, mainly because it is a team of equals, not a parade of primadonnas. The second comes from this paper, my inadequate tribute to Aage: the Danish welfare state was, since its origins, premised on the firm belief that more equality translates into a far more powerful overall outcome. I may read way too much into my results, but this is what societies like the Danish seem capable of accomplishing. And the third, yes, is represented by Aage's career as a sociologist. Aage was the only great sociologist that Denmark ever produced. Alas, greatness will easily suffocate in a calm pond of little ducklings where no one can be allowed to excel. And so Aage's career came to unfold in the United States where, so to speak, islands of excellence dot a large sea of ignorance. Even Denmark, at times, can be fallible.

NOTES

1. Research on the impact of social origin on incomes and earnings has a long history in economics. For a general overview, see Solon (1999) and Corak (forthcoming). A recent study by Harding et al. (2002) shows, surprisingly, that the correlation between offsprings' household income and parental social class declined in the United States for some decades. They also show that inter-generational inheritance patterns are asymmetric, namely especially strong at the bottom end of the income distribution. Similar asymmetries emerge when one focuses on the "rich," namely substantially less downward mobility among the children of the very rich (see Corak, forthcoming).

2. Erikson and Jonsson (1996, pp. 1–63) suggest five possible (and not mutually exclusive) mechanisms behind Sweden's success in reducing inheritance effects. One, educational reform helped universalize secondary education. Two, the virtual abolition of poverty and income insecurity in families should favour greater risk taking in educational transitions. Three, cultural capital differences have declined among families. And, four, it is possible that also social capital inequalities have declined.

3. An alternative rational calculus argument would come to a similar conclusion: if it is parents, rather than offspring, who are the key decision-makers, poor parents may prefer to accelerate the moment of independence of their children, thus tracking them into quick or more vocationally oriented educational lines. Reference group theory may also help explain lower aspirations. If parents' educational level is the son's and daughter's point of reference in terms of achievement, the son and daughter may be content with a level that simply surpasses that of the parent.

4. Both data sets are described in detail in OECD (2000) and OECD (2001), respectively.

5. For an overview of education system characteristics, see Shavit and Blossfeld (1993) and OECD (2001). For welfare state characteristics, see Esping-Andersen (1990, 1999). For differences in economic structure and employment dynamics, see Scharpf and Schmidt (2000).

6. The unemployment effect is even more pronounced for long-term unemployment. For a recent overview of research findings, see Bowles et al. (2001).

7. Estimated from the IALS data. The correlation varies very little across countries.

8. The distributional properties of the test-score data are not ideally suited for decile based computations, such as the Gini coefficient (Allison, 1978). In the context used here, the measures of inequality are meant as heuristic devices. In any case, country rankings change very little if we use alternative dispersión measures, such as OECD's 5-level classification (OECD, 2000).

9. The lowest quintile implies a level of skills at which people would be able to perform little more than routine and wholly unqualified work. Adults at this cognitive level are, for all purposes, probably un-trainable.

10. It is difficult to see how these differences can be attributed to mass extensión of upper secondary education. For the 25–34 age group, between 85–90% have completed secondary education in Denmark, Sweden, and Germany, just like in the U.S. The cognitive gaps are more likely to stem from national inequalities within the school system, on one hand, and from inequalities due to class inheritance, on the other hand (as we shall see shortly). Note that these international differences would have been even more dramatic had we included additional countries, such as Chile, Ireland and Poland.

11. The weak social origins effect for Britain may come as a surprise, not just because the U.K. scores very unequal, but also because Britain has traditionally been associated with strong class cleavages. We shall see below that class effects in Britain vary by cohort.

12. Note that in the following estimations I use the *combined* scores for the three cognitive dimensions: document, prose, and quantitative. In practice, using one, another, or all combined makes very little difference since they correlate around 0.90–0.95.

13. In order to minimize collinearity, we measure father's education in years and mothers' with a series of dummies (less than secondary is reference, secondary, and tertiary level) that capture her level of educational attainment.

14. I have run similar models for years of education (not shown) and the results end up consistent with the ones obtained from transition models.

15. Julio Carabaña (personal commuication) questions this rational choice reasoning. If education is viewed as an investment in prospective employment opportunities, it is probable that an employer will give preference to a candidate who has spent *some* time in, say, college compared to one who has not, regardless of whether that person was a college drop-out. If so, the returns to college failure would be positive and this should induce a rational youth to opt for the transition.

16. As a reminder, I cleanse the cognitive score of the influence of father's education by taking the residuals from a regression of cognitive scores on father's education. Here is cause for warning. The cognitive scores are based on tests when respondents were adults, not when educational transitions were actually made. This may cause some contamination since it is possible that the educational process itself affects later adult cognitive performance. Yet, such contamination should be quite limited considering that it is well-established that one's cognitive development is concentrated in the ages 0–15. *Note also that I have included 2*

years of college as equivalent of upper secondary education for the United States so as to ensure greater comparability across nations' educational systems.

17. These and other estimations not shown here can be obtained directly from the author: gosta.esping@upf.edu.

18. Similar inter-generational educational attainment anállyses were also performed for Italy and the Netherlands. The Italian case is yet another example of a perfect constant flux. The Netherlands, arguably another key test-case, considering that Shavit and Blossfeld (1993) do detect a reduction in the inheritance effect there, could not be estimated due to substantial classification problems in the Dutch IALS file.

19. In the following analyses I ignore school and neighborhood variables. As also the OECD's (2001) analyses of the data show, these variables yield very little explanatory power once we include family-related variables.

20. Interestingly, the immigrant penalty is rather modest in Spanish estimates (not included here).

21. I thank Ernesto Villanueva for alerting me to this posible source of ambiguity.

22. See also Currie (2001) and Barnett and Boocock (1998) for a review of the cognitive effects of day care.

23. For an overview, see Duncan and Brooks-Gunn (1996) and Waldvogel (2002).

24. Ermish and Francesconi's data are no doubt far better suited for these kinds of estimations and we should therefore give preference to their results.

25. To exemplify, the coefficient for boys is −19.2 in The U.S. and −20.2 in the Netherlands. In both cases, the coefficient for girls is non-significant.

26. Muller and Kerbow (1993), for example, show devastating effects on children's grades when parental involvement in their educational experience is low, when parents fail to restrict TV consumption, and when children remain unsupervised after school hours. To cite an example, children left unsupervised for 3+ hours have on average 10% lower grades than those who are never left unsupervised (p. 28). Nevertheless, McCulloch and Joshi (2002) suggest quite convincingly that, *independently of* cultural factors, protracted low income has a substantial effect on children's intellectual development.

ACKNOWLEDGMENTS

The author would like to thank Richard Breen, Julio Carabaña, Christopher Jencks, Karl Ulrich Mayer, Stephen Morgan, Luis Ortiz, Niels Ploug, and Sebastián Sarasa for their generous comments and suggestions.

REFERENCES

Allison, P. (1978). Measures of inequality. *American Sociological Review, 43*, 865–880.

Barnett, W. S., & Boocock, S. (1998). *Early care and education for children in poverty*. Albany: State University of New York Press.

Becker, G. (1964). *Human capital*. New York: Columbia University Press.

Becker, G., & Tomes, N. (1986). Human capital and the rise and fall of families. *Journal of Labor Economics*, *4*, 1–39.

Bell, D. (1976). *The coming of postindustrial society*. New York: Basic Books.

Bjorklund, A., & Jantti, M. (1997). Intergenerational income mobility in Sweden compared to the United States. *American Economic Review*, *87*, 1009–1018.

Blau, D. (2001). *The child care problem, an economic analysis*. New York: Russell Sage.

Blau, F., & Kahn, L. (2000, June). Do cognitive test scores explain higher U.S. wage inequality? Working Paper. Russell Sage.

Bourdieu, P. (1983). The forms of capital. In: J. G. Richardson (Ed.), *Handbook of Theory and Research in the Sociology of Education* (pp. 241–258). Westport, CT: Greenwood.

Bowles, S., Gintis, H., & Osborne, M. (2001). The determinants of earnings: A behavioural approach. *Journal of Economic Literature*, *XXXIX*, 1137–1176.

Breen, R., & Goldthorpe, J. (1997). Explaining educational differentials. Towards a rational action theory. *Rationality and Society*, *9*(3), 275–305.

Brooks-Gunn, J., Duncan, G., Klebanov, P., & Sealand, N. (1993). Do neighborhoods influence child and adolescent development? *American Journal of Sociology*, *99*(2), 353–395.

Card, D. (1998). The causal effect of education on earnings. In: O. Ashenfelter & D. Card (Eds), *Handbook of Labor Economics* (Vol. 3). Amsterdam: North Holland.

Corak, M. (2001). Are the kids all right? Intergenerational mobility and child well-being in Canada. Working Paper No. 171, Family and Labour Studies, Statistics Canada.

Corak, M. (forthcoming). *The dynamics of intergenerational income mobility*. Cambridge: Cambridge University Press.

Currie, J. (2001). Early childhood intervention programs. *Journal of Economic Perspectives*, *15*, 213–238.

DiMaggio, P. (1982). Cultural capital and school success. *American Sociological Review*, *47*, 189–201.

DiMaggio, P., & Mohr, J. (1985). Cultural capital, educational attainment and marital selection. *American Journal of Sociology*, *90*, 1231–1261.

Duncan, G., & Brooks-Gunn, J. (1997). *Consequences of growing up poor*. New York: Russell Sage.

Erikson, R., & Goldthorpe, J. (1992). *The constant flux*. Oxford: Clarendon Press.

Erikson, R., & Jonsson, J. (1996). *Can education be equalized? The Swedish case in comparative perspective*. Boulder, CO: Westview Press.

Ermisch, J., & Francesconi, M. (2002). The effect of parents' employment on children's educational attainment. ISER Working Paper, 21. University of Essex.

Esping-Andersen, G. (1999). *Social foundations of postindustrial economies*. Oxford: Oxford University Press.

Esping-Andersen, G. (2002). *Why we need a new welfare state*. Oxford: Oxford University Press.

Featherman, D., Jones, F., & Hauser, R. (1975). Assumptions of social mobility research in the United States: The case of occupational status. *Social Science Research*, *4*, 329–360.

Gangl, M. (2002). Changing labour markets and early career outcomes: Labour market entry in Europe over the past decade. *Work, Employment and Society*, *16*(1), 67–90.

Ganzeboom, H., De Graaf, P., & Treiman, D. (1992). A standard international socio-economic index of occupational status. *Social Science Research*, *21*(1), 1–56.

Harding, D., Jencks, C., Lopoo, L., & Mayer, S. (2002). The changing effects of family background on the incomes of American adults. In: S. Bowles, H. Gintis & M. Osborne (Eds), *Family Background and Economic Success* (forthcoming). New York: Russell Sage.

Haveman, R., & Wolfe, B. (1995). *Succeeding generations. On the effects of investments in children*. New York: Russell Sage.

Heckman, J. (1999). Doing it right: Job training and education. *The Public Interest* (Spring), 86–106.

Jonsson, J. (1996). Stratification in post-industrial society. In: R. Erikson & J. Jonsson (Eds), *Can Education be Equalized?* (pp. 113–144). Boulder, CO: Westview Press.

Levy, F. (1998). *The new dollars and dreams*. New York: Russell Sage.

Lipset, S. M., & Bendix, R. (1959). *Social mobility in industrial society*. Berkeley: University of California Press.

Machin, S. (1998). Childhood disadvantage and intergenerational transmissions of economic status. In: A. Atkinson & J. Hills (Eds), *Exclusion, Employment and Opportunity*. London School of Economics (CASE).

Mare, R. (1993). Educational stratification and observed and unobserved components of family background. In: Y. Shavit & H. P. Blossfeld (Eds), *Persistent Inequality* (pp. 351–376). Boulder, CO: Westview Press.

Mayer, S. (1997). *What money can't buy*. Cambridge, MA: Harvard University Press.

McCulloch, A., & Joshi, H. (2002). Child development and family resources: Evidence from the second generation of the 1958 British birth cohort. *Journal of Population Economics*, *15*(2), 283–304.

Muller, C., & Kerbow, D. (1993). Parent involvement in the home, school, and community. In: B. Schneider & J. S. Coleman (Eds), *Parents, Their Children, and Schools* (pp. 13–42). Boulder, CO: Westview Press.

OECD (2000). *Literacy in the knowledge society*. Paris: OECD.

OECD (2001). *Knowledge and skills for life*. Paris: OECD.

Scharpf, F., & Schmidt, V. (2000). *Welfare and work in the open economy*. Oxford: Oxford University Press.

Shavit, Y., & Blossfeld, H. P. (1993). *Persistent inequality*. Boulder, CO: Westview Press.

Van Parijs, P. (1986). A revolution in class theory. *Politics and Society*, *15*(4), 453–482.

Vleminckx, K., & Smeeding, T. (2001). *Child well-being, child poverty, and child policy in modern nations*. Bristol: Policy Press.

Waldvogel, J. (2002). Child care, women's employment and child outcomes. *Journal of Population Economics*, *15*, 527–548.

CAREER PATTERNS OVER THE LIFE COURSE: GENDER, CLASS, AND LINKED LIVES

Sonja Drobnič and Hans-Peter Blossfeld

INTRODUCTION

This paper draws on several concepts that are central to Aage Sørensen's work and have been profoundly affected by his theoretical and methodological contributions to sociology: career mobility as process, open and closed positions as structure, social class and social stratification, the life course perspective, his focus on cross-national comparative institutional analysis, and event history analysis. In particular, his conceptual elaboration of the properties of social structure and its impact on the relationship between individual characteristics and socioeconomic attainment, provided new insights into the patterns of social mobility and social stratification, and in many ways, redirected the focus of sociological observations and the interpretations of those observations.

Sørensen (1983, 1986a) argued that mobility among positions that form a social structure, as well as mechanisms of access to positions, determine individuals' life courses. One of his central distinctions regarding the mechanisms of access to positions can be found in the concepts of open- and closed-position systems. These two systems translate individual effort, background, and ability into socioeconomic achievements in very different ways. In open-position systems, market-competition translates individual characteristics into socioeconomic outcomes. In case of occupational positions, for example,

Inequality: Structures, Dynamics and Mechanisms: Essays in Honor of Aage B. Sørensen
Research in Social Stratification and Mobility, Volume 21, 139–164

ISSN: 0276-5624/doi:10.1016/S0276-5624(04)21008-3

individual skills, efforts and abilities are directly translated into social and economic rewards. In closed-position systems, however, there are constraints in access to positions that are independent of individual resources. Individual ability and effort will only bring about the desired outcome, if there is a vacancy and the individual can outperform other candidates for this position. Both the emergence of the vacancy and the characteristics of other competitors are outside of the control of the individual.

These different mechanisms for the allocation of individuals to positions are highly relevant for the variation in socioeconomic outcomes. Stratification research and labor-market research have increasingly incorporated in their models Sørensen's idea of social structure that shape the individual attainment trajectories. It became recognized that an individual's action and outcomes are produced and shaped by structurally given opportunities and constraints, and by institutional arrangements and regulations. In other words, many positions that determine the major dimensions of inequality in society can be described as closed-system-like positions, at least to some degree.[1] Knowing the characteristics of individuals is therefore insufficient to understand the outcomes, such as individual attainment and career processes.

Sørensen's concepts have been effectively applied in life-course research. As Sørensen (1986a, p. 178) himself pointed out, main features of the life course can be described by the major positions individuals occupy during their life-time. In analyzing life courses, sociology should describe and analyze the patterning of positions over the life span. Major positions are generally not occupied in a random order but follow socially produced regularities. Moreover, it is not only important which positions a person occupies, but how he or she gets access to them, at what time in the life course, and in which order or sequence. The modes of access to positions determine how characteristics of individuals and characteristics of positions become associated, and the understanding of these mechanisms should be important for our understanding of how social structure shapes individual lives.

In this paper we both build on Sørensen's central concepts and further develop them for the analysis of coupled careers. We argue that one reason for the mechanisms of access to positions in the labor market not having been fully understood in stratification and labor-market research is the failure to acknowledge the degree to which employment histories and family processes are related. For that purpose, we use an additional aspect that has to a large extent been neglected not only in stratification and labor-market research but also in the life-course approach: the principle of interdependent or linked lives. This conceptual framework addresses the relationship between individual lives and social structure in a specific way, and simultaneously seeks to uncover some of the mechanisms through which these two levels are interconnected. It has been proposed by Elder and Caspi (1990) as one of five principles to help us examine the link between social change and the life course. It locates lives in relation to others who mediate the influence of social change. As they put it, "All lives are lived interdependently, and this connectedness defines a medium through which historical change plays out its influence over time" (*ibid.*, p. 221).

The interdependence of life histories is most salient when the life course perspective is applied to the family unit. The life course of the family underscores the interdependent life histories of its members: the properties of the family as a whole are derived from the properties of the relationships between individuals in the family and not just from the characteristics of the individuals as separate persons (Elder & Caspi, 1990). This conceptual framework suggests that instead of treating individuals as isolated entities, we should consider individuals within their social matrix of relationships. The opportunities and constraints faced by individuals also reflect their position in the web of interpersonal ties, and social change has powerful consequences for the individuals through the lives of related others.

We employ the principle of interdependent or linked lives to better understand the persisting inequalities between men and women in modern labor markets, and persisting cross-national differences in the levels of married women's participation in paid employment. The starting point for our theoretical discussion is the economic theory of the family with its implicit assumptions of an open-position system and gender-neutral mechanisms of allocating individuals to positions in social structure. We then proceed with the discussion of the structural and institutional contexts in countries with various welfare state regimes, and seek empirical support for theoretical propositions in a series of studies on couples' employment patterns in twelve different countries (see the book by Blossfeld & Drobnič, 2001). All empirical studies on which the summary of results and conclusions in this paper are based are longitudinal in their design and analytical methods. In particular, they use event history analysis and most include rich retrospective life history information on work and family transitions of both husbands and wives. We summarize the empirical results in the light of a welfare state regime typology that provides a theoretical orientation and facilitates the interpretation of a wealth of information on differences and similarities found in cross-national comparison. Finally, we bring together gender inequality and class inequality, showing how they intersect with each other in allocating individuals to social positions, and how this intersection occurs through interdependencies between and among lives.

STRATIFICATION AND LABOR-MARKET RESEARCH: INDIVIDUALISTIC VS. FAMILY PERSPECTIVES

Theories of social inequality traditionally defined social class as a market relationship and considered the family as the key unit of social stratification (see Sørensen, 1986b). In this conceptual approach, conjugal families were regarded as collective entities in which family members share the rewards gained by the family head through relationships within labor markets and production units and, as primary agents of socialization and institutions channeling social and economic inheritance, transmit privilege as well as power and prestige to the next generation (Coser, 1973; Davis, 1949; Hyman, 1953). It is therefore not surprising that until the early 1980s, intra- and intergenerational social mobility studies (e.g. Goldthorpe, 1980) as well as status attainment research (Blau & Duncan, 1967; Sewell & Hauser, 1975) regarded variation in the social position of male family heads as the key dependent variable to be explained (see Sørensen, 1986b). Measuring the effects of a father's education and occupation on his son's education and occupational attainment dominated stratification research for many years. When these social mobility models were extended to married women, it was not women's own resources that were studied; rather, the education and occupation of women's fathers were compared with those of their husbands (Handl et al., 1977).

The focus of this early stratification research on male family heads reflected the historical dominance of the traditional family model in the 1950s and 1960s. For this historical period, stratification studies provided valuable insights into the basic relationships between social origin, education, occupation and income among men, but clearly excluded other important forms of inequality (Curtis, 1986). In particular, the division of work between husbands and their wives, the inequality between spouses, and the power structures within the family were almost completely ignored.

The dramatic increase in the labor force participation of married women, accompanied by an increase in the share of family income contributed by wives (e.g. Sørensen & McLanahan, 1987), led to a growing critique of the pervasive "male bias" in the stratification literature (Acker, 1973; Dex, 1990; Huber & Spitze, 1983; Sørensen & McLanahan, 1987). A growing stream of feminist research suggested a complete abandonment of the assumption of the family as the unit of stratification and of class analysis (Acker, 1973). According to this school of thought, the class position of individual men and women measured by their own work position should be the focus of research in social stratification. Indeed, a number of empirical studies followed this recommendation: women, women's employment, and gender inequality in the labor market became visible, and sociological knowledge of the mechanisms behind women's continuing disadvantage in the labor market improved greatly, as Annemette Sørensen (1994) noted in her comprehensive review of the controversy on the unit of stratification. The "individualistic" perspective met a spirited opposition by defenders of the conventional approach, who viewed family as the unit of class analysis (Erikson, 1984; Goldthorpe, 1983, 1984). The issue has not been resolved unequivocally: the appropriate unit of analysis in studying gender and class, particularly the class position of dual earner couples, has remained a controversial issue in stratification research (Plutzer & Zipp, 2001).

Subsequently, the research focus gradually shifted from traditional stratification research to labor market research and from household heads to individual women and men in the marketplace, largely ignoring their family or household context, their income-sharing within the family, and their social security or other benefits enjoyed through family relationships. This individualistic turn also led to the belief that equality between the sexes could be easily achieved by policy interventions in the educational system and the labor market. On the one hand, supply-oriented labor market approaches, such as human capital studies, attempted to show that much of the sex differentials in earnings and job opportunities could in fact be explained by productivity differences, which in turn were seen as a result of differential investments in general and job-specific human capital by men and women (Mincer & Ofek, 1982; Mincer & Polachek, 1974; Polachek, 1981). Thus, this approach suggested that education and training are the strategic variables for change, and that equality between the sexes could be achieved by women investing more in their human capital.

On the other hand, demand-oriented studies of labor market segmentation tried to demonstrate that the labor market could be divided into relatively closed partial markets. Primary and internal labor markets were not equally accessible to equally productive women because employers, implementing mechanisms of statistical discrimination, simply believed women, on average, to be less committed and stable employees (Arrow, 1972; Cain, 1976; Phelps, 1972). Thus, based on this approach, the central policy route to gender equality would clearly be an increase in women's labor force participation over the life course. Finally, many feminist-oriented labor market studies tried to establish that women's paid work, female labor force participation, and women's income opportunities were the result of universal discriminating practices by union officials and employers (Hartmann, 1976; Madden, 1973, 1975). From this perspective, the implementation of equal opportunities legislation would seem to be the key variable to reduce male power and dominance and achieve equality between working men and women.

If one reviews the empirical results of these individual-oriented, work-centered labor market studies, one can conclude that – although women seem to have made some progress in their job opportunities, upward career mobility and earnings across birth cohorts – the picture is dominated by persistent gender inequality across all industrialized societies (cf. Blau, 1999; Blossfeld, 1987; Huber, 1988; Reskin & Roos, 1990; Rubery & Fagan, 1993). This enduring feature of the labor market in different countries is, however, quite surprising in the light of individualistic labor market approaches. From their perspective, one would have expected that as a result of massive social changes in the educational and employment systems in the last decades, sex differences in all important work-related aspects should have declined to a much larger extent than they actually have. First, educational expansion has led to the virtual disappearance of differentials in the educational attainment levels of men and women in nearly all modern societies (Erikson & Jonsson, 1996; Shavit & Blossfeld, 1993). In some countries, the gender gap in educational attainment has actually been reversed, with young women on the average attaining higher levels of education than men. Second, married women's labor force participation has risen virtually everywhere, due to the decline in the propensity of women to withdraw permanently from the labor market on marriage or after the birth of their first child, and with the declining number of children in modern families (cf. Blossfeld & Hakim, 1997; Van der Lippe & Van Dijk, 2002). Third, employers who discriminate against women have to pay an economic premium for hiring men, and should therefore – at least in the long run – suffer from a severe competitive disadvantage. And, finally, the implementation of equal opportunities laws and policies in most of the industrialized countries are increasingly ensuring that jobs must remain formally open to all applicants. In other words, in these individualistic approaches the mechanisms by which gender inequalities have been maintained over decades and continue to be both an individual and an institutional practice remain a puzzle.

Our aim in this paper is to explore this puzzle by introducing an intermediate level between individual characteristics and actions, and the structural properties of the labor markets. We start from the premise that neither the traditional concentration on male household heads nor the individualistic approach with "atomized" men and women is appropriate if we want to understand how gender inequalities are produced and reproduced in the labor market. Rather, the interdependent decision-making processes of men and women from different social classes within families and households have to become an issue of major interest. Families as collective entities send their male and female members out to work, assign household tasks and share wages and resources (cf. Moen & Forest, 1999).

THE ECONOMIC THEORY OF THE FAMILY

None of the theoretical perspectives that have been used to understand gender inequality in market and nonmarket work has received as much attention as the economic theory of the family (Becker, 1981; Mincer & Polachek, 1974; Schultz, 1974). The chief concern of the proponents of this approach was that changes in women's income potential that became widespread in the 1970s and early 1980s would endanger the interdependence between the sexes, produced by the sexual division of labor in the family and the labor market, and destabilize the family as a social institution. This notion can also be found in the writings of Parsons, who believed that one of the main functions of the specialization of men in paid employment and women in work within the family was to prevent disruptive status competition between the spouses (Parsons, 1942; Parsons & Bales, 1966).

The economic theory of the family is thus an approach which relatively early drew attention to the fact that an individual's decision-making regarding the allocation of time and effort to paid work in the labor market and unpaid work in the home can best be understood within the context of the family. The type of family considered in this approach is the traditional married couple with children and a wife who is not in the paid labor force. The decisions of each spouse are viewed as interdependent with the activities and characteristics of the other family members (Mincer & Polachek, 1974).

The economic approach to the family is based on assumptions of utility maximization, stable preferences, and equilibrium in the markets. A core feature of this model is that spouses tend to specialize within the marriage because specialization is the most efficient productive strategy and maximizes the utility for the household as a whole. Since the production and rearing of children is the main purpose of families, families use market goods and services as well as parents' time to achieve this goal. The economic theory of the family predicts that specialization of a husband and a wife towards either market or unpaid household work will follow the principle of comparative or relative efficiency. The person who has more marketable skills, higher productivity and higher earnings capacity will specialize in paid work; the other partner's main responsibility will be the maintenance of the home and childrearing. Based on the comparative advantages of mates at the time of marriage and based on the initial division of labor, spouses will tend to further increase their specialization with increasing marriage duration because that is the most efficient productive strategy for the family.

Even if the economic theory of the family argues that wives normally rely on husbands as providers, and husbands mostly depend on wives for the maintenance of the home as well as for the rearing of children, it is only because young men and young women had invested differently in their earnings capacities during the early life course. Thus, the economic theory of the family holds that the sexual division of labor in the family and in the labor market is not so much based on biological sex-differences – although this aspect still remains a subject of intense debate – but is rather the result of gender-specific educational and training investments. These investments and the connected comparative advantages, however, could in principle be balanced (or reversed) between young men and young women.

Following the logic of this in principle gender-neutral approach, an increasing equalization of educational attainment levels and earning power of young men and women across cohorts should also affect the process of assortative mating and change the structure of couples' sex-specific division of labor within the family and the labor market: First, it should lead to a decline in the proportion of men marrying downwards – or women marrying upwards – with regard to traits determining earnings capacity, simply because the structures of these traits are becoming more equalized across cohorts. In fact, there is empirical evidence that the incidence of these traditional marriages is indeed declining in the course of educational expansion (Blossfeld & Timm, 2003). Second, it should raise the proportion of couples marrying homogamously. Given the increasingly gender-equalized structure of traits determining earnings capacity, the economic theory of the family predicts that mates benefit most from each other when they resemble each other as far as possible in their non-market traits (intelligence, health, education etc.). Third, the likelihood that young women will marry downwards should increase. When young women profit more than young men from educational expansion and career resources, then, from a statistical point of view, the random probability that women will marry downwards – or men upwards – with regard to traits determining earnings capacity (or income and wage) should increase for each younger cohort. And, finally, both an increasing number of homogamous marriages, where the relative earning power of husband and wife is uncertain, and a rising number of women marrying downwards, where the wife has a markedly higher income potential than her husband, should increase the proportion of husbands who rely on wives as providers, and of wives who rely on husbands for the maintenance of the home as well as for the rearing of children. Therefore, from a life course perspective, it should then be the husband who typically schedules his work and family roles sequentially over the life course, and it should be the wife who as the family's primary earner has a fairly uninterrupted employment career over the life course.

In this paper, we address these propositions, using longitudinal life-history data on employment careers of husbands of wives in a number of different countries with various national contexts. In this way, we can simultaneously examine the effects of individual characteristics, institutional contexts, and interdependent decision-making processes within family units. Due to substantive variation in national data sets and difficulties with detailed occupational schemes in cross-national comparisons, we limit the analysis to the patterns of paid employment and unpaid work over the life course of individuals. The distinction between paid and unpaid work can be considered the major determinant of an individual's position in a society because the labor force continues to be the arena for the major socio-economic stratification processes. In Western societies, individuals who are excluded from participation in the labor force, among them traditionally many women, are disfavored in terms of material standards of living as well as social rights, which are claim rights typically acquired by economic activity (Korpi, 2000).

THE COUNTRY CONTEXT

According to the economic theory of the family, the patterns of labor force participation of husbands and wives over the life course can be expected to vary according to their educational and training investments – not only in absolute terms but also relative to each other, which determines who has a comparative advantage in the labor market. Further, employment patterns over the life course may be contingent on a number of structural influences and institutional mechanisms that vary across countries. In this study, we include twelve countries that may be classified into five major groups according to their basic cultural and economic systems: (1) Western capitalist countries with "conservative" welfare states, (West) Germany, the Netherlands, and (the Flemish part of) Belgium; (2) Southern European capitalist countries with "familialistic" welfare states, Italy and Spain; (3) Western capitalist countries with a "liberal" welfare state, the United Kingdom and the United States of America; (4) Western capitalist countries with a "social democratic" welfare state, Denmark and Sweden; and (5) Central and Eastern European (formerly) socialist countries, Poland and Hungary. Finally, and in order to enrich the selection of societies examined here, we have included a study on non-Western socialist China.[2]

These countries do not constitute a representative sample of all contemporary societies, but do represent considerable variation in the following characteristics: the level of industrialization/tertiarization and the standard of living, the political system, the degree of de-commodification by the capitalist welfare state, the degree to which the husband can earn a breadwinner family wage, the package of public policies that support maternal employment, and the variation in women's full-time and part-time employment rates.

The employment structure of a country as a whole, and its gender-specific occupational patterns in particular, shape opportunities and constraints, and in this way influence the choices couples make. However, there is a two-way dynamic relationship where couples' choices in turn produce a renewal as well as changes of these structures. Thus, we have to understand the country-specific employment constraints and their changes within which husbands and wives operate.

In the countries included in this study, whether capitalist or (former) state socialist, whether Western or non-Western, men have normally been employed continuously and full-time, unless they were in school, retired, suffered from health problems, or were employed part-time involuntarily due to low labor demand (Rosenfeld & Birkelund, 1995). Thus, non-employment of men normally has taken the form of unemployment, and part-time employment of men (and its increase) has mainly been a matter of very specific (but growing) groups such as students or (early) retirees, and not an important phenomenon related to men's roles as husbands and fathers. In these countries, the average proportion of part-time working men is about 3–4%, with the Netherlands (16%), the United States of America (11%), and Denmark (10%) as the exceptions (Blossfeld & Hakim, 1997). From a life course perspective, men's part-time work is concentrated at the ages of transition from school to work and from work to retirement. It follows that most husbands during middle age have quite a saturated level of labor force participation – at least as long as they do not suffer from unemployment – and are usually working in full-time "male" occupations which makes them prone to become the providers or at least the primary earners of their families (Hakim, 1998).

On the other hand, women show a substantial variation in the proportion of labor force participation over the life course and the extent to which they work full- or part-time (Van der Lippe & Van Dijk, 2002). Full-time employment levels of married women are relatively high in countries such as Sweden and Denmark (where part-time working women frequently work hours long enough to be classified as full-timers), the United States of America, and the (former) state socialist countries like Poland and Hungary, as well as China. The similarity in women's full-time participation among these otherwise very different countries is highly significant for our cross-national comparison because full-time jobs are particularly important in breaking down sex-stereotypes and cultural barriers to women at all occupational levels. Recent labor market studies indicate that full-time jobs normally give better access to "male" and "gender-mixed" occupations (Hakim, 1998). In particular, the small group of "gender-mixed" occupations, which absorb a disproportionate share of Service Class positions (cf. the class schema developed by Erikson & Goldthorpe, 1992), seems to be growing rapidly as a result of the process of occupational and industrial restructuring in many countries. Thus, the best jobs in terms of earnings, status and prestige are increasingly "gender-mixed" occupations shared proportionately by men and women, and not male-dominated occupations (Hakim, 1998). In other words, declining occupational segregation in the full-time workforce should give full-time employed wives an increasingly better lever to become equal providers or even primary earners for their families (Saltzman Chafetz, 1995).

In many countries, declining occupational segregation in the full-time workforce is, however, counterbalanced and concealed by rising occupational segregation in the part-time workforce. Part-time jobs are not just diminutive versions of full-time jobs, they are jobs that mainly recruit married women who work as secondary earners. This is reflected in today's relatively high proportion of married women in part-time jobs in the Netherlands, West Germany, the United Kingdom, Belgium, Denmark, and Sweden. However, the opportunity to work part-time as well as the composition of part-time workforce differ greatly in various countries. If few part-time options are available, wives either have to work full-time, as in Hungary, Poland and China, where integrating women into paid full-time work was considered a vital strategy to achieve gender equality in the socialist/communist development (Drobnič, 1997), or they have to become economically inactive, which has been the standard situation of wives in Italy and Spain.

WELFARE STATE REGIMES

These country-specific patterns of wives' labor force participation as well as the extent of female full-time and part-time work are closely (inter)related with various types of welfare state regimes. "Regime" here refers to the typical ways in which welfare production is allocated between state, market, and households (Esping-Andersen, 1990, 1999). It is important to approach the country-specific differences from such a broad theoretical perspective because husbands' and wives' employment patterns are not a matter of narrowly defined (fiscal, monetary, family, labor market etc.) policies. In effect, the same sociopolitical goals can be achieved by alternative policies and within broader country-specific policy packages various policies can serve as functional equivalents. For example, childcare provision, which influences wives' decisions to work, can be organized primarily via public-sector provision by the state (e.g. Sweden, Denmark, and (former) state socialist regimes), low-priced family care services via the market (e.g. the United States), or through kinship care networks via the households (e.g. Germany). The diversity of these state-market-family packages reflects cross-national differences in historical origins, cultural models, and contemporary policy goals (Gornick et al., 1997; Pfau-Effinger, 1999).

Along similar lines, DiPrete (2002) argues that occupational-based models of social mobility are insufficient to understand cross-national variation in social mobility. He proposes the concept of "mobility regime," which should capture the institutional mechanisms that can explain the observed cross-national variation in this area. An adequate theoretical treatment of national mobility regimes must be conceptualized and operationalized in terms of the life conditions of the individual's household. The focus should be on the extent to which societal institutions influence the rate of events with the potential to change a household's life conditions through the manipulation of incentives for mobility-generating events, and the extent to which they mitigate the consequences of these events through social insurance.

We believe that typologies of this kind are a useful tool to conceptualize the general contours of institutional characteristics of various societies in cross-national comparison. They also provide a theoretical orientation and facilitate the interpretation of differences and similarities found in cross-national comparisons. We therefore partly follow Esping-Andersen (1990) with his threefold distinction between "liberal," "conservative" and "social democratic" welfare state regimes. This typology has stimulated much research in the comparative study of welfare states but also provoked criticism across a wide range of problems (DiPrete, 2002; Leibfried, 1992; Lewis, 1992; Lewis & Ostner, 1995; Orloff, 1993; Sainsbury, 1996). We extended this typology by adding the Mediterranean welfare state regime and the (former) state-socialist countries, and thus distinguish five main clusters or regimes that are supposed to produce markedly different patterns of couples' careers: the "conservative," the "Mediterranean," the "liberal," the "social democratic," and the (former) "state socialist" regime. We explicitly emphasize that there is no one-to-one relationship between ideal welfare regimes and individual welfare states, and a country might in some aspects significantly digress from a "pure" welfare state regime within which it is placed.

The conservative welfare state in the Netherlands, West Germany, and to a lesser extent in Belgium (Flanders), supports wives and mothers who give priority to family activities (Esping-Andersen, 1999). National policies are generally familialistic in the sense that they favor wives' economic dependence on their husbands and stimulate mothers' choices for non-employment against part-time work, and part-time work against full-time employment. Hence, this welfare state regime tends to preserve the male-breadwinner family model. A strong welfare policy assures the male breadwinner wage, which strengthens wives' economic dependence on their husbands and husbands' social reproduction dependency on their wives. Tax system supports these arrangements; in Germany, for example, dual-earner couples are punished by the tax system which privileges wives' non-employment or part-time employment. Further, conservative welfare states typically provide low levels of childcare and day-care services (cf. Gornick et al., 1997), and the school system is organized under the assumption that children can be taken care of in the families. Based on this welfare state regime, we assume that the higher the husbands' occupational resources, the more wives' employment, in particular full-time employment, is suppressed.

On almost all counts, the Mediterranean welfare states such as Italy and Spain display extremely low public provision (Esping-Andersen, 1999). In fact, they have a limited focus on social assistance, and direct family benefits are truly meager (González López, 1998). They are far less egalitarian and de-commodifying than the social democratic or conservative welfare states and rather resemble the liberal welfare states. However, the familialism of Mediterranean countries is distinct in the centrality of the family as a provider of care and ultimate responsibility-taker for its members' welfare (Bettio & Villa, 1998; Esping-Andersen, 1999). It is characteristic of the Mediterranean model that with women's better education and increasing career opportunities, couples have two alternatives: either they follow the traditional model which is associated with the wife's economic dependency on her husband (Saraceno, 1996), or a dual-earner model, with both spouses working full-time, and constrained fertility. In our context, given the importance of the traditional family model in the Mediterranean welfare state, we assume that the decision for wife's employment is also strongly dependent on the husband's social position.

The liberal welfare states in the United Kingdom and the United States emphasize the principle of individual freedom. They accept the distributional consequences of market forces in terms of class and gender inequalities and do little to stimulate married women's labor supply by direct public policy measures (Esping-Andersen, 1999). Thus, on the one hand, this type of welfare state is far less egalitarian and de-commodifying than the social democratic welfare state, but on the other hand, it is de-familialistic, too. Here, de-familialization is produced via market provisions. The unregulated, market-driven employment structure of the liberal welfare state produces a large pool of low-wage workers in the service sector and a declining wage rate for "middle-class" workers with two consequences: (a) households, especially lower-income families, increasingly have to shift time from domestic activities to market work to enjoy the benefits of the growth in the standard of living; (b) labor-intensive and cost-sensitive market services become affordable for an increasing number of households. Hence, inexpensive services, such as day-care, laundering etc., raise the opportunity costs for families doing unpaid domestic work, particularly in the middle class. Wives in the United States are integrated (often full-time) into the labor market via a decreasing male breadwinner market wage and the availability of inexpensive market services for the household. This implies an erosion of the male-breadwinner model and an increasing importance of wives' income for the socioeconomic status of the family. We expect that the initial negative impact of husbands' resources on wives' employment disappears or even becomes positive.

Social democratic welfare-states in Sweden and Denmark emphasize the principles of "egalitarianism," "de-commodification" and "de-familialization"

(Esping-Andersen, 1999). The egalitarian element is expressed in that most benefits are universal in these countries. De-commodification means that the social democratic welfare state is particularly committed to comprehensive risk coverage and generous benefit levels which weaken the cash nexus. Finally, and most importantly for this study, de-familialization refers to the degree to which households' welfare and caring responsibilities are relaxed via welfare state provision. Thus, a de-familializing regime is one which seeks to unburden the household and diminish individuals' welfare dependence on kinship. Thus, the social democratic welfare state radically increases women's choices in favor of (full-time and part-time) employment and decreases the economic dependence on a husband. The result is an early and fast diffusion of the dual-earner model and also a relatively high fertility rate. The increase in women's employment goes hand-in-hand with an increase in public-sector jobs and growing occupational sex segregation (Esping-Andersen, 1993). Since the public-sector workforce and active labor market policies are very costly, personal tax rates are steeply progressive and relatively high. Accordingly, wives in Sweden and Denmark are integrated into the labor market by a tax system that penalizes a male breadwinner wage and offers public-sector service support to the households. Since wives' employment is ubiquitous, their income has become an important component of the family's social status, and husbands should show strong interests in their wives' labor force participation.

The political and ideological contexts in the (former) state socialist countries such as Hungary, Poland, and China, differ profoundly from Western capitalist economies. A far-reaching redistribution of resources, egalitarian policies with regard to class and gender, and the ideology of equality of conditions were the main principles explicitly pursued by state socialist countries. In most of the former socialist countries of Central and Eastern Europe, official unemployment was non-existent or negligible, and as a rule the demand for labor exceeded the labor supply (Ferge, 1992; Jackson et al., 1995). Work arrangements in these countries could tentatively be described as standard forms of employment, with life-long, secure, permanent, full-time jobs for both men and women. Under state socialism, female labor force participation was extremely high, with women accounting on average for 45–51% of the total labor force in 1989–1990 (Einhorn, 1993). Women as a rule worked full-time; part-time work was not considered a typically female phenomenon (Drobnič, 1997). These countries set up a comprehensive and relatively generous system of family benefits, including lengthy periods of paid maternity and childcare leave. The common employment pattern was based on a family model with two earners working full-time, and husband's resources should therefore have a positive effect on wife's employment.

Finally, China implemented the most determined social engineering policy aimed at eradicating the sexual division of labor in society. The principles of equality between the sexes, monogamy, freedom of choice of a marital partner and the right to sue for divorce were laid down already in the Marriage Law of 1950. This was a radical break from Confucian patriarchal values which supported a conception of the difference between the sexes and sharply segregated roles for men and women (Stockman et al., 1995). In contemporary urban China, there is a prevalence of dual full-time working among spouses and parents of young children. This pattern is associated with a widespread joint conjugal sphere with spouses sharing the domestic tasks of housework and caring for children and with greater equality in domestic decision-making (Stockman et al., 1995, p. 135). China is thus unique on a number of fronts, perhaps the most important being the impact of the state on the role of the family through specific social policies (e.g. the one-child policy) as well as through redistributive economic institutions. It is therefore of great interest how in this context the allocation decisions are being made and to investigate what kind of adaptive family strategies are being developed by Chinese couples.

EMPIRICAL CROSS-NATIONAL COMPARISONS

The focus of our country-specific analyses was to study the interdependent employment careers of couples with longitudinal data, and provide information for comparing these patterns across different contemporary societies. We use the more general term "couples" instead of "spouses" because in the specific case of Sweden the process of family formation and the structure of households have changed to such an extent that the distinction between marital and consensual unions has almost disappeared. The focus of the study, however, was on husbands' and wives' coupled transitions between full-time work, part-time work and unpaid housework over the life course, beginning with the time of entry into the marital union. The distinction between full-time and part-time jobs makes it possible to differentiate between primary and secondary earners. The life-course approach explicitly recognizes the dynamic nature of family roles and circumstances as husbands and wives move through their life paths, the interdependence of lives and life choices among family members, the situational imperatives confronting families in different countries, and the cumulation of advantages and disadvantages experienced by the individual members of the family. In particular, we try to better understand how employment strategies of husbands and wives from different social classes evolve over the family cycle, along with shifts in household composition, family needs, family resources, as well as country-specific constraints and opportunities.

Specifically, we seek answers to the following questions: (1) To what degree do spouses marry homogamously and how does marriage homogamy as well as upward and downward marriage, respectively, affect the employment relationships of husbands and wives over the later family life course in different countries? This aspect should provide a direct test of the economic theory of the family and its principle of comparative advantage as a driving force of the sex-specific division of labor in couples. (2) How important are women's work-related and family-related characteristics for their integration in the labor market and what are the changes across marriage cohorts and across various countries? As predicted by the human capital theory, individual characteristics, such as education, skills, and experience, should translate directly into socioeconomic achievement, as measured by the level of integration in the labor market. (3) Do class-specific differences in the division of labor between husbands and wives over the family life cycle become more or less important across marriage cohorts in different countries, and if so, how can we interpret these variations? Here, we expect the welfare state regimes to play a major role in shaping structurally given opportunities and constraints for individual action. Moreover, we seek to explore the effects of interdependencies in couples, and the ways through which social change is mediated via linked lives.

Data requirements for an analysis of life-course career processes of couples are substantial. We need employment and family histories not only for individuals but for couples. Researchers who conducted the country-specific studies (with the exception of the United States, where data from respondents in four cities in upstate New York were used, and China, where data are based on 20 cities) employed relatively recent nationally representative data, covering couples' employment patterns over broad historical periods. Since each of the twelve countries represents various unique features which are important for the substantive conclusions, a complete standardization of the statistical analysis was not a requirement. Rather, we attempted to maintain, as far as possible, a sufficient standardization to enable a systematic comparison of the results. Thus, most of the country-specific analyses followed a common set of guidelines and, at the same time, explicated the important aspects specific to each country. The country-specific analyses employed panel as well as life history data and used event history and sequence analysis in order to study the development of husbands' and wives' employment patterns over the life course. The longitudinal event history analysis of couples' interdependencies is a methodologically complex endeavour. Most of the country-specific studies applied a "causal approach" to the analysis of interdependent systems that was suggested by Blossfeld and Rohwer (2002).

RESULTS

In Table 1 we summarize the main results for all twelve countries, and present them separately for different welfare state regimes. The first column shows the level of marriage homogamy. Due to differences in data sources, the indicators used to measure the socio-economic position of men and women around the time of formation of marital union differ somewhat among the countries; however, they all carry long-term implications for job placement and occupational and earnings attainment: educational level, occupational score, socio-economic status, income, or type of work organization in which spouses are employed. Based on these indicators, marriage homogamy was found to be high in all countries without exception. In several countries where the data allow the study of trends in the level of marriage homogamy, such as Germany, the Netherlands, and urban China, it was found that the proportion of homogamous couples is increasing. This development

Table 1. Summary of Main Results.

Country	Marriage Homogamy	Effects of Wife's Resources on her Labor Force Participation	Effects of Husband's Resources on Wife's Labor Force Participation	Consequences for Pre-Tax, Pre-Transfer Income Inequality Between Couple Households
Conservative welfare state				
Germany	high	positive	negative	reduced
The Netherlands	high	positive	negative	reduced
Belgium (Flanders)	high	positive	negative	reduced
Mediterranean welfare state				
Italy	high	positive	negative	reduced
Spain	high	positive	negative	reduced
Liberal welfare state				
Great Britain	high	positive	no effect	no effects
U.S.A.	high	not studied	not studied	not studied
Social democratic welfare state				
Denmark	high	positive	positive	increased
Sweden	high	positive	positive	increased
(Former) state socialist countries				
Hungary	high	positive	positive	increased
Poland	high	positive	negative	reduced
Urban China	high	positive	positive	increased

Note: Results for China refer to the "preferred" job shift patterns in organizational hierarchy.

is not surprising in the light of the rising educational attainment among women which augments structural opportunities for homogamy. However, it also has to be kept in mind that educational stratification is a persistent phenomenon in modern societies and a mere increase in women's educational level would not automatically lead to higher marriage homogamy if the selection of a marriage partner were random.

The implication of high marriage homogamy is that more couples are emerging where there is an approximate equality of earnings. Also, the situation where women have higher earnings potentials than their partners is becoming more common. This development questions the view that the male partner should automatically be viewed as the breadwinner and should influence the decision-making process that leads to an allocation of time and effort to paid and unpaid work between the partners. In other words, an increasing symmetry in occupational chances and earnings potentials should also lead to a more symmetric allocation of time by husbands and wives, at least within the neoclassical household production framework, as exemplified by Gary Becker's work (1965, 1981). However, when examining the allocation of time to market work and household production within couples, the principle of competitive advantage has not been supported in any of the countries studied. Specialization in unpaid work – scheduling work and family roles sequentially over the life course – is so uncommon among men that no parallel analyses of transitions between paid and unpaid work for men and women is feasible. In spite of dramatic improvements in women's employment resources in all countries, there is no indication that there has been a change in employment and family roles of men.

There has been, however, a direct impact of women's occupational resources on their participation in the labor market (the second column of Table 1). The estimates presented are summarized net effects of occupational resources, such as education, occupational score, income, or type of work organization in the case of China. That is, these are estimated effects when other factors, such as social origin, number and ages of children, work experience, husband's/partner's characteristics, and marriage cohorts are controlled. The prevailing pattern is that women with higher occupational resources have a higher participation rate in the labor market. Their risk of employment exit tends to be considerably lower and the re-entry rate higher. Or, in the case of Flanders and Sweden, women with higher occupational resources tend to move from full-time into part-time jobs instead of leaving the labor market. These universal findings underline the importance of educational expansion for women's socioeconomic positions and indicate a support for human capital arguments that explain the increase in female labor market supply in terms of the increase in women's market wage opportunities or the opportunity cost of women's time in non-market production. However, these arguments do not explain the substantial differences in the level of married women's employment participation and differences in their career patterns over the life course in various countries.

Only when we examine the impact of partners' resources and class position on women's work careers can significant diversity among countries can be detected (Table 1, third column). In the Netherlands, Germany and Belgium – grouped under the conservative welfare state regime – the tendency is that men with higher occupational resources suppress spouse's participation in paid employment. Due to the diversity of data sources and indicators, it is not possible to make precise quantitative comparisons between the countries; nevertheless, it seems that this effect is strongest in (West) Germany. Here, the simulated examples show that even when the wife has substantial resources of her own at her disposal, high career resources of the husband can override her career potentials and drive her out of the labor market. The consequences include the traditional division of labor in couples, a growing gap between male and female careers over the course of the marriage, and an increasing dependency of married women on their spouses over the life course. Although the effects in the Netherlands and Flanders are not as strong as in Germany, the general overall tendency in these countries is asymmetry in couples: the higher the occupational resources of the male partner, the lower the economic activity of the women.

Similar patterns can be found in the Mediterranean welfare state regimes. In Italy, husband's resources affect the wife's career trajectory in two stages; in the decision to quit the labor market and in suppressing re-entry. In Spain, higher husband's resources increase exit rates while the effects on re-entry are mixed. In general, the higher the occupational position of the husband, the lower the employment participation of the wife.

In Great Britain, a liberal welfare state, there is no effect of husband's occupational resources on their wives' employment transitions. In the U.S. study, this particular question was not examined in a way that would allow a straightforward comparison. However, we know from previous research that the situation in the U.S. has undergone a major change in recent decades. Until the 1980s, a number of studies demonstrated that men with high earnings tended to be married to women with relatively good earnings prospects but these wives participated less in the labor force than women married to less well-paid men (Mincer, 1974; review in Treas, 1987). By the end of the 1980s, however, the correlation between spouses' earnings became positive, implying that highly paid husbands had wives with above-average earnings (Karoly & Burtless, 1995). It might well be that an examination of the long-term employment patterns of American couples, without taking the changes in historical periods into account, would have produced a similar effect for the U.S. as in Great Britain.

In the social democratic welfare state regime, male's occupational resources have the opposite effect on their partner's participation rates than that found in the conservative and Mediterranean welfare state regimes: husbands'/partners' resources increase women's labor market activity. Women married to well educated husbands in Denmark as well as women with high income partners in Sweden are less likely to leave the labor market than women with low-resource partners.

Finally, the (former) socialist countries tend to exhibit a pattern similar to that of the social democratic welfare regimes. In Hungary, wives with husbands that have more resources are less likely to exit employment and thus manifest a higher labor force attachment. In China, the spousal effects are symmetrical. The "preferred" workplace status of one partner tends to facilitate the job shifts of the other, thus increasing the homogamy of the couple's socio-economic status. Poland, however, deviates from this model. Here, women with better educated husbands show a higher tendency of exiting employment and specializing in household production. We interpret this with the specific role of religious values and church influence in the country. More traditional family values and a lower female employment rate than in other Central and East European countries make Poland in this respect more similar to countries belonging to the conservative and Mediterranean welfare state regime.

In sum, cross-national analyses portray the following dynamic picture: the majority of couples are fairly similar in terms of their occupational resources when they enter the union. However, over the course of the marriage the paths of men and women diverge in spite of high marital homogamy. Husbands follow the traditional career patterns and only in exceptional cases interrupt employment for family reasons. Women, however, exhibit a great diversity across countries. On the one hand, there are common patterns across countries: women's higher occupational resources increase their participation in paid employment. On the other hand, there are distinct differences in the impact of husbands' resources on their spouses' employment behaviour and these differences in broad contours correspond to the welfare state regimes. In countries associated with the conservative and Mediterranean welfare state regime, the employment paths over the course of the marriage are clearly gendered, leading to an increasing division of labor within couples, specialization of spheres, economic dependency of wives on their partners, and the prevalence of a breadwinner family model. Women's paid employment is negatively correlated with the occupational position of their husbands. In the social democratic welfare state regime and generally in (former) socialist countries, the trend is reversed: high occupational resources cumulate in couples and get translated into more symmetric employment paths over the life course and the dual-earner family model. Finally, there are countries where no impact of husbands' resources is detected, such as Great Britain, or where other studies indicate that a country rapidly moved from a typical breadwinner to a modern dual-earner family type, such as the USA.

STRATIFICATION RESEARCH AND LINKED LIVES

We have argued in this article that understanding the interdependency of paid employment and family processes in the life course is an important piece in the remaining puzzle of the persistence of gender inequality in the labor market. If we conceptualize the life course through the major positions that individuals occupy during their life-time, as suggested by Sørensen (1986a), we can detect patterns and regularities that are generated by the individual's characteristics, background and abilities, by institutional arrangements and regulations that provide structurally given opportunities and constraints, as well as by interpersonal ties that modify individuals' employment positions and socioeconomic outcomes in a systematic way.

The results of our study also highlight the way in which gender inequality within couples affects the process of socio-economic stratification and material inequality generated in the stratification process. Research on the development of inequalities in the distribution of household income indicate that after the early 1980s, in many countries the tendency towards declining inequalities was halted and even reversed, most dramatically so in the United States and Great Britain (Atkinson et al., 1995; Gottschalk & Smeeding, 1997; Gustafsson & Johansson, 1999; Karoly & Burtless, 1995).

An important reason for the rise in family income inequality is the composition and structure of families and households, such as family size and single-headed vs. married couple households, and the employment patterns of household members, in particular participation in paid employment of husbands and wives. The level of women's participation in the labor force has an impact on the inter-household distribution of economic well-being and class status. Thus, an interesting and still under-researched aspect of the diffusion of dual-earner couples in male breadwinner societies is that it will probably enhance social inequality – at least during a transition period. Since in most modern societies, couples tend to marry homogamously with regard to traits determining earnings capacity, husbands and wives with high wages and influential social networks pool their resources and reinforce social differences between families. This is illustrated in column 4 of Table 1, which presents hypothesized effects of couples' division of labor over the duration of marriage on social stratification in the countries included in the study.

The general trend would seem to be that the decrease in gender inequality in terms of labor force participation is accompanied by an increase in social class inequalities. In countries where husbands' occupational resources facilitate wives' labor force participation, we can expect a cumulation of pre-tax income and other social advantages within households. Again, with few anomalies, the predictions concerning the effects of couples' career trajectories on socio-economic inequalities between the households fit the welfare state regime scheme. The conservative and Mediterranean welfare state regimes potentially reduce social inequalities between the households, the social democratic welfare state regime and (former) socialist countries with less gendered patterns of labor force participation increase inter-household inequalities, and the liberal welfare state regime can be expected to fall somewhere in between.

As long as wives are secondary earners, their earnings have a generally equalizing effect on inter-household income. Wives most likely to be employed in such a situation are those married to low income husbands and their contribution to the total family income reduces inter-household inequalities. But when working women become more ubiquitous, other household members' income becomes less and less of a predictor of who works and who does not. The working and non-working groups encompass more socio-economic diversity and resemble one another more in terms of other income (Treas, 1987). This can double the advantage of couples at the upper end of the income scale. So, when women married to men with high earnings enter the labor force, this can increase the inequality between spouses and households.

The trend towards increasing labor force participation of married women is observed in all contemporary modern societies; however, if and when the threshold that divides the prevailing male breadwinner family model from the prevailing dual-earner family model is reached, depends on institutional constellations, social policies and cultural traditions in individual countries. Thus, the way that couples in diverse circumstances negotiate their actions in order to coordinate the family and work sphere is also structurally given. Often, as Krüger (2001, p. 413) argues, the modern life-course regime counts on couples, not on individuals. Not only are lives regulated and structured by institutions and the state with its policies, but so are the interdependencies between lives, which themselves must be studied in their embeddedness in the structural and institutional context.

NOTES

1. Open and closed positions are end points on a continuum. No labor market, for example, is completely open and no labor market is completely closed (Sørensen, 1983).

2. Results of this cross-national comparative research project are reported in detail in Blossfeld and Drobnič (2001). Individual country-specific analyses were performed by national teams of researchers with an intimate knowledge of the country in question:

Belgium/Flanders (M. Corijn), China (X. Zhou and P. Moen), Denmark (S. Leth-Sørensen and G. Rohwer), Germany (H.-P. Blossfeld, S. Drobnič, and G. Rohwer), Hungary (P. Róbert, E. Bukodi, and R. Luijkx), Italy (F. Bernardi), the Netherlands (J. Hendrickx, W. Bernasco, P. de Graaf), Poland (S. Drobnič and E. Frątczak), Spain (M. González-López), Sweden (U. Henz and M. Sundström), UK (A. McCulloch and S. Dex), USA (S.-K. Han and P. Moen).

REFERENCES

Acker, J. (1973). Women and social stratification: A case of intellectual sexism. *American Journal of Sociology*, *78*, 936–945.

Arrow, K. (1972). Models of job discrimination. In: A. H. Pascal (Ed.), *Racial Discrimination in Economic Life* (pp. 83–102). Lexington, MA: Lexington, Heath.

Atkinson, A. B., Rainwater, L., & Smeeding, T. M. (1995). *Income distribution in OECD countries: Evidence from the Luxembourg Income Study (Social Policy Studies No. 18)*. Paris: Organisation for Economic Co-operation and Development.

Becker, G. S. (1965). A theory of the allocation of time. *Economic Journal*, *75*, 493–519.

Becker, G. S. (1981). *A treatise on the family*. Cambridge, MA: Harvard University Press.

Bettio, F., & Villa, P. (1998). A Mediterranean perspective on the breakdown of the relationship between participation and fertility. *Cambridge Journal of Economics*, *22*, 137–171.

Blau, F. D. (1999). Women's economic well-being, 1970–1995: Indicators and trends. *Focus*, *20*, 4–10.

Blau, P. M., & Duncan, O. D. (1967). *The American occupational structure*. New York: Wiley.

Blossfeld, H.-P. (1987). Labor market entry and the sexual segregation of careers in the Federal Republic of Germany. *American Journal of Sociology*, *93*, 89–118.

Blossfeld, H.-P., & Drobnič, S. (Eds) (2001). *Careers of couples in contemporary societies. From male breadwinner to dual-earner families*. Oxford: Oxford University Press.

Blossfeld, H.-P., & Hakim, C. (Eds) (1997). *Between equalization and marginalization. Women working part-time in Europe and the United States of America*. Oxford: Oxford University Press.

Blossfeld, H.-P., & Rohwer, G. (2002). *Techniques of event history modeling. New approaches to causal analysis*. Mahwah, NJ: Erlbaum.

Blossfeld, H.-P., & Timm, A. (2003). *Who marries whom? Educational systems as marriage markets in modern societies*. Dordrecht: Kluwer.

Cain, G. G. (1976). The challenge of segmented labor market theories to orthodox theory: A survey. *Economic Literature*, *14*, 1215–1257.

Coser, L. (1973). *Greedy institutions: Patterns of undivided commitments*. New York: Free Press.

Curtis, R. F. (1986). Household and family in theory of inequality. *American Sociological Review*, *51*, 168–183.

Davis, K. (1949). *Human society*. New York: Macmillan.

Dex, S. (1990). Goldthorpe on class and gender: The case against. In: J. Clark, C. Modgil & S. Modgil (Eds), *John H. Goldthorpe: Consensus and Controversy* (pp. 135–152). London: Falmer Press.

DiPrete, Th. A. (2002). Life course risks, mobility regimes, and mobility consequences: A comparison of Sweden, Germany, and the United States. *American Journal of Sociology*, *108*, 267–309.

Drobnič, S. (1997). Part-time work in Central and East European countries. In: H.-P. Blossfeld & C. Hakim (Eds), *Between Equalization and Marginalization. Women Working Part-time in Europe and the United States of America* (pp. 71–89). Oxford: Oxford University Press.

Einhorn, B. (1993). *Cinderella goes to market. Citizenship, gender and women's movements in East Central Europe*. London and New York: Verso.

Elder, G. H., & Caspi, A. (1990). Studying lives in a changing society: Sociological and personological explorations. In: A. I. Rabin et al. (Eds), *Studying Persons and Lives* (pp. 201–247). New York: Springer Publishing Company.

Erikson, R. (1984). Social class of men, women, and families. *Sociology*, *18*, 500–514.

Erikson, R., & Goldthorpe, J. H. (1992). *The constant flux: A study of class mobility in industrial societies*. Oxford: Clarendon Press.

Erikson, R., & Jonsson, J. O. (Eds) (1996). *Can education be equalized?* Boulder, CO: Westview Press.

Esping-Andersen, G. (1990). *The three worlds of welfare capitalism*. Cambridge: Polity Press.

Esping-Andersen, G. (Ed.) (1993). *Changing classes: Stratification and mobility in postindustrial societies*. London: Sage.

Esping-Andersen, G. (1999). *Social foundations of postindustrial economies*. Oxford: Oxford University Press.

Ferge, Z. (1992). Unemployment in Hungary: The need for a new ideology. In: B. Deacon (Ed.), *Social Policy, Social Justice and Citizenship in Eastern Europe* (pp. 158–175). Aldershot: Avebury.

Goldthorpe, J. H. (1980). *Social mobility and class structure in modern Britain*. Oxford: Clarendon Press.

Goldthorpe, J. H. (1983). Women and class analysis: In defence of the conventional view. *Sociology*, *17*, 465–488.

Goldthorpe, J. H. (1984). Women and class analysis: A reply to the replies. *Sociology*, *18*, 491–499.

González López, M. J. (1998). Do modern welfare states foster democratic family arrangements? Comparative studies of Britain and Spain. *South European Society & Politics*, *3*(2), 98–123.

Gornick, J. C., Meyers, M. K., & Ross, K. E. (1997). Supporting the employment of mothers: Policy variation across fourteen welfare states. *Journal of European Social Policy*, *7*, 45–70.

Gottschalk, P., & Smeeding, T. M. (1997). Cross-national comparisons of earnings and income inequality. *Journal of Economic Literature*, *35*, 633–687.

Gustafsson, B., & Johansson, M. (1999). In search of smoking guns: What makes income inequality vary over time in different countries? *American Sociological Review*, *64*, 585–605.

Hakim, C. (1998). *Social change and innovation in the labor market*. Oxford: Oxford University Press.

Handl, J., Mayer, K. U., & Müller, W. (1977). *Klassenlagen und sozialstruktur*. Frankfurt a. M. and New York: Campus.

Hartmann, H. (1976). Capitalism, patriarchy, and job segregation by sex. *Signs*, *1*, 137–169.

Huber, J. (1988). A theory of family, economy, and gender. *Journal of Family Issues*, *9*, 9–26.

Huber, J., & Spitze, G. (1983). *Sex stratification*. New York: Academic Press.

Hyman, H. (1953). The value systems of different classes. In: R. Bendix & S. M. Lipset (Eds), *Class, Status and Power* (2nd ed. 1960). London: Routledge and Kegan Paul.

Jackson, M., Koltay, J., & Biesbrouck, W. (Eds) (1995), *Unemployment and evolving labor markets in Central and Eastern Europe*. Aldershot: Avebury.

Karoly, L. A., & Burtless, G. (1995). Demographic change, rising earnings inequality, and the distribution of personal well-being, 1959–1989. *Demography*, *32*(3), 379–405.

Korpi, W. (2000). Faces of inequality: Gender, class and patterns of inequalities in different types of welfare states. *Social Politics*, *4*, 127–191.

Krüger, H. (2001). Social change in two generations: Employment patterns and their costs for family life. In: V. W. Marshall, W. R. Heinz, H. Krüger & A. Verma (Eds), *Restructuring Work and the Life Course* (pp. 401–423). Toronto: University of Toronto Press.

Leibfried, S. (1992). Towards a European welfare state: On integrating poverty regimes in the European community. In: Z. Ferge & J. E. Kolberg (Eds), *Social Policy in a Changing Europe* (pp. 245–280). Frankfurt: Campus.

Lewis, J. (1992). Gender and the development of welfare regimes. *Journal of European Social Policy, 2*, 159–173.

Lewis, J., & Ostner, I. (1995). Gender and the evolution of European social policy. In: S. Leibfried & P. Pierson (Eds), *European Social Policy: Between Fragmentation and Integration*. Washington, DC: Brookings Institution.

Madden, J. F. (1973). *The economics of sex discrimination*. Lexington, MA: Lexington Books.

Madden, J. F. (1975). Discrimination – A manifestation of male market power? In: C. B. Lloyd (Ed.), *Sex, Discrimination and the Division of Labor* (pp. 146–174). New York: Colombia University Press.

Mincer, J., & Ofek, H. (1982). Interrupted work careers: Depreciation and restoration of human capital. *Journal of Human Resources, 17*, 3–24.

Mincer, J., & Polachek, S. (1974). Family investments in human capital: Earnings of women. *Journal of Political Economy, 82*, S76–S108.

Moen, P., & Forest, K. B. (1999). Strengthening families. Policy issues for the twenty-first century. In: M. Sussman, S. K. Steinmetz & G. W. Peterson (Eds), *Handbook of Marriage and the Family* (pp. 633–663). New York: Plenum Press.

Orloff, A. S. (1993). Gender and the social rights of citizenship: The comparative analysis of gender relations and welfare states. *American Sociological Review, 58*, 303–328.

Parsons, T. (1942). Age and sex in the social structure of the United States. *American Sociological Review, 7*, 604–616.

Parsons, T., & Bales, R. (1966). *Family, socialization, and interaction process*. New York: Free Press.

Pfau-Effinger, B. (1999). The modernization of family and motherhood in Western Europe. In: R. Crompton (Ed.), *Restructuring Gender Relations and Employment. The Decline of the Male Breadwinner* (pp. 60–79). Oxford: Oxford University Press.

Phelps, E. (1972). The statistical theory of racism and sexism. *American Economic Review, 64*, 59–63.

Plutzer, E., & Zipp, J. F. (2001). Class, gender, and the family unit: A dynamic model of stratification and class politics. *Social Science Research, 30*, 426–448.

Polachek, S. (1981). Occupational self-selection: A human capital approach to sex differences in occupational structure. *Review of Economics and Statistics, 58*, 60–69.

Reskin, B. F., & Roos, P. A. (1990). *Job queues, gender queues: Explaining women's inroads into male occupations*. Philadelphia: Temple University Press.

Rubery, J., & Fagan, C. (1993). Occupational segregation of women and men in the European Community, Social Europe, Supplement 3/93, Luxembourg: OOPEC.

Rosenfeld, R. A., & Birkelund, G. E. (1995). Women's part-time work: A cross-national comparison. *European Sociological Review, 11*, 111–134.

Sainsbury, D. (1996). *Gender, equality, and welfare states*. Cambridge: Cambridge University Press.

Saltzman Chafetz, J. (1995). Chicken or egg? A theory of the relationship between feminist movements and family change. In: K. Oppenheim Mason & A.-M. Jensen (Eds), *Gender and Family Change in Industrialized Countries* (pp. 63–81). Oxford: Clarendon Press.

Saraceno, C. (1996). Family change, family policies and the restructuration of welfare. Paper presented at the OECD Conference 'Beyond 2000: The New Social Policy Agenda', Paris: OECD.

Schultz, T. W. (Ed.) (1974). Marriage, family human capital, and fertility. *Supplement to the Journal of Political Economy*, 82.

Sewell, W. H., & Hauser, R. M. (1975). *Education, occupation and earnings*. New York: Academic Press.

Shavit, Y., & Blossfeld, H.-P. (1993). *Persistent inequality*. Boulder, CO: Westview Press.

Sørensen, A. B. (1983). Processes of allocation to open and closed positions in social structure. *Zeitschrift für Soziologie*, *12*, 203–224.

Sørensen, A. B. (1986a). Social structure and mechanisms of life-course processes. In: A. B. Sørensen, F. E. Weinert & L. R. Sherrod (Eds), *Human Development and the Life Course: Multidisciplinary Perspectives* (pp. 177–197). Hillsdale, NJ and London: Lawrence Erlbaum.

Sørensen, A. B. (1986b). Theory and methodology in social stratification. In: U. Himmelstrand (Ed.), *The Sociology of Structure and Action* (pp. 69–95). London: Sage.

Sørensen, A. (1994). Women, family and class. *Annual Review of Sociology*, *20*, 27–47.

Sørensen, A., & McLanahan, S. (1987). Married women's economic dependency, 1940–1980. *American Journal of Sociology*, *93*, 659–687.

Stockman N., Boney, N., & Xuewen, S. (1995). *Women's work in East and West: The dual burden of employment and family life*. London: UCL.

Treas, J. (1987). The effect of women's labor force participation on the distribution of income in the United States. *Annual Review of Sociology*, *13*, 259–288.

Van der Lippe, T., & Van Dijk, L. (2002). Comparative research on women's employment. *Annual Review of Sociology*, *28*, 221–241.

STRUCTURAL INEQUALITY AND RENTS

SOURCES OF STRUCTURAL INEQUALITY IN MANAGERIAL LABOR MARKETS

Rakesh Khurana and Mikołaj Jan Piskorski

ABSTRACT

This article proposes two mechanisms that allow actors to obtain unearned advantages in labor markets. The first mechanism is consistent with collusive closure arguments. However, it questions the assumption that those who seek to benefit from collusive closure will always initiate it. Instead, it suggests that under certain cultural conditions, closure may arise through a series of self-reproducing social constructions that restrict access to a position to those who conform to certain socially defined criteria. The second mechanism is consistent with Sørensen's discussion of the role of composite rents in generating unearned advantages. Whereas Sørensen focused on composite rents between actors and productive assets, the mechanism presented here suggests that actors can obtain unearned advantages even if workers are not specific to productive assets, as long as there are composite rents between these productive assets. Data in support of the models are provided from the executive labor market.

INTRODUCTION

If there is one characteristic that forcefully distinguishes sociology from other social sciences, it is the differentiation between an actor and an actor's position

Inequality: Structures, Dynamics and Mechanisms: Essays in Honor of Aage B. Sørensen
Research in Social Stratification and Mobility, Volume 21, 167–185

ISSN: 0276-5624/doi:10.1016/S0276-5624(04)21009-5

in the social structure (Simmel, 1950). Central to this distinction is the claim that rewards are attached to positions rather than to actors' performances. Thus, inequality between actors is generated by occupation of different positions and is largely independent of their efforts or resources (Sørensen, 1990, 1994). This line of reasoning forms the cornerstone of structural explanations of earnings inequality and stands in a marked contrast to individualistic theories, which postulate that actors are rewarded mainly on the basis of their individual resources (Coleman, 1990; Parsons, 1953).

The usefulness of structural explanations of inequality critically depends on the process of allocation of actors to positions (Sørensen, 1990). If actors are accorded a privileged position as soon as they possess appropriate resources, or lose it as soon as they lose their resources, positions reflect nothing more than the resources of the incumbent. In these circumstances, we can fully account for observed inequality by examining actors' resources. The fact that rewards are attached to positions gives us little theoretical insight into the sources of inequality (Granovetter, 1994). In contrast, when actors retain their privileged positions despite a loss of valued resources, or are unable to attain them despite possession of appropriate resources, structural advantages or disadvantages can occur. As incumbents obtain payments in excess of what is required to attract another occupant to that position, Sørensen (1996) suggested that these positional advantages represent rents. These rents are received at the expense of those actors who are unable to attain the position despite possession of appropriate resources.

Given the critical role of allocation processes to the emergence of structural advantages and disadvantages, social scientists have long sought to identify conditions under which such processes emerge in a number of social contexts (Parkin, 1979). Such analyses date back to Smith's (1776) discussion of collusive social relations in markets whereby actors seek to create artificial restrictions on the supply of available actors or supply of available positions. These collusive relations are often institutionalized through political institutions, professional societies or even caste systems (Weber, 1947). Once established, these institutions dictate that potential occupants of privileged positions must possess social or physical attributes of the dominant group or face exclusion. This exclusionary strategy allows the dominant group to secure for itself certain resources and advantages at the expense of other groups. Empirical research in settings as broad as inequality in income in the economy as a whole (Weeden, 2002) or as specific as venture capital (Piskorski & Anand, 2003) lends significant empirical support to the importance of collusive closure in generating structural inequality.

Whereas the collusive closure explanation presumes that structural advantages and disadvantages will appear only once power subverts the efficiency logic,

Sørensen argued that under certain conditions structural advantages and disadvantages could emerge even if actors seek to maximize efficiency gains. Specifically, he focused on the role of composite rents between actors and positions and the emergence of internal labor markets. Composite rents exist when two separate resources are so specific to each other that the benefit from their joint use exceeds the combined benefits from the separate use of each resource (Marshall, 1948). For example, composite rents between actors and assets arise when workers obtain specific on-the-job training and therefore are more productive in one firm than in another. Although both the employer and the employee would benefit from such investments, they first need to overcome significant incentive problems (Kahn & Huberman, 1988). A worker acquires skills only if there is a promise of a higher wage for doing so. However, the employer has an incentive to claim that the worker has not acquired these skills even when he in fact has, in order to save on wage costs. As the firm has an incentive to renege, the worker has no incentive to acquire the specific skills. To solve this problem, a firm can commit to a labor contract which attaches wages to different tasks, rather than to individual worker performances (Prendergast, 1993). In this case, a worker can be rewarded for skill acquisition by promotion to another job. The promise of reward through promotion, rather than through wage, gives rise to internal labor markets.

Although the creation of internal labor markets appears to be an efficient solution to contracting problems in the presence of composite rents, Sørensen (1994) argued that it had significant implications for earnings inequality between actors. Once internal labor markets are established, closed employment relationships emerge with vacancy chains replacing market allocation process (Sørensen, 1996). Since advancement in vacancy chains is driven by the availability of positions and actors' positions in the system (Sørensen, 1974; White, 1970), and not necessarily by an actor's performance in the position, actors may be allowed to occupy a position even though their performance or qualities do not justify it. Similarly, other actors may be prevented from occupying a privileged position, even though they possess appropriate skills or resources, because that position is not open to competition. Consequently, certain positions in a vacancy chain may give their incumbents a structural advantage or disadvantage.

In this article, we propose two additional mechanisms of allocation of actors to positions that generate positional inequality. The first one, proposed by Khurana (1998), is aligned with the view that traces the sources of positional inequality to collusive closure. However, in contrast to earlier arguments, Khurana questions the assumption that collusive closure will always be initiated by those who seek to benefit from it. Instead, he argues that under certain cultural conditions, closure may arise through a series of self-reproducing social constructions that restrict access to a position to those who conform to certain socially defined criteria. The second model, proposed by Piskorski (2001), is consistent with Sørensen's model in that it seeks to explicate causes of structural advantages and disadvantages that are consistent with economic notions of efficiency. Whereas Sørensen traced structural inequality to composite rents generated by the relationship between workers and productive assets, Piskorski endeavors to show that structural inequality can emerge even if workers are not specific to assets. As long as occupation of a position requires an actor to work with two or more assets that are specific to each other, the process of allocation to such positions will generate structural advantages and disadvantages.

We find significant empirical support for both of our models in the context of labor markets for top executives. As we discuss in the conclusion, our evidence has broader implications for the understanding of inequality in external labor markets. Most accounts of external labor markets suggest that there should be no unearned advantages or disadvantages in these markets. This is because if anyone offered a wage below marginal productivity for occupation of a position, then it would always be profitable for another actor to offer a higher wage. Similarly, if anyone demanded a wage above his or her marginal productivity for occupation of a position, then it would always be profitable for another actor to demand a lower wage. Competition between the two classes of actors ensures that wage is equal to marginal productivity and there are no unearned advantages or disadvantages. However, our models show that under a set of specific conditions structural advantages and disadvantages can be present even in external labor markets. The presence of unearned advantages in such markets flies in the face of today's uncritical faith in markets as a mechanism for achieving such socially desirable goals as equal opportunity based on open competition, or advancement on the basis of merit.

LEGITIMACY CONSIDERATIONS AND CEO SUCCESSION

Collusive closure has long been held to be the primary mechanism through which certain actors secure advantages at the expense of others. Central to this explanation is the assumption that those who will benefit from the closure will seek to engage in collusive behavior. However, Khurana's research highlights that neither such pernicious motivations nor the implied solidarity among the selecting group is required for market closure. Instead, closure can emerge when those who control access to positions must respond to the interests and scrutiny of a number of constituencies, who seek to make sure that the selection of occupants of positions is legitimate. In these circumstances, a social matching process emerges and applies a "legitimate, taken-for-granted and rational" set of principles in identifying and sorting candidates for the position.

As documented by Khurana's research on the role of directors in the CEO search process, these legitimacy concerns are particularly acute in the external CEO market. There are two interconnected factors that elevate the board members' concern with legitimacy, leading to the social matching mechanism and consequent structural inequality. The primary reason for board members' concern with legitimacy is that the external CEO labor market is not a "market" in the ordinary sense. It is not even like the market for other executive positions. Instead of a perfect market with a large numbers of buyers and sellers engaged in relatively anonymous exchange, there is a small market in which buyers and sellers are few. Instead of principals directly transacting with agents, there is a disconnect between the interest of principals (shareholders) and their agents (directors). Instead of a low-risk transaction in which all the necessary information is freely available and widely circulated, there is a significant lack of information about potential candidates and about the position itself. Thus, the question of who is ultimately chosen depends, in part, on whether a firm's board can gather detailed information about potential external candidates.

The second reason for the board's concern with legitimacy in an external CEO search is the weakening of the boundaries between firms and markets. Choosing a new CEO is no longer considered a divine right of the incumbent or even of the board. In the past, the CEO or the board chose the successor through peer review on the assumption that people who have been in positions of leadership should decide who should run the corporation. Today, by contrast, it is increasingly treated as an event in which external constituencies have a strong interest and where they have a right to influence the outcome. These external constituencies – namely, shareholders, the Wall Street analysts and business journalists who claim to represent their interests – now constitute a recognized key constituency for most organizations. Investors, and especially institutional investors, increasingly rely on the judgments of these audiences when making investment decisions (Zuckerman, 1999). In these conditions, the best searches serve to legitimate both the search process itself and the final choice of the search committee and board, so that a new CEO can have a smooth transition into the position. Missteps during the search process can leave organizational observers and constituents alike seething about the search and hostile to its outcome. The search ends up an abysmal failure, not because the wrong candidate was selected, but because the mishandling of the process handicaps someone who may have been right for the organization. Both internal and external constituents, because of the manner in which the process was executed, may reject the outcome of a search that may have been appropriate from a strategic perspective.

ACHIEVING LEGITIMACY THROUGH THE SOCIAL MATCHING PROCESS

The context of difficulty in information gathering, as well as concern with the perceptions of external stakeholders, interacts with the structural nature of the external CEO labor market to close this market to all but a small number of candidates. Specifically, the process leads to a social matching approach toward identifying candidates. Social matching is a filtering process that takes place when individual and organizational actors are confronted with selections that are difficult to make because limited information hampers their ability to reliably distinguish one from another. Social matching leads to a closed CEO labor market because directors seize upon one or more externally identifiable characteristics of potential candidates to construct a narrowly defined candidate pool.

The term social *matching* has its roots in a study of the careers of school superintendents (March & March, 1978). Using data on one state's school superintendents, the researchers found that most of the superintendents were nearly indistinguishable across a range of criteria, including behaviors, career paths, credentials, and prior performance evaluations. Drawing on social psychological research on decision-making under uncertainty, the researchers' explanations for this lack of variation was that when matching individuals to jobs, organizational decision-makers relied on socially defined criteria or social matches – such as certification or adherence to an institutionally legitimate career – when matching individuals to jobs. In an external CEO search, agreement on which social criteria are most important is evidenced by an overwhelming consensus in favor of three observable standards: the candidate's current position; the performance of the candidate's current firm; and the status of the candidate's current firm.

Position Matching

Like most paths to power and status in established organizations, the path to the CEO position combines selection and socialization to ensure that a person occupying this position will act in an appropriate manner. Useem's (1984) study of corporate executives highlighted that most corporate chieftains move either horizontally or vertically through a similar career path. They arrive in the executive suite after a series of selection processes lasting years. Socialization, self-selection, and filtering significantly reduce the variability of plausible candidates. Difficulties in assessing performance due to limited information and impression management increase the difficulty of selecting among them. Because differences among plausible candidates are likely to be small, similar candidates may appear to be different, and different candidates may appear to be similar. One empirical consequence is that firms choosing a CEO from outside the firm will more likely select external CEO candidates who have already been in top positions at other firms. In fact, 75% of new CEOs in the Standard and Poor 500 companies from 1990 to 2000 were either CEOs or presidents of the firms from which they originated.

Performance Attribution

Not only are plausible candidates likely to be similar in terms of experience, but they are likely to be similar in terms of their perceived effectiveness as well. The problem of discriminating among such candidates has been referred to as "selecting at the right tail" – that is, the extreme right-hand portion of the bell-shaped normal distribution curve. Most such candidates will be well qualified. It is possible that there will be speculation as to how the fortunes of the firm will vary based upon which candidate is selected. But the differences among candidates are usually so small, and the effects of external factors so large, that it is rarely possible to predict *ex ante* the performance consequences for the firm of selecting among the top candidates. In fact, dozens of academic studies have found that the relationship between leaders and organizational performance is at best tenuous and at worst non-existent. Despite the lack of conclusive evidence linking leadership to organizational performance, several scholars have noted the strong cultural, social, and psychological forces that lead to the attribution of organizational performance directly to individual leaders. As a result, Khurana (1998) finds, in choosing among external CEO candidates, firms attach great value to observable performance metrics in making their selection decision. Consequently, firms choosing a CEO from outside select external CEOs from firms that have positive performance.

Status Matching

The process that generates the selection in favor of individuals with prior experience as CEOs and associations with high-performing firms raises the question of whether boards are simply acting on the best information they have available. Yet if this were so, the issue of the status of a candidate's current firm would not loom nearly so large as it does in an external CEO search. Prestige is, in fact, particularly important in CEO searches, and search committees see the status of the institution that a candidate comes from as potentially amplifying or reducing the status of their own firms. Similarly, candidates for CEO positions see the status of the potential employer as a source of their own status and hence are unlikely to choose to head organizations of lower status. Consequently, both searching firms and candidates can plausibly consider only a match that maintains, or preferably increases, their reputations, and this mutual interest in reputation enhancement sets constraints that severely limit the positions to which candidates can aspire, and which vacancies appear attractive to potential candidates. Thus there is a process of self-selection that serves to limit the participants in a search. There should be little overlap, for example, between candidates considering jobs at low-reputation firms and those seeking positions at high-reputation firms. As is revealed by using a Bonacich (1987) centrality measure for firm status measured through director interlocks, 80% of outsider CEOs in the S&P 500 were coming from firms of similar or higher status.

IMPLICATIONS FOR STRUCTURAL INEQUALITY

Considered as either a process for filling vacancies or one for advancing careers, the external CEO search appears at first glance to offer almost unlimited opportunities for identifying candidates. However, the social matching process that lies at the heart of an external CEO search is likely to produce candidates who have passed through a series of promotional filters and who have been extensively socialized in institutions similar to the ones at which they are candidates to become outsider CEOs. Because of this, directors of searching firms are likely to find that those individuals who end up in the pool of candidates judged to merit serious consideration are quite similar to one another when it comes to the characteristics believed to be most important for the CEO position. It is true, of course, that each candidate is different from the others in certain respects, and that there will be a wide range of personalities, temperaments, and leadership styles evident among them. But compared to the important ways in which candidates who make it into the pool of finalists are similar, the consequences of these differences may be marginal.

The closure process in the CEO labor market has direct implications for rent-extraction. Because the corporate elite form a distinctive and identifiable network, they control valuable resources that support network activities such as continual recruitment from a restricted set of individuals. Moreover, such restrictions are subsequently supported through an extensive set of beliefs and practices that sustain network control of the resource. These restrictions, in turn, generate rent-extracting opportunities. In the case of the CEO labor market, these rent-extraction opportunities present themselves in the CEO compensation process. Because boards of directors are notoriously social organizations, where the goal is not to maximize profits but to avoid personal embarrassment while maintaining social cohesion within the board and the larger corporate community, directors do not drive a hard bargain when negotiating CEO pay. For directors, it is simply bad form to nitpick over a couple of million dollars with another member of the group, particularly one who helps set director fees or serves on the compensation committee of other corporations. Moreover, boards often legitimate the compensation of their CEOs by hiring a compliant executive compensation consultant and then arguing that the pay is set in an arm's-length market transaction. One implication, then, is that executive compensation would have a weak relation to firm performance and result in a pay-setting process that is economically distortive. Recent corporate scandals around CEO pay levels and corporate disclosure practices suggest this may be true.

THREATS FROM THE MARKET FOR CORPORATE CONTROL

The foregoing discussion of the external search for executives clearly indicates that executive succession is heavily constrained by legitimacy concerns, which restricts access to only a few legitimate candidates. Although these access restrictions are enforced by boards of directors, and not executives themselves, they allow executives to reap benefits that would otherwise be dissipated by more equal competition for executive positions. However, the initiation of the executive succession process is not restricted only to the boards of directors. Executives and boards of directors also have to reckon with a powerful market for corporate control that can quickly eradicate any collusive efforts at closure.

In the market for corporate control, managers compete for the right to control organizations on behalf of shareholders. These managers look for profitable opportunities to assume the management of organizations. When the stock price of a company is high, it is unlikely that contesting managers can profit from replacing the incumbent managers. In contrast, such an opportunity is present in poorly managed firms, whose market value is low. Once the opportunity is identified, the contesting managers launch a takeover bid by offering to buy, at a premium, the stock held by the firm's shareholders. Although the firm's board members and incumbent managers can resist the takeover, shareholders are the sole decision makers (Walking & Long, 1984). The incumbents can only affect the outcome of a takeover bid by proposing a counter offer that would result in greater financial benefits for shareholders. Such an offer could in turn elicit a counter-offer from the hostile bidder. The whole process leads to a price contest between incumbents and contestants for the right to control the firm. As shareholders decide whether to change the control of the firm largely on the basis of the outcome of this contest, the whole process resembles an efficient market for corporate control in which control over assets is allocated to those who value them most (Manne, 1965). Thus, the market for corporate control can be thought of as a mechanism for competitive allocation of managers to organizations.

The operation of the market for corporate control in the 1980s formed a particular threat to the entrenched process of executive selection. Prior to the 1980s, managerial social networks, reputations, and class interests played an important role in the incidence of takeovers (Zeitlin, 1974), leading to unequal exposure of firms to the market for corporate control (Marris, 1964). Firms managed by the members of the inner circle of the corporate elite were unlikely to receive a takeover bid, while other firms did not enjoy similar protection (Palmer et al., 1995). However, changes in corporate governance in the 1980s erased these differences. Developments in the financial industry allowed outsiders to secure short-term debt financing through junk bonds or other financial vehicles to complete the takeover (Baker & Smith, 1998). These changes removed financial constraints on these outsiders and allowed entrepreneurial firms and individuals to bid for the corporate control of firms (Jensen, 1993). The Supreme Court also lessened state laws limiting takeovers (Edgar vs. MITE, 1982), allowing outsiders to undertake even the largest deals. The increase in the number of potential participants in the market for corporate control – groups that had little reverence for the existing corporate pecking order (Hirsch, 1986) – eradicated the protective elements of the intercorporate social structure. In fact, empirical research on the topic suggests that in the 1980s neither size (Morck et al., 1988) nor connections to other large corporations or to banks (Davis & Stout, 1992) were likely to protect a firm from a hostile takeover bid.

The foregoing discussion suggests that the market for corporate control in the 1980s presents itself as a competitive arena where actors are matched to positions on the basis of performance, and with little regard to the social processes surrounding executive succession. However, against this general trend, Piskorski (2000) observed that numerous large American corporations avoided a hostile takeover bid, despite their poor performance. In fact, in apparent defiance of the prevailing climate that forced the great majority of organizations to increase shareholder value or face a hostile takeover, executives of certain organizations engaged in a set of value destroying strategies as if they considered themselves immune to a takeover. Such actions supported the managerial agendas and represented a rent transfer from shareholders to the managers.

COMPOSITE RENTS AND ALLOCATION OF ACTORS TO POSITIONS

In order to explain the apparent ability of certain actors to derive rents from their positions in this very competitive environment, Piskorski (2001) followed

Sørensen's footsteps and re-examined the effect of composite rents on the process of competitive allocation of actors to positions. Sørensen focused on composite rents derived from the relationship between actors and assets, such as those that emerge when workers have obtained specific on-the-job training. In contrast, Piskorski examined the role of composite rents between two non-human productive assets. These rents emerge when two firms tailor their investments to the exchange of goods and services they plan to undertake with each other. The main difference between the two types of composite rents lies in the solution to the problem of bargaining over the composite rent. In the case of composite rents between actors and assets, the internal labor market provides the solution. When composite rents between assets are present, a substantial amount of economic literature suggests that assets should be integrated and that one actor should be given control rights over both. Integration avoids costly bargaining between autonomous actors, as the single actor resolves the bargaining problems by fiat (Williamson, 1981). Piskorski (2001) has developed the implications of this basic economic observation for the process of allocation of actors to positions in labor markets. He argued that from a labor-market perspective, asset integration is akin to creating a position in a labor market in which the occupant of the position has to be capable of simultaneously managing two assets. As discussed in the model below, occupants of such positions are unlikely to be replaced following a decline in performance, leading to the development of positional advantages.

The model examines allocation of actors to positions in which contestants for a position replace the incumbent when they can offer higher performance at the same cost. Essential to the model are two assumptions. First, the model assumes that the probability of finding a generalist simultaneously capable of working with two assets is smaller than the probability of finding a pair of specialists, each of whom is capable of providing the same performance with one of the assets. Second, the incumbent of a position can be replaced either by a generalist, who occupies the entire position. Alternatively, the incumbent is replaced by a pair of specialists, in which case, the position is divided into separate components, each with control over a particular asset. This process of competitive replacement of incumbents of a position by generalists and specialists is consistent with widespread incidence of "bust-up" takeovers, events in which multi-business-unit firms were split into separate business units following a takeover (Davis et al., 1994; Davis & Stout, 1992). Empirical data for the 1980s suggest that following a takeover, approximately 80% of firms were quickly restructured, with numerous divisions sold off (Jensen, 1989). In practice, bust-up takeovers could take two forms. Consider, for example, a firm with two business units, one in forestry and another in paper production. In one form of the bust-up takeover, an arbitrageur, such as Carl Icahn, could launch a bid for a company after having secured buyers for its constituent parts, and without any intention of managing the firm after takeover (Lipton & Steinberger, 1988). Once the bid was successful, the company was split apart and sold to specialists, with one acquiring the forestry business unit and the other the paper-production operation. In an alternative form of such a takeover, one of the two specialists could act as the arbitrageur. In this case, the specialist would launch a takeover bid for the firm as a whole. After the takeover was complete, the successful bidder would sell the unwanted business to the other specialist. Despite the differences in the actual mechanics of the takeover, in both cases a set of specialists would replace the incumbents.

The model is best explained by a stylized example of allocation to high-composite-rent positions and low-composite-rent positions, as illustrated in Fig. 1. In the figure, the dots represent different assets, while the dotted lines represent the boundary of a position. The width of the line between the dots represents the existence of composite rent between assets. Thus, there is no composite rent between assets associated with the position on the left-hand side. In contrast, there is substantial composite rent between assets associated with the position on the right-hand side. I assume that the composite rent amounts to 1 unit of performance. This rent would be lost if the position were separated. Each asset within the position has a queue of specialist contestants. Each contestant can provide different level of performance if they could control the asset. In the figure, I illustrate this condition with contestants A' and B', who can each deliver 1 unit of performance if given control over one of the two assets in the position, and contestants A'' and B'', who can each deliver 0.5 units of performance if given control over one of the two assets in the position. The incumbents of both positions are performing at 2.

For occupants of both positions, the process of replacement by a generalist is the same. A generalist contestant will replace the incumbent as long as the generalist contestant can perform better in that position than the incumbent for the same reward. In contrast, the replacement by specialists differs across the two positions. In order to replace the incumbent of the position with no composite rent, the contestants have to be able to perform at least at the incumbent's level. The only combination of contestants capable of reaching this level is A'B'. Each of them can perform up to the level of 1 with their asset, so the sum of their performance is 2. They can separate the position and each of them can manage one of the assets separately. The replacement of the incumbent of the position with substantial composite rent between assets, whose performance is also 2, is more difficult. Contestants have to be able to perform better than the incumbent in order to compensate for the costs imposed by the separation. Thus, the total performance of contesting specialists has to be at least 3. Since there is no combination of specialist contestants capable of delivering this performance, the incumbent is safe from replacement under these circumstances. In this example, the only threat of replacement for this incumbent comes from a generalist contestant. Thus, for

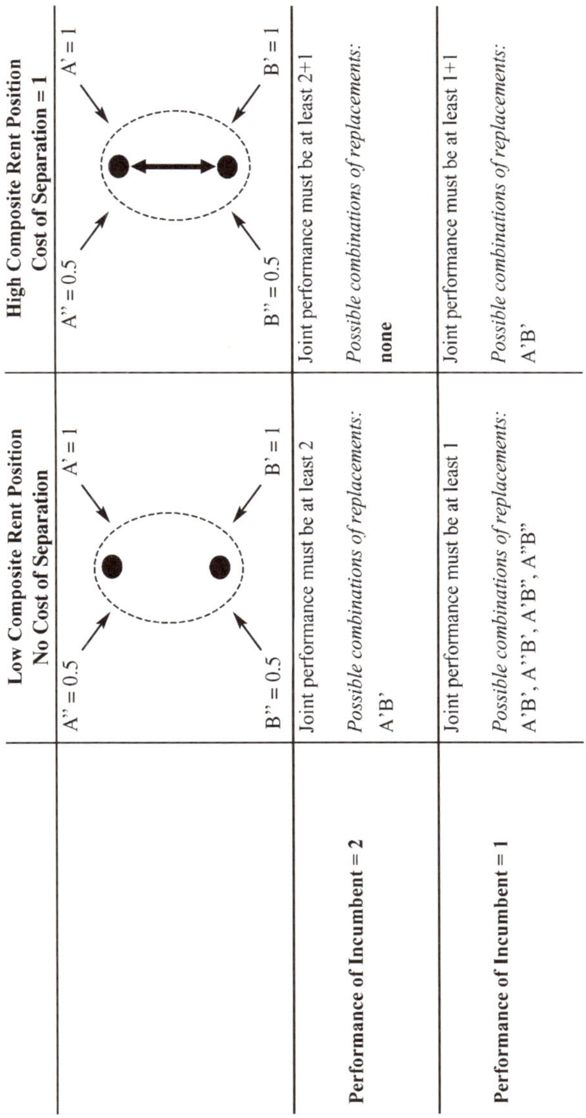

Fig. 1. Composite Rent and Closure.

an equivalent level of performance, incumbents of high-composite-rent positions are less likely to be replaced.

Not only does composite rent associated with a position have an effect on the absolute likelihood of replacement for a given level of performance of the incumbent, but also it determines how sensitive that likelihood is to performance. Consider the effect of declining performance of the incumbent of both positions from 2 to 1. Now there are two more combinations of contestants capable of reaching this level for the position with no composite rent between assets. These additional combinations are: A'B" and A"B'. In order to replace the incumbent of the position with high composite rent, the contestants have to be able to perform at the level of the incumbent and bear the costs of separation of the position. Thus, the total performance of specialists has to be at least 2. The only combination of contestants capable of reaching this level is A'B'. Thus, for the position with high composite rent, the decline in the incumbent's performance increased the number of potential specialist replacements by one. Thus, an equivalent decline in the incumbent's performance has a different effect on the likelihood of replacement of the incumbents of the two positions. The increase is larger for the incumbent of the position with no composite rent than for the incumbent of the position with high composite rent.

IMPLICATIONS FOR STRUCTURAL INEQUALITY

The foregoing discussion shows that an equivalent decline in the incumbent's performance has a different effect on the likelihood of replacement for the incumbent of low- and high-composite-rent positions, respectively. Occupants of low-composite-rent positions are very likely to be replaced following a decrease in their performance. In contrast, occupants of high-composite-rent positions are likely to keep their positions, despite the decline in their performance. The results of empirical analysis of the incidence of takeovers in the 1980s, reported in Piskorski (2001), are consistent with these predictions. When composite rents inside a firm are low, the incidence of takeover bids is driven by the performance of incumbents relative to other market participants. When the incumbent creates less value than an alternative actor could, the incumbent will be replaced. However, when composite rents inside a firm are high, the traditional characterization of the market for corporate control does not reflect the reality. Specifically, when performance of such firms declines, the increase in the likelihood of takeover is substantially lower. In fact, when composite rents are sufficiently high, the relationship between firm performance and the likelihood of takeover no longer exists, protecting the managers of these companies from replacement despite their poor performance.

This result points to a paradoxical situation whereby an efficient internalization of difficult transactions between business units, which is beneficial from the point of view of shareholders, also protects the managers from the market for corporate control, and thus provides scope for managerial agency.

The hypotheses put forward by the model together with the empirical results suggest that the existence of composite rents has substantial effects on structural inequality between actors in the labor market. Specifically, occupants of low-composite-rent positions cannot enjoy structural advantages or disadvantages. As soon as their performance declines, they lose their position and all of the economic privileges associated with it. This was the fate of many managers who were in charge of diversified companies that engaged in multiple businesses that were easily separated from each other. In contrast, occupants of high-composite-rent positions were structurally advantaged. Although their performance declined, they continued to occupy the position, and were able to enjoy the economic benefits over and above what they would be able to obtain if they occupied a low-composite-rent position. This apparent ability to extract rents from the position has been borne out in Piskorski's (2000) qualitative research of the behavior of managers in charge of firms that comprised numerous tightly integrated business units. For example, his analysis of the business strategy of a large chemical company reveals that managers of this company were able to embark on a number of strategies that satisfied their own empire-growing goals at a significant expense to shareholders.

CONCLUSION

The examination of the two models has important implications for our understanding of inequality in markets. Theoretically, markets are systems of exchange in which actors are matched to positions on the basis of actors' performances. In the ideal case, each buyer and seller acts independently of every other, so that positions and actors are matched impersonally through competitive dynamics. There are no relations of control in this market – any individual position is supposed to be able to be occupied by any competent laborer. Nor are there supposed to be any relations of authority in the market, except those necessary to provide rules of exchange and the enforcement of contracts. The distinctive feature of a market is the absence of such controlling mechanism and authoritative directions. Collectively, sellers might wish to keep the prices of their services higher than their marginal cost, but so long as they act individually, they are driven to bring them down into equilibrium to secure for each individual as large a share of the market as possible. As many sociologists and economists have emphasized, this is not a prospect that sellers usually enjoy and, whenever the means are available, it is one that they quickly subvert. As Marshall (1948) notes, market participants abhor competition intensely and will often collude and resist market competition.

This line of reasoning suggests that as long as one is able to keep these collective efforts in check, the market will not generate any unearned advantages or disadvantages. Our models suggest otherwise. Khurana's description of the role of directors in the CEO search process highlights that neither such motivations nor any solidarity among the selecting group is required for the existence of unearned benefits. The closure process starts early in the CEO succession process, beginning with a reliance on directors' own suggestions of potential candidates, being furthered by the reliance on generally accepted criteria to sort candidates, and ending with directors gathering information about candidates largely through their own trusted contacts, primarily with other directors. The paradox and, perhaps, irony of the reliance on ties and other aspects of the social matching process, is that even when directors bypass the internal process of CEO succession to get away from its restrictiveness, they often end up duplicating a similar structure and order in their own processes. Directors, as they pursue the identification of candidates, establish and maintain a certain set of readily identifiable characteristics to narrow the number of potential candidates. While the directors may use their selection criteria to identify a manageable set of candidates, they are clearly at the same time maintaining and reproducing a structure.

Piskorski's model suggests that even if one eliminated all efforts at collusion, as well as all the social-matching processes in the market, structural advantages and disadvantages would still persist. Actors occupying positions with high composite rents would still enjoy advantages that would otherwise be foreclosed to them. This has important implications for the debate concerning the suitability of markets for corporate control as mechanisms to constrain managerial agency. "Marketists" argue that markets for corporate control are the most efficient means of controlling managerial agency (Jensen & Ruback, 1983; Manne, 1965). Kaufman and Zacharias (1992) summarize this view:

> In unfettered markets, corporate managers would be disciplined by a simple rule: a decline in a market value below the replacement cost of the firm would induce outsiders to bid for control with the intention of enhancing their wealth by the liquidation or reorganization of the acquired business [...] A perfectly fluid system would allow discipline to be imposed on inefficient managers and firms in a perfectly competitive environment with recontracting for all managerial talent with short-term contracts.

In contrast, sociologically informed accounts underscore the critical role of social instruments of control, such as boards of directors (Khurana, 2002) and organized shareholder action (Kang, 1996). Instead of proposing that the markets for corporate control provide a better method of managerial oversight than such social instruments of control, Piskorski's model proposes an important contingency. The appropriateness of each control mechanism critically depends on the nature of the firm. When composite rents inside the firm are low and the incidence of takeover bids is tightly related to firm performance, managers need to maximize shareholder value in order to avoid a takeover bid. Under these conditions, therefore, markets for corporate control are appropriate mechanisms for controlling managerial agency. In contrast, when composite rents inside the firm are high, the incidence of takeover bids is not related to firm performance. Consequently, managers can pursue their own interests, at the expense of shareholders, without the threat of being replaced by market forces. Under these conditions, markets for corporate control no longer seem to be able to control managerial agency. Instead, active control by boards of directors and shareholders is important to ensuring that managers do not engage in behaviors that fulfill their goals at the expense of the population that owns stock in those companies.

ACKNOWLEDGMENTS

Both authors have equally contributed to the writing of this article and their names are listed in alphabetical order. We are forever indebted to Aage Sørensen for instigating our interest in social inequality and for being a patient advisor as we developed our ideas. Arne Kalleberg and Steve Morgan provided us with valuable feedback on this article. All errors are ours.

REFERENCES

Baker, G. P., & Smith, G. D. (1998). *The new financial capitalists: Kohlberg Kravis Roberts and the creation of corporate value*. Cambridge, NY: Cambridge University Press.

Bonacich, P. (1987). Power and centrality: A family of measures. *American Journal of Sociology, 92*, 1170–1182.

Coleman, J. S. (1990). *Foundations of social theory*. Cambridge, MA: Harvard University Press.

Davis, G. F., Diekmann, K. A., & Tinsley, C. H. (1994). The decline and fall of the conglomerate firm in the 1980s: A study in the deinstitutionalization of an organizational form. *American Sociological Review, 59*, 547–571.

Davis, G. F., & Stout, S. K. (1992). Organization theory and the market for corporate control: A dynamic analysis of large takeover targets, 1980–1990. *Administrative Science Quarterly, 37*, 605–634.

Edgar vs. MITE. In *457 U.S. 624 [1982]*.

Granovetter, M. (1994). Toward a sociological theory of income differences. In: D. B. Grusky (Ed.), *Social Stratification: Class, Race and Gender in Sociological Perspective*. Grusky. Boulder, CO: Westview Press.

Hirsch, P. M. (1986). From ambushes to golden parachutes: Corporate takeovers as an instance of cultural framing and institutional integration. *American Journal of Sociology, 91*, 800–837.

Jensen, M. C. (1989). Eclipse of a public corporation. *Harvard Business Review, 67*, 61–74.

Jensen, M. C. (1993). The modern industrial revolution, exit, and the failure of internal control systems. *Journal of Finance, 48*, 831–880.

Jensen, M. C., & Ruback, R. S. (1983). The market for corporate control: The scientific evidence. *Journal of Financial Economics, 11*.

Kahn, C., & Huberman, G. (1988). Two sided uncertainty and up-or-out contracts. *Journal of Labor Economics, 6*, 423–444.

Kang, D. L. (1996). *The impact of ownership type on organizational performance*. Ph.D. Thesis, Organizational Behavior Department, Harvard University, Cambridge, MA.

Kaufman, A., & Zacharias, L. (1992). From trust to contract: The legal language of managerial ideology, 1920–1980. *Business History Review, 66*, 547–559.

Khurana, R. (1998). *The changing of the guard: Causes, process and consequences of CEO turnover*. Ph.D. Thesis, Organizational Behavior Department, Harvard University, Cambridge, MA.

Khurana, R. (2002). *Searching for a corporate savior: The irrational quest for charismatic CEOs*. Princeton, NJ: Princeton University Press.

Lipton, M., & Steinberger, E. H. (1988). *Takeovers and freezeouts* (Vol. 1). New York, NY: Law Journal Seminars Press.

Manne, H. G. (1965). Mergers and the market for corporate control. *Journal of Political Economy, 73*, 110–120.

March, J. C., & March, J. G. (1978). Performance sampling in social matches. *Administrative Science Quarterly, 23*, 434–453.

Marris, R. (1964). *The economic theory of managerial capitalism*. New York, NY: Free Press.

Marshall, A. (1948). *Principles of economics*. London: Macmillan.

Morck, R., Shleifer, A., & Vishny, R. W. (1988). Characteristics of targets of hostile and friendly takeovers. In: A. J. Auerbach (Ed.), *Corporate Takeovers: Causes and Consequences*. Chicago, IL: University of Chicago Press.

Palmer, D., Zhou, X. G., Barber, B. M., & Soysal, Y. (1995). The friendly and predatory acquisition of large U.S. corporations in the 1960s – the other contested terrain. *American Sociological Review, 60*, 469–499.

Parkin, F. (1979). *Marxism and class theory*. New York, NY: Columbia University.

Parsons, T. (1953). A revised analytical approach to the theory of social stratification. In: R. Bendix & S. Lipset (Eds), *Class, Status and Power* (pp. 99–128). New York, NY: Free Press.

Piskorski, M. J. (2000). Against the tide: How dow chemical avoided a takeover bid. Harvard Business School Working Paper, Boston, MA.

Piskorski, M. J. (2001). *Structural closure and exposure: Performance and autonomy of american corporations*. Ph.D. Thesis, Organizational Behavior Department, Harvard University, Cambridge, MA.

Piskorski, M. J., & Anand, B. N. (2003). Power, brokerage and prestige in the formation of structural advantages in exchange networks. Working Paper, Graduate School of Business, Stanford University. Stanford, CA.

Prendergast, C. (1993). The role of promotion in inducing specific human capital acquisition. *Quarterly Journal of Economics, 108*, 523–534.

Simmel, G. (1950). Fundamental problems of sociology: Individual and society. In: K. H. Wolff (Ed.), *The Sociology of Georg Simmel* (pp. 3–23). New York: NY: Free Press.

Smith, A. (1776). *An inquiry into the nature and causes of the wealth of nations*. London: Printed for W. Strahan and T. Cadell.

Sørensen, A. B. (1974). A model for occupation careers. *American Journal of Sociology*, *80*, 44–57.

Sørensen, A. B. (1990). Processes of allocation to open and closed positions in social structure. In: J. Berger & M. Zelditch, Jr. (Eds), *Sociological Theories in Progress* (Vol. III, pp. 256–287). New York, NY: Sage.

Sørensen, A. B. (1994). An outline of a theory of the matching of persons to jobs. In: D. B. Grusky (Ed.), *Social Stratification: Class, Race and Gender in Sociological Perspective*. Boulder, CO: Westview Press.

Sørensen, A. B. (1996). The structural basis of social inequality. *American Journal of Sociology*, *101*, 1333–1365.

Useem, M. (1984). *The inner circle: Large corporations and the rise of business political activity in the U.S. and UK*. New York: Oxford University Press.

Walking, R. A., & Long, M. (1984). Agency theory, managerial welfare, and takeover bid resistance. *Rand Journal of Economics*, *15*, 54–68.

Weber, M. (1947). *Economy and society*. University of California Press.

Weeden, K. A. (2002). Why do some occupations pay more than others? Social closure and earnings inequality in the United States. *American Journal of Sociology*, *108*, 55–101.

White, H. C. (1970). *Chains of opportunity: System models of mobility in organizations*. Cambridge, MA: Harvard University Press.

Williamson, O. E. (1981). The economics of organization: The transaction cost approach. *American Journal of Sociology*, *87*, 548–577.

Zeitlin, M. (1974). Corporate ownership and control: The large corporation and the capitalist class. *American Journal of Sociology*, *79*, 1073–1119.

Zuckerman, E. W. (1999). The categorical imperative: Securities analysts and the illegitimacy discount. *American Journal of Sociology*, *104*, 1398–1438.

TOWARDS A STRUCTURAL THEORY OF STATUS INEQUALITY: STRUCTURES AND RENTS IN POPULAR MUSIC AND TASTES

Michèle Ollivier

ABSTRACT

In this paper, I use Aage Sørensen's theory of structural inequality as a point of departure to develop a framework for understanding status in contemporary social life. Contrary to the view that status is now fragmented into a multiplicity of localized spaces of distinction, I argue that status structures, consisting of mutually-sustaining sets of cultural schemas and resources, are transposed in a wide variety of social situations in such a way that enduring patterns of inequality are reproduced over time and space. These status structures provide advantages which correspond to Sørensen's earlier definition of rents as returns obtained from positions in social structure rather than from individual talent and effort. To illustrate the usefulness of this framework, I present two examples from my work in the sociology of culture. In a study of prestige among popular music artists in Quebec, I show that status schemas which appear to be context-specific are related to similar schemas found in other art fields, are not entirely detached from other dimensions of inequality, and provide advantages which are rents. In an exploratory study of tastes, I show how status structures can change over time in a way that reproduces existing inequalities. Drawing a parallel with

---

Inequality: Structures, Dynamics and Mechanisms: Essays in Honor of Aage B. Sørensen
Research in Social Stratification and Mobility, Volume 21, 187–213

ISSN: 0276-5624/doi:10.1016/S0276-5624(04)21010-1

the rhetoric of diversity expressed in a variety of fields, including economics, marketing, and politics, I argue that conspicuous openness to diversity may be emerging as one of the master cultural schemas of our times.

INTRODUCTION

Aage Sørensen was my dissertation advisor at Harvard University in the early 1990s. I'm a sociologist of culture, and I wrote my doctoral dissertation on prestige among popular music artists in Quebec. I interviewed artists, producers, and critics to understand how people's classification and evaluation of the work of artists influence the types of career that artists pursue. Halfway through my dissertation, Professor Sørensen asked me to write a book with him entitled *Class, Status, and Privilege: A Conceptual Analysis*. The plan was that he would write two chapters on class (class as lifestyle and class as exploitation), I would write two chapters on status (socioeconomic status and prestige), with a common introduction and conclusion. Needless to say, I was both honoured and excited by the project.

From the start, this was a very strange collaboration. Aage Sørensen and I come from very different sociological backgrounds. He was mainly interested in the so-called infrastructure, that is, in understanding structures of opportunity in education, occupations, and organisations, and in the processes of allocation of people among these positions. The focus of my work has always been the superstructure – symbolic representations, discourse, ideologies, knowledge, classification systems, and artistic hierarchies. He used the language of economics, and once lamented the interest of sociologists for "non-existing entities" such as postmodernism. My early training in French critical sociology in the late 1970s had made me familiar with authors whose work inspired the postmodern turn in cultural studies.

In spite of our differences, we shared an interest for what Sørensen referred to as the "central idea of sociology" (1994, p. 232), that of social structure. One of the main thrust of his work on class and allocation has been the attempt to develop a "genuine sociological theory" of social inequality (2000, p. 1524). As opposed to the more individualist approach of standard economic theory, this theory focussed on inequality arising from positions in social structure rather than from individual talent and effort. Similarly, in my recent work on status and tastes (Fridman & Ollivier, 2002, 2004; Ollivier & Fridman, 2001), I've tried to understand how status operates in a world where social representations, including status beliefs and rules of distinction, are seen as fragmented, individualised, and "radically detached from the social matrix" (Pakulski & Waters, 1996, p. 125). Coming from different horizons and working within different theoretical traditions, we shared an interest for structural bases of inequality, that is, for patterns of unequal social relations which constrain social agents and are reproduced over time. We worked mostly in parallel, commenting on each other's work as it evolved. Unfortunately, he passed away before the project could be completed.

In this paper, I examine recent debates about status in contemporary societies, in dialogue with Aage Sørensen's work to develop a structural theory of social inequality. My main argument is that certain current conceptions of status greatly overestimate the fragmentation of social representations and the individualisation of inequality in contemporary social life. Using examples from my recent work on status, culture, and tastes, I argue that some status schemas continue to be widely held, are transposable from one situation to another, are not detached from other dimensions of inequality, and provide rents in social interaction. In the first section, I briefly review the transformation of status concepts in sociology, from a society-wide aspect of integration (Parsons, 1954) or domination (Bourdieu, 1979) mirroring macro structures of power, to a strictly local phenomenon detached from other dimensions of inequality. In the second section, I build on Aage Sørensen's structural theory of social inequality to develop the outline of a framework for understanding status, in a way that takes into account the increased fluidity of social relations without abandoning the search for structural forms of inequality. In the third section, I illustrate the usefulness of this framework with two examples from my work on status, culture, and tastes.

STATUS IN CONTEMPORARY SOCIOLOGY: BOURDIEU, POSTMODERNISM, AND BEYOND

Status has many meanings in sociology, most of which involve a combination of two different elements. First, status refers to the esteem or contempt, deference or derogation, granted to individuals or groups perceived as superior or inferior. It refers to people's positive and negative evaluations of one another and it is synonymous with prestige. Status in this sense is a "sentiment in the minds of people" (Gilbert & Kahl, 1982, p. 21) and it pertains to a distinctly symbolic aspect of inequality. Second, status also refers to positions in social structure, in a way that is sometimes totally independent from social evaluations. When social structure is represented as a gradation, we get concepts of socio-economic status, that is, rankings of positions with regard to socioeconomic resources. When social structure is conceptualised as discrete social categories, status refers to the rights and duties attached to these categories, for example in legal concepts of marital status and citizenship. Whereas status in the symbolic sense and status as social structure may be conceptualised as independent from one another, in practice they are most often associated together. In its quintessential sociological sense, status refers to collective evaluations of superiority and inferiority, which have acquired an existence beyond individual beliefs and which influence social relations in various ways.

The combination of status in the symbolic sense with various conceptions of social structure has given rise to the three main perspectives on status in sociology. First, the combination of status in the symbolic sense with a gradational view of social structure forms the basis of Neo-Durkheimian and functionalist theories of social stratification (Barber, 1957; Durkheim, 1967; Shils, 1975). In this perspective, social positions are graded in the social consciousness according to their functional or charismatic importance in the social system. These shared gradings of positions form a moral classification which sets limits to individual appetites and legitimates the unequal allocation of rewards. Second, the combination of status in the symbolic sense with a discrete view of social structure constitutes the basis of Neo-Weberian concepts. Status is seen here as an attribute of groups, whose successful claims to social esteem typically lead to the monopolisation of opportunities and rewards through legal or customary closure (Weber, 1978). Third, the interactional or exchange concepts of status (Blau, 1967; Homans, 1950) focus on the micro-interactional underpinnings of these status processes, showing how status arises in the course of social exchange, becomes institutionalised as gradations within groups or as legal/customary monopolies between them, and then feeds back into social interaction.

These status concepts have not been equally successful in recent years. After remaining a core concept in community studies (Warner et al., 1960) and in sociological theories of inequality (Barber, 1957, Davis & Moore, 1945, Parsons, 1954) from the 1940s to the 1960s, status as shared values became increasingly marginal in stratification research in the 1970s. With the development of socioeconomic status scales, social structure was reconceptualized as a hierarchy of positions based on socioeconomic resources rather than on values, and status came to be seen as "a function of power and privilege rather than the other way around" (Lenski, 1984, p. 430). As a result, status in the symbolic sense was virtually eliminated as an independent explanatory factor from models of stratification.

At the same time, status emerged as a major concept in the sociology of culture, in large part through Bourdieu's work on tastes, cultural capital, and class domination. Building on Weber's concept of status as domination as well as on Marx's view of the primacy of class in social relations, Bourdieu shows that non-material resources such as know-how, tastes, and knowledge of the arts are essential for understanding social inequality. The power of dominant classes and groups arises not only from their economic assets, but also from the status they gain through possession and display of cultural resources. Bourdieu's concept of cultural capital rests on the assumption that a unified and hegemonic set of evaluative standards, reflecting the social position and aesthetic dispositions of dominant classes, imposes itself as legitimate culture in a given society. In this sense, Bourdieu's Neo-Weberian conception of status shares certain functionalist assumptions about social life. In both cases, symbolic representations, including status beliefs, are seen as part of a unified and all-encompassing cognitive structure which closely mirrors macro structures of power.

While Bourdieu is widely praised for having developed a comprehensive analysis of the role of symbolic power in shaping patterns of inequality, this aspect of his work has come under intense criticism. Most importantly, Bourdieu has been criticised for postulating the existence of a single, objective space of distinction, in which cultural capital operates as a universally recognised currency of exchange (Erickson, 1996; Hall, 1992). Bourdieu acknowledges that cultural distinctions are expressed differently in various fields, but he maintains that a unique organising principle ultimately accounts for these variations. Bourdieu further assumes a strict homology between class position and class dispositions, and subsumes under the concept of class the entire spectrum of status distinctions based for example on race, ethnicity, gender, language, and age.

In the field of stratification, many argue that the concept of class, as defined by Bourdieu, is no longer useful for understanding contemporary forms of inequality (Pakulski & Waters, 1996; Schecter & Paquet, 2000). Contemporary societies, they argue, have witnessed a phenomenal increase in the breadth and anonymity of social relations, as more people come into more fleeting contact with others in a diversity of social settings. High levels of geographical and social mobility, coupled with the extraordinary increase in the amount and diversity of information available through the mass media, have led to major changes in processes of identity formation and status competition. As opposed to relatively small communities, where status is linked to personal knowledge of fixed identities based on family name, reputation, kinship, and place of residence, enlarged and anonymous social spaces provide individuals with vastly increased possibilities of experimenting with strategies of self-presentation in everyday life. Contemporary societies are seen as highly complex and segmented, so that people have multiple social affiliations which do not necessarily coincide (Blau & Schwartz, 1984; DiMaggio & Mohr, 1985).

The classical sociological metaphor of hierarchically arrayed groups or positions has given way to pictures of a network society in which "boundaries are more permeable, interactions are with diverse others, linkages switch between multiple networks, and hierarchies (when they exist) are flatter and more recursive" (Wellman & Hampton, 1999). In more radical perspectives, the network society is presented as "horizontal" (Collins, 2000), that is, as comprising a patchwork of microsituational encounters which remain largely disjuncted from one another as well as from macro structures of power. The horizontal society is not one where inequality has disappeared, but one in which it has become individualised (Beck, 1992) or too complex to be apprehended (Schecter & Paquet, 2000). Far from being based on exclusion, the horizontal society is sometimes presented as a space of inclusion, in which talent and chance are the main determinants of social inequality (Schecter & Paquet, 2000).

In the sociology of culture, Bourdieu's critics argue that it is no longer possible to envision the existence of a single, unified, and hegemonic legitimate culture based on knowledge of high culture. In a process celebrated by some (Lipovetsky, 1994) and lamented by others (Bloom, 1987; Finkielkraut, 1995), the Enlightenment ideal of liberal arts education, which is at the root of Bourdieu's vision of legitimate culture, has been seriously challenged in universities, the media, and other cultural institutions by feminist, poststructuralist, and postcolonial activists seeking greater recognition for minority cultures. The last decades of the 20th century have also witnessed a considerable erosion of the boundaries between high and popular culture, as high culture institutions gradually adopted the marketing strategies of commercial mass culture and some popular genres such as comic books borrowed the complex stylisation of form commonly associated with high culture. As a result, contemporary tastes and cultures are seen either as fragmented along a multiplicity of localised spaces of distinction (Hall, 1992), or as an expression of individual preferences and private choices (Lipovetsky, 1994). If "under postmodernism there is no absolute standard of taste or opinion," there is therefore "no ground for closure and exclusivity" (Pakulski & Waters, 1996, p. 121). Being reduced to an array of local currencies with no significance outside specific social settings, cultural capital no longer serves as a basis of class domination.

Late modern societies are thus seen as comprising multiple, segmented, and sometimes incommensurable normative orders, in which status operates predominantly at micro or local levels, for example among popular music artists (Ollivier, 1997), carnival strippers (Meiselas, 1976), upper class philanthropists (Ostrower, 1995), and adolescents (Milner, 1996). Rather than representing a society-wide normative structure, status is linked to the multilayered symbolic boundaries of race, gender, class, and lifestyle that people draw between themselves and others in processes of inclusion and exclusion (Lamont & Fournier, 1992). It organises relationships in local settings but has little society-wide significance. To borrow the terminology developed by DiMaggio in relation to artistic classification systems (1987), status in contemporary societies is seen as exhibiting a high degree of *differentiation* (status cultures are separated into several as opposed to few categories) but a low degree of *universality* (few status distinctions are universally recognised and accepted as legitimate outside specific social circles), low *symbolic potency* (status boundaries tend to be weak and permeable), and low levels of *hierarchisation* (status cultures tend to be considered of equal value as opposed to being arranged hierarchically).

Under the joint influence of the demise of functionalist theories of stratification, the growing influence of Neo-Weberian theories of status as an attribute of groups within a collectivity, and the postmodern critique of classical sociology, status was thus successively reconceptualized, from a moral canopy holding society together to a by-product of socioeconomic resources and, more recently, to a strictly local phenomenon. However, while modernist perspectives emphasising stable identities and strong homologies between levels (micro/macro) or dimensions (structure/consciousness) of social reality no longer seem appropriate for understanding contemporary forms of inequality, postmodern visions of extreme fluidity and radical individualisation seem to defeat the purpose of sociological analysis altogether. Bourdieu undoubtedly exaggerated the universality and symbolic potency of high culture as a means of domination. As convincingly argued by his critics, cultural dispositions may not be shaped exclusively or even primarily by class position (Hall, 1992); consumption may be driven by existential anxiety (Bauman, 1988) or by a quest for personal autonomy (Lipovetsky, 1994) much more than by status competition; cultural capital, to the extent that it exists at all, may function as a means of inclusion across classes as often as it works as a means of exclusion between them (Erickson, 1996); and we may need to relinquish the notion that classes, as homogeneous groupings held together by stable sets of acquired dispositions, constitute a useful analytical tool for understanding inequality. Accepting these arguments, however, does not justify the conclusion that status should now be conceptualised exclusively as a local phenomenon detached from other dimensions of inequality. Sørensen's structural theory of inequality, I argue in the next section, provides a useful starting point for conceptualising status in a way that takes into account the current fluidity and segmentation of social relations while avoiding the more radical implications of postmodernist interpretations.

STATUS, STRUCTURES, AND RENTS

The main objective of Sørensen's structural theory of inequality is to identify conditions under which inequality arises from positions in social structure rather than from the skills and efforts of incumbents of these positions. In his most recent formulation of the question (2000), positions in social structure are defined on the basis of economic property rights. Property rights are "the ability to receive the return on an asset, directly or indirectly through exchange" (2000, p. 1525). Returns on assets may be monetary or they may take the form of prestige or status. It is property rights over different types of assets which define class positions. Exploitation classes arise from property rights over rent-producing assets, which provide returns "exceeding the competitive price or the price sufficient to cover costs and therefore exceeding what is sufficient to bring about the employment of the asset" (2000, p. 1536). Rents always involve some degree of closure, that is, some form of collective action which limits the supply of the rent-producing asset or the free flow of information about it. Because rents represent deviations from perfect competition, they create economic inefficiencies which result in an overall decrease in collective welfare (2000, p. 1544). Rents thus create conditions of exploitation, since owners of rent-producing assets obtain benefits at the expense of the collectivity. Because rents generate advantages attached to positions in social structure, they create durable antagonistic interests. Those who benefit from rents have an interest in protecting them while others have an interest in abolishing them.

Sørensen's structural theory of inequality, I argue, contains two useful elements for understanding status inequality in what Mary Douglas (1979) refers to as "low-grid, weak-group" social contexts, with highly fluid social classifications, few restrictions on social interaction, and weak community control over individuals. The first element is the concept of structural inequality, which implies that various dimensions of inequality interlock in some way to create long-lasting effects on social interaction. The second one is the concept of rent, with its assumption that part of the return received for using an asset is in some way problematic. Both elements, however, need to be slightly revised in order to provide a "sounder basis" for understanding contemporary forms of status inequality.

Status and Structures

Much of stratification research since the demise of functionalism in the 1960s was based on a dualist conception of social life opposing structure and culture. Structure was defined as things material, objective, durable, and determining, while culture was seen as ideational, subjective, fleeting, and derivative. Accordingly, terms such as class, wealth, income, education, power, and authority were defined as structural, and therefore as explanatory factors in processes of social inequality, while status beliefs and ideologies were seen as cultural, and thus as by-products of more fundamental social forces (Hodge et al., 1982; Lenski, 1984). In Sørensen's approach to inequality, the *structuring* element of life chances is property rights. Property rights, however, do not exist in a social vacuum. They are inherently cultural in nature, since they necessarily rest on ideas about social rights and entitlements. Modern property rights are thus thoroughly embedded in cultural schemas which presuppose a conception of individual autonomy and of contractual market relations.

Recognising that structures can only function as such by virtue of the cultural meanings attached to them, many sociologists have proposed much broader conceptions of social structure which go beyond the one-way causation of material and ideational, objective and subjective, determining and derivative (Bourdieu, 1977; Giddens, 1984; Sewell, 1992). Sociologists interested in cognitive processes, in particular, have recently called attention to the role of cultural schemas in structuring social action (DiMaggio, 1997). Schemas may be defined as "intersubjectively available rules or procedures" (Sewell, 1992, p. 8) which organise our knowledge of the world into systems of categorisation and evaluation. They are constitutive of what Bourdieu calls *doxa*, that is, taken-for-granted, default assumptions about events and objects in everyday life. They are powerful and pervasive in part because they can be transposed or generalised to novel situations. The concept of schemas, as widely-available cognitive structures, has been extremely popular in the sociology of culture in recent years, starting with Ann Swidler's (1986) conception of culture as a "tool-kit" of symbols, ideologies, images, habits, and skills, to Lamont and Thévenot's work on national cultural repertoires (Lamont & Thévenot, 2000), and Alexander and Smith's (1993) conception of culture as a structure comprising basic sets of binary symbolic codes.

However, if cultural schemas are to be considered as structures in any sociological sense, they need to be sustained and reproduced over time. The unequal distribution of resources, defined as "anything that can serve as a source of power in social interaction" (Sewell, 1992, p. 9), functions as a validation of cultural schemas. Material resources make visible and tangible the categories of culture and the evaluative schemes associated with them. Resources and schemas are thus interdependent, in so far as resources can only function as sources of power by virtue of the cultural meanings embodied in them. It is the existence of these schemas which makes it possible for resources such as a college degree, a factory, or a position of authority in a bureaucracy to function as sources of social power. Sets of schemas and resources thus "constitute *structures* when they mutually imply and sustain each other over time" (Sewell, 1992, p. 13).

In their efforts to critique the rigidity of past models of inequality, advocates of postmodern fragmentation and individualised inequality, I argue, underestimate the prevalence of widely-shared cultural schemas which transcend local situations and organise interaction in similar ways in different contexts. As acknowledged by most sociologists working along these lines (DiMaggio, 1997; Lahire, 1998; Sewell, 1992; Swidler, 1986), such a conception of mutually reinforcing schemas and resources is perfectly compatible with the idea that structures are multiple, contingent, unstable, and constantly challenged or reaffirmed in interaction. The important point, however, is that some schemas or superschemas (Ridgeway, 1997), pertaining for example to gender, race, and class, are readily available as part of national cultural repertoires (Lamont & Thévenot, 2000) or sets of binary codes (Alexander & Smith, 1993). These schemas are in no way "radically detached from the social matrix" (Pakulski & Waters, 1996, p. 125) and they have implications which go much beyond "the cacophony of conflicting local beliefs" (Ridgeway & Erickson, 2000, p. 583). Schemas anchored in unequal distributions of resources, especially if they provide benefits which are rents, may prove especially resistant to change because of the advantages attached to them.

Status and Rents

Implicit in all theories of social stratification is some conception of distributive justice according to which certain types of social arrangements are considered acceptable while others are not. Sørensen's concept of rent is interesting because it points to a type of inequality which is in some way unacceptable. Rents, he argues, constitute a source of exploitation because they increase the welfare of those who benefit from them while decreasing the overall welfare of society. In common language, the term exploitation has very strong normative connotations. The Merriam-Webster Online Dictionary, for example, defines exploiting as making "use of *meanly* or *unjustly* for one's own advantage" (Merriam-Webster Online, 2002, emphasis added). In his attempt to ground exploitation in objective features of social structure, however, Sørensen tries to avoid normative issues, arguing for example that "there is nothing intrinsically desirable about perfectly competitive markets" (2000, p. 1544) or that eliminating exploitation would not necessarily "create good lives" (2000, p. 1535). Exploitation arises from a more abstract conception of overall system equilibrium, which assumes that deviations from perfect competition "create a 'deadweight' loss that is an externality *reducing the welfare of society*" (2000, p. 1544).

This odd use of the term exploitation has been noted by his critics (Goldthorpe, 2000; Rueschemeyer & Mahoney, 2000), who argue that deviations from market equilibrium do not necessarily constitute exploitation. What is considered a loss in terms of economic efficiency may constitute a gain in other ways. Rents may provide collective benefits, for example social peace, higher quality consumer goods, and qualified medical doctors, over and above the private benefits obtained by owners of rent-producing assets. As noted by Rueschemeyer and Mahoney (2000), Sørensen's conception of exploitation also creates difficulties when linking structural interests and social action. If rents are perceived as providing public goods rather than as sources of economic inefficiency, it is hard to imagine that social agents would take action to destroy them. Structural interests need to be framed in terms of moral or justice issues in order to lead to collective action.

One way to solve these difficulties, I argue, while retaining the power of rents to identify returns which are in some way unfair or unjustified, is to go back to Sørensen's earlier concept of rent (1996). In this earlier formulation, the salient property of rents is not that a component of the payment is obtained "in excess of what is needed to bring out the supply of the assets" (2000, p. 1537). Rather, the salient property is that "a component of the payment obtained from using the asset is obtained *independently of the effort and past actions* of the person who has the right to that income" (1996, p. 1338). Rents, in this sense, are "advantages that are *unearned*" (1996, p. 1363, emphasis added). While the later formulation rests on a systemic conception of economic efficiency, the earlier concept makes no such assumption. It defines rents in relation to a historically contingent theory of distributive justice and as such it identifies conditions under which rents may be *considered* unfair by social scientists and other people alike.

In market democratic societies based on the ideal of meritocratic achievement, some measure of inequality is usually considered fair as long as it has been earned through individual talent and efforts. Advantages which are unearned, that is, which are obtained from membership in social categories or from positions in social structure as opposed to individual skills and effort, are generally considered unfair, especially when they cannot be justified on the basis of some contribution to the public good. Rents will thus generate antagonistic interests not because of departures from perfect competition, but because the returns they generate will be *perceived* as illegitimate. Conceiving of rents as departures from the conception of distributive justice prevalent in democratic, market-based societies provides a benchmark for social scientists and social agents alike to assess the unequal allocation of rewards.

To summarise, Sørensen's structural theory of social inequality contains two elements – a concern with structure and the concept of rent – which provide useful foundations for a structural theory of status inequality whose aim is to identify pervasive and enduring forms of status inequality leading to social action. Structures are defined as patterns of schemas (status beliefs) and resources which are mutually reinforcing and transposable to a wide variety of social situations. Positions in these structures generate rents in so far as at least part of the benefits they provide come from these positions rather than from individual talent and effort. In the next section, I examine recent efforts by sociologists to develop theories of status inequality which are in line with Sørensen's conception of structural inequality.

Towards a Structural Theory of Status Inequality

A structural theory of status inequality emphasising the distinction between status obtained from individual attributes and status arising from positions in social structures was recently developed by Guillermina Jasso (2000). The central feature of her framework is a distinction between status attached to individuals and status pertaining to social categories. As "socially organized systems of distinction" (Tilly, 1998, p. 4), social categories based for example on gender, race, class, age, or language may be considered as positions in social structures in so far as they are sustained through specific socioeconomic arrangements (viz resources) and widely held cultural beliefs (viz schemas). On the basis of the distinction between individuals and social categories, Jasso identifies three types of status. First-order status is a property of individuals based on a linear ranking of valued characteristics. Individuals are accorded high or low status for attributes, performances, or services which are highly valued within a community, e.g. for producing much-cited scientific papers (Hagstrom, 1965), growing big yams in traditional New Guinea societies (Forge, 1970), writing songs which articulate feelings of national identity (Ollivier, 1997), providing useful advice in a group (Blau, 1963), or staying ahead of fashion trends in high school (Milner, 1996).

Second-order status is based on qualitative characteristics which serve to classify individuals into categories but have no inherent order. Categorical status is a summary measure of the first-order status of its individual members. For example, if brown-eyed individuals on average grow bigger yams than blue-eyed ones, they will acquire, as a social category, higher status compared to others. Finally, third order status is a property of individuals which is based either entirely on categorical second-order status, when individual first-order status is unknown, or on a weighted average of individual and categorical status when information about both is available. For example, the third-order status of an academic would be a composite of her own performance on a valued characteristic (e.g. scientific productivity) and of her membership in relevant social categories (e.g. institutional affiliation, ethnicity, gender, etc.). Using Sørensen's terminology, the component of third order status obtained from membership in social categories may be considered a rent in so far as it is payment which is independent from individual skills and effort.

By distinguishing between individual and categorical status, Jasso's framework allows for the identification of returns on assets which are rents. However, her framework also presents a somewhat static and benign picture of status structures. She briefly mentions the various means through which status structures may change over time, but she does not incorporate these comments into the process through which first order individual status is instituted in the first place. As argued by Bourdieu (1983), groups possessing different amounts and types of resources compete in various fields so that their own attributes come to be considered as legitimate criteria for allocating first-order individual status. Groups occupying positions of dominance in existing power structures often – though not always – find themselves in better positions to make their own attributes perceived as desirable. Furthermore, Jasso seems to assume that second order categorical status arises from the bottom up, as a simple average of the status of individual members of the category. Categorical status, however, may emerge in a number of different ways.

First, and most important for the argument developed here, categorical status often results from the transposition of existing status schemas from one context to another. Recent developments of status generalisation theory (Ridgeway & Erickson, 2000), in particular, show that in situations where categorical identities correspond to differential access to power and resources, people develop expectations about the performance of members of each group – high expectations for members of dominant groups and low expectations for members of subordinate ones. These expectations influence how individuals interact with others, how well they perform, and how their achievements are evaluated. Members of positively evaluated categories benefit from advantages in face-to-face relations since they tend to display higher levels of confidence and to send signals of competence, which, in turn, result in more favourable evaluations by others regardless of their actual performance. These expectations give rise to consensual status beliefs according to which one group is widely accepted as more competent or worthy than another (Ridgeway & Erickson, 2000). Second, categorical status may also arise simply from the possession and display of valued resources. In task-oriented groups, individuals identified as possessing assets such as authority, education, or income are likely to be perceived as more competent and to acquire high status as a social category, *regardless of their performance on task-specific criteria of evaluation* (Ridgeway & Erickson, 2000).

Categorical status therefore not only arises from the bottom up, but also the top down, as people's positions in existing sets of schemas and resources are transposed to novel situations. In discussing the persistence over time of gender inequality in the labour market, for example, Ridgeway (1997) and Valian (1998) point to the structuring effect of gender schemas, whereas both men and women "implicitly expect (or expect that others will expect) greater competence from men than from women, other things being equal" (Ridgeway, 1997, p. 222). These status beliefs create expectations which have self-fulfilling effects, shaping people's perception of their own competence, their levels of assertiveness, and their actual performance. In societies where formally open contests are organised into "hierarchically ordered chains of opportunity" (Murphy, 1988, p. 222), small advantages at the start get magnified over time as individuals move through a series of sequential competitions. The transposition of gender schemas and the accumulation of advantages over time are thus two major mechanisms accounting for the persistence of gender inequality in the labour market (Valian, 1998).

To summarise, a structural theory of status inequality as envisioned by Sørensen is premised on the distinction between status arising from positions in social structures and status granted on the basis of individual talent and efforts. Social structure is defined here as mutually-reinforcing sets of cultural schemas and resources. Social categories constitute positions in social structure in so far as they correspond to specific configurations of schemas and resources. Status structures are pervasive and enduring because cultural schemas are transposed from one situation to another, in such a way that similar patterns of inequality are reproduced over time and space. Criteria of evaluation which appear to be context-specific are often – though by no means always – transpositions of existing status schemas. This *does not* mean that *all* status structures should ultimately be considered as transpositions of a master set of schemas and resources, as implied by Bourdieu in much of his empirical work (1979, 1984). However, it means that some status structures are more wide-spread and long-lasting than warranted by postmodernist accounts.

In societies based on meritocratic conceptions of distributive justice, advantages derived from membership in social categories, as opposed to those arising from individual effort, tend to be considered unfair. According to Sørensen's earlier framework, they constitute a rent, that is, advantages that are unearned. As such, they give rise to antagonistic interests and they are likely to be contested. Conflicts over rents may take different forms. As illustrated by the debates over Sørensen's "sounder basis for class analysis" (Goldthorpe, 2000; Rueschemeyer & Mahoney, 2000), one source of disagreement is whether rents represent unfair returns to members of social categories who successfully restrict access to an asset, or fair rewards for the provision of public goods to a collectivity. Where status beliefs come from and who benefits from them is also a central theme in disputes between order and conflict theories of stratification (Boudon, 1995). Proponents of order theories assume that status beliefs provide directions for social action in a way which benefits an entire collectivity, and that high prestige is a fair reward for contributions to the public good. Advocates of conflict perspectives, by contrast, argue that dominant groups within a collectivity struggle to impose status beliefs reflecting their own interests, and then use these beliefs as a means of legitimating exclusive access to opportunities and rewards. These scholarly disputes on collective and private benefits, while difficult to resolve empirically, shape the status structures in which we live in so far as they contribute to making existing arrangements appear more or less legitimate.

Conflicts over rents may also take the form of disagreements concerning whether returns on assets derive from membership in social categories or whether they come from individual skills and effort. As argued by theorists of social closure

(Collins, 1979; Murphy, 1988; Parkin, 1979), status in contemporary societies is most often ostensibly granted on the basis of individual attributes and skills. Rents arise through social closure when the capacity to acquire these skills is unequally distributed across social groups. This is at the core of Bourdieu's argument on the role of cultural capital in class reproduction (Bourdieu & Passeron, 1977). Soares's (2002) recent study of admissions at an elite college in the United States provides an illustration of this process. He shows that preference for highbrow arts among two cohorts who graduated from an Ivy League college in the 1960s is a strong predictor of whether or not their children gain admission in the most prestigious colleges. It is primarily through the interviews conducted as part of the admissions process, he argues, that prospective students have an opportunity to display the cultural capital acquired in their family. While apparently based on individual achievement, the admissions process systematically rewards students whose background includes large amounts of cultural capital. The portion of students' evaluation obtained from membership in a social category (upper classes with high levels of cultural capital), as opposed to individual effort and ability, constitutes an invisible rent.

Again, my argument is not that a master status schema, mirroring some objective distribution of material resources, is unconsciously reproduced by social agents in all fields, at all times. Rather, I argue that some status structures, consisting of mutually-sustaining sets of cultural schemas and resources, are reproduced in a variety of social situations and provide social agents with advantages and disadvantages which accumulate over time and space. In the following section, I illustrate the usefulness of this framework with two examples from my work on cultural schemas and status. In a study of prestige among popular music artists in Quebec, I show that status beliefs which appear to be context-specific are transposed from similar situations; they are not detached from other dimensions of inequality and they provide advantages corresponding to Sørensen's earlier definition of rents. In my recent work on tastes, I cast a critical look on the recent flourishing of interest in, and celebration of, diversity, eclecticism, and cosmopolitanism in scholarly, governmental, and popular discourse.

STATUS SCHEMAS AND RESOURCES IN POPULAR MUSIC AND TASTES

Prestige among Popular Music Artists in Quebec

In a study of prestige among French-speaking popular music artists conducted in Quebec in the early 1990s, I interviewed artists, producers, and critics to understand how they picture the field of popular music and how they evaluate the work of artists

(Ollivier, 1994, forthcoming). I asked them to sort artists into categories in any way which was meaningful to them and to rate artists according to the admiration they personally felt for their work. On the basis of these interviews, I argue that in the 1990s, the field of popular music in Quebec remained quite sharply divided along a symbolic boundary, established in the 1960s, opposing a highly prestigious group of songwriters/rock/pop-rock artists, most of whom write and sing their own music and lyrics, to a less prestigious group of interpreters/*artistes populaires*/country singers, who sing songs written by others and/or who perform in the less valued light pop or country genres.[1]

The distinction between songwriters and interpreters is arguably a local one, in the sense that it was shaped by the particular historical conditions which gave rise to a strong nationalist movement in Quebec in the 1960s. In the context of emerging nationalism, the ability to write original songs came to be seen as emblematic of the struggle of French-speaking Quebeckers to articulate a new identity and to gain greater control over social, political, and economic institutions. Songwriters were seen as expressing the soul of the nation and therefore as making a major contribution to the profound transformation of Quebec society. Local adaptations of French *chansonnettes* and translations of foreign pop hits of the day, which had dominated radio and record production until the 1950s, came to be perceived, at least by art critics and other cultural authorities, as a sign of subservience to outside cultural models. Even when interpreters subsequently started singing songs written by Quebec songwriters, their work remained undervalued.

The salience of the distinction between songwriters and interpreters in Quebec popular music is intimately linked to specific historical conditions, but it is not entirely detached from other, more pervasive, cultural schemas. First, it became clear during the interviews that the distinction between songwriters and interpreters is closely related to similar oppositions, for example between art and entertainment, artistic quality and commercial success, or authenticity and fabrication, structuring so many other art fields (Bourdieu, 1983; Greenfeld, 1989; Lowenthal, 1961). For some respondents, writing music and lyrics is inherently more creative, and therefore more authentic, than singing songs written by others. Others saw the distinction between interpreters and songwriters as an opposition between light entertainment on the one hand and songs conveying more profound aesthetic, social, or political content on the other. Terms such as courage, creativity, integrity, emotion, artistic intention, and content were opposed to the desire to please at all cost, following fads, conformity, commercial orientation, as well as to a concern with image and packaging. With some degree of simplification, the distinction between songwriters and interpreters may be considered as a transposition, in the particular historical context of 1960s Quebec society, of a cultural schema ubiquitous in other art fields.

Second, as a cultural schema, the distinction between songwriters and interpreters is not independent from other dimensions of inequality, most importantly from gender and socioeconomic inequality. Although this was *never* explicitly mentioned by respondents as criteria of classification and evaluation, artists in the most prestigious group of songwriters are overwhelmingly male, and they tend to have much higher levels of education compared to artists in the less prestigious categories. The superior second order status granted to songwriters as a social category undoubtedly reflects the average performance of individual members on a series of valued characteristics, but it also results from the transposition of status schemas pertaining to gender as well as from existing inequality in the distribution of cultural capital. Artists who occupy privileged positions in terms of gender and education are also those whose professional role is most highly valued (songwriters as opposed to interpreters), whose work is more likely to be perceived as authentic, and whose songs are considered as significant contributions to popular music and national identity. Far from being "radically detached from the social matrix" (Pakulski & Waters, 1996, p. 125), the local distinction between songwriters and interpreters remains thoroughly embedded in existing sets of cultural schemas and resources.

As argued above, status schemas are more likely to persist over time when they give rise to, and are sustained by, unequal allocation of resources. Analysing the careers of artists, I show that artists in the most prestigious group of songwriters derive two main advantages from their structural location. First, compared to interpreters/*artistes populaires*/country singers, they receive more honorific awards granted by governments, private foundations, and professional associations in recognition for the quality of their work. In addition to the prestige attached to them, honorific awards affect artistic careers in different ways: they provide greater visibility, increase record sales, and facilitate access to foreign markets (ADISQ, 1989). Second, songwriters are more likely to be invited to perform at special cultural events. Participation in special cultural events also affects artistic careers by providing opportunities for artists, who may not be very successful commercially, to perform for large audiences. For example, songwriters are much more likely than interpreters to participate in outdoor concerts organised every year to celebrate Quebec's national day. Being associated with this event provides strong legitimation for artists seeking recognition beyond commercial success. It increases the likelihood that their work will be considered as a major contribution to Quebec culture and, as a result, their ability to persist over time, even if they are only moderately successful. Having more limited access to these types of rewards, interpreters need to rely almost exclusively on commercial success to gain prestige and to pursue their careers.

Do the symbolic and material rewards granted almost exclusively to songwriters constitute a rent? The third order status of individual artists – and the rewards attached to it – undoubtedly reflects their performance on valued characteristics such as their ability to write good songs, their charisma when performing these songs, their commercial success, and their perceived contribution to Quebec culture and society. Part of their third order status, however, comes from membership in social categories. Regressing the prestige scores of individual artists on various features of their careers, I show that being associated with the most prestigious category of songwriters/rock/pop-rock artists has by far the strongest impact on prestige scores, much more so than individual characteristics such as being a songwriter as opposed to an interpreter, record sales, position on radio charts, and gender. This analysis supports the conclusion that a component of the third order status of artists constitutes a rent. It is derived from membership in the highly valued category of songwriters, which is itself linked to cultural schemas and resources based on gender and cultural capital.

Overall, my analysis of prestige among popular music artists in Quebec satisfies the main requirement of Sørensen's structural theory of inequality, which calls for the identification of advantages arising from positions in social structures rather than from individual talent and effort. I show how cultural schemas are transposed from one social context to another in a way that reproduces existing patterns of inequality. As a status schema, the distinction between songwriters and interpreters is related to other commonly-found cultural schemas opposing art to entertainment, artistic intention to profit-making, and authenticity to fabrication. It is also shaped by existing schemas and resources pertaining to gender and cultural capital. Part of the symbolic and material rewards obtained by artists comes from their membership these social categories.

My concern with structural sources of inequality should not be taken as an indication that I see status structures as static and immune to change. On the contrary, my research shows that the exclusion of interpreters/*artistes populaires*/country singers from certain honorific awards, as well as the lack of recognition of their contribution to Quebec culture and society, have been strongly contested over the years in the music industry, in the popular press, and in scholarly publications (ADISQ, 1988; Côté, 1983; Grenier, 1997). Efforts to rehabilitate the work of these artists have been partly successful, leading to a considerable erosion of the symbolic and organisational boundaries between songwriters and interpreters over the years. Comparing songwriters and interpreters at different stages in their careers, I show that differences in musical styles, organisational support, marketing strategies, educational attainment, prestige, honorific awards, and participation in cultural events are much less pronounced among younger artists than among older ones. More recent studies of popular music in Quebec documenting the coexistence of a plurality of musical styles within a unified music industry also support this conclusion (Grenier, 1997; Grenier & Guilbault, 1997).

Paradoxically, these trends could be taken as an indication that the configuration of schemas and resources identified in my study is a remnant of times past, thereby supporting postmodern predictions that status structures are being dismantled and replaced by more individualised forms of inequality. While there is clear evidence that the status structure identified in my study has lost much of its potency over the years, I argue, in the final section of this paper, that we may be witnessing the emergence of a new set of status schemas based on variations around the theme of openness to diversity. These status schemas offer a reservoir of socially valued significations, which can be transposed in a variety of social situations in ways which both reflect and sustain existing structures of inequality.

Conspicuous Openness to Diversity as a Master Cultural Schema

One of the most intriguing findings of recent research on tastes is the omnivore-univore pattern identified by Peterson in 1992. Research conducted in different countries, on various topics, and using a range of methodologies consistently show that high socioeconomic status respondents report preferences for, and participation in, the broadest range of cultural genres and activities, while low status respondents display more restricted tastes and practices (Bryson, 1996; Coulangeon, 2003; Donnat, 1994; Erickson, 1996, Holt, 1997; Peterson, 1992; Van Eijck, 2001; Warde et al., 1999). On the basis of these findings, several authors argue that what we call "conspicuous openness to diversity" (Fridman & Ollivier, 2004) has replaced high culture as a means of distinction among cultural elites. As argued by Peterson (1992), the model of the educated person is no longer the snob, displaying exclusive tastes for high culture and shunning commercial mass culture. Rather, the new ideal is the omnivore, who displays tastes for a diversity of multicultural objects and practices, which include high culture but are not restricted to it. Offering a slightly different interpretation, others argue that broad tastes serve not only as a means of distinction, but also as a conversational resource which facilitates access to wide social networks (Erickson, 1996). Wide networks, in turn, offer diversified sources of information which increase people's ability to act strategically in their personal and professional lives (Granovetter, 1995). In a world where relationships are increasingly anonymous and segmented, knowledge of a diversity of cultural codes appropriate in various social milieus, coupled with the ability to culture-switch according to circumstances, have become much more useful socially than knowledge of a restricted range of high culture symbols: eclectic *tastes* signal membership in exclusive elite circles while broad *cultural resources* facilitate interaction in widely-different social situations.

What is interesting in these studies is that diverse, eclectic, and cosmopolitan tastes are presented in a positive light, as an attribute of dominant groups and as sources of status and power. In exploratory research on the rhetoric of diversity in different fields, we found a strikingly similar pattern (Fridman & Ollivier, 2004).[2] Examples include: newspaper articles emphasising and celebrating the eclectic tastes of members of Quebec's cultural elites, with individual tastes described as ranging from baroque cello to rap music, from caviar to peanut butter, and from classical plays to romance novels (Germain, 2001a, b, c); government research on youth culture which argues that the rich and diversified cultural practices of young people "constitute a major asset for the economic and social development of Quebec" (Séguin-Noël & Garon, 2000, my translation); a *New York Times* supplement in which diversity is presented as a winning strategy in the competitive environment of the knowledge-based economy (*New York Times*, 2001); Naomi Klein's (2000) analysis of the marketing strategies of multinational corporations, which identify diversity as the key characteristic of the global youth market and as the core element of their brand identities; and political debates around multiculturalism, in which cosmopolitan multiculturalism, anchored in open, fluid, and elective identities, is presented as a means of social integration and thus as highly desirable, while pluralistic multiculturalism, based on the preservation of stable and permanent cultural identities, is seen as a potential source of divisive ethnic conflict (Hollinger, 2001).

These examples are arguably anecdotal, but taken together, they show a remarkably similar pattern. Invariably, terms such as diversity, openness, and cosmopolitanism are opposed to what is defined as unitary, homogeneous, and closed upon itself. The former terms are associated with what is dominant and desirable while the latter have more negative connotations. On the basis of these similarities, we developed two working hypotheses. Our first hypothesis is that the prevalence of the rhetoric of diversity across different fields may be symptomatic of the emergence of a new type of legitimate culture. The positive effects associated with diversity in social discourse may have over time a normative effect, prescribing new criteria for defining what is desirable and undesirable in the acquisition of culture. This legitimate culture, in turn, may be part of a larger discursive configuration based on a series of binary oppositions, whereby terms such as diverse, open, eclectic, global, cosmopolitan, educated, enlightened, dominant, and desirable on the one hand are opposed to what is defined as homogeneous, local, closed upon itself, uneducated, regressive, dominated, and undesirable on the other. These oppositions constitute a set of closely related cultural schemas, that is, intersubjectively shared cognitive structures used by social agents to organise their knowledge of the world into systems of categorisation and evaluation. Far from indicating that identities and social representations have become fragmented and localised, the emphasis on diversity, hybridity, eclecticism, and cosmopolitanism in social discourse could be taken as a sign that cultural schemas are transposed in highly similar ways across different situations.

In a globalize world, there is no question that broad cultural repertoires and attitudes of openness are highly desirable, whether as a superior moral stance, as a source of status and power for individuals, or as a means of maintaining peaceful relations within and between nations. What is problematic from our point of view, however, is that whereas openness to diversity is widely recognised as desirable, the capacity to acquire and express this attitude is not equally distributed among all social groups. Our second working hypothesis, then, is that the cultural schemas pertaining to diversity function as ideological codes (Alexander & Smith, 1993; Smith, 1999) or rhetorical devices, used by social agents to challenge or sustain unequal relations of power. Openness to diversity, we argue, is often most easily available to, and it frequently furthers the interests of, groups occupying positions of power in any given field.

In the field of tastes, valuing what is diverse, eclectic, and exotic as opposed to what is limited, unitary, and banal reintroduces some measure of scarcity, and thus of closure, among the infinite choices available under postmodern conditions. How to distinguish oneself when no clear distinction can be drawn between Bach's cello and Eminem's rap, or between classical plays and popular action movies? Conspicuous openness to diversity, we argue, presents a solution to this postmodern problem of distinction. As argued by Donnat, the display of eclectic tastes, which is the foundation of elite attitudes, "requires the combination of many assets in terms of cultural capital, personal availability, and proximity to the cultural events" (Donnat, 1994, p. 343, my translation). To the extent that people generally *like* what they *know* (Donnat, 1994), openness to diversity among high-status respondents is not only a question of *attitude*, but also a question of *resources*. Liking caviar as much as peanut butter, baroque cello as much as rap music, and classical plays as much as romance novels assumes that one has had the opportunity to taste caviar, to read classical plays, and to listen to Bach's cello. To the extent that tastes reflect people's strategies for defining themselves in relation to others, these strategies remain shaped in part by the resources available to them by virtue of their positions in social structures. Conspicuous openness to diversity and broad cultural resources may function, in some circumstances, as one source among others of cultural capital, in the bourdieusian sense of being *widely considered desirable* but *unequally distributed*. As a set of interlocking schemas and resources which "mutually imply and sustain each other over time" (Sewell, 1992, p. 13), they would thus constitute a new status structure.

Will broad cultural repertoires and openness to diversity ever provide rents to individuals in social interaction, just like knowledge of high culture has been shown to provide advantages in processes of educational attainment (DiMaggio & Mohr, 1985; Soares, 2002; Sullivan, 2002) and marital selection (DiMaggio & Mohr, 1985)? In other words, will the display of eclectic tastes and cosmopolitan attitudes become, in some circumstances, a criterion for allocating first-order status in a way that systematically advantages some social categories over others? This issue remains to be further investigated. Our research is still exploratory, the processes discussed here are in their infancy, and much work remains to be done to determine whether our working hypotheses represent figments of our imagination or fruitful directions for future research.

CONCLUSION

My main objective in this paper was to argue that despite any trend towards the fragmentation of social representations and the individualisation of inequality, some status structures continue to transcend local situations and to create enduring patterns of inequality between social categories. The framework presented here substantially departs from the structural theory of inequality developed by Sørensen (2000) in his "sounder basis for class analysis." Nonetheless, I believe that it stays true to his general vision of structural inequality as advantages obtained from positions in social structure rather than from the individual talent and effort of incumbents of these positions. It also remains true to his general objective of identifying positions in social structure which give rise to antagonistic interests and lead to social action. I define social structures as sets of mutually-sustaining schemas and resources which can be transposed in many different situations. Jasso's status framework provides a useful extension of Sørensen's approach because it defines positions in social structures as membership in social categories. Her distinction between the first-order status granted to individuals, the second-order status attached to social categories, and the third-order status arising from a combination of the two allows for the identification of returns that are rents according to Sørensen's earlier conception of the term. In societies based on the ideology of meritocratic achievement, status and other advantages arising from membership in social categories rather than from individual talent and effort are likely to be considered, by social scientists and most other people, as *unearned* and therefore as unfair and illegitimate. These advantages give rise to antagonistic interests and they are likely to be contested.

Using this framework, I show in my work on popular music in Quebec that the distinction between songwriters and interpreters, far from being a strictly local phenomenon, is linked to more pervasive sets of cultural schemas and resources. It is closely related to the commonly-found opposition between art and entertainment as well as to schemas and resources pertaining to gender and cultural capital. Part of the third-order prestige of songwriters comes from their own performance on valued, first-order characteristics, but part of it may be considered a rent in so far as it comes from membership in the category of songwriters, whose prestige is in turn linked to gender and cultural capital. The high prestige granted to songwriters as well as the advantages derived from it were contested over the years, leading to a gradual erosion of the status structure which had shaped popular music in Quebec since the 1960s. My work on tastes, while still exploratory, proposes that openness to diversity may be emerging as one of the master cultural schemas of our times. The prevalence of the rhetoric of diversity in different fields suggests that openness to diversity may become a criterion for allocating first-order status in a variety of social circumstances. If and when openness to diversity is more easily available to members of some social categories, it may give rise to benefits that are rents.

The framework outlined above provides some direction for future research on status. Without reducing all status beliefs to manifestations of a master cultural schema reproducing itself *ad infinitum*, studies of status in local settings should remain open to the possibility that status beliefs which appear to be context-specific are linked to similar patterns found in other social settings. Since rents are likely to be considered unfair, studies of status should also seek to identify situations in which the allocation of status is contested. For example, agents may compete in different fields so that their own attributes are accepted as legitimate criteria for allocating status; to make their own practices considered as embodying these valued characteristics; so that the advantages they receive from using their assets are perceived as resulting from individual effort rather than from membership in social categories; or to ensure that the rewards they receive from using an asset are perceived not as rents, but as a legitimate return for the provision of a public good. I'm not advocating a return to visions of status as a monolithic and all-encompassing set of beliefs, which closely reflects the distribution of material resources and tightly constrains social action. More simply, I argue that postmodern visions of fragmentation and individualisation capture only one aspect of current social change. Some cognitive structures continue to be widely-shared, to provide taken-for-granted assumptions about desirable and undesirable features of social life, and to supply members of social categories who embody these features with enduring collective advantages.

NOTES

1. In this context, the term *artistes populaire* refers to artists whose songs are aimed at a wide audience and do not seek to convey a profound message. The classification of artists

into groups was achieved through multidimensional scaling and hierarchical clustering of the sorting data obtained from respondents. At the most general level of analysis, one category includes primarily songwriters, rock, and pop-rock artists, while the other comprised mostly interpreters, *artistes populaires*, and country singers. The distinction between songwriters and interpreters is by far the most salient criteria of demarcation between the two categories. Each of these categories is further subdivided into older and younger artists. The older generation of songwriters/rock/pop-rock artists has the highest average prestige scores followed by their younger counterparts. Younger interpreters/*artistes populaires*/country singers come next while older artists in this category have the lowest prestige.

2. This section is based on my work with Viviana Fridman from the Université du Québec à Montréal.

ACKNOWLEDGMENTS

I remain deeply indebted to Aage Sørensen for the warm and intellectually challenging support he so generously provided over the years. I also thank François Gobeil, Stephen L. Morgan, and John Myles for their helpful comments on earlier drafts. Research presented here was supported by several grants from the Social Science and Humanities Research Council of Canada.

REFERENCES

ADISQ (1988). *Les retombées promotionnelles, artistiques et économiques du Gala des Félix, 1979–1987*. Montréal: ADISQ.

ADISQ (1989). *Disponibilité de la musique vocale de langue française: Le contexte économique et industriel*. Montréal: ADISQ.

Alexander, J., & Smith, P. (1993). The discourses of American civil society: A new proposal for cultural studies. *Theory and Society*, *22*(2), 151–207.

Barber, B. (1957). *Social stratification: A comparative analysis of structure and process*. New York: Harcourt, Brace, and World.

Bauman, Z. (1988). *Freedom*. Milton Keynes: Open University Press.

Beck, U. (1992). *Risk society: Towards a new modernity*. London: Sage.

Blau, P. (1963). *The dynamics of bureaucracy*. Chicago: University of Chicago Press.

Blau, P. (1967). *Exchange and power in social life*. New York: Wiley.

Blau, P., & Schwartz, J. E. (1984). *Crosscutting social circles*. Orlando: Academic Press.

Bloom, A. (1987). *The closing of the American mind*. New York: Simon & Shuster.

Boudon, R. (1995). *Le juste et le vrai : Études sur l'objectivité des valeurs et de la connaissance*. Paris: Fayard.

Bourdieu, P. (1977). *Outline of a theory of practice*. Cambridge: Cambridge University Press.

Bourdieu, P. (1979). *La distinction*. Paris: Les Éditions de Minuit.

Bourdieu, P. (1983). The field of cultural production, or: The economic world reversed. *Poetics*, *12*, 311–356.

Bourdieu, P. (1984). *Homo academicus*. Paris: Éditions de Minuit.

Bourdieu, P., & Passeron, J.-C. (1977). *Reproduction in education, society, and culture*. London: Sage.

Bryson, B. (1996). Anything but heavy metal: Symbolic exclusion and musical dislikes. *American Sociological Review*, *61*, 884–899.

Collins, R. (1979). *The credential society*. New York: Academic Press.

Collins, R. (2000). Situational stratification: A micro-macro theory of inequality. *Sociological Theory*, *18*(1), 17–43.

Côté, C. (1983). La musique Pop au Québec. *La revue Yé-Yé*, *1*(7), 4–7.

Coulangeon, P. (2003). La stratification sociale des goûts musicaux. Le modèle de la légitimité culturelle en question. *Revue française de sociologie*, *44*(1), 3–33.

Davis, K., & Moore, W. E. (1945). Some principles of stratification. *American Sociological Review*, *10*, 242–249.

DiMaggio, P. (1987). Classification in art. *American Sociological Review*, *52*, 440–455.

DiMaggio, P. (1997). Culture and cognition. *Annual Review of Sociology*, *23*, 263–287.

DiMaggio, P., & Mohr, J. (1985). Cultural capital, educational attainment, and marital selection. *American Journal of Sociology*, *90*(6), 1231–1261.

Donnat, O. (1994). *Les Français face à la culture. De l'exclusion à l'éclectisme*. Paris: Éditions la Découverte.

Douglas, M. (1979). *In the active voice*. London: Routledge & Kegan Paul.

Durkheim, É. (1967). *Le suicide*. Paris: Presses universitaires de France.

Erickson, B. (1996). Culture, class, and connections. *American Journal of Sociology*, *102*(1), 217–235.

Finkielkraut, A. (1995). *The defeat of the mind*. New York: Columbia University Press.

Forge, A. (1970). Prestige, influence, and sorcery: A New Guinea example. In: M. Douglas (Ed.), *Witchcraft Accusations and Confessions*. London: Tarrstock.

Fridman, V., & Ollivier, M. (2002). Les cretons autant que le caviar ou l'érosion des hiérarchies culturelles. *Loisirs et sociétés/Leisure and Society*, *25*(1), 37–54.

Fridman, V., & Ollivier, M. (2004). Ouverture ostentatoire à la diversité et cosmopolitisme. Vers une nouvelle configuration discursive? *Sociologie et sociétés*, *36*(1), 105–126.

Germain, G.-H. (2001a). Plamondon à la recherche d'un goût perdu. *Le Devoir* (January 20–21), A1.

Germain, G.-H. (2001b). Du rap au violoncelle. *Le Devoir* (March 17–18), A1.

Germain, G.-H. (2001c). Profession: junkie culturel. *Le Devoir* (April 28–29), A1.

Giddens, A. (1984). *The constitution of society: Outline of the theory of structuration*. Cambridge: Polity Press.

Gilbert, D., & Kahl, J. A. (1982). *The American class structure: A new synthesis*. Homewood, IL: Dorsey Press.

Goldthorpe, J. H. (2000). Rent, class conflict, and class structure: A commentary on Sørensen. *American Journal of Sociology*, *105*(6), 1572–1582.

Greenfeld, L. (1989). *Different worlds: A sociological study of taste, choice and success in art*. Cambridge: Cambridge University Press.

Grenier, L. (1997). '*Je me souviens*' ... en chansons: Articulations de la citoyenneté culturelle et de l'identitaire dans le champ musical populaire au Québec. *Sociologie et sociétés*, *29*(2), 31–47.

Grenier, L., & Guilbault, J. (1997). *Créolité* and *Francophonie* in music: Socio-musical repositioning where it matters. *Cultural Studies*, *11*(2), 207–234.

Granovetter, M. (1995). *Getting a job: A study of contacts and careers*. Chicago: University of Chicago Press.

Hagstrom, W. O. (1965). *The scientific community*. New York: Basic Books.

Hall, J. R. (1992). The capital(s) of culture: A nonholistic approach to status situations, class, gender, and ethnicity. In: M. Lamont & M. Fournier (Eds), *Cultivating Differences: Symbolic Boundaries and the Making of Inequality* (pp. 257–288). Chicago and London: University of Chicago Press.

Hodge, R. W., Krauss, V., & Schild, E. O. (1982). Consensus in occupational prestige ratings: Response to Guppy. *Social Forces*, *60*(4), 1190–1196.

Hollinger, D. A. (2001). Not universalists, not pluralists: The new cosmopolitans find their own way. *Constellation*, *8*(2), 236–248.

Holt, D. B. (1997). Distinction in America? Recovering Bourdieu's theory of tastes from its critics. *Poetics*, *25*, 93–120.

Homans, G. (1950). *The human group*. New York: Harcourt, Brace and Company.

Jasso, G. (2000). Studying status: An integrated framework. *American Sociological Review*, *66*(1), 96–124.

Klein, N. (2000). *No logo: Taking aim at the brand bullies*. Toronto: Random House.

Lahire, B. (1998). *L'homme pluriel. Les ressorts de l'action*. Paris, Nathan.

Lamont, M., & Fournier, M. (1992). *Cultivating differences: Symbolic boundaries and the making of inequality*. Chicago and London: University of Chicago Press.

Lamont, M., & Thévenot, L. (Eds) (2000). *Rethinking comparative cultural sociology: Repertoires of evaluation in France and the United States*. London: Cambridge University Press.

Lenski, G. E. (1984). *Power and privilege: A theory of social stratification*. Chapel Hill: University of North Carolina Press.

Lipovetsky, G. (1994). *The empire of fashion: Dressing modern democracy*. Princeton: Princeton University Press.

Lowenthal, L. (1961). *Literature, popular culture, and society*. Englewood Cliffs, NJ: Prentice-Hall.

Merriam-Webster Online (2002). Online at www.m-w.com/home.htm. Consulted in August.

Meiselas, S. (1976). *Carnival strippers*. New York: Farrar, Strauss & Giroux.

Milner, M., Jr. (1996). Geeks, weirdos, and cool kids: Status among American adolescents. Paper presented at the Annual Meeting of the American Sociological Association, New York.

Murphy, R. (1988). *Social closure: The theory of monopolization and exclusion*. Oxford: Clarendon Press.

Ollivier, M. (1994). *Prestige and social closure in the arts: The case of popular music artists in Québec*. Doctoral Thesis presented to the Department of Sociology, Harvard University, Cambridge, MA.

Ollivier, M. (1997). Measuring symbolic boundaries among artists. *Poetics*, *24*, 299–328.

Ollivier, M. (forthcoming). Snobs and quétaines: Prestige and boundaries in popular music in Quebec. *Popular Music*, *24*.

Ollivier, M., & Fridman, V. (2001). Taste/taste cultures. *International Encyclopedia of the Social and Behavioral Sciences*. London: Elsevier.

Ostrower, F. (1995). *Why the wealthy give: The culture of elite philanthropy*. Princeton: Princeton University Press.

Pakulski, J., & Waters, M. (1996). *The death of class*. London, Thousand Oaks, Calif: Sage.

Parkin, F. (1979). *Marxism and class theory: A bourgeois critique*. London: Tavistock.

Parsons, T. (1954). An analytical approach to the theory of social stratification. In: *Essays in Sociological Theory*. New York: Free Press.

Peterson, R. A. (1992). Understanding audience segmentation: From elite and mass to omnivore and univore. *Poetics*, *21*, 243–258.

Ridgeway, C. L. (1997). The conservation of gender inequality. *American Sociological Review*, *62*, 218–235.

Ridgeway, C., & Erickson, K. G. (2000). Creating and spreading status beliefs. *American Journal of Sociology*, *106*(3), 579–615.

Rueschemeyer, D., & Mahoney, J. (2000). A neo-utilitarian theory of class? *American Journal of Sociology*, *105*(6), 1583–1591.

Schecter, S., & Paquet, B. (2000). Inclusion et exclusion à l'aune de la sociologie Luhmanienne: l'exemple de la pauvreté au Canada. *Sociologie et Sociétés*, *32*(2), 211–232.

Séguin-Noël, R., & Garon, R. (2000). *Les pratiques culturelles des jeunes de 15 à 35 ans en 1999*. Ministère de la Culture et des Communications, online at http://mcc.quebectel.qc.ca/Mcc/ClinStat.nsf/Theme?OpenView.

Sewell, W. H., Jr. (1992). A theory of structure: Duality, agency and transformation. *American Journal of Sociology*, *98*, 1–29.

Shils, E. (1975). *Centre and periphery: Essays in macrosociology*. Chicago: University of Chicago Press.

Smith, D. E. (1999). *Writing the social: Critique, theory, and investigations*. Toronto, University of Toronto Press.

Soares, J. (2002). Cultural capital and elite educational reproduction of ivy league families in the 1960s and 1970s. Paper presented at the Meeting of the American Sociological Association, Chicago.

Sørensen, A. (1994). The basic concepts of stratification research: Class, status, and power. In: D. B. Grusky (Ed.), *Social Stratification: Race, Class, and Gender in Sociological Perspective* (pp. 229–241). Boulder, CO: Westview.

Sørensen, A. (1996). The structural basis of social inequality. *American Journal of Sociology*, *101*(5), 1333–1365.

Sørensen, A. (2000). Toward a sounder basis for class analysis. *American Journal of Sociology*, *105*(6), 1523–1558.

Sullivan, A. (2002). Cultural capital and educational attainment. *Sociology*, *35*(4), 893–912.

Swidler, A. (1986). Culture in action: Symbols and strategies. *American Sociological Review*, *51*, 273–286.

Tilly, C. (1998). *Durable inequality*. Berkeley: University of California Press.

Valian, V. (1998). *Why so slow? The advancement of women*. Cambridge: MIT Press.

Van Eijck, K. (2001). Social differentiation in musical taste pattern. *Social Forces*, *79*(3), 1161–1184.

Warde, A., Martens, L., & Olsen, W. (1999). Consumption and the problem of variety: Cultural omnivorousness, social distinction, and dining out. *Sociology*, *33*, 105–127.

Warner, L. W., Meeker, M., & Eels, K. (1960). *Social class in America*. New York: Harper & Row.

Weber, M. (1978). *Economy and society*. Berkeley: University of California Press.

Wellman, B., & Hampton, K. (1999). Living networked on and offline. *Contemporary Sociology*, *28*(6), 648–655.

SOCIAL CLASS, RENT DESTRUCTION, AND THE EARNINGS OF BLACK AND WHITE MEN, 1982–2000

Stephen L. Morgan and Mark W. McKerrow

ABSTRACT

Adopting a consistent social class schema for March CPS data, we analyze trends from 1982 to 2000 in social class and black-white differences in the earnings of men. After presenting the well-known recent growth in earnings inequality within an EGP social class framework, we then show that the steady decline in the black-white gap among full-time, full-year workers is concentrated among semi-skilled and unskilled workers (classes VI and VIIa) and is particularly pronounced among supervisors of manual workers (a large proportion of class V). Three explanations account for this pattern. First, in the context of growing wage inequality across the entire labor market, white men at the bottom of the class distribution have been unable to maintain their wage advantages over their black counterparts to the same degree that white men at the top of the class distribution have. Second, rates of labor market non-participation among low-skilled black men increased in the 1980s and 1990s (though not as much as they increased in the 1960s and 1970s), and this selection out of the labor force has accentuated the decline in the relative earnings gaps observed for classes V, VI, and VIIa. Third, the tight labor market of the 1990s has disproportionately helped low-skilled black men. The relative weighting of these three explanations cannot

Inequality: Structures, Dynamics and Mechanisms: Essays in Honor of Aage B. Sørensen
Research in Social Stratification and Mobility, Volume 21, 215–251

ISSN: 0276-5624/doi:10.1016/S0276-5624(04)21011-3

be determined definitively with any available data, but the first explanation deserves at least as much attention as the latter two, has not been sufficiently developed in the literature on the black-white gap, and is consistent with the heretofore unevaluated rent destruction explanation for increases in inequality of Sørensen (2000). Taken together, the findings demonstrate the continued value of traditional modes of social class analysis for the study of inequality in post-industrial society.

INTRODUCTION

Examining social class differences in the earnings of black and white men from 1982 through 2000, we will show that the significance of race for labor market inequality among men has changed in the economic transformation of the 1980s and 1990s. In the course of analysis, we will argue that there has been a relative decline in the importance of race at the bottom of the earnings distribution of men and that this change can be explained in large part by general increases in earnings inequality. In developing this argument, we engage three related strands of literature – explanations for growth in earnings inequality in the U.S. labor market since the early 1980s (see Card & DiNardo, 2002; Katz & Autor, 1999), empirical examinations of the relative position of black men over the same time period (e.g. Grodsky & Pager, 2001; Wilson, 1987, 1996), and recent theoretical elaborations of the structural foundations of social class (Goldthorpe, 2000; Sørensen, 1996, 2000).[1]

PAST FINDINGS ON CHANGES IN INEQUALITY AND BLACK-WHITE DIFFERENCES IN EARNINGS

In the transformation of the U.S. economy in the 1980s and 1990s, labor market inequality increased dramatically across years of completed education and even more comprehensively within almost all measured categories of workers (see Katz & Autor, 1999). As a result, earnings inequality in the U.S. labor market is now more pronounced than perhaps at any time since World War II. Despite the theoretical importance and public recognition of these trends, relatively little sociological literature has investigated the causal mechanisms responsible for generating them (see Morris & Western, 1999). Even a descriptive agenda has not been pursued seriously, as there is little or no published literature on the growth in earnings gaps between social classes.[2]

Within the relevant economics literature, no strong evidence in support of a single explanatory narrative has emerged. Where there was some initial agreement, surrounding the explanation of skill-biased technological change (see Berman et al., 1994, 1998), Morris and Western (1999, p. 635) surmise that "something other than science" fortified the initial enthusiasm.[3] And, thus, in addition to technological change, many labor economists are willing to accept that an unknown mixture of demographic shifts in the early 1980s, globalization, deindustrialization, and associated declines in union membership and negotiating power also seem responsible for a substantial portion of the increase (see the SDI framework of Katz & Autor, 1999; see also Bernstein & Mishel, 2001; Card & DiNardo, 2002).

Alongside these more general changes in inequality, the black-white gap in the earnings of men has changed over the past several decades as well. Here again no explanation has achieved dominance, and the extant sociological literature is rather thin. Certainly sociologists have studied trends in black-white differences in occupational attainment (e.g. Hout, 1984) and in labor force participation (e.g. Jargowsky, 1997).[4] Again, however, economists have dominated the study of trends in black-white earnings differentials (see Bound & Freeman, 1992; Bound & Holzer, 1993; Card & Lemieux, 1994, 1996; Juhn et al., 1991). Altonji and Blank (1999) summarize the economics literature, highlighting several common empirical findings. Although the black-white earnings gap decreased dramatically between 1960 and 1980, it has since remained relatively stable. And for the last two decades, two countervailing trends must be separated. Black men continued to narrow some of the wage gap by acquiring more education, and perhaps also by securing higher occupational attainments above and beyond that which can be attributed to their increased educational attainments. But because the earnings of low-skilled workers have not kept pace with high-skilled workers over the same period and because black men still on average have lower educational attainments than white men, the gains won by increased educational attainment have been wiped out almost entirely in the aggregate.

Although this basic two-part narrative seems to have been widely accepted in the mid-1990s, considerable ferment emerged in the late 1990s over fine points that do and do not support it. The work collected in Cherry and Rodgers (2000), especially Freeman and Rodgers (2000), argues that the tight labor market of the 1990s disproportionately benefitted black men relative to their white counterparts. Not only did unemployment fall relatively more for blacks throughout the 1990s, but the wages of blacks appear to have increased relative to whites, particularly at the bottom of the distribution of educational attainment. Others, however, have countered these claims, arguing that race differences in patterns of incarceration (see Western & Pettit, 2000) and slight increases in relative non-employment among blacks (even in the context of declining unemployment) may have created illusory gains (see also Juhn, 2001). This counter-argument represents a re-birth of arguments that as much as 50% of the wage gains observed in the 1960s and 1970s for blacks represent artefactual increases attributable to gradually increasing labor market non-participation (see Brown, 1984; Heckman et al., 2000; Jaynes, 1990; Juhn, 1992; Smith & Welch, 1989; Welch, 1990).

WHAT ROLE FOR CLASS ANALYSIS?

To the extent that sociologists are more predisposed than economists to regard labor market positions as more fundamental than individuals' attributes, a *prima facie* sociological depiction of changes in inequality would focus on the linkage between earnings levels and alternative occupational positions, the latter being conceptualized broadly as social class position. And yet, as we noted earlier, a straightforward and sufficiently complete class-based descriptive analysis of recent trends in earnings inequality cannot be found in the literature. Should such an agenda be pursued?

Debates over the optimal form of class analysis for future research have proliferated in recent years (see Grusky & Weeden, 2001; Portes, 2000; Sørensen, 2000; along with their associated comments and replies). These debates are crucial for refining the conceptual foundations of research on social inequality, but they should not be allowed to crowd out empirical research with the tools at our disposal. New empirical work gives these debates more material with which to grapple, extending the terrain of contestation beyond the classic conjectures of the 1960s through 1980s on patterns of social fluidity and styles of life.

In this article, we aim primarily to move the empirical literature forward and hence will offer a straightforward social class decomposition of trends in earnings inequality, focusing narrowly on the earnings of black and white men (see Note 1). And, we will use only one of the social class schemas that is available, the one variously known as the EGP schema (after Erikson et al., 1979), Goldthorpe's class schema (after Goldthorpe, 1987), or the CASMIN coding (after Goldthorpe & Müller, 1982). Although many class mappings exist in the sociological literature, in the past two decades the EGP schema has become the most prominent, primarily because it has been effectively deployed in a wide variety of substantive contexts, such as in studies of social mobility (e.g. Erikson & Goldthorpe, 1992; Hout, 1989) and voting (e.g. Heath et al., 1985; Manza & Brooks, 1999). The EGP schema has also received a recent theoretical justification (see Goldthorpe, 2000) grounded on a broad set of literature from both economics and sociology, and has been introduced into the economics literature (see Erikson & Goldthorpe, 2002). Table 1 presents descriptions of the EGP social classes. Our analysis is based on our own coding of the 1980 and 1990 census occupation codes and is available from the authors by request.

Table 1. Descriptions for the EGP Social Class Schema.

Social Class	Description
I	Higher-grade professionals, administrators, and officials; managers in large industrial establishments; large proprietors
II	Lower-grade professionals, administrators, and officials; higher-grade technicians; managers in small industrial establishments; supervisors of non-manual employees
IIIa	Routine non-manual employees, higher-grade (administration and commerce)
IIIb	Routine non-manual employees, lower-grade (sales and service)
IVa and IVb	Small proprietors, artisans, and other self-employed workers
IVc	Farmers and small-holders and other self-employed workers in primary production
V	Supervisors of manual workers; lower grade technicians
VI	Skilled manual workers
VIIa	Semi- and unskilled manual workers (not in agriculture)
VIIb	Agricultural and other workers in primary production, not self-employed

Note: A detailed account of our coding of the class schema is provided in a supplementary appendix.

For our analysis, EGP classes serve as attractive vantage points from which to track the evolution of earnings differentials in the U.S. labor market. We do not regard the fine contours of labor market outcomes as the residue of overt class struggle, and hence we do not maintain that earnings are distributed according to the EGP class structure. Rather, the EGP class schema merely furnishes for us a useful grouping of structural positions in the labor market, clustered along specific (but not exhaustive) dimensions of employment relations.[5] We leave arguments for the general superiority of the EGP class schema, vis-à-vis its alternatives, to its creators (see Erikson & Goldthorpe, 2002; Goldthorpe, 2000), but we will offer some justification for its adoption in this application.

As a predictive tool, the EGP schema performs well in accounting for changes in inequality.[6] Indeed, as we will show later, had it been deployed in the late 1980s and early 1990s when economists were documenting movement in the college wage premium, sociologists may have discovered the growth in inequality.

And yet, predictive power, although attractive, is surely an insufficient justification on its own for deploying the EGP schema. We therefore offer four additional reasons for adopting the EGP schema for an analysis of changes in inequality in sociology:

(1) Why should sociology allow labor economists to define the explananda of interest for sociologists? The increase in the college wage premium is surely worthy of investigation, but narrowly focusing on the divergence between the mean earnings of classes I and V in the EGP framework is likewise interesting, especially when examining cross-cutting patterns of ascriptive inequality that have traditionally been framed with the language of social class.

(2) Although gross measures of inequality (e.g. Gini coefficients, Theil indices) will continue to be the dominant metric for cross-national comparisons of earnings distributions, EGP classes represent a more promising basis for first-order decompositions of any such cross-national differences. There appears to be considerably less variability across industrialized countries in the division of labor than in educational institutions. And, even more narrowly within the U.S., there is a great deal of unexamined heterogeneity, which arises from different types of educational institutions, within typical "years completed" measures of educational attainment. While EGP classes can be decomposed to the unit-occupation-level, with data such as the CPS no similar decomposition can be performed for different levels of educational attainment. Thus, while one can offer careful within-class adjustments for compositional change (as we will offer in Tables 3 and 4), no similarly direct adjustment can be offered for groups delineated by years of completed education.

(3) A class-based approach allows for a more explicit connection of studies of earnings inequality to traditional modes of analysis in social stratification research, primarily in social mobility studies (e.g. Erikson & Goldthorpe, 1992). Certainly, at some point in the future, we will want to answer the questions: Have these changes in earnings inequality affected regimes of social mobility? And if so, have the changes in mobility patterns been more dramatic in the U.S. where the increase in earnings inequality has been the greatest, perhaps thus lending support to the currently out-of-favor contention of American exceptionalism (see Erikson & Goldthorpe, 1985)?

(4) Narrative accounts of structural change are more naturally constructed using results generated by a class schema, especially when collective action and institutional constraints are important elements of the plot. Class analysis provides actors, albeit of an aggregated sort, that can be used to construct compelling accounts. How such narratives are best developed has become a contentious issue in the recent literature. For detailed "realist" narratives, Grusky and Sørensen (1998) and Grusky and Weeden (2001) have argued that aggregate actors considerably more narrowly defined than those suggested by the EGP schema are required. And yet, for sufficiently parsimonious and compelling narratives, Portes (2000) has argued that some sort of nominalist big class schema must be adopted, although not necessarily the EGP schema which we surmise he would regard as too rigidly bound by the occupational categories invented for national censuses and surveys.

For our application, we are satisfied that the EGP schema allows us to effectively and elegantly convey the descriptive findings of our analysis and hence serves justifications 1 through 3 outlined here. However, as will become clear in our discussion section, where we invoke the rent-based social class framework of Sørensen (1996, 2000), the EGP schema must also be supplemented conceptually in this particular application in order to account for within-class race differences. We do not regard the need for such supplementation as a fundamental limitation of the EGP class schema. Rather, to us, it demonstrates the utility of the schema, as it can accommodate many such types of supplementation, and hence allows for refinements in pursuit of a compelling explanatory narrative.

PLAN FOR EMPIRICAL ANALYSIS

Against this background of literature, we pursue answers to a series of descriptive questions:

(1) How has the black-white gap in the earnings of men evolved over the last several decades?
(2) How have EGP class differentials in the earnings of black and white men evolved since 1982?

In response, we show that a slight decline in the black-white gap has occurred in spite of generalized growth in earnings inequality across social classes. Attempting to reconcile these findings, we then ask:

(3) Is the decline in the black-white gap entirely attributable to changes in class entry rates?
(4) If not, is the black-white gap in earnings among men declining at the same modest rate within each class? Or, alternatively, is there interpretable variation in the decline across social class?

Although straightforward, these questions require careful modeling, especially when the limitations of the Current Population Surveys are recognized and the potential impact of self-selection out of the labor force is assessed. Nonetheless, the effort is justified, as the findings suggest important implications for the evolution of inequality in the late-twentieth century U.S. labor market. In the concluding section, we discuss these implications, drawing upon the rent destruction explanation for increases in inequality promoted by Sørensen (1996, 2000).

DATA AND VARIABLES

We analyze labor force data drawn from the 1964 through 2001 March Current Population Surveys. For the majority of our analysis, however, we restrict attention to the 1983 through 2001 March CPS data, and hence the analysis of prior-year earnings data from 1982 through 2000. We chose this more limited time frame to allow for a consistent and detailed coding of social class using 1980 and 1990 3-digit census occupation codes. Nonetheless, this nineteen-year time period is the focus of the literature on recent increases in earnings inequality and also nicely brackets the two most recent economic expansions (1983–1989 and 1992–2000, interrupted by the 1990–1991 downturn). In some of our analysis, we will explicitly compare the last five years of these two most recent economic expansions in an attempt to remove business cycle effects from our over-time comparisons. Presumably, at some point in the future, the 1990–1991 recession should be compared to the recession of the early 2000s, but we do not attempt such a comparison here (in part because it is unclear whether the latter has yet been completed). For all of our models, we analyze weekly earnings, converted to constant 2000 dollars using the Personal Consumption Expenditures Deflator (PCED). For the CPS, earnings values are top-coded to preserve the anonymity of respondents, and the top codes change periodically over the years. To create a uniform dataset, we imposed the lowest top-code for any year on all years, after having converted each year's values to 2000 dollars. We then multiplied the common topcode by a multiplier calculated using a method inspired by Pareto, which varied from 1.50 to 1.76 over the years.[7]

Our detailed coding of the EGP class schema (from the 1980 and 1990 census occupations codes and the employer size variable) is available in an extensive supplementary appendix that is available from the authors by request. For the regression models reported in Tables 3 and 4, we used standard codings of CPS variables for education, marital status, urbanicity, and region. Details of these coding decisions, along with those used to analyze more general patterns of labor force participation, are also available in the supplementary appendix.

RESULTS

The Evolution of Earnings Differentials Among Men in the 1980s and 1990s

We begin our empirical analysis by linking our findings to the established literature on the black-white gap in the earnings of men. Figure 1 presents five-year moving averages from 1963 to 2000 of the difference in log weekly earnings between

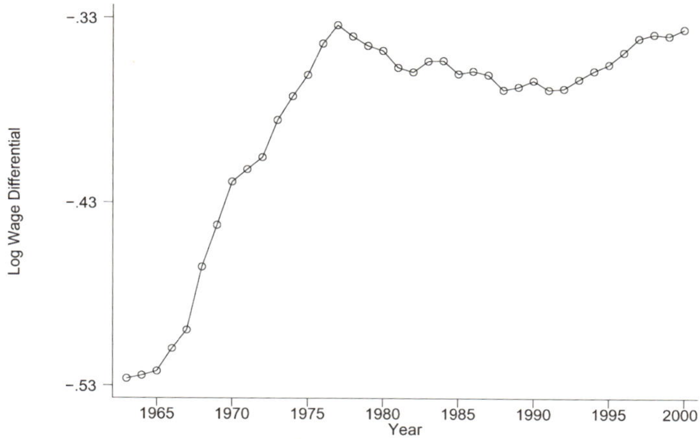

Fig. 1. Raw Earnings Gap of Black Men Relative to White Men, Log Weekly Earnings, 1963–2000.

black and white men employed full-time, full-year (i.e. working at least 35 hours per week in a typical week and employed for at least 50 weeks per year).[8] Over the entire time series, a sizable race gap in the earnings of men is present, never falling below 0.33 on the log scale for weekly earnings (which corresponds to a difference, for example, of approximately 835 dollars per week for whites and only 600 dollars per week for blacks). Even though the black-white gap remains large over the entire time series, Fig. 1 shows that the measured gap has declined, as argued in the literature summarized earlier. However, the initial increase in the gap in the 1980s, followed by its decline thereafter, awaits a compelling explanation. And, it is therefore this last period on which we focus in this article, as it also corresponds to the main period of growth in earnings inequality across the entire labor market.

Figure 2 presents five-year moving averages of the weekly earnings of all white and black men employed full-time, full-year (hereafter, FTFY) in classes I, II, IIIa, IIIb, V, VI, and VIIa from 1982 to 2000. The well-documented growth in earnings inequality is evident, although here for the first time we can see it as growth in between-class inequality. In particular, the class-specific trend lines diverge from 1982 onward and do not narrow substantially even in the robust economic expansion of the late 1990s that lifted the wages of all workers. The weekly earnings of workers in class V, which includes supervisors of manual workers, fell below the average wages of workers in class II. Likewise, the weekly earnings of semi-skilled and unskilled manufacturing workers in classes VI and VIIa fell below those of

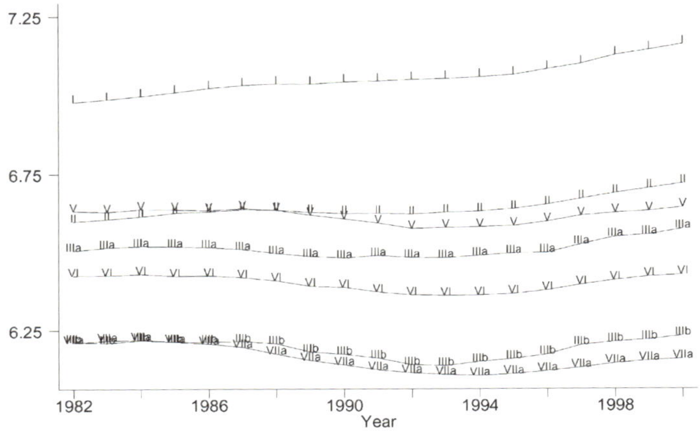

Fig. 2. Log Weekly Earnings by EGP Social Class for Black and White Males Who Work Full-time, Full-Year.

routine non-manual workers in classes IIIa and IIIb. All three trends reflect the relative decline in the fortunes of those employed in the manufacturing sector.

To examine how changes in the black-white gap are associated with general increases in inequality across the labor market, the first step is to examine changes in the distributions of white and black men across social classes. Accordingly, we analyze pooled data from the last five years of the two most recent economic expansions in the United Sates, 1985 through 1989 and 1996 through 2000.[9]

For each of these two time periods, Table 2 presents the proportion of FTFY workers employed in each of the EGP classes summarized in Table 1 separately for white and black men. Two trends are clear. First, the black-white difference in the distribution of men across social classes declined from the late 1980s through the 1990s. Sizable differences still remain, with blacks much less likely to be employed in classes I and II, but their proportional representation within classes continued to converge to that of whites. Second, the class distribution among white and black men has changed slightly, and this structural shift is most clearly revealed in over-time differences in the proportions of white men in each of the EGP classes (since the changes over time for blacks are confounded by inter-generational upward mobility). In particular, the proportion of whites who are employed in classes I and VIIa increased while the proportion employed in classes II and V decreased.

As shown in Fig. 2, the earnings advantages that classes I, II, IIIa, and IIIb have over classes V, VI, and VIIa increased in the 1980s and 1990s. Even though black men moved out of classes VI and VIIa over this time period, the declining relative earnings of these classes, in which blacks were still much more likely

Table 2. Proportion of Full-time, Full-year White and Black Males in Each Social Class for the Last Five Years of the Two Most Recent Economic Expansions.

	White Males (Ages: 18–64)		Black Males (Ages: 18–64)	
	1985–1989	1996–2000	1985–1989	1996–2000
I	0.193	0.199	0.082	0.097
II	0.236	0.227	0.137	0.163
IIIa	0.061	0.059	0.086	0.082
IIIb	0.022	0.025	0.019	0.031
IVab	0.035	0.032	0.014	0.019
IVc	0.009	0.008	0.0003	0.001
V	0.076	0.067	0.067	0.068
VI	0.158	0.156	0.136	0.128
VIIa	0.197	0.213	0.449	0.407
VIIb	0.011	0.014	0.010	0.005

to be employed, limited the progress that otherwise would have been achieved in mitigating the unconditional black-white gap. We therefore conclude that the basic social class decomposition presented jointly in Fig. 2 and Table 2 is consistent with the dominant interpretation of economists through the mid-1990s (see the discussion of Altonji & Blank, 1999, earlier). Blacks may have experienced increasing educational and occupational attainment, but declines in the overall black-white gap in earnings were modest at best because of general increases in inequality.

We now look within social classes at the black-white gap in order to understand how the gap varies across social classes and, more importantly, how this variation has changed over time. The social class breakdown allows for a theoretically-grounded exploration of the heterogeneity of the black-white gap across different locations in the labor market. Of course, there is considerable controversy over whether the EGP schema locates theoretically meaningful categories of positions (see debates cited earlier), centering on whether one is willing to accept the general employment relations perspective of Erikson and Goldthorpe (1992), most recently elaborated in Goldthorpe (2000). Although we do not wish to strongly endorse such arguments, we would argue that: (1) they have not been refuted by anyone; and (2) at least for our project, as we will now show, the EGP schema does generate a pattern of interpretable heterogeneity of the black-white gap that we see as compelling.

Accordingly, for Fig. 3, we calculated the raw wage gap within each of the EGP classes analyzed for Fig. 2, again only for black and white male FTFY workers.

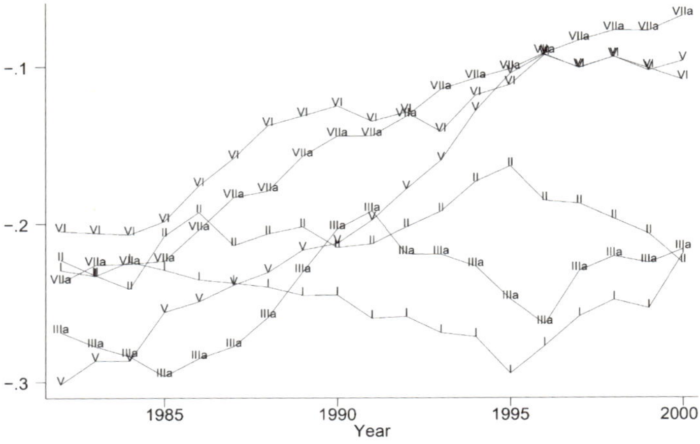

Fig. 3. Black-White Earnings Gap by Social Class.

To be precise, the estimates plotted in Fig. 3 are five-year moving averages within each EGP class of a simple difference in sample expectations:

$$E_N[Y_i|B_i = 0, \text{FTFY}_i = 1] - E_N[Y_i|B_i = 1, \text{FTFY}_i = 1], \quad \text{(E1)}$$

where FTFY_i is a dummy variable for full-time, full-year workers.[10]

Figure 3 demonstrates that there is substantial heterogeneity across social class of the black-white gap in the weekly earnings of men. In particular, the black-white gap seems to have narrowed dramatically for class V (supervisors of manual workers and lower grade technicians) and to a lesser but still substantial degree for classes VI and VIIa (skilled, semi-skilled, and unskilled manual workers). At the same time, however, the gap may have increased slightly for class I (higher-grade professionals and managers) and decreased only slightly for class II (lower-grade professionals and managers; higher-grade technicians; supervisors of non-manual workers) and class IIIa (higher-grade non-manual workers).[11]

If this pattern is genuine, then it has important implications for explanations of both the black-white gap in the earnings of men and general increases in earnings inequality across classes. Before laying out these implications, in the next section we will show that the trends are, as best we can tell, genuine. They are substantively non-trivial, statistically significant, cannot be explained by trends in the observable characteristics of black and white men, and are not produced by self-selection out of employment because of race-specific costs or other institutional factors.

A Formal Linear Test of the Relative Decline in the Black-White Gap

Although results such as those presented in Figs 1 through 3 can be regarded as primarily descriptive, when enacting adjustments for observed and unobserved characteristics, one inevitably confronts the challenges of causal inference. In an attempt to be as explicit as possible about how we will interpret the results of this section, we will adopt the counterfactual model of causality (see Winship & Morgan, 1999 for a review).[12] Our basic strategy is to form estimates of the potential earnings of blacks if they were instead white and then average these differences over the distribution of: (1) blacks who are employed full-time, full-year; or (2) the predicted distribution of blacks who would be employed full-time, full-year if they were as likely as whites to be employed full-time, full-year. We denote the potential earnings of each individual if black as Y_i^{b} and the potential earnings of each individual if white as Y_i^{w}. In the CPS data we analyze, we have at our disposal individual realizations of two related but substantially more limited random variables: Y_i, an individual's observed earnings and B_i, a dummy variable equal to 1 if a sampled individual self-identifies as black. The most general gap we will consider is:

$$E[\gamma_{i\in \mathrm{B}}] \equiv E[Y_{i\in \mathrm{B}}^{\mathrm{w}}] - E[Y_{i\in \mathrm{B}}^{\mathrm{b}}] \qquad \text{(G1)}$$

where B denotes the subset of the population that, if asked, would self-identify as black. Gap G1 is explicitly defined as the average black-white gap among blacks, and, as a result, it focuses attention on the earnings penalties associated with being black. Accordingly, we will ignore the earnings penalties whites would suffer if they were suddenly found to be black. And, we will not attempt to estimate the black-white gap across all white and black men, $E[Y_i^{\mathrm{w}} - Y_i^{\mathrm{b}}]$, as it is not clear that (1) it is at all practical to do so or (2) that there are any analytic benefits to modeling this more encompassing gap.

We maintain two types of conditions when estimating and then interpreting our adjusted results. First, the contrasts we will attempt to estimate will be very narrow (indeed, as we will show below when defining gaps G2 and G3, more narrow than even gap G1). The baseline race contrast we will attempt to estimate is the average earnings gain an employed black male working full-time, full-year would expect to capture if he were suddenly found to be white. When we move beyond this contrast, we do so only very minimally, attempting to estimate the gap among a set of hypothetically employed blacks who would be employed full-time, full-year if they were as likely as whites to have access to stable employment in the core full-time, full-year labor market.

We will not proceed any further in this regard, such as by trying to estimate what the black-white gap would be if black men had grown up in families with as much family income as whites, and hence would have had the available resources with which to purchase higher quality secondary and post-secondary education. If we were to attempt to statistically equalize all possible pre-market characteristics (see Neal & Johnson, 1996) across white and black men (i.e. switching to the contrast "what if a black male were to have been born white and into a white family"), we would need to assert additional assumptions on top of those we assert below, clouding the basic labor market contrasts that we regard as the subject of primary theoretical interest in this study. Attempting to estimate the average gains that black labor market participants would capture if they were subject to race-neutral hiring and compensation policies is challenging enough already.

Second, we stipulate that our estimates inform us only about potential wage gains that a few blacks might capture if the equilibrium of the labor market remained the same. That is, because we cannot infer how the entire distribution of earnings would be altered if, in theory, all employers were simultaneously to become race-blind, the estimates we will offer are only informative about the expected gain that a few black men could expect to receive if they were suddenly found to be white by a few randomly chosen employers.[13]

Adjustments for Observed Characteristics

Table 3 reports results from a formal linear test of the relative decline in the black-white gap for classes V, VI, and VIIa between 1982 and 2000. We fit nine variants of the model:

$$Y_i = \mathbf{Z}_i\beta + \tau_i[B_i \times T_i] + \delta_{II}[B_i \times T_i \times II_i] + \delta_{IIIa}[B_i \times T_i \times IIIa_i] + \cdots + \delta_{VIIa}[B_i \times T_i \times VIIa_i] + \varepsilon_i \quad (1)$$

where B_i is a dummy variable for blacks, T_i is a linear term for time (in years), and II_i through $VIIa_i$ are dummy variables for classes II through VIIa (and hence, where class I is the omitted reference class). For all models in Table 3, the covariate vector $\mathbf{Z}_i$ includes a constant, main effects for race, time, and social class (B_i, T_i, and II_i through $VIIa_i$) as well as two-way interactions between race and class ($B_i \times II_i$ through $B_i \times VIIa_i$). In the second panel, main effects for basic human capital and demographic characteristics are added to $\mathbf{Z}_i$: years of education, years of potential experience and its square, three region dummies, two dummies for urbanicity, and four dummies for types of marital status. In the third panel, two-way interactions are included between each of the class dummies and the additional variables for human capital and demographic characteristics.

Within each panel, three separate sets of weights are used for the regressions. For the first column of each panel, the weights are the individual sampling probabilities of being included in the CPS, standardized by the relative size of

Table 3. Variations of a Linear Test for a Greater Relative Decline in the Race Gap in Classes V, VI, and VIIa.

	No Covariates			Human Capital and Demographic Covariates			Human Capital and Demographic Covariates Interacted with Class		
		Weights 1985–1989	Weights 1996–2000		Weights 1985–1989	Weights 1996–2000		Weights 1985–1989	Weights 1996–2000
τ_I	−0.123	0.020	−0.005	0.086	0.025	−0.013	0.135	0.065	0.032
	(0.207)	(0.192)	(0.117)	(0.187)	(0.178)	(0.121)	(0.193)	(0.183)	(0.134)
δ_{II}	0.371	0.487	0.481	0.261	0.419	0.432	0.205	0.402	0.413
	(0.364)	(0.249)	(0.222)	(0.335)	(0.249)	(0.218)	(0.341)	(0.264)	(0.235)
δ_{IIIa}	0.503	0.803	0.658	0.240	0.586	0.572	0.136	0.525	0.502
	(0.279)	(0.302)	(0.193)	(0.234)	(0.248)	(0.193)	(0.253)	(0.247)	(0.236)
δ_{IIIb}	0.689	0.672	0.551	0.337	0.140	0.024	0.307	0.248	0.119
	(0.447)	(0.694)	(0.635)	(0.427)	(0.499)	(0.433)	(0.406)	(0.494)	(0.441)
δ_V	1.492	1.225	1.168	1.172	0.934	0.895	1.142	0.963	0.927
	(0.330)	(0.248)	(0.214)	(0.289)	(0.301)	(0.247)	(0.289)	(0.305)	(0.254)
δ_{VI}	0.751	0.836	0.959	0.509	0.599	0.744	0.456	0.592	0.735
	(0.290)	(0.243)	(0.204)	(0.298)	(0.228)	(0.190)	(0.304)	(0.229)	(0.198)
δ_{VIIa}	1.168	0.857	0.886	0.597	0.543	0.565	0.576	0.529	0.559
	(0.214)	(0.243)	(0.164)	(0.189)	(0.207)	(0.135)	(0.186)	(0.195)	(0.136)
Average decline in the race-gap within classes V, VI, and VIIa	1.013	0.993	0.999	0.845	0.692	0.721	0.860	0.760	0.772
	(0.084)	(0.099)	(0.098)	(0.087)	(0.227)	(0.001)	(0.083)	(0.001)	(0.001)
Average decline in classes V, VI, and VIIa relative to classes I, II, IIIa, and IIIb	0.746	0.482	0.582	0.549	0.406	0.478	0.563	0.401	0.482
	(0.126)	(0.216)	(0.174)	(0.001)	(0.228)	(0.002)	(0.001)	(0.221)	(0.002)
p-value for relative decline	<0.001	0.038	0.004	<0.001	0.092	0.010	<0.001	0.086	0.010

Note: Standard error are in parentheses and are robust, heteroskedastic-consistent standard errors, further adjusted for the clustering of respondents within CPS years. All coefficients and standards errors are multiplied by 100. The average decline is stipulated to be the linear combination of coefficients: $[(\tau_I + \delta_V) + (\tau_I + \delta_{VI}) + (\tau_I + \delta_{VIIa})]/3$, and the relative decline is stipulated to be the linear combination of coefficients: $[(\tau_I + \delta_V) + (\tau_I + \delta_{VI}) + (\tau_I + \delta_{VIIa})]/3 - [\tau_I + (\tau_I + \delta_{II}) + (\tau_I + \delta_{IIIa}) + (\tau_I + \delta_{IIIb})]/4$. The *p*-value is for a two-tailed test where the null hypothesis is that the relative decline is 0. Within each panel, the *N*s for the models in the first through third columns are 450,982, 444,554, and 443,339.

the CPS sample in each year. For the second and third columns within each panel, these standardized sampling weights are multiplied by additional scaling factors in order to generate estimates of average wage gaps while aligning the within-class occupational distributions of both whites and blacks in every year to the same unit-level occupational distribution of blacks for two alternative reference time period periods, 1985–1989 and 1996–2000. These modeling weights were generated by multiplying the sampling weights of each individual by additional occupation- and race-specific yearly scaling factors:

$$\pi^{\mathrm{w}}(k,t) = \frac{\text{\% of black FTFY workers in occupation } k \text{ in the reference time period}}{\text{\% of white FTFY workers in occupation } k \text{ in year } t}$$

for white males and

$$\pi^{\mathrm{b}}(k,t) = \frac{\text{\% of black FTFY workers in occupation } k \text{ in the reference time period}}{\text{\% of black FTFY workers in occupation } k \text{ in year } t}$$

for black males.[14] When deployed in weighted OLS models, these weights balance unit-occupation-level differences across race, and as a result, adjust for within-class race differences in occupational attainment. At the same time, they sweep away heterogeneity bias of the form that Grusky and Weeden (2001) claim weakens the claims of all big class models. And, moreover, they do so not simply by pushing the heterogeneity aside, but instead by normalizing it across race in the accordance with the definition of gap G1 and with reference to two separate and theoretically meaningful time periods.

The model reported in the first column of Table 3 does not include any human capital or demographic covariates. As a result, the reported coefficient estimate of τ_{I} represents the linearly interpolated slope of the line for class I in Fig. 3. Similarly, the coefficient estimates of δ_{II} through δ_{VIIa} represent the differences in the linearly interpolated relative slopes of the lines in Fig. 3 for classes II through VIIa in comparison with class I. For economy of space, each of the estimated coefficients and standard errors is multiplied by 100.

The coefficients reported in the first column imply that over the nineteen year time period, the gap for class I increased slightly. The coefficient for τ_I reported in the first row is -0.123. When divided by one hundred and multiplied by nineteen, the coefficient implies that the black-white gap increased by 0.0234 on the log scale. In contrast, on average for classes V through VIIa, the black-white gap declined by 0.192 on the log scale (which is the linear combination of coefficients, $[(\tau_I + \delta_V) + (\tau_I + \delta_{VI}) + (\tau_I + \delta_{VIIa})]/3$, reported in the third row from the bottom of the table as 1.013, and which was then divided by one hundred and multiplied by nineteen). Picking reasonable values for the initial black-white gap, and converting to a dollar metric over 52 weeks of work, the model in the first column implies that the black-white gap for class I increased from 12,614 dollars to 13,641 dollars whereas the black-white gap averaged over classes V, VI, and VIIa declined from 7,650 dollars to 1,949 dollars.[15]

Although this contrast compares the trend in the black-white gap within class I to those within classes V, VI, and VIIa, it ignores classes II, IIIa, and IIIb, and hence is perhaps too narrow of a test. As shown in Fig. 2, the earnings of workers in classes V, VI, and VIIa generally fell behind those of workers in classes I, II, IIIa, and IIIb. If the overall increase in earnings inequality is driving this change, we should expect a relatively greater decline in V, VI, and VIIa in comparison to all other classes. The second to last row of the table reports the average class-specific linear trend in the black-white gap for classes V, VI, and VIIa relative to the average class-specific linear trend in the black-white gap for classes I, II, IIIa, and IIIb:

$$\frac{(\tau_I + \delta_V) + (\tau_I + \delta_{VI}) + (\tau_I + \delta_{VIIa})}{3} - \frac{\tau_I + (\tau_I + \delta_{II}) + (\tau_I + \delta_{IIIa}) + (\tau_I + \delta_{IIIb})}{4}$$

along with its corresponding standard error (again where both are multiplied by 100 for economy of space). The last row of the table then reports the p-value for a two-tailed t-test, where the null hypothesis is that this linear combination of coefficients is 0. According to frequentist standards, if there were no average class difference in the decline in the black-white gap between classes I, II, IIIa, and IIIb relative to classes V, VI, and VIIa (under the specification of the model in column 1), the probability that we would observe a relative difference between classes as large in absolute value as is reported in column 1 is less than 0.001.

For the remaining eight models reported in Table 3, the same general pattern holds. The unreported main effect coefficients in $\mathbf{Z}_i$ change substantially when covariates are added, such that overall class differences in earnings are partialled out across both class and educational training. But the overall within-class trends in the black-white gap follow the same pattern, as shown in the rows for the average decline in the gap for classes V, VI, and VIIa.

Additional Adjustments for Selection Patterns into the Labor Force

Underlying labor force participation patterns vary by race, complicating the development of a consistent estimator for the black-white gap. To focus on the essential problem, consider the estimation challenges introduced by the following self-selection narrative. According to the literature on urban labor markets, a spatial mismatch between jobs and the residence locations of blacks generates greater relative costs of employment for blacks (e.g. greater transportation costs;

see Holzer, 1991). As a result of this difference in costs, blacks at the bottom of the distribution of potential occupational attainment may have higher wage thresholds above which they would choose to work rather than remain idle. Accordingly, blacks who would receive the lowest wages in the lowest-paying occupations are less likely to enter employment than comparable whites, and hence those blacks who are observed in low-paying occupations receive relatively higher wages on average than their unemployed counterparts would necessarily receive if they chose to work. This line of argument suggests that a smaller within-occupation earnings gap is observed at the lower end of the occupational distribution because the average wages of blacks in classes VI and VIIa are artificially inflated by self-selection out of employment.[16]

As fully described in the appendix, we assess the robustness of our conclusions based on Fig. 3 and Table 3 to these types of selection bias by first stipulating that the gap of primary theoretical interest is the gap at the core of the labor market for FTFY workers. We then perform an adjustment for selection patterns by artificially equalizing across race the proportion of workers employed FTFY and then calculating the gap assuming that the additional black workers who are added to the "what if" FTFY sample had the lower weekly earnings typical of full-time, part-year (hereafter, FTPY) workers in the same social class.

Our implementation of this strategy follows several steps. First, for each class c in each year t, we calculated the proportion of observed white and black FTFY and FTPY workers who were FTFY workers:

$$\lambda^{\mathrm{w}}(c, t) = \frac{\%\text{ of white FTFY workers in class } c \text{ in year } t}{\%\text{ of white FTFY and FTPY workers in class } c \text{ in year } t}$$

and:

$$\lambda^{\mathrm{b}}(c, t) = \frac{\%\text{ of black FTFY workers in class } c \text{ in year } t}{\%\text{ of black FTFY and FTPY workers in class } c \text{ in year } t}$$

We then used the CPS data (along with external data on the yearly incarceration rates of the black and white male adult population) in order to estimate a broad-based rate of FTFY employment:

$$\theta^{\mathrm{b}}(c, t) = \frac{\%\text{ of black FTFY workers observed in class } c \text{ in year } t}{\begin{array}{c}\%\text{ of all blacks who would be in class } c \text{ in year } t \text{ if they were as likely}\\ \text{as whites to be employed as FTFY workers in class } c \text{ in year } t\end{array}}$$

where we invoked a reasonable (and pessimistic) assumed distribution for the employment of additional blacks across the class distribution. Values for these three rates, along with the specific components on which they are based, are presented as averages over the 1985–1989 and 1996–2000 time periods in appendix Tables A1 and A2.

For execution of the selection adjustment models, we then added all FTPY black males to the analysis sample and reestimated the models in Table 3 with the augmented sample. While doing so, we multiplied the model-specific weights used for the nine columns of Table 3 by additional year-specific scaling factors for black workers only. For FTFY blacks, the weights were multiplied by:

$$\psi^{b}(c,t) = \frac{\theta^{b}(c,t)}{\lambda^{w}(c,t)},$$

and for FTPY blacks, the weights were multiplied by:

$$\psi^{b}(c,t) = \left(\frac{\lambda^{b}(c,t)}{1-\lambda^{b}(c,t)}\right)\left(\frac{\lambda^{w}(c,t)-\theta^{b}(c,t)}{\lambda^{w}(c,t)}\right).$$

In combination, the modified weights for FTFY and FTPY blacks lower the relative representation of FTFY blacks and raise the relative representation of FTPY blacks. And since FTPY blacks have earnings that are approximately 20% less than FTFY blacks (see columns eight through twelve of Table A2), the modified weights have the effect of lowering the average earnings of blacks by an amount that is proportional to the difference between observed white and black FTFY participation rates in each year.

The resulting models are presented in Table 4. Comparing the first column of this table with that of Table 3, the coefficient for the relative average decline is reduced from 0.746 to 0.699. Thus, only approximately six percent of the baseline relative decline can be attributed to trends in race differences in selection into the FTFY labor force. A similar pattern is revealed in the remaining columns of the table, using covariance adjustments alongside the weighting estimators. In the last six columns, however, the effect of the selection adjustment is mitigated by the human capital covariates; FTPY blacks have substantially lower educational attainment, as do all other categories of the "what if" blacks.[17]

Selection into the labor force is an important consideration, and the unreported main effects show that the relative size of the wage gap within classes V, VI, and VIIa is indeed substantially reduced when the sample is augmented with FTPY black workers and then weighted according to our selection-adjustment scheme. But, this does not appear to explain away the time trend that is revealed in Fig. 3 and Table 3. As shown in the appendix, between the 1980s and 1990s, the trend toward greater incarceration and "voluntary" non-participation of blacks seems roughly counterbalanced by shifts out of unemployment and relative shifts out of part-year work. Thus, even though black males remained substantially less likely to be employed FTFY by the end of the time series, the race difference in the rate of FTFY employment changed less than might be expected.

Table 4. Selection-Adjusted Linear Tests for a Greater Relative Decline in the Race Gap in Classes V, VI, and VIIa.

	No Covariates			Human Capital and Demographic Covariates			Human Capital and Demographic Covariates Interacted with Class		
		Weights 1985–1989	Weights 1996–2000		Weights 1985–1989	Weights 1996–2000		Weights 1985–1989	Weights 1996–2000
τ_I	−0.192	−0.078	−0.063	−0.055	−0.037	−0.034	−0.007	0.015	−0.007
	(0.206)	(0.192)	(0.123)	(0.198)	(0.195)	(0.155)	(0.204)	(0.217)	(0.177)
δ_{II}	0.401	0.517	0.538	0.335	0.531	0.495	0.317	0.503	0.495
	(0.340)	(0.326)	(0.325)	(0.329)	(0.337)	(0.333)	(0.326)	(0.351)	(0.343)
δ_{IIIa}	0.416	0.806	0.635	0.215	0.653	0.547	0.158	0.593	0.475
	(0.331)	(0.360)	(0.283)	(0.256)	(0.285)	(0.229)	(0.276)	(0.304)	(0.243)
δ_{IIIb}	1.071	0.898	0.782	0.548	0.327	0.112	0.611	0.446	0.210
	(0.381)	(0.519)	(0.574)	(0.375)	(0.416)	(0.439)	(0.384)	(0.406)	(0.426)
δ_V	1.571	1.306	1.059	1.250	1.033	0.826	1.312	1.081	0.892
	(0.312)	(0.287)	(0.170)	(0.299)	(0.272)	(0.199)	(0.302)	(0.288)	(0.218)
δ_{VI}	0.847	0.905	0.973	0.611	0.715	0.809	0.604	0.692	0.823
	(0.270)	(0.239)	(0.209)	(0.294)	(0.259)	(0.235)	(0.304)	(0.279)	(0.260)
δ_{VIIa}	1.095	0.779	0.749	0.626	0.527	0.529	0.637	0.525	0.579
	(0.217)	(0.238)	(0.148)	(0.189)	(0.212)	(0.149)	(0.187)	(0.219)	(0.168)
Average decline in the race-gap within classes V, VI, and VIIa	0.979	0.919	0.864	0.774	0.721	0.687	0.843	0.781	0.758
	(0.071)	(0.090)	(0.018)	(0.077)	(0.094)	(0.111)	(0.076)	(0.092)	(0.106)
Average decline in classes V, VI, and VIIa relative to classes I, II, IIIa, and IIIb	0.699	0.441	0.439	0.554	0.381	0.433	0.579	0.381	0.469
	(0.001)	(0.178)	(0.168)	(0.104)	(0.165)	(0.151)	(0.001)	(0.154)	(0.144)
p-value for relative decline	<0.001	0.023	0.018	<0.001	0.033	0.010	<0.001	0.024	0.004

Note: See Table 3. Within each panel, the *N*s for the models in the first through third columns are 459,321, 454,109, and 451,505.

Although more research is surely needed on the consequences of selection into the labor force, the decline in the wages of white males appears to be driving the trends we have presented, not artefactual increases in the wages of black males. Taken together, the more refined results we have presented in Tables 3 and 4 do not change the basic result revealed in Fig. 3. The black-white gap among men has declined relatively more at the bottom of the class distribution.

DISCUSSION

Between 1982 and 2000, the black-white gap in the earnings of men decreased slightly while aggregate social class differences in earnings increased. The black-white gap for class I is either constant or slightly increasing, and yet it emerges as the largest gap across all classes primarily because the relative wages of white men from classes V, VI, and VIIa have fallen consistently over the past two decades. In the context of growing wage inequality in general, white men at the bottom of the class distribution have been unable to maintain their wage advantages over their black counterparts to the same degree that white men at the top of the class distribution have. In this concluding section, we will interpret the relative decline as consistent with the rent destruction explanation for increases in earnings inequality developed by Sørensen (1996, 2000). However, before proceeding to a discussion of rent destruction, and its implications for research on social class and social stratification in post-industrial societies, we first discuss other plausible explanations for the findings we present.

Kaufman (1983) argued that gains in the average occupational placement of blacks would generate a paradoxical increase in the net wage gap between white and black men, since he found when analyzing 1970 census data that the race gap was slightly larger at the top of the distribution of occupations (after a variety of covariance adjustments). Grodsky and Pager (2001) then analyzed 1990 census data to show that in spite of demonstrable gains in the occupational attainment of black men, the black-white gap in earnings persists and also seems to remain largest at the top of the distribution of occupational prestige and average earnings. These findings are consistent with Kaufman's prediction, even though they do not explicitly demonstrate an increase in the gap. In addition, Grodsky and Pager supplement Kaufman's explanatory narrative, offering a new explanation for the pattern of heterogeneity across the occupational distribution. They argue that white professionals serve clients that on average have a greater capacity to pay high fees for their services. Whites in these occupations occupy structural job niches that command greater profitability than do blacks. Although we have no direct evidence to support Grodsky and Pager's explanation, we are quite captivated by its potential, especially since it is complementary to and consistent with the rent destruction interpretation we adopt below.[18]

At the same time, two other explanations could generate our findings (and those of Grodsky & Pager as well). First, as detailed earlier, patterns of selection out of the labor force could generate the relative decline in the race gap, even though our analysis suggests otherwise. Second, a relatively greater decline in discriminatory compensation practices at the bottom of the class distribution could also give rise to the same empirical pattern. Again, however, it is not clear that a relative decline in discriminatory compensation practices should be interpreted as an alternative to rent destruction, rather than as part and parcel of the same mechanism. To explain why, we now present an explanation that we see as the most compelling and theoretically intriguing, even though we recognize that we have little direct evidence to favor it over these alternatives.

Sørensen (1996, 2000) argued that when examining labor market processes, stratification researchers should be interested in the distribution of three different quantities: (1) Y^a, actual wages paid in the labor market; (2) Y^c, wages that would be paid under perfect competition; and (3) $r^c = Y^a - Y^c$, rent. Adopting this simple but broad framework, Sørensen argued that increases in labor market inequality in the U.S. reflect pervasive but selective rent destruction since the 1970s.

Even though Sørensen offered little detail on precisely how this rent destruction occurred, one can develop a set of implied claims using the EGP class schema. Since the 1970s, individuals in the most privileged jobs within classes I and II have been able to retain (or even increase) their wage advantages over others in less privileged jobs (both within classes I and II and in comparison with all jobs in other social classes). In contrast, in classes V, VI, and VIIa, the wage advantages associated with the best jobs in the 1960s and 1970s have declined so that all wages paid to workers within classes V, VI, and VIIa have converged to wage levels for the least paid.

Sørensen's argument is more subtle than claims about the hollowing out of the class distribution in post-industrial society, since the motivation for the framework is to transcend the simple story of how the decline in the prevalence of jobs in heavy industry produced a new market equilibrium in which an over-supply of unskilled workers reduced the average wage levels of classes V, VI, and VIIa. Rather, according to Sørensen, the recent increases in earnings inequality reflect a fundamental shift in employment relations, organized around new norms for firm management of individuals' careers. Although workers at the top of the class distribution continue to be paid according to lifetime earnings schemes, which often include loyalty and efficiency wage components, workers at the bottom of the class distribution have become increasingly likely to be paid according to managers' calculations of workers' instantaneous marginal contributions to output.

Our finding of a relative decline in the black-white earnings gap among men within classes V, VI, and VIIa is consistent with Sørensen's rent destruction explanation *if* one is willing to assert assumptions about race differences in access to rent-advantaged positions. For example, relying on the classic split-labor market argument of Bonacich (1972, 1976), or, alternatively, the characterization of black-white differences in Sørensen (1975, 1979), one could assume that prior to 1980 black men were more likely to be excluded from rent-advantaged positions across the entire spectrum of available occupations, and that, after 1980, access to such rent-advantaged positions increased no more for those in classes V, VI, and VIIa than for classes I and II (and perhaps IIIa and IIIb). If selective rent destruction is a plausible explanation for increases in inequality between social classes after 1980, then the destruction of rent-advantaged positions should be greatest at the bottom of the class distribution, and a *ceteris paribus* implication follows immediately from the assumption above: The black-white gap in earnings among men should have decreased relatively more within classes V, VI, and VIIa than within classes I and II (and perhaps IIIa and IIIb).[19] This is precisely the pattern revealed in the analysis we report.

We therefore conclude that the rent destruction hypothesis promoted by Sørensen (1996, 2000) is a useful explanatory narrative for the specific set of findings that we present, and one which can be used to supplement rather than supplant first-order interpretations suggested by the EGP-class-based analysis on its own. A larger implication of our analysis, if this interpretation is convincing, is that class analysis in its traditional modes is not irrelevant and need not be completely overhauled to remain useful. When big classes based on reasonable codings of census occupational schemes are deployed in analysis, a compelling descriptive picture of labor market outcomes can be generated. Thereafter, if it is so desired, supplementary explanatory effort can be mounted to elucidate the consequences of unappreciated heterogeneity, as argued by Grusky and Weeden (2001), or more basic structural processes, as argued by Sørensen (1996, 2000).

NOTES

1. In this article, we will not investigate gender differentials or contrasts with racial/ethnic groups other than those identified for the Current Population Surveys as white and black. These differentials are worthy of analysis as well. However, the gap between white and black men has been the subject of much targeted research and represents, we would argue, the best starting point for developing an EGP-class-based analysis of changes in earnings inequality.

2. Hout et al. (1993) is the only published class-based decomposition of earnings inequality in the U.S. that we have found which uses the EGP class schema (which

is what we regard as the dominant class schema employed in empirical research; see below).

3. The technological explanation has not gone completely unexamined in sociology, as Fernandez (2001) provides a fascinating account of how technological innovation in one plant resulted in the skill-upgrading of occupations associated with that plant. Whether or not this study "provides strong evidence for the importance of skill-biased technological change as an explanation of rising wage inequality" (Fernandez, 2001, p. 316) is a matter for debate, one which should properly rest on the logic of Fernandez's claim that his study's "natural-experiment design solves the self-selection problem that plagued past skill-bias studies" (Fernandez, 2001, p. 315).

4. Sociologists have offered explanations for persistent race differences in labor market outcomes, focusing on the ways in which discriminatory hiring practices are institutionalized in job creation and staffing decisions, grounded either in the dual labor market conceptualizations of Bonacich (1972, 1976) or the spatial mismatch hypotheses of Wilson (1987). Complementing these structural explanations, attention has also focused on differentials in opportunities to acquire marketable skills and credentials prior to entering the labor market (e.g. Farley, 1984), differences in cultural competencies that are rewarded in the labor market (see Lamont, 1999), and the systematically incorrect beliefs that employers maintain about the skills of non-white workers (see Moss & Tilly, 2001). Our claim is only that these explanations have not been deployed by sociologists in explicit attempts to model change in the past two decades in black-white differences in earnings.

5. In this sense, it is not especially problematic, from our perspective, that we leave out of our descriptive picture all women and those men not identified as white or black for the CPS data. Clearly, however, if one regards classes as holistic entities, then such truncation of the class structure would be very problematic, especially if one were interested in characterizing comprehensively how the race and gender compositions of social classes are evolving in postindustrial society.

6. Consider the following comparison. For the 450,982 respondents in the first panel of Table 3, we fit a regression equation predicting weekly earnings with parameters for time, experience, experience squared, region, urbanicity, and marital status. The R^2 for this baseline model was 0.1551. Adding to this baseline model linear and quadratic terms for years of education, each interacted with time, the R^2 increased to 0.3281. However, when adding six dummy variables for social class, each interacted with time, to the same baseline model, the R^2 increased to 0.3353. Of course, EGP uses more parameters, but by the criterion of variance explained, it does outperform a standard Mincerian human capital rate of return model, even when augmented with a quadratic term for education.

7. Our procedures for handling topcodes allow us to estimate conditional means, but they do not determine the qualitative conclusions we report to any substantial degree. The models in Tables 3 and 4 were re-estimated using median regression procedures and the results were only trivially different.

8. For comparability with later results, Fig. 1 is further restricted to those in one of the seven main social classes we will analyze throughout the article (i.e. excluding farmers and most self-employed workers; see below).

9. For now, we do not analyze recessionary years (1982, 1990, and 1991) and early recovery years (1983, 1984, and 1992 through 1995) in order to focus analytically on stable full-employment distributions of social classes. In the more formal regression tests, these years are included in analysis.

10. In this article, we use $E[\cdot]$ to denote the population expectation and $E_N[\cdot]$ to denote the sample expectation (i.e. the estimated mean from a sample of size *N*). This notation, drawn from the method of moments literature, allows for economy of expression when making claims about the large sample properties of estimators.

11. For Fig. 3, we do not present the estimated race gap for class IIIb. There are very few black men who hold such occupations in the CPS (approximately 50–80 per year spread across 20 different occupations), and as a result, estimates of the wage gap vary dramatically from year to year, reflecting little more than sampling error. We do, however, include class IIIb in the more formal tests of heterogeneity reported later.

12. We fully recognize that some researchers maintain that counterfactuals cannot be used to profitably examine non-manipulable discrete variables, such as race and gender (see Holland, 1986). In our opinion, Glymour (1986) provides a cogent defense of using counterfactuals to elucidate effects that are presumed to have been caused by a set of potentially manipulable factors that are merely referred to collectively by nominal labels.

13. We fully recognize that these assumptions are very stringent, and that the use of counterfactual models for examining race differences within the labor market will be controversial for some readers. However, we challenge others to be similarly specific in laying out their assumptions and the causal inferences their results can sustain (or, if not making causal claims, why a descriptive analysis is useful).

14. See Handcock and Morris (1999) for a comprehensive treatment of non-parametric weighting estimators, of which our weighting procedures are one variant. See Barsky et al. (2002) for a similar application.

15. These calculations assume a black-white gap of 0.25 on the log scale at the beginning of the time series for both groups. For class I, the initial gap is assumed to be 7 and 6.75 on the log scale (or 57,025 and 44,411 in dollars over 52 weeks). For classes V through VIIa, the gap is assumed to be 6.5 and 6.25 on the log scale (or 34,587 and 26,937 dollars over 52 weeks). The implied decreased average earnings of blacks in class I is 6.7266 on the log scale (or 43,384 in dollars over 52 weeks), while for classes V through VIIa it is 6.442 on the log scale (or 32,638 in dollars over 52 weeks).

16. This argument implicitly assumes that the wage offers received by all individuals at the upper end of the distribution of potential occupational attainment exceed their reservation wages. Thus, there is no similar tendency for self-selection out of employment among blacks at the top of the distribution of potential occupational attainment.

17. For models reported in the second and third columns of each panel, the occupational alignment scaling factors that are utilized for the non-parametric weighting estimators are altered slightly to:

$$\phi^{w}(k,t) = \frac{\text{\% of black FTFY and FTPY workers in occupation } k \text{ in the reference time period}}{\text{\% of white FTFY workers in occupation } k \text{ in year } t}$$

for white males and

$$\phi^{b}(k,t) = \frac{\text{\% of black FTFY and FTPY workers in occupation } k \text{ in the reference time period}}{\text{\% of black FTFY and FTPY workers in occupation } k \text{ in year } t}$$

for black males.

18. That is, as we discuss below, whites at the top of Grodsky and Pager's prestige distribution have held on to their rents, whereas those at the bottom of the distribution have lost some of theirs.

19. A more formal derivation of this implication could be developed as follows. Suppose that all measurable effects of skill differences have been partialled out of Y^a within each class. Suppressing subscripts for individuals i and time t (for compactness of notation), continue to define rent as $r^c \equiv Y^a - Y^c$. Now suppose that competitive wages and the sizes of rents for those who receive rents are independent of race within class: $E[Y^c|C] \perp B$ and $E[r|r > 0, C] \perp B$. Defining a disproportionate share of whites who occupy rent-advantaged positions as $\rho^{\text{w-b}} \equiv \Pr[r > 0|C, B = 0] - \Pr[r > 0|C, B = 1]$, suppose $\rho^{\text{w-b}}$ is positive in all classes. If $E[Y^a|C = c, B = 0] - E[Y^a|C = c, B = 1]$ is shown to be decreasing in time for class c, then $(\rho^{w-b}|C = c)E[r|r > 0, C = c]$ is decreasing in time, which implies that either $\rho^{\text{w-b}}$ or $E[r|r > 0]$ (or both) is decreasing in time for class c. The crucial assumption, of course, is that $\rho^{\text{w-b}}$ remains positive (or, more specifically in this application, that it remains relatively more positive in classes V, VI, and VIIa than in class I).

ACKNOWLEDGMENTS

A prior version of this paper was presented in August 2002 at the meetings of the American Sociological Association in Chicago and in December 2002 at the Center for Statistics in the Social Sciences at the University of Washington. We are thankful for the comments of attendees, and also for the written comments of Arne Kalleberg and Arthur Sakamoto. This research was supported by a seed grant from the Center for the Study of Inequality at Cornell University and by NSF Grant #0213642 for a project entitled "Rent and Social Class, 1982–2000."

REFERENCES

Altonji, J. G., & Blank, R. M. (1999). Race and gender in the labor market. In: O. C. Ashenfelter & D. Card (Eds), *Handbook of Labor Economics* (Vol. 3, pp. 3143–3259). Amsterdam: Elsevier.

Barsky, R., Bound, J., Charles, K. K., & Lupton, J. P. (2002). Accountin for the black-white wealth gap: A nonparametric approach. *Journal of the American Statistical Association, 97*, 663–673.

Berman, E., Bound, J., & Griliches, Z. (1994). Changes in the demand for skilled labor within U.S. manufacturing: Evidence from the Annual Survey of Manufactures. *Quarterly Journal of Economics, 109*, 367–397.

Berman, E., Bound, J., & Machin, S. (1998). Implications of skill-biased technological change: International evidence. *Quarterly Journal of Economics, 113*, 1245–1279.

Bernstein, J., & Mishel, L. (2001). Seven reasons for skepticism about the technology story of U.S. wage inequality. In: I. Berg & A. L. Kalleberg (Eds), *Sourcebook of Labor Markets: Evolving Structures and Processes* (pp. 409–427). New York: Kluwer/Plenum.

Bonacich, E. (1972). A theory of ethnic antagonism: The split labor market. *American Sociological Review, 37*, 547–559.

Bonacich, E. (1976). Advanced capitalism and black/white race relations in the United States: A split labor market interpretation. *American Sociological Review, 41*, 34–51.

Bound, J., & Freeman, R. B. (1992). What went wrong? The erosion of relative earnings and employment among young black mean in the 1980s. *Quarterly Journal of Economics*, *107*, 201–232.

Bound, J., & Holzer, H. J (1993). Industrial shifts, skill levels and the labor market for white and black males. *The Review of Economics and Statistics*, *75*, 387–396.

Brown, C. (1984). Black-white earnings ratios since the Civil Rights Act of 1964: The importance of labor market dropouts. *Quarterly Journal of Economics*, *99*, 31–44.

Card, D., & DiNardo, J. E. (2002). Skill-biased technological change and rising wage inequality: Some problems and puzzles. *Journal of Labor Economics*, *20*, 733–783.

Card, D., & Lemieux, T. (1994). Changing wage structure and black-white wage differentials. *The American Economic Review*, *84*, 29–33.

Card, D., & Lemieux, T. (1996). Wage dispersion, returns to skill and black-white wage differentials. *Journal of Econometrics*, *74*, 319–361.

Cherry, R., & Rodgers, W. M., III (Eds) (2000). *Prosperity for all? The economic boom and African Americans*. New York: Russell Sage.

Erikson, R., & Goldthorpe, J. H. (1985). Are American rates of social mobility exceptionally high? New evidence on an old issue. *European Sociological Review*, *1*, 1–22.

Erikson, R., & Goldthorpe, J. H. (1992). *The constant flux*. Oxford: Clarendon Press.

Erikson, R., & Goldthorpe, J. H. (2002). Intergenerational inequality: A sociological perspective. *Journal of Economic Perspectives*, *16*, 31–44.

Erikson, R., Goldthorpe, J. H., & Portocarero, L. (1979). Intergenerational class mobility in three Western European societies: England, France, and Sweden. *British Journal of Sociology*, *30*, 415–430.

Farley, R. (1984). *Blacks and whites: Narrowing the gap?* Cambridge: Harvard University Press.

Fernandez, R. M. (2001). Skill-biased technological change and wage inequality: Evidence from a plant retooling. *American Journal of Sociology*, *107*, 273–320.

Freeman, R. B., & Rodgers, W. M., III (2000). Area economic conditions and the labor market outcomes of young men in the 1990s expansion. In: R. Cherry & W. M. Rodgers, III (Eds), *Prosperity for All? The Economic Boom and African Americans* (pp. 50–87). New York: Russell Sage.

Glymour, C. (1986). Comment: Statistics and metaphysics. *Journal of the American Statistical Association*, *81*, 964–966.

Goldthorpe, J. H. (1987). *Social mobility and class structure in Britain* (2nd ed.). Oxford: Clarendon Press.

Goldthorpe, J. H. (2000). *On sociology: Numbers, narratives, and the integration of research and theory*. Oxford: Oxford University Press.

Goldthorpe, J. H., & Müller, W. (1982). *Social mobility and class formation in industrial nations: Proposal for a comparative research project*. Oxford/Mannheim.

Grodsky, E., & Pager, D. (2001). The structure of disadvantage: Individual and occupational determinants of the black-white wage gap. *American Sociological Review*, *66*, 542–567.

Grusky, D. B., & Sørensen, J. B. (1998). Can class analysis be salvaged? *American Journal of Sociology*, *103*, 1187–1234.

Grusky, D. B., & Weeden, K. A. (2001). Decomposition without death: A research agenda for the new class analysis. *Acta Sociologica*, *44*, 203–218.

Handcock, M. S., & Morris, M. (1999). *Relative distribution methods in the social sciences*. New York: Springer.

Heath, A., Jowell, R., & Curtice, J. (1985). *How Britain votes*. London: Pergamon.

Heckman, J. J., Lyons, T. M., & Todd, P. E. (2000). Understanding black-white wage differentials, 1960–1990. *American Economic Review*, *90*, 344–349.

Holland, P. W. (1986). Statistics and causal inference. *Journal of the American Statistical Association*, *81*, 945–960.

Holzer, H. J. (1991). The spatial mismatch hypothesis: What has the evidence shown? *Urban Studies*, *28*, 105–122.

Hout, M. (1984). Occupational mobility of black men, 1962–1973. *American Sociological Review*, *49*, 308–322.

Hout, M. (1989). *Following in father's footsteps: Social mobility in Ireland*. Cambridge: Harvard University Press.

Hout, M., Brooks, C., & Manza, J. (1993). The persistence of classes in post-industrial societies. *International Sociology*, *8*, 259–277.

Jargowsky, P. (1997). *Poverty and place*. New York: Russell Sage.

Jaynes, G. (1990). The labor market status of black Americans: 1939–1985. *Journal of Economic Perspectives*, *4*, 9–24.

Juhn, C. (1992). The decline of male labor market participation: The role of declining market opportunities. *Quarterly Journal of Economics*, *107*, 79–121.

Juhn, C., Murphy, K. M., & Pierce, B. (1991). Accounting for the slowdown in black-white wage convergence. In: M. H. Kosters (Ed.), *Workers and their Wages* (pp. 107–143). Washington, DC: AEI Press.

Katz, L. F., & Autor, D. H. (1999). Changes in the wage structure and earnings inequality. In: O. C. Ashenfelter & D. Card (Eds), *Handbook of Labor Economics* (Vol. 3, pp. 1463–1555). Amsterdam: Elsevier.

Kaufman, R. (1983). A structural decomposition of black-white earnings differentials. *American Journal of Sociology*, *89*, 585–611.

Lamont, M. (Ed.) (1999). *The cultural territories of race: Black and white boundaries*. Chicago: University of Chicago Press.

Manza, J., & Brooks, C. (1999). *Social cleavages and political change: Voter alignments and U.S. party coalitions*. Oxford: Oxford University Press.

Morris, M., & Western, B. (1999). Inequality in earnings at the close of the twentieth century. *Annual Review of Sociology*, *25*, 623–657.

Moss, P., & Tilly, C. (2001). *Stories employers tell: Race, skill, and hiring in America*. New York: Russell Sage.

Neal, D. A., & Johnson, W. R. (1996). The role of pre-market factors in black-white wage differences. *Journal of Political Economy*, *104*, 869–895.

Portes, A. (2000). The resilient importance of class: A nominalist interpretation. *Political Power and Social Theory*, *14*, 249–284.

Smith, J. P., & Welch, F. R. (1989). Black economic progress after myrdal. *Journal of Economic Literature*, *27*, 519–564.

Sørensen, A. B. (1975). The structure of intragenerational mobility. *American Sociological Review*, *40*, 456–471.

Sørensen, A. B. (1979). A model and a metric for the analysis of the intragenerational status attainment process. *American Journal of Sociology*, *85*, 361–384.

Sørensen, A. B. (1996). The structural basis of social inequality. *American Journal of Sociology*, *101*, 1333–1365.

Sørensen, A. B. (2000). Toward a sounder basis for class analysis. *American Journal of Sociology*, *105*, 1523–1558.

Welch, F. (1990). The employment of black men. *Journal of Labor Economics*, *8*, S26–S74.

Western, B., & Pettit, B. (2000, March). Black-white earnings inequality, employment rates, and incarceration. Mimeo, Princeton University.

Wilson, W. J. (1987). *The truly disadvantaged: The inner city, the underclass, and public policy*. Chicago: University of Chicago Press.

Wilson, W. J. (1996). *When work disappears: The world of the new urban poor*. New York: Knopf.

Winship, C., & Morgan, S. L. (1999). The estimation of causal effects from observational data. *Annual Review of Sociology*, *25*, 659–707.

APPENDIX

Details of Model Specification

To estimate gap G1, we could attempt to: (1) take the observed earnings Y_i of each black respondent; (2) subtract these observed earnings from plausible estimates of each black respondent's potential earnings if white, $\hat{Y}_i^{\text{w}}$; and then (3) average the resulting individual differences, $Y_i - \hat{Y}_i^{\text{w}}$, over the distribution of black respondents. Unfortunately, estimating individual-level counterfactual wage levels is a daunting, if not impossible, task. It is customary to instead estimate only the two expectations on the right-hand side of gap G1. The main challenge, however, is that the simple difference in sample expectations:

$$E_N[Y_i|B_i = 0] - E_N[Y_i|B_i = 1] \tag{E0}$$

does not converge in probability to $E[\gamma_{i\in \text{B}}]$ (i.e. gap G1) because

$$E_N[Y_i|B_i = 0] \underset{p}{\rightarrow} E[Y_{i\notin \text{B}}^{\text{w}}] \tag{A1}$$

and[20]

$$E[Y_{i\notin \text{B}}^{\text{w}}] > E[Y_{i\in \text{B}}^{\text{w}}]. \tag{A2}$$

In other words, estimator E0 is inconsistent for gap G1 because blacks differ from observed whites on characteristics, such as educational attainment, that are relevant for labor market earnings. The inconsistency of Estimator E0 cannot be addressed by simply conditioning or stratifying on observed variables in the CPS. To explain more completely why this is the case, we proceed by first more carefully specifying the black-white gap of interest.

Aside from the lack of opportunity to acquire "pre-market" skills, which we do not explicitly model in this article, there are likely two important penalties associated with being a black male: fewer opportunities for obtaining stable work and lower wages when in stable work. Gap G1 conflates these two penalties in unknown ways. To separate these effects, we use analogous race-conditioned potential outcome and observed variables for full-time, full-year work – $FTFY_i^{\text{b}}$, $FTFY_i^{\text{w}}$, and $FTFY_i$ – corresponding to dummy variables for working FTFY if black, working FTFY if instead white, and observed FTFY status. With these additional variables, we can more carefully specify the counterfactuals of primary theoretical interest.

We start with the assumption that blacks would be more likely to be employed FTFY if they were instead white:

$$\Pr[FTFY_{i\in \text{B}}^{\text{w}} = 1] > \Pr[FTFY_{i\in \text{B}}^{\text{b}} = 1]. \tag{A3}$$

This assumption of differential propensity to find stable work suggests two separate black-white gaps of interest:

$$E[\gamma_{i\in \text{B}}|FTFY_{i\in \text{B}}^{\text{b}} = 1] \equiv E[Y_{i\in \text{B}}^{\text{w}}|FTFY_{i\in \text{B}}^{\text{b}} = 1] - E[Y_{i\in \text{B}}^{\text{b}}|FTFY_{i\in \text{B}}^{\text{b}} = 1] \tag{G2}$$

and

$$E[\gamma_{i\in \text{B}}|FTFY_{i\in \text{B}}^{\text{w}} = 1] \equiv E[Y_{i\in \text{B}}^{\text{w}}|FTFY_{i\in \text{B}}^{\text{w}} = 1] - E[Y_{i\in \text{B}}^{\text{b}}|FTFY_{i\in \text{B}}^{\text{w}} = 1] \tag{G3}$$

where gap G2 is the black-white gap among blacks who are typically employed FTFY and where gap G3 is the black-white gap among blacks who would be employed FTFY if they were instead white (but again, assuming that a hypothetical shift for a black respondent from the potential state $FTFY_i^{\text{b}}$ to its alternative $FTFY_i^{\text{w}}$ does not entail any change in educational preparation or any other observed or unobserved covariate).

Now, returning to the main text, is estimator E1 consistent for either gap G2 or G3? No, just as estimator E0 is not consistent for gap G1, neither is estimator E1 consistent for either G2 or G3 because it is reasonable to assume that:

$$E_N[Y_i|B_i = 0, FTFY_i = 1] \underset{p}{\rightarrow} E[Y_{i\notin \text{B}}^{\text{w}}|FTFY_{i\notin \text{B}}^{\text{w}} = 1], \tag{A4}$$

$$E[Y_{i\notin \text{B}}^{\text{w}}|FTFY_{i\notin \text{B}}^{\text{w}} = 1] > E[Y_{i\in \text{B}}^{\text{w}}|FTFY_{i\in \text{B}}^{\text{b}} = 1], \tag{A5}$$

and

$$E[Y_{i\notin \text{B}}^{\text{w}}|FTFY_{i\notin \text{B}}^{\text{w}} = 1] > E[Y_{i\in \text{B}}^{\text{w}}|FTFY_{i\in \text{B}}^{\text{w}} = 1], \tag{A6}$$

The earnings of FTFY whites are (asymptotically) upwardly biased estimates of the FTFY earnings of blacks if they were instead white. But, this is only the simplest possible case, and as discussed informally in the selection-adjustment section in the main text there may be cases where the inequalities in assumptions A5 and A6 are entirely misleading.

Non-parametric Weighting Estimators

The estimator we introduce in this section (and deploy in columns 2 and 3 of each panel of Tables 3 and 4) allows for the explicit formulation of answers to useful counterfactual questions, such as: How would the earnings gap for each EGP class have evolved between 1982 and 2000 if both whites and blacks had the distribution across occupations that resulted for blacks in the final stages of the last two economic expansions in the United States?

The non-parametric estimator we deploy can be specified in general form as class and year-specific variants of:

$$E_N[\pi^{\mathrm{w}}(k, t)Y_i|B_i = 0, FTFY_i = 1] - E_N[\pi^{\mathrm{b}}(k, t)Y_i|B_i = 1, FTFY_i = 1] \quad \text{(E2)}$$

where the weights $\pi^{\mathrm{w}}(k, t)$ and $\pi^{\mathrm{b}}(k, t)$ are as specified in the main text. Estimator E2 provides a more reasonable estimator for G2 than E1, in the sense that the asymptotic bias of E2 is almost surely lower than for E1. Moreover, as shown in Tables 3 and 4, this non-parametric estimator can be deployed within a regression set-up, which allows for simultaneous covariance adjustments.

Adjustments for Selection Patterns

When conditioning on class, or any other stratifying variable S, the inequalities in assumptions A5 and A6 may not hold if there are complex selection patterns that generate the data. In particular, even though it may be reasonable to assume that:

$$E[Y^{\mathrm{w}}_{i\in \mathrm{B}}|FTFY^{\mathrm{b}}_{i\in \mathrm{B}} = 1, S_i = s] > E[Y^{\mathrm{b}}_{i\in \mathrm{B}}|FTFY^{\mathrm{b}}_{i\in \mathrm{B}} = 1, S_i = s] \quad \text{(A7a)}$$

and

$$E[Y^{\mathrm{w}}_{i\in \mathrm{B}}|FTFY^{\mathrm{w}}_{i\in \mathrm{B}} = 1, S_i = s] > E[Y^{\mathrm{b}}_{i\in \mathrm{B}}|FTFY^{\mathrm{w}}_{i\in \mathrm{B}} = 1, S_i = s], \quad \text{(A7b)}$$

it may also be the case that:

$$E[Y^{\mathrm{b}}_{i\in \mathrm{B}}|FTFY^{\mathrm{b}}_{i\in \mathrm{B}} = 1, S_i = s] > E[Y^{\mathrm{b}}_{i\in \mathrm{B}}|FTFY^{\mathrm{w}}_{i\in \mathrm{B}} = 1, S_i = s] \quad \text{(A8)}$$

and, even more abstractly, that:

$$E[Y^{\mathrm{w}}_{i\in \mathrm{B}}|FTFY^{\mathrm{b}}_{i\in \mathrm{B}} = 1, S_i = s] > E[Y^{\mathrm{w}}_{i\in \mathrm{B}}|FTFY^{\mathrm{w}}_{i\in \mathrm{B}} = 1, S_i = s]. \quad \text{(A9)}$$

For example, for class VIIa, if whites are more likely to be employed FTFY (e.g. by assumption A3) because blacks have higher reservation wages, then the average potential wages of blacks in class VIIa would be lower if blacks were employed as frequently as whites. Thus, the asymptotic bias of a conditional-on-S variant of estimator E1 could be either positive or negative. This is the claim of the contrarian selection narratives outlined in the main text, where the bias is declining in time, possibly generating illusory gains for blacks.

Table A1. Distribution of the Population of White and Black Males Across Types of Labor Market Participation.

	White Males (Age: 18–64)				Black Males (Ages: 18–64)			
	Proportion of CPS Sample		Mean Years Education		Proportion of CPS Sample		Mean Years Education	
	1985–1989	1996–2000	1985–1989	1996–2000	1985–1989	1996–2000	1985–1989	1996–2000
Worked one or more weeks last year								
Full-time, full-year	0.661	0.684	13.36	13.42	0.497	0.528	12.40	12.87
Full-time, part-year	0.159	0.122	12.41	12.56	0.175	0.124	11.82	12.40
Part-time, full-year	0.033	0.038	12.98	13.00	0.029	0.033	11.85	12.53
Part-time, part-year	0.046	0.039	12.68	12.79	0.065	0.044	11.50	12.18
Other (full-time and less than $50/week earnings)	0.004	0.005	12.47	12.37	0.003	0.004	11.33	12.20
Worked zero weeks last year								
Could not find work	0.008	0.006	11.03	11.60	0.036	0.020	11.11	11.62
Disabled	0.035	0.043	9.89	10.99	0.083	0.098	9.12	10.86
Keeping house	0.002	0.005	11.50	11.69	0.004	0.012	10.95	11.44
Retired	0.032	0.030	11.82	12.72	0.024	0.025	9.64	11.69
In school full-year	0.011	0.015	13.63	13.09	0.029	0.031	12.63	12.46
Other	0.004	0.006	11.44	11.58	0.014	0.017	10.63	11.52
Incarcerated	0.006	0.010			0.042	0.069		

To understand how important these complications may be, we first present basic results in Table A1 on race differences in labor market participation, again separately for the final five years of the two most recent economic expansions. The first 11 rows of the table are based on analysis of the entire CPS sample of black and white males between the ages of 18 and 64. For these groups of respondents, we also present in Table A1 measured levels of skill, as the mean years of education attained by respondents. The incarceration rates in row 12 of the table are drawn from the *Sourcebook of Criminal Justice Statistics 2000* (see http://www.albany.edu/sourcebook/1995/pdf/t619.pdf). The distribution across the first 11 rows within year-specific variants of Table A1 was determined by dividing the proportion of the CPS sample observed in each of the categories by $1/(1 +$ the race-specific incarceration rate) in that year.[21]

As shown in the first row of Table A1, a greater proportion of the non-institutionalized population of both white and black males was employed FTFY in 1996–2000 than in 1985–1989. In particular, the proportion of white males working FTFY increased from 66.1 to 68.4% while the proportion of blacks working FTFY increased from 49.7 to 52.8% (which is a net gain of 0.7% for blacks). And, consistent with the greater relative aggregate upward mobility of black males over this time period demonstrated in Table 2, the measured skills of blacks increased more than those of whites, from 12.40 to 12.87 years of education for blacks and from 13.36 to only 13.42 years of education for whites.

For whites, the major difference across the two time periods appears to be movement out of part-year employment into full-year employment. FTPY employment decreased from 15.9 to 12.2% of all white males, and PTPY employment decreased from 4.6 to 3.9%. These trends can be attributed to the record low unemployment levels achieved in the late 1990s economic expansion. And for this reason as well, the core long-term unemployed, those who worked no weeks in the prior year but looked for work, decreased from 0.8 to 0.6%. For blacks, the same trends are evident, although the proportion of respondents in non-FTFY categories was generally higher than for whites in each time period. Nonetheless, FTPY employment decreased from 17.5 to 12.4% of all black males, and PTPY employment decreased from 6.5 to 4.4%. Likewise, the core long-term unemployed decreased from 3.6 to 2.0%. Even though blacks generally made gains relative to whites, this is somewhat misleading, as it is in part generated by the growing racial disparity in imprisonment. The incarceration rate for blacks increased from 4.2 to 6.9% while the incarceration rate for whites increased from 0.6 to 1.0%.

Can these trends account for a substantial portion of the relative decline in the race gap in classes V, VI, and VIIa? The type of estimator we deploy to address this possibility is specified in three main steps, all with the goal of generating a lower average estimate of the wages of blacks in classes V, VI, and VIIa in proportion to the lower propensity for blacks to be observed working as FTFY workers. First, all FTPY blacks were added to the analysis sample. Then, we calculated a set of scaling factors for black FTFY and FTPY workers within each class in each year. These scaling factors are functions of the observed rate of FTFY employment for whites within each year and a more complex "what if" rate of FTFY employment for blacks within each year, as specified below. Finally, we re-estimated all of the models in Table 3 with the sample that includes the FTPY black workers, weighted as specified below.

For comparison with Estimator E2, the selection-adjusted estimator can be written in general form as class and year-specific variants of:

$$E_N[\phi^{\mathrm{w}}(k,t)Y_i|B_i = 0, FTFY_i = 1] \\ - E_N[\phi^{\mathrm{b}}(k,t)\psi^{\mathrm{b}}(c,t)Y_i|B_i = 1, FTFY_i = 1 \,\mathrm{or}\, FTPY_i = 1]. \quad \text{(E3)}$$

Notice that the first term of estimator E3 is nearly identical to the first term of estimator E2, and only differs because the term $\phi^{\mathrm{w}}(k,t)$ is utilized instead of $\pi^{\mathrm{w}}(k,t)$.[22] The selection adjustment is generated by the alternative "what if" estimate for blacks in the second term. The key to the selection adjustment is the scaling factor $\psi^{\mathrm{b}}(c,t)$ for blacks, which, as defined in the main text, is a function of $\lambda^{\mathrm{w}}(c,t)$, $\lambda^{\mathrm{b}}(c,t)$, and $\theta^{\mathrm{b}}(c,t)$. Averaged across the two time periods within each class, the values of these component rates are presented in Table A2, along with the weekly earnings of FTFY and FTPY blacks. The rates $\lambda^{\mathrm{w}}(c,t)$ and $\lambda^{\mathrm{b}}(c,i)$ are straightforward, as they are simply the year and class-specific percentages of observed FTFY and FTPY workers who are observed FTFY workers, respectively for white and black men. As shown in the first four columns of Table A2, values for these rates are mostly between 0.7 and 0.9 and are highest for classes I, II, and V. Likewise, $\lambda^{\mathrm{w}}(c,t)$ is more often than not greater than $\lambda^{\mathrm{b}}(c,t)$, in part because blacks are more likely to experience unemployment spells.

The key to the selection adjustment, however, is the "what if" rate of FTFY employment, $\theta^{\mathrm{b}}(c,t)$. This rate is calculated for a wider population of blacks, augmented proportionally to the greater representation of whites in FTFY employment. This "what if" rate is generated in three steps:

(1) Calculate the gross additional percentage of blacks who would be FTFY workers if the black rate of FTFY employment was as high as the white rate of FTFY employment. For the categories in Table A1, there are six distinct groups in each year t, defined as the proportion of blacks minus the proportion of whites who: (1) Worked zero weeks last year because they could not find work; (2) worked zero weeks last year because they were disabled; (3) worked zero weeks last year because they were keeping house; (4) worked zero weeks

Table A2. Breakdown of Specific Components of Estimator E3 by Class and Time Period.

	$\lambda^{w}(c)$		$\lambda^{b}(c)$		$\theta^{b}(c)$		Log Weekly Earnings of Black, FTFY Workers		Log Weekly Earnings of Black, FTPY Workers	
	1985–1989	1996–2000	1985–1989	1996–2000	1985–1989	1996–2000	1985–1989	1996–2000	1985–1989	1996–2000
I	0.914	0.926	0.913	0.918	0.897	0.891	6.80	6.89	6.54	6.58
II	0.889	0.905	0.892	0.884	0.878	0.859	6.43	6.51	6.32	6.38
IIIa	0.834	0.851	0.817	0.823	0.806	0.801	6.27	6.36	5.94	5.93
IIIb	0.741	0.780	0.651	0.775	0.637	0.753	5.97	6.06	5.56	5.80
V	0.883	0.897	0.876	0.894	0.859	0.861	6.42	6.54	6.19	6.35
VI	0.743	0.814	0.715	0.811	0.698	0.769	6.27	6.32	6.02	6.16
VIIa	0.698	0.775	0.708	0.774	0.681	0.709	6.05	6.08	5.77	5.85

last year for "other reasons"; (5) worked zero weeks last year because they were incarcerated; and (6) worked full-time last year for some amount of weeks but earned on average less than 50 dollars per week.

(2) Assume that these additional blacks would be employed according to the following class distribution: 0.05 for class I, 0.08 for class II, 0.04 for class IIIa, 0.015 for class IIIb, 0.045 for class V, 0.12 for class VI, and 0.65 for class VIIa. This distribution is arbitrary, but it is similar to the distribution of black employment in Table 2, although weighted more heavily toward class VIIa. Then, multiply the two distributions together: the year-specific percentage of gross additional blacks and the stipulated "what-if" class distribution of employment for the gross additional blacks. The result is a distribution of additional blacks, denoted as a set of proportions $\eta^b(c, t)$ which vary over classes c and years t.

(3) Define an adjusted rate of observed FTFY employment among a more broad-based set of blacks, assuming that there are now additional blacks in the denominator:

$$\theta^{\mathrm{b}}(c, t) = \frac{\omega^{\mathrm{b}}(c, t)\lambda^{\mathrm{b}}(c, t)}{\omega^{\mathrm{b}}(c, t) + \eta^{\mathrm{b}}(c, t)}$$

where $\omega^{\mathrm{b}}(c, t)$ is the observed percentage of all black FTFY and FTPY CPS respondents who are in class c in year t. In all years, $\theta^{\mathrm{b}}(c, t)$ is lower than $\lambda^{\mathrm{b}}(c, t)$ for all classes.

Finally, the three rates $\lambda^{\mathrm{w}}(c, t)$, $\lambda^{\mathrm{b}}(c, t)$, and $\theta^{\mathrm{b}}(c, t)$ are then combined into the selection-adjustment scaling factor $\psi^{\mathrm{b}}(c, t)$ that is applied to black FTFY and FTPY workers in the augmented sample. As the difference between $\lambda^{\mathrm{w}}(c, t)$ and $\theta^{\mathrm{b}}(c, t)$ grows, the amount of weight given to the lower FTPY wages of blacks increases, in line with the selection narratives outlined in the main text.

A key assumption of the selection-adjustment framework is that, within class c and year t, the additional "what if" blacks summarized in the aggregate by $\eta^{\mathrm{b}}(c, t)$, would on average receive lower wages than those blacks who are observed working FTFY. In particular, we assume that they would receive the wages typical of black FTPY workers, which are on average 15–20% lower (see Table A2). Since there is virtually no way to know what these hypothetical "what if" black workers would earn if they were employed FTFY, we have no firm justification for this assumption. We regard it as a rather pessimistic assumption, since one might instead assume that if these "what if" black workers were actually employed FTFY they might be earning wages much closer to what observed black FTFY workers typically earn (which would still place their wages below those of whites with comparable measured covariates). Despite our judgement, we experimented with even more pessimistic assumptions. In these ad hoc explorations, our models remained surprisingly robust, primarily because the trends in the black-white gap are largely a function of the consistent relative decline in the earnings of white men in classes V, VI, and VIIa.

NOTES TO APPENDIX

20. Again, $E_N[\cdot]$ denotes the sample expectation. Thus, assumption A1, for example, states that, as N increases to infinity, an implied sequence of sample estimates, compactly denoted as $E_N[Y_i|B_i = 0]$, converges in probability to a precisely defined conditional population expectation $E[Y^{w}_{i\notin B}]$ that is regarded as a theoretical constant.

21. The incarceration rate is the percentage of the adult population, respectively for whites and blacks, resident in federal and state prisons and local jails. We used raw values from 1985 to 1997, and then formed linear extrapolations for 1982–1984 and 1998–2000 from 1985–1988 to 1994–1997, respectively.

22. The weights $\phi^{w}(k, t)$ and $\phi^{b}(k, t)$ are nearly identical to $\pi^{w}(k, t)$ and $\pi^{b}(k, t)$, except that they calculate the percentage representation in each occupation using both black FTFY and FTPY workers. When not invoking the non-parametric occupational alignment, they are implicitly set equal to 1, as in models in the first column of each panel of Table 4. For other models, they take on values in order to align the occupational distributions of whites and blacks to the occupational distribution of blacks in the chosen reference time period, as in the models in the second and third column of each panel in Table 4.

FIRMS, WAGES, AND INCENTIVES: INCENTIVE SYSTEMS AND THEIR IMPACTS ON WAGES, PRODUCTIVITY, AND RISKS

Trond Petersen and Vemund Snartland

ABSTRACT

We address the relationship between output-related wage systems, wage levels, productivity, and risks. Four broad themes are in focus. First, *we investigate the effects of payment systems on wage levels and wage inequality.* Second, *we investigate how output-related payment systems may induce workers to expend more effort and hence lead to increased output.* Third, *we investigate the risk-sharing aspects of output-related payment systems.* Fourth, *we attempt to adjudicate between the productivity and risk-sharing effects of output-related payment systems. We use unique individual-, occupational-, and establishment-level data, covering a wide array of industries, from Norway for the year 1990, with about 165,000 employees in about 6,000 establishments.*

INTRODUCTION

Payment systems based on commissions, piece rates, and production bonuses are common in many jobs. Their historical stronghold was in manufacturing, but with a

Inequality: Structures, Dynamics and Mechanisms: Essays in Honor of Aage B. Sørensen
Research in Social Stratification and Mobility, Volume 21, 253–286

ISSN: 0276-5624/doi:10.1016/S0276-5624(04)21012-5

steady decline since the 1960s. They have however emerged in other work settings, such as in services, sales, and many professional jobs, for example, among doctors. They are thus still central in many employment relationships. And in developing countries, they are to this date practiced in the same manner as they used to be in the West.

Concordant with their historical and contemporary importance, such systems are also one of the most thoroughly studied labor market institutions. Sociologists have examined their operation for more than half a century, resulting in a series of important studies (e.g. Burawoy, 1979; Lupton, 1963; Mathewson, 1931; Roethlisberger & Dickson, 1939; Roy, 1953; Whyte, 1955). Similarly, a considerable economics literature has emerged over the last thirty years addressing the theoretical properties of such systems (e.g. Holmström, 1979; Lazear, 1995; Milgrom & Roberts, 1992, Chap. 7; Shavell, 1979; Stiglitz, 1975).[1]

Yet in spite of the extensive empirical studies in the sociology and organizations literature and the impressive theoretical studies in economics there is a striking paucity of studies addressing in a comprehensive empirical manner the perhaps most salient features of such systems: their effects on wage levels and productivity.[2] These are essential to workers as well as employers. As Sørensen (1994, p. 517) notes: "Surprisingly, little attention has been focused on the distributional consequences of these systems, that is, on how they affect earnings."

Such output-related systems are typically thought to serve two primary purposes. The *first* is to induce workers to expend more effort, that is, to work harder so that more is produced. There are however uncertainties at the point of production, due to faulty materials, machine breakdowns, changing market conditions, and other random events. So the *second* purpose is to allocate some or all of the output risks at the point of production to the workers, as wages vary with output and thus are uncertain. In the economics literature on agency problems the first is referred to as the incentive purpose,[3] while the second is referred to as the risk-sharing purpose.

With respect to wages, it is thus thought that workers paid according to output-related wage systems on average are given extra compensation in part for working harder and in part for the additional risks they face. On average the pay differential between incentive and time-rate workers should consist of compensation for extra effort and for sharing risks.

In this article we shall address the relationship between payment systems, pay, productivity, and risks. Four broad themes are in focus.

First, we will investigate the effects of payment systems on wage levels. Do employees paid on output-related payment systems receive higher wages? This relates to concerns about the distribution of wages as well as to whether such systems are worthwhile from the worker's perspective as well as to the employer's concern about total wage costs.[4]

Second, we investigate how output-related payment systems may induce workers to expend more effort, which we refer to as their incentive, productivity, or performance effect, for short, just their productivity effects.

Third, we investigate the risk-sharing aspects of output-related payment systems. We analyze the extent to which the potentially larger uncertainties lead to some compensation in terms of expected wages.

Fourth, we attempt to adjudicate between the productivity and risk-sharing effects of output-related payment systems. We try to assess the weight given to risk-sharing versus increased effort and hence productivity.

Addressing the first goal will give a useful baseline against which goals 2–4 can be viewed. We underline that while the analysis of the effects of wage systems on wage levels yields a fairly objective and from a data-analytic point of view unmediated description of the situation, accomplishing goals 2–4 requires more speculation and leads to less straightforward evidence.

Several issues will not be considered. One is the determinants of payment systems. Another is the potential role of payment systems in sorting high- and low-productivity workers into incentive and time-rate jobs (e.g. Lazear, 1986). A third is the importance of social rewards in regulating shop-floor behavior, as extensively documented in the industrial sociology literature (see Edwards, 1986, Chaps 1 and 7), for example, those that arise in connection with team production (see Petersen, 1992a, b, 1993).

This is one of few extensive empirical analyses of these issues. It uses unique individual, occupational, and establishment-level data which do not suffer from many of the problems of previous studies, covering a wide array of industries, with 165,250 employees in 6,202 establishments, from Norway for the year 1990. Previous studies have either been case based, on a single industry, or have suffered from various data problems.

Even though the use of output-related payment systems has seen a secular decline in developed countries since about 1960 to the present, there is currently renewed interest in their reintroduction on a wide basis, not only for blue- but also for white-collar workers. The management-scholar Kanter (1990, p. 152) argues for more performance-related pay, recommending a "Move toward reducing the fixed portion of pay and increasing the variable portion." In the Scandinavian context, in Sweden, since 1983 with the breakdown of centralized wage setting, there is renewed interest in such systems. As the *Swedish Delegation on Productivity* stated (SOU, 1991, p. 33, our translation): "A well-functioning wage system will be decisive for capacity utilization, employment, and productivity." So even though our empirical analysis focuses on blue-collar workers, the results may have implications for other types of employees. It is, however, among blue-collar workers that one has the widest experience with output-related wage systems and we will document part of this experience.

The remainder of the paper is organized as follows. The second section develops our four broad research themes. The third section presents the data, while the fourth section the methods. The fifth through to the ninth sections give the results and the tenth section the conclusions.

WAGE LEVELS, PRODUCTIVITY, AND RISK-SHARING

Wage Levels

Before assessing the deeper issues of whether payment systems have an effect on productivity, as well as their risk-sharing effects, we document their impact on wage levels and wage inequality. This addresses their distributional consequences and is of particular relevance in the Scandinavian context because wage inequality there is a central concern. Organizational wage systems must take into account their effects on inequality.[5]

In order to assess this, we address two aspects of the wage distribution. First, we investigate the extent to which workers paid on output-related payment systems on average earn more than those paid on time rates.[6] It is important that the comparison is made among those working in the same occupation and establishment (see SOU, 1991, p. 198). Our basic analysis concerns occupation-establishment units that use time- and piece-rate systems side-by-side. Second, we investigate the extent to which there is more inequality in wages among those paid on incentives than those paid on time-rate systems. Payment systems need not only induce inequality between those on time rates and those on incentives, but may also induce considerable inequality among the latter.

In summary, the main objective of this part of the analysis is:

Objective 1. To investigate whether output-related payment systems lead to increased wages and to increased wage inequality.

Productivity Effects of Payment Systems

It is difficult to measure individual productivity, in part because it is hard to observe. Ideally, one should observe individual employees as they shift between the two payment systems, while performing the same tasks in the same job, and then record at the individual level if there are productivity differences under the two. But such data are rarely available. Lazear (2000) is an exception. But often, what constitutes productivity is ambiguous, as in many types of service and professional work, and how to measure it at the individual level is clear neither to employers nor to social scientists.

However, in some work settings one has better access to reasonable measures of productivity than in others. Where piece-rate work is performed, wages earned on average should match productivity, so that variation in wages, for the same work for the same employer, in principle should reflect variations in productivity. As Phelps Brown (1977, p. 269) stated: "Wherever workers are on piece-rates or any form of 'payment by results,' differences in the outputs credited to them individually result in differences of earnings."

On the basis of this premise, that wages under piece-rate work should match productivity differences when it is for the same work for the same employer, one can in fact make some investigations into the potential productivity effects of payment systems, in several ways.

For employees who switch between time- and piece-rate jobs, we can observe the wages earned under each of these, and can thus make intra-indvidual comparisons of wages, assuming that those reflect productivity differences.

Another exploration of Phelps Brown's claim can be made using a simple idea. In some lines of work productivity should be strongly correlated with other observable characteristics.

One such characteristic is sex. Men should be more productive in some lines of work and women more productive in other lines of work. For example, where considerable physical strength is required, such as in much sawmill work, men should on average be more productive, whereas in lines of work requiring dexterity, such as in much textile work, women should be more productive.[7] If wages reflect productivity, one should expect to observe that under piece-rate work men on average earn more than women in the lines of work where men are at a productivity advantage, whereas the opposite should occur in lines of work where women are at a productivity advantage.[8]

Thus, dividing lines of work, such as detailed occupational groups, into those deemed male and those deemed female advantageous, and then next checking if male-female wage differences under piece-rate work vary accordingly, one should be able to assess whether payment systems have their intended effects on productivity, or at a minimum that wages under piece-rate contracts reflect productivity. It is very important that these comparisons are made for men and women doing the same work for the same employer. It is not sufficient that they work in the same detailed occupation as production technology might vary across employers and there may be self-selection and sorting of employees between establishments that may confound the analyses (see Lazear, 1986). We clearly cannot filter out all the self-selection effects, in part because women in male-advantageous occupations may be more suited for that work than the average female, and vice versa for men in female-advantageous occupations.

In summary, the main objective of this part of the analysis is:

> **Objective 2.** To assess whether output-related payment systems have their intended effects on productivity, to increase it.

Risk-Sharing Effects of Payment Systems

Having discussed the impact of output-related payment systems on wage inequality and their potential impact on effort and productivity we turn to another aspect of such systems: their role in allocating output risks at the point of production to workers. This occurs due to faulty materials, machine breakdowns, the worker having a bad month, and more (e.g. Sørensen, 1994, p. 518). For a given level of effort, there is uncertainty with respect to the amount produced and hence earned because of the uncertainties which are beyond the worker's control. In addition comes uncertainties arising from market conditions. When demand is low, the firm produces less, and there are fewer pressures and opportunities for workers to exert themselves to earn high piece-rate wages.

We shall attempt to assess the extent to which the wage differential between incentive and time-rate workers also is due to compensation for extra risks, not only compensation for extra effort.

This goal is harder to attain. It requires specifying a model for the preferences of workers and what goes on at the point of production. Nevertheless, with some simplifying assumptions, ones that are not unreasonable, it is possible to derive an estimate of the part of the wage that is due to risk compensation. Using a model from Petersen (1991), which in turn was derived from Holmström and Milgrom (1987), we can do so. Fortunately, from the viewpoint of the statistical analysis, this decomposition is quite simple. Even if one does not accept the assumptions used to derive the model yielding the specific interpretations, the reported measures make sense and are of interest in themselves.

To be more specific, we perform two analyses to approach these issues. In the first we establish whether there is evidence of more uncertainty among incentive than time-rate workers. We analyze data on workers employed in the same occupation-establishment unit, but where some are paid on time-rate and others on output-related systems. We analyze the proportion of incentive workers who receive a wage that is less than the: (a) lowest; (b) average; and (c) highest paid time-rate worker. The comparable time-rate workers are employed in the same occupation-establishment unit. These analyses will give some insight into the extent of wage risks faced under output-related payment systems.

The second analysis we will do is to see how the amount of uncertainty in wages at the occupation-establishment level among incentive-rate workers influence the average wages they earn. We thus assess whether the incentive-rate workers that face larger uncertainties in wages also tend to earn higher average wages, a comparison made among incentive-rate workers only. Our measure of uncertainty is the variance in wages among incentive-rate workers at the occupation-establishment level, a simple measure whose properties are known.[9]

We underline that this second analysis is more speculative. The analyses for Objective 1, and to some extent for Objective 2, give unmediated observations. They describe what goes on. In trying to assess the risk premium, we present measures that are statistically straightforward. It is the particular interpretation given to them that may be questionable, as reflecting risk premia.

In summary, the main objective of this part of the analysis is:

Objective 3. To assess whether workers under output-related payment systems are compensated for the increased wage risks they face.

Productivity Versus Risk-Sharing Effects

We finally attempt to assess the amount of the wage differential between incetive- and time-rate workers that is due to the productivity effects of output-related payment systems. The central idea in this analysis is that the part of the wage differential between incentive- and time-rate workers not due to risk-sharing is due to compensation for extra effort and hence productivity, assuming that the wage differential consists of only two parts, a risk-sharing and an effort part.

This analysis hence provides insight into the nature of the institution studied: Is it one that primarily induces workers to expend more effort, that is, extracts labor power, or is it one that primarily allocates risks at the point of production to the workers? We attempt to assign weights to the relative importance of the two purposes for wage differences between the two groups.

In summary, the main objective of this part of the analysis is:

Objective 4. To assess which is more important in the wage premium incentive workers receive: productivity or risk-sharing effects.

DATA

The data were collected by the main employers' association in Norway, the Confederation of Business and Employers (NHO), and were routinely used as input in wage negotiations. They come from establishment records and Norwegian employers are bound by law to collect and report the data, which should be extraordinarily reliable. They are described in detail in Petersen et al. (1997).

We use the comprehensive wage statistics from 1990 on blue-collar workers in the manufacturing, oil extraction, mining, quarrying, and auto repair shops, for simplicity referred to as *Blue-Collar Workers*. They contain information about 165,250 workers, in 428 occupations, 6,202 establishments, and 26,687 occupation-establishment units.

The data cover practically the entire occupational spectrum. For every employee information was obtained on sex, age, occupation (an industry-specific code), and wage form (time- versus piece-rate). Wages and hours worked are reported separately for regular and overtime hours, and by the type of wage system under which they were earned. For employees who alternate between time- and incentive-rate jobs, the wages are specified separately for the two. Wages are given in hourly units.

We use the information on hourly wages earned on regular hours. We do not conflate the wages with those earned on overtime and irregular hours.

Few data sets available are as comprehensive in their coverage of employees and establishments, have such good occupational characteristics, and, in particular, have such detailed and accurate wage information.

METHODS

Here we outline the central aspects of the methods we will use, for each of the four research objectives.

Methods for Objective 1: Effects on Wage Levels

The first objective is to assess the impact of payment systems on wage levels and wage inequality. We compute first the average wages of incentive workers as percentage of the average wages of time-rate workers, separately for each unit at several different levels: total, establishment, occupation, and occupation-establishment. Then an average of this gap is taken across the units that use both wage forms. For example, in each occupation-establishment unit employing both piece- and time-rate workers, we computed the average wages of piece-rate workers as a percent of the average wages of time-rate workers, and then took an average of this ratio across the units. This is explained at more length in the section discussing the results.

Methods for Objective 2: Effects on Productivity

The second objective is to assess whether output-related payment systems have their intended productivity effects. This involves two separate analyses.

First, among workers who switch between piece- and time-rate jobs, we compare their wages under the two systems, at the various levels, total, establishment, occupation, and occupation-establishment. This also involves an intra-individual comparison, where we compute the piece-rate wages as percent of the time-rate wages at the individual level.

Second, we do an analysis of the gender wage gap for a selection of occupations that we judge to be either female or male advantageous in terms of the productivity of the sexes, doing similar computations as above, but now only at the occupation-establishment level.

Methods for Objective 3: Effects on Risk-Sharing

We report the proportion of incentive workers who receives a wage less than the: (a) lowest; (b) average; and (c) highest paid time-rate worker, where the comparable time-rate workers work in the same occupation-establishment unit. These three analyses give insight into the amount of risks faced under output-related payment systems.

To see if incentive workers receive compensation for higher risks, we estimate a regression equation, using only information on incentive workers:

$$w_{ioe} = \beta x_{ioe} + \alpha\hat{\sigma}^2_{w_{I,oe}} + \eta_o + \varepsilon_{ioe} \tag{4.1}$$

where i indexes individuals, o occupations, and e establishments, and w_{ioe} is the wage for individual i in occupation-establishment unit oe and $\hat{\sigma}^2_{w_{I,oe}}$ is the sample variance of wages among incentive workers in the same unit.[10] η_o is a fixed effect for occupation, and gets included in one model, ε_{ioe} is an error term, while x_{ioe} are other covariates and ß their effects.

From the estimate of α from (4.1), we can get an estimate of the risk-sharing part of the pay differential in occupation-establishment unit oe as

$$\Delta\hat{w}_{R,oe} = \hat{\alpha}\hat{\sigma}^2_{w_{I,oe}}. \tag{4.2}$$

We report the average of this quantity across all occupations and establishments.

Methods for Objective 4: Productivity Versus Risk-Sharing

The pay differential between incentive- and time-rate workers in occupation-establishment unit *oe* ($\Delta w_{I,oe}$) consists of one part due to effort ($\Delta w_{E,oe}$) and one part due to risks ($\Delta w_{R,oe}$), namely

$$\Delta w_{I,oe} = \Delta w_{E,oe} + \Delta w_{R,oe}. \tag{4.3}$$

Two of the three quantities in (4.3) have already been estimated. The estimate of the pay differential $\Delta w_{I,oe}$ between the two groups is explained under the methods for Objective 1. The estimate of the risk-sharing differential $\Delta w_{R,oe}$ comes from (4.2) above, as explained in methods for Objective 3. From these two quantities one may obtain an estimate of the part of the pay differential due to effort or productivity, $\Delta w_{E,oe}$. It follows directly as the difference between the other two quantities: $\Delta w_{E,oe} = \Delta w_{I,oe} - \Delta w_{R,oe}$.

We report the percentage of the wage gap between incentive- and time-rate workers estimated to be due to risk-sharing and the percentage due to effort or productivity, following the procedures in Petersen (1991).

USE OF PIECE-RATE SYSTEMS

The workers are divided into three groups, one group for each of three wage forms. The first group is workers who receive all their wages from time-rate jobs, called *time-rate workers*. The second is workers who receive all their wages from piece-rate jobs, called *piece-rate workers*. The third is workers who receive part of their wages from piece-rate jobs and part from time-rate jobs, called *mixed-rate workers*. They shift between working on piece- and time-rate jobs. Often we refer to the piece-rate and mixed-rate workers as just incentive workers or as workers on output-related wage systems. Note that on the piece-rate jobs, be it for piece- or mixed-rate workers, the pay usually consists of a guaranteed baseline wage plus a piece-rate part. As Sørensen (1994, p. 518) noted: "A system where workers will be paid only by the output they produce would make it impossible to keep the workers, ..."

Table 1 gives the distribution of workers on the three pay systems, first for all, and then separately by sex. Of the 165,250 workers, 13.7% are paid on one of the two output-related wage systems. Among these workers, about two-thirds are employed under piece- and one-third under mixed-rate systems.

We next report on the use of wage systems from the perspective of a different unit of analysis than the worker. We report the extent to which the systems are used in industries, establishments, occupations, and occupation-establishment units. At

Table 1. Distribution of Workers on Payment System, for All, and by Sex (Norway 1990).

Payment System	All	Men	Women
Time-rate	86.4	87.4	81.8
Piece-rate	9.2	8.8	10.7
Mixed-rate	4.5	3.8	7.6
Sum	100.1	100.1	100.1
N	165,250	133,812	31,437

Note: There are three groups of workers: (1) time-rate workers, who receive all their wages from time-rate jobs; (2) piece-rate workers, who receive all their wages from piece-rate jobs; and (3) mixed-rate workers, where part of the wages are earned on time-rate jobs and another part on piece-rate jobs.

those levels there are seven possibilities for the use and combination of the three wage systems: (1) only time rates; (2) only piece rates; (3) only mixed rates; (4) both time and piece rates; (5) both time and mixed rates; (6) both piece and mixed rates; and (7) all three wage systems are used.

Table 2 gives in Panel A the distribution of industries, establishments, occupations, and occupation-establishment units on the seven combinations of wage systems used.

At the industry level, eleven (84.6%) of the 13 industries use all three wage systems. Of the remaining two industries, one uses only time-rate and one both time- and piece-rate systems.

At the establishment level, 88.5% of the 6,202 establishments use only time-rate systems for their workers, 2.6% use only piece-rate systems, while 2.5% use all three wage systems.

At the occupation level, 43.2% of the 428 occupations use only time-rate systems for their workers, while 27.6% of occupations use all three wage systems.

At the occupation-establishment level, 90.3% of the 26,687 occupation-establishment units use only time-rate systems for their workers, while only 0.6% of occupation-establishment units use all three wage systems. An entire 96.7% of the units use only one wage system. Thus, from the workers' viewpoint, opportunities to choose between wage systems occur more often between than within occupation-establishment units.

Panel B of Table 2 gives the distribution of the workers on the same seven categories. In column 4 we see that 82.3% of the workers are employed in occupation-establishment units where only time-rate systems are used, while 18,776 or 11.4% are employed in units where two or three wage systems are used side-by-side.

Table 2. Distribution of Industries, Establishments, Occupations, and Occupation-Establishment Units on Combinations of Wage Systems in Use (Panel A), and Distribution of Workers on those Categories (Panel B) (Norway 1990).

	Industry		Establishment		Occupation		Occ-Est	
	1		2		3		4	
Wage Systems in Use	*N*	%	*N*	%	*N*	%	*N*	%
Panel A: Distribution of units on categories								
1. Only time rates	1	7.7	5,490	88.5	185	43.2	24,104	90.3
2. Only piece rates	0	0.0	161	2.6	23	5.4	1,328	5.0
3. Only mixed-rate systems	0	0.0	20	0.3	3	0.7	384	1.4
4. Time rates and piece rates	1	7.7	160	2.6	80	18.7	201	0.8
5. Time rates and mixed rates	0	0.0	189	3.0	18	4.2	373	1.4
6. Piece rates and mixed rates	0	0.0	24	0.4	1	0.2	134	0.5
7. All three systems	11	84.6	158	2.5	118	27.6	159	0.6
Sum	13	100.0	6,202	99.9	428	100.0	26,687	100.0
Panel B: Distribution of workers on categories								
1. Only time rates	3,307	2.0	127,634	77.2	8,898	5.4	135,968	82.3
2. Only piece rates	0	0.0	5,015	3.0	89	0.1	9,133	5.5
3. Only mixed-rate systems	0	0.0	149	0.1	4	0.0	1,373	0.8
4. Time rates and piece rates	1,224	0.7	11,126	6.7	7,300	4.4	3,650	2.2
5. Time rates and mixed rates	0	0.0	5,619	3.4	1,541	0.9	5,406	3.3
6. Piece rates and mixed rates	0	0.0	1,207	0.7	3	0.0	2,504	1.5
7. All three systems	160,719	97.3	14,500	8.8	147,415	89.2	7,216	4.4
Sum	165,250	100.0	165,250	99.9	165,250	100.0	165,250	100.0

Note: In Panel A, the entries give the distribution on the combination of wage systems used within industries, establishments, occupations, and occupation-establishment units. Within each of the four numbered columns (cols. 1–4), the first subcolumn refers to the number of units (e.g., occupations) falling into each of the seven categories, while the second subcolumn refers to the percent of the units that do so. For example, in column 2, the number 88.5 in line 1 means that 88.5% of the establishments pay all their workers on only time rates, corresponding to 5,490 establishments, while line 7 means that 2.5% of the establishments utilize all three wage systems, corresponding to 158 establishments. Or, for column 4, the number 90.3 in line 1 means that 90.3% of the occupation-establishment units pay all their workers on only time rates, while line 4 means that 0.8% of the units pay some of their workers on time-rate systems and others on piece-rate systems. Panel B gives the distribution of workers on the seven categories in Panel A. For example, in column 2, the number 8.8 in line 7 means that 8.8% of the workers are employed in establishments that use all three wage systems.

That most occupation-establishment units use only one wage system is perhaps not surprising. Use of wage systems sometimes reflects technological possibilities, which tend to vary more between than within establishments and occupation-establishment units. And even when more than one system is technologically feasible, it may be more costly to operate two or three systems than only one. Each system has its administrative costs in addition to its incentive and motivation properties, and those costs must be factored in when choosing which and how many systems to operate.

RESULTS 1: EFFECTS ON WAGES

Our first question concerns the impact of the wage system on wage levels: Is there a wage payoff from working under output-related systems? We make several comparisons.

Table 3 gives the mean and standard deviation of hourly wages for each group of workers. Piece-rate workers on average earn 86.20 Norwegian *kroner* (NOK), a miniscule 1.86% more than time-rate workers. Among mixed-rate workers, their average wage on piece-rate jobs is NOK 93.88, or 25.5% higher than on their time-rate jobs.

The standard deviation of wages is somewhat higher for piece- than time-rate workers, 21.36 versus 17.30, reflecting higher wage dispersion among the former. The standard deviation of wages on the piece-rate jobs of mixed-rate workers is quite large, 32.23. But for the total hourly wages of mixed-rate workers, combining wages on piece- and time-rate jobs, its standard deviation is smaller than among both time-rate workers and piece-rate workers.

Table 3. Descriptive Statistics for Wages by Wage System (Norway 1990).

			Mixed-Rate Workers		
	Piece-Rate Workers	Time-Rate Workers	Total Wages	Piece-Rate Jobs	Time-Rate Jobs
	1	2	3	4	5
Mean	86.20	84.63	83.37	93.88	74.78
S.D.	21.36	17.30	15.57	32.23	16.47
N	15,122	142,712	7,414	7,414	7,414

Note: Piece-rate workers receive all their wages from piece-rate jobs. Time-rate workers receive all their wages from time-rate jobs. Mixed-rate workers receive part of their wages from piece-rate jobs and part from time-rate jobs.

We now turn to our main task. Table 4 compares the two groups of workers on output-related payment systems to those on time rates. In column 1 we compare piece-rate workers, those who receive all their pay from piece-rate jobs, to time-rate workers, those who receive all their pay from time-rate jobs. We compute the piece-rate wages as percent of the time-rate wages. This we do for five different levels, reported in lines 1–5. In the first line we compute the average wages of piece-rate workers as a percent of the average wages of time-rate workers. In the second line we do the same, but now controlling for industry. For each industry, we first computed the average wages of piece-rate workers as a percent of the average wages of time-rate workers. Thereafter we took the mean of this percent across the industries. In lines 3–5 we make the same types of computations, but now at the establishment, occupation, and occupation-establishment levels respectively. Especially the last line is important. Here we computed, in each occupation-establishment unit employing both piece- and time-rate workers, the average wages of piece-rate workers as a percent of the average wages of time-rate workers. Then the average of this was taken across the units. As reported above, only a small percent of the occupation-establishment units employ piece- and time-rate workers side-by-side. Table 2 gives the number of units and workers included in each combination of wage systems at the five levels.

In columns 2–4 we make the same type of comparisons but now between mixed-rate and time-rate workers. In column 2 we compare the average wages of the two groups, at the five different levels. In column 3 we compare the wages on the piece-rate jobs of mixed-rate workers to the wages of time-rate workers. In column 4, we compare the time-rate wages of mixed-rate workers to the wages of time-rate workers. These computations are done again for each of the five levels, overall, industry, establishment, occupation, and occupation-establishment.

No matter how one looks at it, as soon as one goes down to a finer level than the total or overall, it pays in terms of wages to work on one of the output-related wage systems. Starting with piece-rate workers, overall they earn a miniscule 1.86% more than time-rate workers. However, at the occupation and occupation-establishment levels they earn 7.78 and 11.83% more.

For mixed-rate workers, combining wages on the piece- and time-rate jobs, overall they earn 1.28 percent less than time-rate workers. However, once they work in the same occupation and same occupation-establishment unit, they earn 6.70 and 8.29% more than time-rate workers. The piece-rate wages of mixed-rate workers are considerably higher than the wages of time-rate workers, by 26.86 and 27.47% at the occupation and occupation-establishment levels respectively. On time-rate jobs the wages of mixed-rate workers are a little below those of time-rate workers: At the occupation and occupation-establishment levels 2.64 and 0.29% lower.

Table 4. The Mean Wages of Piece-Rate Workers (Col. 1) and of Mixed-Rate Workers (Cols. 2–4) as Percent of the Mean Wages of Time-Rate Workers, at Five Different Levels (Norway 1990).

		Mixed-Rate Workers Relative to Time-Rate Workers		
	Piece-Rate Relative to Time-Rate Wages	Total Mixed-Rate Wages to Time-Rate Wages	Piece-Rate Jobs Relative to Time-Rate wages	Time-Rate Jobs Relative to Time-Rate wages
	1	2	3	4
Panel A: Relative wage differentials				
Overall	101.86	98.52	110.94	88.36
Industry	103.63	103.13	113.78	94.80
Establishment	113.63	107.24	122.25	97.84
Occupation	107.78	106.70	126.86	97.36
Occupation-Establishment	111.83	108.29	127.47	99.71
Panel B: Absolute wage differentials				
Overall	1.57	−1.25	9.26	−9.85
Industry	2.84	2.19	11.22	−4.59
Establishment	9.29	4.78	16.38	−2.31
Occupation	5.35	4.75	21.78	−2.60
Occupation-establishment	8.09	5.39	20.04	−0.78

Note: There are three groups of workers: Those who receive all wages from piece-rate jobs, called piece-rate workers; those who receive all wages from time-rate jobs, called time-rate workers; and those who receive part of their wages from piece-rate jobs and part from time-rate jobs, called mixed-rate workers. In Panel A, the numbers in the table give the wages of each group as percentage of the wages of time-rate workers. For column 1, the first line gives the average wage of piece-rate workers as percent of the average wage of time-rate workers. For column 1, the second line obtains in two steps. First, one computes the average wage of piece-rate workers as percent of the average wage of time-rate workers, separately within each industry. Then an average of this is taken across industries. For column 1, lines 3–5 are computed in the same manner, but now for establishment, occupation, and occupation-establishment. For columns 2–4, the computations are analogous to those in column 1. The difference is that the comparison groups differ. The wages of mixed-rate workers are computed relative to the wages of time-rate workers. For the mixed-rate workers there are three different wage measures: Their total wages, combining wages on piece- and time-rate jobs, their wages on piece-rate jobs, and their wages on time-rate jobs. For example, in column 3, line 1, the mean wages of mixed-rate workers earned on piece-rate jobs is taken as a percent of the mean wages of time-rate workers. Then in lines 2–5, this gets computed at the industry, establishment, occupation, and occupation-establishment levels, in the same manner as in column 1. Panel B gives the absolute wage differences between the groups at the five levels.

Table 5. Mean Wages of Mixed-Rate Workers as Percent of Mean Wages of Piece-Rate Workers (Norway 1990).

	Total Wages	Piece-Rate Jobs Compared to Piece-Rate Wages	Time-Rate Jobs Compared to Piece-Rate Wages
	1	2	3
Overall	96.72	108.92	86.75
Industry	99.78	109.98	91.48
Establishment	97.06	102.57	88.46
Occupation	100.11	118.43	91.68
Occupation-establishment	98.01	101.85	89.36

Note: In this table we compare mixed-rate workers to piece-rate workers. In column 1, we compare the average wages of mixed-rate workers, combining wages on piece- and time-rate jobs, to the wages of piece-rate workers. In column 2, we compare the wages on the piece-rate jobs of the mixed-rate workers to the wages of piece-rate workers. In column 3, we compare the wages on the time-rate jobs of mixed-rate workers to the wages of piece-rate workers. In each column, this is done at five different levels, overall, industry, establishment, occupation, and occupation-establishment. See note to Table 4 and text for details on computation.

We next turn to a comparison of mixed-rate to piece-rate workers. Table 5 gives the same types of statistics for the two groups. In terms of the average wages earned, combining wages on the piece- and time-rate jobs, mixed-rate workers earn about the same as piece-rate workers: At the occupation and occupation-establishment levels they earn respectively 0.11 more and 1.99% less. On the piece-rate jobs, however, mixed-rate workers do better than piece-rate workers: At the occupation and occupation-establishment levels they earn 18.43 and 1.85% more. But on the time-rate jobs of mixed-rate workers the wages are considerably below those of piece-rate workers, with 8.32 and 11.64% at the occupation and occupation-establishment levels respectively.

An unusual opportunity for analysis arises for the mixed-rate workers. Table 6 gives the same kinds of statistics but for the mixed-rate workers alone, comparing their wages on piece-rate jobs to their wages on time-rate jobs. This is computed for the same five levels as in Table 5. Additionally, in line 6 we report the following. First, for each worker, her piece-rate wages was computed as a percentage of her time-rate wages. Thereafter an average of this percentage was taken across all workers. This gives how much on average a worker employed on a mixed-rate systems earns on piece- compared to time-rate jobs.

Table 6 shows clearly that mixed-rate workers earn more on piece- than on time-rate jobs: At the occupation and occupation-establishment levels the pay

Table 6. Mean Wages on Piece-Rate Jobs as Percent of Mean Wages on Time-Rate Jobs of Workers on Mixed-Rate Payment Systems, at Six Different Levels (Norway 1990).

Overall	125.55
Industry	120.48
Establishment	124.96
Occupation	134.52
Occupation-establishment	127.43
Intra-individual	129.07

Note: The numbers in this table pertain to workers who are employed on mixed-rate payment systems. It gives the wages from piece-rate jobs as a percent of wages on time-rate jobs, at various levels. The first line gives the average wages from the piece-rate jobs as a percent of the average wages of the time-rate jobs. The second line is obtained in two steps. First one computes, for all the workers in a given industry who are on mixed-rate systems, the average wages on the piece-rate jobs as percent of the average wages on the time-rate jobs. Then an average of this percent is taken across the industries. Lines 3–5 are computed in the same manner, but now for establishment, occupation, and occupation-establishment. The last line obtains by first computing, at the individual level, the ratio (in percent) of wages on piece-rate jobs to time-rate jobs, separately for each individual paid on a mixed-rate system, and then by taking an average of this across individuals. This is hence an intra-individual comparison, where individuals are compared to themselves in terms of what they earn on the two separate wage systems, the piece- and the time-rate jobs.

differentials are 34.52 and 27.43% respectively. At the individual level in line 6, wages on piece-rate jobs are 29.07% higher than on time-rate jobs.

In summary, there is no question that there is a clear wage premium from being paid on an output-related wage system, be it a piece-rate or mixed-rate system. Whether it is a big premium is a matter of judgment. At the occupation and occupation-establishment levels it is 7.78 and 11.83% for piece-rate workers and 6.70 and 8.29% for mixed-rate workers. From the workers' viewpoint, as far as wages are concerned, the advantages are considerable, and they are biggest for those who receive all their pay from piece-rate jobs. For comparison, the difference between incentive- and time-rate workers at the occupation and occupation-establishment levels are considerably bigger than the gender wage gaps found at those levels (e.g. Petersen et al., 1997).

The Norwegian situation differs markedly from the Finnish. In Finland the wage payoff to being on piece-rate systems is more substantial. For example, at the occupation and occupation-establishment levels, piece-rate workers earn 27.60 and 25.20 more than time-rate workers, with somewhat smaller differences for mixed-rate workers (Meyersson-Milgrom et al., 2002).

RESULTS 2: EFFECTS ON PRODUCTIVITY

The fact that wages are higher under output-related than time-rate systems for workers in the same occupation and occupation-establishment unit, gives indirect support to the claim that such systems increase output. This was illustrated in Tables 4–6 above. The perhaps strongest evidence in this regard comes from the results for the mixed-rate workers in Table 6. Comparing the same group of workers as they shift between the two wage systems, on average they receive considerably higher wages on piece- than time-rate jobs. Most telling is the intra-individual comparison made in line 6: On average, individual workers earn 29% more when on piece- than time-rate jobs. Taken at face value, relying on Phelps Brown's claim: Productivity increases with 29% when a worker shifts from time- to piece-rate jobs. This of course assumes that pay under time rates also reflects productivity, which it of course may not do, but probably it is not entirely divorced from it either.

Further insight into the productivity effects can be gained from a different line of reasoning. As discussed earlier, one should expect women to be at a productivity advantage in some lines of work, while men to be at an advantage in other lines. Under piece-rate work, where pay is linked to productivity, women should earn more than men when they are at an advantage and less when they are at a disadvantage. Such issues are now explored.

We selected some occupations (industry specific) where we thought men to be at a productivity advantage and some where women were thought to be at an advantage. The selections mirror stereotypes about the kinds of skills needed in different occupations and industries, such as strength and dexterity, and how the characteristics may be unevenly distributed between the sexes. Such stereotypes have been around for a long time and some are probably accurate statistical generalizations. To identify occupations with the relevant characteristics we relied on the detailed occupational descriptions for the data.

Table 7 reports the gender wage gaps under time- and piece-rate systems for selected occupations, with presumed male-advantageous ones in Panel A and presumed female-advantageous ones in Panel B. Column 1 gives the gap among incentive workers, where we combine piece-rate workers and the piece-rate jobs of mixed-rate workers. Column 2 gives the gap for time-rate workers.

Under piece rates it matters strongly for the gender wage gap whether one is in a male- versus a female-advantageous occupation. In male-advantageous settings, women suffer a pay gap of about 4%, while in female-advantageous settings they enjoy a wage premium, earning on average 4% more than men. Under time-rate work it does not matter much for the wage gap whether the setting is male or female advantageous. On average it is in favor of men, of about 2.0–2.5 %. It is only slightly higher in male-advantageous settings.

Table 7. Gender Wage Gap at the Occupation-Establishment Level Among Workers on Piece-Rate (Col. 1) and Time-Rate Wage Systems (Col. 2) in Male- and Female-Adventagous Occupations (Norway 1990).

Occupation by Industry	Piece-Rate 1	Time-Rate 2
Panel A: "Male-advantageous occupations"		
General maintenance		
Freight handler, truck operator	96.09	97.69
Mining and quarrying laborer	90.07	98.74
Mining		
Miner	97.08	
Meat		
Apprentice	94.07	96.61
Butcher	92.75	99.58
Machine operator	93.51	91.48
Fisheries		
Fish receiving	99.64	97.47
Forestry		
Sawmill worker	100.89	96.93
Metals		
Skilled worker	98.98	98.38
Across occupations (unweighted)	95.89	97.11
Across occupations (weighted)	95.48	97.17
Panel B: "Female-advantageous occupations"		
Fisheries		
Filet cutter	107.77	100.69
Filet packing and weighting	103.42	99.59
Thawing and cleansing of shrimp	98.54	86.57
Textiles		
Knitter	98.18	94.80
Clothing		
Seamstress whole cloth	106.07	97.96
Assembly seamstress	109.96	104.47
Across occupations (unweighted)	103.99	97.34
Across occupations (weighted)	104.47	98.11

Note: For procedures, see text and note to Table 4. For mixed-rate workers, in column 1, only their wages on piece-rate jobs are used, while in column 2, only their wages on time-rate jobs are used. In column 1, the gender wage gap is computed for wages on piece-rate jobs. In column 2, the gender wage gap is computed for wages on time-rate jobs. The number of cases, in terms of occupation-establishment units (N_{oe}), number of women (N_f), and number of men (N_m), are as follows: In male-advantageous occupations, under piece rates, $N_{oe} = 47$, $N_f = 210$, $N_m = 1{,}610$, and under time rates, $N_{oe} = 202$, $N_f = 1{,}841$, $N_m = 4{,}865$; in female-advantageous occupations, under piece rates, $N_{oe} = 27$, $N_f = 463$, $N_m = 192$, and under time rates, $N_{oe} = 57$, $N_f = 627$, $N_m = 290$.

Furthermore, in male-advantageous settings, where women are thought to be less productive, the gap is about 1.5 % higher under piece- than time-rate work. Conversely, in female-advantageous settings, where women are thought to be more productive than men, they get penalized under time-rate work, on average earning 2.0–2.5% less than men, while reaping the benefits of their productivity advantages under piece-rate work, earning 4% more than men.

Note here the female wage advantage among "Filet Cutters" on piece rates: Women earn 7.77% more than men (in Panel B). Not only does this correspond to stereotypes, it corresponds also to perceived realities among employers. In 2003, the Finnish Equality Ombudsperson wrote a letter of complaint to the counterpart in Norway accusing Norwegian fish factories of refusing to hire Finnish men as filet cutters, while routinely hiring Finnish women for the same jobs, claiming that refusal to hire was because of their sex. The Norwegian daily *Aftenposten* (Nilsen, 2003) called several employers in the industry. One response was: "This is so simply because Finnish women produce more than the men. This is not the case only for Finnish women, but also for Norwegian. The women have smaller hands and are faster. We don't want Norwegian men either." Our data show that the stereotype appears to be a correct statistical generalization, one that employers take into account when hiring.

These results thus give further support to the claim that piece-rate systems increase productivity, and especially that wages under output-related systems tend to reflect productivity. In the settings where one sex is thought to be more productive than the other, there is under piece-rate systems a wage gap in favor of the more productive sex, but not one under time-rate pay.

RESULTS 3: EFFECTS ON RISK-SHARING

In this section we first establish the extent to which there is uncertainty in wages of piece- and mixed-rate workers. Then we address whether there is wage compensation for the extra uncertainty among workers who receive all or some of their wages from piece-rate work, trying to estimate the amount of risk compensation. The issues are addressed below in two separate subsections.

Is There Uncertainty in the Wages of Incentive Workers?

One aspect of all output-related wage systems is that they make wages less predictable. They go up and down with productivity. And the productivity depends not only on the effort of the worker but also on other factors outside his or her control, such as faulty materials, machine breakdown, noncooperative co-workers, market conditions, and more. Such uncertainty may lead to incentive workers sometimes earning lower wages than time-rate workers.

We have established that incentive workers on average earn higher wages than time-rate workers in the same occupation and occupation-establishment unit. But that does not mean that all incentive workers do so. Some may earn lower wages due to the uncertainty. This was initially documented in Table 3: the standard deviation of wages was larger on piece-rate than time-rate jobs, reflecting more wage variability under output-related systems.

We report how often it occurs that incentive wages fall below the wages of time-rate workers. Table 8 gives, in Panels A, B, and C, the percent of incentive workers who receives a wage less than: (a) the lowest paid time-rate worker; (b) the average wage of time-rate workers; and (c) the highest paid time-rate worker. The time-rate workers to whom comparisons are made work in the same occupation-establishment unit. Among piece-rate workers, the three percentages are 25.7, 36.2, and 60.6. Among the mixed-rate workers, the percentages are 7.6, 18.2, and 43.8 for the piece-rate jobs, and 10.1, 25.2, and 60.5 for the total wages. A non-trivial percent of incentive workers thus earn less than the lowest, average, and highest paid time-rate worker in the same occupation-establishment unit.

Based on the evidence in Table 8 one may say that wages under output-related wage systems contain some amount of uncertainty. They often fall below the wages of time-rate workers in the same occupation-establishment unit. Similar results were found for Finland in 1996 (Meyersson-Milgrom et al., 2002).

Are Piece-Rate Workers Compensated for Extra Uncertainty?

In Tables 3–5 we showed that there was a significant wage payoff to being paid on some incentive system. This wage differential may be due to compensation for extra effort: When more effort is exerted, more is produced, and more is earned. That is likely the most important part of the differential. But part of it may also be due to compensation for the extra wage risks under piece rates. This can be thought of as follows. Suppose there is no effort differential between incentive and time-rate workers, for example because the pace of work is controlled by the machinery. In that case, the two groups will on average produce as much. The wages of a time-rate worker are fixed, while those of an incentive worker will vary with the amount produced, and will drop when input materials are faulty or market conditions bad. For a worker to accept working on a piece-rate contract, where wages may be either lower or higher than under time rates, it is often thought that on average some compensation needs to be offered for the added uncertainty.

Table 8. Percent of Workers, Either on Piece-Rate (Col. 1) or on Mixed-Rate Systems (Cols. 2–3), for Whom the Wage is Lower than the Lowest, the Average, and the Highest Paid Time-Rate Worker in the Same Occupation-Establishment Unit (Norway 1990).

		Mixed-Rate Workers	
	Piece-Rate Workers	Total Wages of Mixed-Rate Workers	Piece-Rate Wages of Mixed-Rate Workers
	1	2	3
Panel A: Comparison with lowest time-rate wage			
Not lower	74.3	89.9	92.4
Lower	25.7	10.1	7.6
Sum	100.0	100.0	100.0
N	4,315	5,212	5,212
Panel B: Comparison with average time-rate wage			
Not lower	63.8	74.8	81.8
Lower	36.2	25.2	18.2
Sum	100.0	100.0	100.0
N	4,315	5,212	5,212
Panel C: Comparison with highest time-rate wage			
Not lower	39.4	39.5	56.2
Lower	60.6	60.5	43.8
Sum		100.0	100.0
N	4,315	5,212	5,212

Note: Panel A makes comparisons to the wage of the lowest paid time-rate worker employed in the same occupation-establishment unit. In column 1, for each piece-rate worker in a given occupation-establishment unit we computed whether or not the worker received a lower wage than the lowest wage of time-rate workers in the same occupation-establishment unit. Column 1 then reports the percent of piece-rate workers for whom this is the case. In column 2, we make the same computation but now for the total wage (combining wages on the piece- and time-rate jobs) of mixed-rate workers. In column 3, the same computation is done for the wage under the piece-rate jobs for mixed-rate workers. In Panel B, the same kinds of comparisons are made, but now to the average wages of time-rate workers employed in the same occupation-establishment unit. In Panel C, the same kinds of comparisons are made, but now to the wage of the highest paid time-rate worker employed in the same occupation-establishment unit.

The incentive workers will then know that they can expect to earn higher wages, but are not assured of it. Without an expected compensation for uncertain wages, workers will not take on piece-rate work. That compensation is referred to as a risk premium or as a risk-sharing differential.

In reality, incentive workers also exert more effort, otherwise there would be no point to an incentive system, neither for employers nor workers, since it would result in no sharable gain. With more effort expended, and hence on average more produced, the wage differential relative to time-rate workers will reflect both compensation for extra effort (and output) and for risk-sharing.

In what follows we attempt to estimate the extent to which the wage differential between piece- and time-rate workers reflects compensation for extra effort versus compensation for risk-sharing. We start by estimating the risk-sharing part. With this in hand, we can recover the effort part, in the next section.

How to explore this issue is not obvious. But one simple approach is this. A measure of uncertainty at the occupation-establishment level is the variance of wages among piece-rate workers at that level. This can be computed for occupation-establishment units employing two or more incentive workers. We use the so-called unadjusted variance, where one divides by the number of workers rather than by the number of workers minus one.

Then one can next regress the wages of incentive workers on the variance of their wages at the occupation-establishment level and on other characteristics, especially dummy variables for occupation. The coefficient for variance of wages, assuming it is positive, gives how much on average the wages of incentive workers increase when the variance of wages at the occupation-establishment level increases with one unit. From this measure we can see how much on average uncertainty in wages gets compensated in the size of wages. This seems like a plausible procedure, yielding effects that are easy to interpret.[11]

We repeat the caveat that the interpretation of the results relies on various assumptions, some of which likely are not met. The results should hence be viewed as illustrations rather than decisive descriptions of the issues.

With this caveat in hand, Table 9 gives the results from the regression analyses, presenting the estimate of the coefficient for the variance of wages at the occupation-establishment level on the wage of the worker. Column 1 gives the results for piece-rate workers. Here the variance of wages is computed for that group of workers and only those workers enter into the regression analysis. Column 2 gives the results for the piece-rate jobs for mixed-rate workers. Only the piece-rate wages of those workers enter into the computation of the variance and only those workers contribute to the analysis. Finally, in column 3 we combine the two groups from columns 1 and 2. The variance of wages is computed from the wages of piece-rate workers and the wages on the piece-rate jobs of the mixed-rate workers.

From Table 9 we see that the effects of the variance of wages vary with the group of workers considered. It is smallest among piece-rate workers. The many decimals in the coefficients reflect that the variance is a large number.

To see what these numbers mean it is useful to compute how much the average wages of incentive workers increases when uncertainty (i.e. variance of

Table 9. Effect on Wages of Variance of Wages at the Occupation-Establishment Level Among Piece-Rate Workers and Mixed-Rate Workers (Norway 1990).

	Piece-Rate Workers	Mixed-Rate Workers	Mixed-Rate and Piece-Rate Workers
	1	2	3
Model 1. No additional control variables	0.0014*	0.0104*	0.0056*
Model 2. Controlling for occupation	0.0013*	0.0123*	0.0063*
Mean of within Occ-est. variance of wages	153.52	275.35	195.78

Note: The dependent variable in the regression is the hourly wages for the worker. In column 1, the analysis is based on piece-rate workers, in column 2 on the wages on the piece-rate jobs of mixed-rate workers, and in column 3 the two groups are combined, using the wages of piece-rate workers and the wages on the piece-rate jobs for mixed-rate workers. In Model 1, we control only for the variance of wages. In Model 2, we have in addition controlled for occupation by a set of dummy variables. The entries in the table give the estimated coefficient for the variable variance of wages. It is measured at the occupation-establishment level for respectively piece-rate workers and the piece-rate jobs of mixed-rate workers. We use the unadjusted variance, where we divide by the number of workers on piece rates in the occupation-establishment unit. In the adjusted variance one would divide by number of workers minus 1. Line 3, gives the mean of the within occupation-establishment variance of wages across all occupation-establishment units that entered into the regression analyses in the column.

*Significantly different from 0 at 5-percent level (two-tailed test).

wages) increases. The thinking is that average wages are higher in occupation-establishment units with considerable uncertainty of wages than in units with less uncertainty.

Table 10 gives some examples. When one goes from an occupation-establishment unit where the variance of wages equals zero to one where it equals its mean and next twice its mean, the average wage among piece-rate workers increases with NOK 0.22 and 0.43, trivial increases of about 0.25–0.50% of their average wages overall. Among mixed-rate workers, the impact of uncertainty is more substantial. The mean wages increases with NOK 2.89 and 5.69 as uncertainty of wages increases with amounts equal to one and two times the mean of the variance. These are increases of about 3–7% relative to the mean wages of mixed-rate workers. We readily see from Table 9 why the impact is so much bigger among mixed- than piece-rate workers: The coefficient for the variance of wages is 6–10 bigger in the former group and the mean occupation-establishment level variance of wages is about twice as large. When the coefficient and the variance get multiplied, the impact is much bigger among mixed-rate workers.

Table 10. Estimated Amount of Increase in Average Hourly Wages for Different Values of the Variance of Wages at the Occupation-Establishment Level, NOK (Norway 1990).

Amount of variance in wages	Piece-Rate Workers	Mixed-Rate Workers	Piece-Rate and Mixed-Rate Workers
	1	2	3
From model 1: No additional control variables			
Zero variance	0.00	0.00	0.00
Mean (σ^2)	0.22	2.89	1.10
Mean (σ^2) times two	0.43	5.78	2.20
From model 2: Controlling for occupation			
Zero variance	0.00	0.00	0.00
Mean (σ^2)	0.19	3.40	1.23
Mean (σ^2) times two	0.39	6.79	2.46

Note: We use the regression coefficients and the mean of the within occupation-establishment level variance in wages from Table 9. In column 1, the analysis is based on piece-rate workers (from col. 1 in Table 9), in column 2 on the piece-rate jobs of mixed-rate workers (from col. 2 in Table 9), and in column 3 the two groups are combined, using the wages of piece-rate workers and the wages on the piece-rate jobs for mixed-rate workers (from col. 3 in Table 9). For the results from Model 1, we control only for the variance of wages at the occupation-establishment level, in which case we use the results from Model 1 in Table 9. For the results from Model 2, we have in addition controlled for occupation by a set of dummy variables, in which case we use the results from Model 2 in Table 9. The entries in the table obtain as the estimated coefficient for the variable for variance of wages multiplied with the average value of the variable itself, from Eq. (4.2). This gives the estimated average risk compensation, evaluated when uncertainty is at its average value, the mean of the variance of wages at the relevant occupation-establishment level. Which coefficient and which value for the variable is used vary with the column, so that columns 1, 2, and 3 above come from respectively columns 1, 2, and 3 in Table 9, corresponding to the three groups of workers. For example, the entry of 0.22 in column 1 above obtains from column 1 of Table 9 as 0.0014 multiplied with 153.52, while 6.79 in column 2 in the last line above obtains from column 2 of Table 9 as 0.0123 multiplied with 275.35. We use the unadjusted variance, where we divide by the number of workers on piece rates in the occupation-establishment unit. In the adjusted variance one would divide by number of workers minus 1.

Substantively, it may make sense that mixed-rate workers get more risk compensation. They have the time-rate jobs to make comparisons to, or even to fall back on. They may thus require more risk compensation in order to be willing to take on the piece-rate jobs. Piece-rate workers in contrast to a smaller extent have time-rate jobs to fall back on. The conclusion is that the mean wages of incentive workers increase with uncertainty of wages. There appears to be some compensation for uncertainty. But it appears to be small.

RESULTS 4: PRODUCTIVITY VERSUS RISK-SHARING?

Finally, we attempt to decompose the average wage differential between incentive and time-rate workers into one part due to compensation for extra risks and another due to compensation for extra effort that on average leads to increased output. This goes to the heart of two of the central purposes of output-related wage systems, to induce workers to expend more effort and to allocate some of the risks at the point of production to the workers.

We again make the caveat that the interpretations given to these computations rely on various assumptions. The numbers themselves are straightforward to interpret in plain empiricist terms, but the more ambitious interpretations we here try to make require specific assumptions, and clearly can be questioned.

We make several computations, taking their departure in Tables 3, 4, 9 and 10. Recall from Tables 3 and 4 that for the overall wage differential, there is a small positive difference between piece- and time-rate workers, and a small negative one between mixed-rate and time-rate workers; thus not much of a positive wage differential to decompose in the first comparison and none in the second. But these average differences are computed across industries, establishments, occupations, and occupation-establishment units, lumping together workers employed in widely varying setting, under different technologies, and so forth. Once comparison of wages are done at the occupation and especially occupation-establishment level an entirely different picture emerges, with clear wage advantages to incentive over time-rate workers. The occupation-establishment level is the most relevant level at which to decompose the wage differential that accrues to incentive work.

Table 11 gives a decomposition first of the total wage premium (Panel A) for output-related wages and next of the premium at the occupation-establishment level (Panel B). Other comparisons could here have been made.

For Panel A, comparing piece- to time-rate workers, the overall average wage differential is NOK 1.57, from Table 4. Of this differential, NOK 0.22 is on average due to compensation for the extra uncertainty faced by piece-rate workers, from Table 10, computed as the amount with which the average wage increases when uncertainty increases from zero to its mean value, using Eq. (4.2). This amount of 0.22 makes up 14.0% of the wage differential ($0.140 = 0.22/1.57$). The remainder of the wage differential, NOK 1.35 ($=1.57-0.22$), using Eq. (4.3), is then compensation for the extra effort that on average may lead to greater output, an entire 86.0% of the differential ($0.86 = 1.35/1.57$). In short, 14% is compensation for risks, 86% for effort. Columns 3 and 4 of Table 11 contain an analogous decomposition of the wage differential between the piece- and time-rate jobs of mixed-rate workers. The results are the same as in the first comparison.

Table 11. Decomposition of the Average Hourly Wage Differential of Piece- Versus Time-Rate Workers (Cols. 1–2) and Piece- Versus Time-Rate Jobs of Mixed-Rate Workers (Cols. 3–4) into One Part Due to Risk Compensation and Another Due to Effort Compensation (Norway 1990).

	Wages of Piece-Rate Workers Versus Time-Rate Workers		Wages on Piece-Rate Versus Time-Rate Jobs of Mixed-Rate Workers	
	NOK	Percent	NOK	Percent
	1	2	3	4
Panel A				
Overall wage differential	1.57	1.86	19.10	25.54
The two parts				
Risk compensation	0.22	14.0	2.89	15.1
Effort compensation	1.35	86.0	16.21	84.9
Sum	1.57	100.0	19.10	100.0
Panel B				
Occ-Estab-level wage differential	8.09	10.14	20.04	26.27
The two parts				
Risk compensation	0.22	2.7	2.89	14.4
Effort compensation	7.87	97.3	17.15	85.6
Sum	8.09	100.0	20.04	100.0

Note: In columns 1 and 2, the comparison is between piece-rate workers and time-rate workers. The average wage differential in Panel A, column 1, line 1, is computed from the average wages presented in Table 3. For piece-rate workers it is 86.20, for time-rate workers 84.63, yielding a differential of 1.57. The average risk-sharing compensation of NOK 0.22, in column 1 in both Panels A and B, line 2 within each, is taken from Table 10, column 1, line 2: On average NOK 0.22 of the wage differential of 1.57 is due to risk compensation, that is, 14.0 % of the differential (0.140 = 0.22/1.57). The rest of the wage differential is compensation for effort or productivity. The average effort compensation is thus the average wage differential minus the average risk compensation, in Panel A as 1.35 (=1.57−0.22), from Eq. (4.3). The other decompositions are computed in the same manner. In Panel B, column 1, line 1, the wage differential of NOK 8.09 is taken from Table 4, Panel B, column 1, line 5. The average risk-sharing compensation is the same as in Panel A. The average effort compensation is then 7.87 (=8.09−0.22). In columns 3 and 4, the comparison is between the piece-rate jobs and time-rate jobs of mixed-rate workers. The average wage differential in Panel A, column 3, line 1, is computed from the average wages presented in Table 3. For piece-rate jobs it is 93.88, for time-rate jobs 74.78, yielding a differential of 19.10. The average risk-sharing compensation of NOK 2.89, in column 1 in both Panels A and B, line 2 within each, is taken from Table 10, column 2, line 2: On average NOK 2.89 of the wage differential of 19.10 is due to risk compensation, that is, 15.1% of the differential (0.151 = 2.89/19.10). The rest is compensation for effort or productivity. Again, the average effort compensation is the average wage differential minus the average risk compensation, in Panel A as 16.21 (=19.10−2.89). In Panel B, column 3, line 1, the wage differential of NOK 20.04 is taken from Table 4, Panel B, column 3, line 5. The average risk-sharing compensation is the same as in Panel A. The average effort compensation is then 17.15 (=20.04−2.89).

But what do these results look like for the wage differential at the occupation-establishment level? Panel B of Table 11 gives the answer. Piece-rate workers earn NOK 8.09 or 11.83% more than time-rate workers (from Table 4, Panel B, col. 1, line 5). The risk-compensation part of the wage differential is in absolute terms the same as in Panel A (0.22), but in relative terms much smaller, 2.7% (0.027 = 0.22/8.09). For the mixed-rate workers, comparing their wages on piece- to those on time-rate jobs, the risk compensation in percentage terms is of same magnitude as in Panel A.

The conclusion is that output-related payment systems primarily lead to increased output, which gets translated into higher wages. Only secondarily do they contain a risk-sharing component. It is not absent from the wage. It is just not a substantial part of the wage differential.

CONCLUSIONS

We have shown, unambiguously, that there is a substantial average wage payoff from working on some incentive system. When employed in the same occupation and in the same occupation-establishment unit, piece-rate workers on average earn respectively 7.78 and 11.83% more per hour than those on time-rate systems. The wage advantage to workers on mixed-rate systems is almost as pronounced, of 6.70 and 8.29% at the occupation and occupation-establishment levels. And when comparisons are made for the piece-rate jobs of mixed-rate workers, the wage advantage relative to time-rate workers is considerable, 27.47% at the occupation-establishment level.

Second, we have illustrated that there probably are productivity effects of incentive systems. For workers on mixed-rate systems, at the individual level, wages are 29% higher on piece- than time-rate jobs. This likely reflects some productivity differences induced when switching to piece-rate jobs, as documented using actual output data in Lazear (2000). Additionally, from a different angle, we report that the gender wage gap at the occupation-establishment level closely reflects presumed productivity differences between the sexes in different lines of work. In occupations where men are thought to be at a productivity advantage, the wage gap is bigger, while in occupations where women are thought to be more productive, the wage gap is in their favor.

Third, we have shown that there is uncertainty in wages under output-related systems. A noticeable percent of the incentive workers earn lower wages than the time-rate workers in the same occupation-establishment unit. Related to this, we documented that there is some risk compensation for working on output-related systems. The higher the uncertainty of wages at the occupation-establishment level, the higher the average wages at that level.

And finally, we illustrated how the wage differential between time- and piece-rate workers probably mostly consists of compensation for extra effort, while a small part consists of compensation for extra risks. About 14% of the overall wage differential is due to risk compensation, while 86% to effort compensation. At the occupation-establishment level, an even higher percentage of the pay differential is due to effort compensation, an entire 97%.

The last result makes sense. For the employer there would be little point in using output-related payment systems if these primarily allocate risks to the workers and only secondarily increase output. With no or little increase in output, paying the workers the risk compensation associated with working on piece rates would seem futile. It would increase the average wage bill, increase variation in wages among workers, but would not lead to an increase in output. The only observable change would be in decreased expected profits. The employer would be worse off and workers would not be better off. There would be no sharable gain from output-related wage systems.

Returning to our original concern, and those of Sørensen (1994), there is no question that wage systems have distributional consequences. At the occupation and occupation-establishment level these are substantial, of the same magnitude as the gender wage gap for the former and considerably larger for the latter, in the case of Norway (Petersen et al., 1997). We repeat Sørensen's (1994, p. 517) view: "Surprisingly, little attention has been focused on the distributional consequences of these systems, that is, on how they affect earnings." This is one of a few extensive empirical papers on the effects of output-related payment systems on wage levels, wage inequality, productivity, and risk-sharing, using unique data from Norway.

As to the generalizability of our findings, this is unproblematic. Our data cover the entire occupational spectrum, a wide array of establishments, and virtually every manufacturing industry in the private sector in Norway. For wages of blue-collar workers, we think our results give as accurate a picture as can currently be had, clearly ignoring many details, but without question extensive in its coverage.

But do the results extend to other kinds of employees? Many of the processes in connection with output-related wage systems clearly operate in a similar way among sales and even among some clerical and office workers. For example, among workers in insurance companies, number of insurance policies sold and number of claims processed have a status comparable to number of shirts stitched. Similarly in banks, number of calls answered and number of customers served are central performance measures, and individual employees may be rewarded for these. The same holds in many other types of jobs: in hotels, restaurants, hospitals, laundries, parts of transportation (taxis), garbage collection, mortgage industry, and more.

But what about professional jobs? While it is true that additional factors enter into professional work, such as perhaps a larger emphasis on quality, and certainly a larger array of output and performance aspects to measure and evaluate, especially those related to face time with clients, it is still the case that many of the processes relevant for blue-collar workers matter here too. Doctors diagnose patients and perform medical procedures, the number of which corresponds to piece-rate output, and the absence of medical malpractice complaints corresponds to quality. Professors advise undergraduate and graduate students, and are sometimes given what amounts to piece-rate credits for this. Lawyers serve clients, the number of which can be rewarded by piece rates, and the success in winning cases corresponds to quality. And also among blue-collar workers, which we have studied, is not only quantity but also quality central. Firms that consistently produce lower quality at same prices as competitors will sooner or later be in financial trouble. On balance, the commonalities in the use of output-related wage systems between blue-collar and other types of work may be larger than the differences.

NOTES

1. Sørensen (1994, p. 524) points out: "There are few areas of research that provide a more fruitful arena for interdisciplinary research than the study of how incentives are used by firms to increase the productivity of workers . . .."

2. As Holmlund (1991, pp. 40–41, our translation) writes: "This lively theoretical analysis has however resulted in surprisingly few studies of the relationship between payment systems and productivity . . . Here there is beyond doubt considerable room for more refined studies."

3. Many of the same concerns have been in focus in the Marxist labor-process literature, referred to as the purpose of extracting labor power (e.g. Burawoy, 1979, Chaps 3–4; Lazonick, 1990, Chaps. 1–2).

4. There is considerable research on the impact of such systems on pay among executives (e.g. Jensen & Murphy, 1990; and for Sweden, Meyerson, 1994, 1995), but very little for other kinds of employees.

5. There is of course important research on inequality more generally in Scandinavia (Holmlund, 1994; Westergård-Nielsen, 1994), including research on differences between men and women (e.g. le Grand, 1991), but little that studies this in connection with payment systems.

6. Very few studies have been made of the effects of payment system on wages. Pencavel (1977) studied the wages of 183 punch-operators in a Chicago factory, Seiler (1984) studied workers in the footwear and clothing industries, Mitchell et al. (1990) reported average wage differentials by payment system across several industries, and Petersen (1991, 1992c) studied production workers in the nonferrous foundries industry and salespersons in department stores. Paarsch and Shearer (1999, 2000) provide evidence among Canadian mine workers in the 1920s. For Sweden, Östros (1990) studied the engineering industry

while le Grand (1989) included a dummy variable for piece-rate work in a wage equation using data from the Swedish Level of Living from 1981. See also le Grand (1996). These studies all find a pay premium for piece-rate work. Meyersson-Milgrom et al. (2002) use the same design as below and similar data from Finland.

7. In his study of piece-rate work and productivity Max Weber remarked: "On the work suitability of the genders there are hardly any exact investigations." This is followed by the statement that on the one hand, "It is beyond doubt that within the linen textile factory men are at an advantage on the wide machine (for bed clothing and the like)," while on the other hand, "At the handkerchief machine it appears to me that females decidedly are best suited" (Weber, [1908]1924, p. 163, our translation).

8. Remarkably little has been done on this since Weber's (1908[1924]) study. Some work has been done on productivity in agriculture (Saito, 1994; Smith, 1943). Closer in spirit to the analyses we propose are the results from the Swedish machinery industry reported in Chen and Edin (1994), however, using more restricted data.

9. See Hey (1979, p. 52) for a discussion of when the variance is an appropriate measure of uncertainty.

10. Note that $\hat{\sigma}^2_{w_{I,oe}}$ is an estimated regressor (Pagan, 1984), which raises some statistical problems that we will not deal with.

11. As already mentioned, the procedure can also be given a justification from a more elaborate mathematical model, as in Petersen (1991), based on Holmström and Milgrom (1987).

ACKNOWLEDGMENTS

Trond Petersen wrote his Ph.D. thesis (1987), *Incentives and Wage Inequality*, the topic of the present paper, at the University of Wisconsin, Madison, with Aage B. Sørensen as the thesis chair. Vemund Snartland wrote his MA thesis (1995) at the University of Oslo, with Trond Petersen as the thesis chair, also on the topic of incentive systems and wages. Aage B. Sørensen (1994) wrote the article "Firms, Wages, and Incentives." The present article takes its title from Sørensen's article and draws on empirical results in Snartland's MA thesis, especially Tables 1, 3–5 and 7–9 below. The article follows the framework in Meyersson-Milgrom et al. (2002), which in turn relied heavily on Snartland (1995), Petersen and Snartland (1993), and Petersen (1991). We thank Karen Modesta Olsen for comments.

REFERENCES

Burawoy, M. (1979). *Manufacturing consent*. Chicago: University of Chicago Press.

Chen, P., & Edin, P.-A. (1994). Gender wage differentials, discrimination and work effort across methods of pay. In: B. Holmlund (Ed.), *Pay, Productivity, and Policy* (Chap. 3). Stockholm: Trade Union Institute for Economic Research.

Edwards, P. K. (1986). *Conflict at work*. Oxford, UK: Basil Blackwell.

le Grand, C. (1989). *Interna arbetsmarknader, ekonomisk segmentering och social skiktning*. Stockholm, Institutet för social forskning.

le Grand, C. (1991). Explaining the male-female wage gap: Job segregation and solidarity wage bargaining in Sweden. *Acta Sociologica*, *34*(4), 261–278.

le Grand, C. (1996). Lön för mödan? Arbetsmotivation och nya löneformer. In: Å. Sandberg (Ed.), *Ledning För Alla*. Stockholm: Förlag SNS.

Hey, J. D. (1979). *Uncertainty in economics*. New York: New York University Press.

Holmlund, B. (1991). Produktivitetsutveckling och belöningssystem. In: *Arbetskraft, arbetsmarknad och produktivitet* (pp. 21–44). Expertrapport Nr. 4 till Produktivitetsdelegationen. Stockholm: Allmänna Förlaget.

Holmlund, B. (Ed.) (1994). *Pay, productivity, and policy*. Stockholm: Trade Union Institute for Economic Research.

Holmström, B. (1979). Moral hazard and observability. *Bell Journal of Economics*, *10*(1), 74–91.

Holmström, B., & Milgrom, P. (1987). Aggregation and linearity in the provision of intertemporal incentives. *Econometrica*, *55*(2), 303–328.

Jensen, M. C., & Murphy, K. (1990). Performance pay and top management incentives. *Journal of Political Economy*, *98*, 225–263.

Kanter, R. M. (1990). The attack on pay. In: V. R. Vroom (Ed.), *Manage People, Not Personnel. Motivation and Performance Appraisal* (pp. 137–152). Boston, MA: Harvard Business School Press.

Lazear, E. P. (1986). Salaries and piece rates. *Journal of Business*, *59*(3), 406–431.

Lazear, E. P. (1995). *Economics of personnel*. Cambridge, MA: MIT Press.

Lazear, E. P. (2000). Performance pay and productivity. *American Economic Review*, *90*(5), 1346–1361.

Lazonick, W. (1990). *Competitive advantage on the shop floor*. Cambridge, MA: Harvard University Press.

Lupton, T. (1963). *On the shop floor*. London: Pergamon Press.

Mathewson, S. B. (1931, rpt. 1969). *Restriction of output among unorganized workers*. Carbondale, IL: Southern Illinois Press.

Meyerson, E. M. (1994). *Kompensationskontrakt i Börsnoterade Företag. En Studie av Ledningsgruppsmedlemmars Inkomster och Förmåner under 1980–talet*. Industriens Utredningsinstituts Skriftserie. Stockholm.

Meyerson, E. M. (1995). Kompensationskontrakt i svenska börsnoterade företag. *Ekonomisk debatt*, *23*(3), 217–224.

Meyersson-Milgrom, E. M., Petersen, T., & Asplund, R. (2002). Pay, risk, and productivity. The case of Finland, 1980–1996. *Finnish Economic Papers*, *15*(1), 3–23.

Milgrom, P., & Roberts, J. (1992). *Economics, organization, and management*. Englewood Cliffs, NJ: Prentice-Hall.

Mitchell, D. J. B., Lewin, D., & Lawler, E. E., III (1990). Alternative pay systems, firm performance, and productivity. In: A. S. Blinder (Ed.), *Paying for Productivity. A Look at the Evidence* (pp. 15–94). Washington, DC: Brookings Institution.

Nilsen, J. (2003). Finske menn får ikke napp i norske fiskerier. Newsreport in *Aftenposten* April 11, 2003.

Östros, T. (1990). *Lönestruktur i verkstadsindustrien – en empirisk studie*. Forskningsrapport nr. 33, FIEF. Stockholm.

Paarsch, H. J., & Shearer, B. S. (1999). The response of worker effort to piece rates. *The Journal of Human Resources*, *34*, 643–667.

Paarsch, H. J., & Shearer, B. S. (2000). Piece rates, fixed wages, and incentive effects: Statistical evidence from payroll record. *International Economic Review*, *41*(1), 59–92.

Pagan, A. (1984). Econometric issues in the analysis of regressions with generated regressors. *International Economic Review*, *25*(1), 221–247.

Pencavel, J. H. (1977). Work effort, on-the-job screening, and alternative methods of remuneration. In: R. G. Ehrenberg (Ed.), *Research in Labor Economics* (Vol. 1, pp. 225–258). Greenwich, CT: JAI Press.

Petersen, T. (1987). *Incentives and wage inequality*. Ph.D. thesis, Department of Sociology, University of Wisconsin, Madison, Wis.

Petersen, T. (1991). Reward systems and the distribution of wages. *Journal of Law, Economics, and Organization*, *7*(Special Issue), 130–158.

Petersen, T. (1992a). Individual, collective, and systems rationality in work groups: Dilemmas and market-type solutions. *American Journal of Sociology*, *98*(3), 469–510.

Petersen, T. (1992b). Individual, collective, and systems rationality in work groups: Dilemmas and nonmarket solutions. *Rationality and Society*, *4*(3), 332–355.

Petersen, T. (1992c). Payment systems and the structure of inequality: Conceptual issues and analysis of salespersons in department stores. *American Journal of Sociology*, *98*(1), 64–107.

Petersen, T. (1993). Recent developments in the economics of organization: The principal-agent relationship. *Acta Sociologica*, *36*(3), 277–293.

Petersen, T., & Snartland, V. (1993). *En vurdering av datas egnethet for videre analyse av belønningssystemer i formelle organisasjoner*. Report to NHO. Oslo: University of Oslo.

Petersen, T., Snartland, V., Becken, L.-E., & Olsen, K. M. (1997). Within-job wage discrimination and the gender wage gap, the case of Norway. *European Sociological Review*, *13*(2), 199–213.

Phelps Brown, H. (1977). *The inequality of pay*. Oxford, UK: Oxford University Press.

Roethlisberger, F. J., & Dickson, W. J. (1939). *Management and the worker: An account of the research program conducted by the Western Electric Company*. Hawthorne Works, Chicago. Cambridge, MA: Harvard University Press.

Roy, D. F. (1953). Work satisfaction and social rewards in quota achievement: An analysis of piecework incentive. *American Sociological Review*, *18*(5), 505–514.

Saito, K. (1994). *Raising the productivity of women farmers in sub-Saharan Africa*. Washington, DC: World Bank.

Seiler, E. (1984). Piece rate vs. time rate: The effects of incentives on earnings. *Review of Economics and Statistics*, *66*(3), 363–375.

Shavell, S. (1979). Risk-sharing and incentives in the principal and agent relationship. *Bell Journal of Economics*, *10*(1), 55–73.

Smith, J. H. (1943). Work output capacity of women employed in agriculture. *Welsh Journal of Agriculture*, *17*, 51–58.

Snartland, V. (1995). *Lønnssystemer i industrien: en empirisk undersøkelse*. MA thesis in Sociology, Oslo, University in Oslo.

Sørensen, A. B. (1994). Firms, wages and incentives. In: N. J. Smelser & R. Swedberg (Eds), *Handbook of Economic Sociology* (pp. 504–528). Princeton University Press.

SOU (1991). *Drivkrafter för Produktivitet och Velstand. Produktivitetsdelegationens Betänkande*. Stockholm: Allmänna Förlaget.

Stiglitz, J. E. (1975). Incentives, risk, and information: Notes towards a theory of hierarchy. *Bell Journal of Economics*, *6*(2), 552–579.

Weber, M. ([1908] 1924). Zur psychophysik der industriellen arbeit. In: *Gesammelte Aufsätze zur Soziologie und Sozialpolitik* (pp. 61–255). Tübingen: Verlag von J. C. B. Mohr.

Westergård-Nielsen, N. (Eds) (1994). *The Nordic labor markets in the 1990s. Wage differentials in the Nordic countries*. Amsterdam: North-Holland.

Whyte, W. F. (1955). *Money and motivation: An analysis of incentives in industry*. New York: Harper.

ABOUT THE AUTHORS

Hans-Peter Blossfeld is Professor and Chair in Sociology at the Otto Friedrich University of Bamberg. Since 1990 he has been editor of the *European Sociological Review*. He has published 16 books and over 120 articles on social inequality, youth, family, and educational sociology, labor market research, demography, social stratification and mobility, the modern methods of quantitative social research, and statistical methods for longitudinal data analysis.

Sonja Drobnič is Professor of Sociology at the University of Hamburg, Germany. Her main research interests include life-course research and gender, in particular the employment dynamics of couples and their retirement patterns, as well as issues in social stratification, comparative research, and longitudinal research methods.

Gøsta Esping-Andersen is Professor of Sociology and Dean at Universitat Pompeu Fabra (Barcelona). His most recent book is *Why We Need a New Welfare State* (with Duncan Gallie, Anton Hemerijck and John Myles, Oxford, 2003). Has also worked extensively for the OECD, the World Bank, and the UN, as well as for several European Union Presidencies. He received a doctor honoris causis from Roskilde University in 2001.

Maureen T. Hallinan is White Professor of Sociology at the University of Notre Dame and Director of the Center for Research on Educational Opportunities. She conducts research in the sociology of education, examining the effects of school organization on student achievement and social development. She is currently principal investigator in a five-year study, funded by the U.S. Department of Education, on school sector effects on student outcomes.

Robert M. Hauser is Vilas Research Professor of Sociology at the University of Wisconsin-Madison. His current research interests include trends in educational progression among racial and ethnic groups, policy uses of educational assessments, effects of families on social and economic inequality, and changes in socioeconomic standing, health, and well-being across the life course.

Peter Hedström is an Offical Fellow of Nuffield College, Oxford University. His interests focus on action-based theorising, macro-level outcomes of individual actions, and quantitative methods appropriate for analyzing such processes. Currently he is completing a book manuscript entitled *Dissecting the Social: On the Principles of Analytical Sociology*.

Arne L. Kalleberg is a Kenan Distinguished Professor of Sociology and Senior Associate Dean for the Social Sciences at the University of North Carolina at Chapel Hill. He has published over 100 articles and chapters, and has co-authored or co-edited eight books, dealing with topics related to the sociology of work, organizations, occupations and industries, labor markets, and social stratification. His current research addresses issues related to job quality and changing work attitudes in the United States, the meaning of time at work, the mismatching of persons and jobs, and changing employment relations in the United States and Norway.

Rakesh Khurana is an Assistant Professor at Harvard Business School. His research examines the social context of business leadership and the allocation of leadership positions. He is the author of *Searching for a Corporate Savior: The Irrational Quest for Charismatic CEOs* (Princeton University Press, 2002).

Warren N. Kubitschek is a Research Associate in the Center for Research on Educational Opportunity at the University of Notre Dame. His research is primarily in the sociology of education. His current work examines school organization and climate, sector differences, and educational achievement.

Mark W. McKerrow, M.A., is a Ph.D. candidate in Sociology, Cornell University, Ithaca, NY. His interests include lifetime-earnings inequality, labor market discrimination, and quantitative methodology. He is currently working on his dissertation, which deals with the role of selection on intergroup differences in the relationship between earnings and education.

Stephen L. Morgan, Ph.D., is Associate Professor, Department of Sociology at Cornell University. His areas of interest include social stratification, sociology of education, economic sociology, and quantitative methodology. His recent projects include investigations of changes in earnings inequality over the past two decades and the social organization of apprenticeship education among shoemakers in Kano, Nigeria. He has just completed a book on models of educational attainment, entitled *On the Edge of Commitment*, to be published by Stanford University Press in January 2005.

John Myles is Canada Research Chair and Professor of Sociology at the University of Toronto and Visiting Research Scholar at Statistics Canada. His recent research has focused on themes related to income security and public policy in Europe and North America. Most recently, he collaborated with Gosta Esping-Andersen, Duncan Gallie and Anton Hemerijck on *Why We Need a New Welfare State* (Oxford, 2002). With colleagues at Statistics Canada, he complements this program of macro-level, institutional, research with on ongoing program of micro-level, quantitative, analysis of income inequality and poverty.

Michèle Ollivier is Associate Professor of Sociology at the University of Ottawa. Her main research area is culture and inequality. Her current research interests include the transformation of tastes in contemporary societies, minority francophone women's access to and use of information and communication technologies, and feminist research methodologies.

Trond Petersen is a Professor of Sociology (and a 0 percent professor in the Haas School of Business) at the University of California, Berkeley. His research and teaching are in the areas of inequality and social stratification, organizations, and quantitative methods. He has also taught at the University of Oslo and previously at Harvard University. His most recent publication is "The Opportunity Structure for Discrimination," *American Journal of Sociology, 108*(4), January 2004 (with Ishak Saporta).

Mikołaj Jan Piskorski is an Assistant Professor of Organizational Behavior at the Graduate School of Business at Stanford University. His research focuses on sources of structural inequality in markets. He examines the emergence of structural advantages and disadvantages in three types of markets: labor markets, production markets and prestige markets.

Rachel A. Rosenfeld (1948–2002) was a William R. Kenan, Jr. Distinguished Professor of Sociology at the University of North Carolina at Chapel Hill. She was president of the Southern Sociological Society in 2001–2002. Her research focused on the influence of social stratification on career and job mobility, particularly for women. Her recent research included studies of the U.S. Women's movement, work histories of women, academic careers, and work-family policies in advanced industrialized countries.

Vemund Snartland teaches statistical methods in sociology at the University of Bergen, Norway, and conducts research at the Institute for Research in Economics and Business Administration. He is currently working on a project studying the careers of entrepreneurs, including the mechanisms that initiate entrepreneurship.

APPENDIX A: AAGE B. SØRENSEN'S PUBLICATION LIST

BOOKS AND MONOGRAPHS

Sørensen, A. B., & Christensen, L. (1966). *De studerendes sociale og geografiske oprindelse* (The Social and Geographical Origin of Students). Copenhagen: Nyt fra Samfundsvidenskaberne (Vol. 3).

Sørensen, A. B., & Sørensen, A. (1977). *Mathematical sociology: A trend report and an annotated bibliography* (Vol. 23, No. 2, of *Current Sociology*). Hague: Mouton.

Sørensen, A. B., Weinert, F., & Sherrod, L. (Eds) (1986). *Human development: Multidisciplinary perspectives*. Hillsdale, NJ: Lawrence Erlbaum.

Allardt, E., Lysgaard, S., & Sørensen, A. B. (1988). *Sociologin i sverige: Vetenskap, miljö och organisation* (Sociology in Sweden: Science, Culture and Organization). Uppsala: Swedish Science Press.

Sørensen, A. B., & Spilerman, S. (Eds) (1993). *Social theory and social policy: Essays in honor of James S. Coleman*. Westport, CT: Praeger Publishers.

RESEARCH ARTICLES

Sørensen, A. B. (1969). Social ulighed i fordelingen af uddannelse i et uddannelsessystem i vaekst. *Sociologiske Meddelelser*, *13*(1–2), 5–22.

Sørensen, A. B. (1970). Organizational differentiation of students and educational opportunity. *Sociology of Education*, *43*(Fall), 355–376.

Sørensen, A. B. (1971). Simulation. In: K. Svalastoga (Ed.), *Sociologisk Metodik II* (pp. 106–128). Copenhagen: Jørgen Paludans Forlag.

Sørensen, A. B. (1971). Equality of educational opportunity in an expanding educational system. *Acta Sociologica*, *14*(3), 151–161.

Coleman, J. S., Blum, Z. D., Sørensen, A. B., & Rossi, P. H. (1972). White and black careers during the first decade of labor force experience, Part I: Occupational status. *Social Science Research*, *1*(3), 243–270.

Holland, J. L., Sørensen, A. B., Clark, J. P., Nafziger, D. H., & Blum, Z. D. (1973). Applying an occupational classification to a representative sample of work histories. *Journal of Applied Psychology*, *53*(1), 34–41.

Kalleberg, A. L., & Sørensen, A. B. (1973). The measurement of the effects of overtraining on job attitudes. *Sociological Methods and Research*, *2*(2), 215–238.

Greenberger, E., & Sørensen, A. B. (1974). Toward a concept of psycho-social maturity. *Journal of Youth and Adolescence*, *3*(4), 329–358.

Sørensen, A. B. (1974). A model for occupational careers. *American Journal of Sociology*, *80*(1), 44–57.

Michener, H. A., Cohen, E. D., & Sørensen, A. B. (1975). Social exchange: Predicting interpersonal outcomes in 4-event, 3-person systems. *Journal of Personality and Social Psychology*, *32*(2), 283–293.

Myles, J. F., & Sørensen, A. B. (1975). Elite and status attainment models of inequality of opportunity. *Canadian Journal of Sociology*, *1*(1), 75–88.

Sørensen, A. B. (1975). Growth in occupational achievement: Investment in human capital or social mobility. In: K. C. Land & S. Spilerman (Eds), *Social Indicator Models* (pp. 335–360). New York: Russell Sage.

Sørensen, A. B. (1975). Models of social mobility. *Social Science Research*, *4*(2), 65–92.

Sørensen, A. B. (1975). The structure of intragenerational mobility. *American Sociological Review*, *40*(4), 456–471.

Sørensen, A. B. (1975). Uddannelse og ulighed (Education and inequality). *Dansk Pædagogisk Tidskrift*, *25*(7), 285–292.

Sørensen, A. B. (1976). Models and strategies in research on attainment and opportunity. *Social Science Information*, *15*(1), 71–91.

Sørensen, A. B., & Hallinan, M. T. (1976). A stochastic model for change in group structure. *Social Science Research*, *5*(1), 43–61. Also in: P. Krishnan (Ed.) (1977), *Mathematical Models in Sociology. The Sociological Monograph Series* (pp. 143–166). Keele: Keele University Press.

Michener, H. A., Cohen, E. D., & Sørensen, A. B. (1977). Social exchange: Transactional outcomes in five-event, four-person systems. *American Sociological Review*, *42*(3), 522–535.

Sørensen, A. B. (1977). Estimating rates from retrospective questions. In: D. Heise (Ed.), *Sociological Methodology 1977* (pp. 209–223). San Francisco: Jossey-Bass.

Sørensen, A. B. (1977). The structure of inequality and the process of attainment. *American Sociological Review*, *42*(6), 965–978.

Sørensen, A. B., & Hallinan, M. T. (1977). A reconceptualization of school effects. *Sociology of Education*, *50*(4), 273–289.

Sørensen, A. B. (1978). Causal analysis of cross-sectional and over time data: With special reference to the study of occupational achievement. In: W. Wesolowski, K. M. Slomczynski & B. W. Mach (Eds), *Social Mobility in Comparative Perspective* (pp. 111–129). Warszawa: Ossolineum.

Sørensen, A. B. (1978). Mathematical models in sociology. *Annual Review of Sociology*, *4*, 345–371.

Sørensen, A. B. (1978). Education, the process of attainment and the structure of inequality. In: R. Girod (Ed.), *Effets Economiques et Sociaux de L'enseignement* (pp. 221–242). Vevey, Switzerland: Delta Publishing Company.

Sørensen, A. B. (1978). Reconceptualizing school effects: A reply to Hauser. *Sociology of Education*, *50*(3), 233–236.

Sørensen, A. B., & Fuerst, S. (1978). Black-white differences in the occurrence of job shifts. *Sociology and Social Research*, *62*(4), 537–557.

Kalleberg, A. L., & Sørensen, A. B. (1979). The sociology of labor markets. *Annual Review of Sociology*, *5*, 351–379.

Rosenfeld, R. A., & Sørensen, A. B. (1979). Sex differences in patterns of career mobility. *Demography*, *16*(1), 89–101.

Sørensen, A. B. (1979). A model and a metric for the process of status attainment. *American Journal of Sociology*, *85*(2), 361–384.

Sørensen, A. B. (1979). Theory and models of mobility. *Institut für Höheren Studien Journal*, *3*, B79–B97.

Sørensen, A. B. (1980). Analysis of change in discrete variables. In: J. Clubb & E. K. Scheuch (Eds), *Historish-Sozialwissenschaftliche Forschungen* (pp. 284–299). Stuttgart: Klett-Cotta.

Sørensen, A. B., & Kalleberg, A. L. (1981). An outline of a theory of the matching of persons to jobs. In: I. Berg (Ed.), *Sociological Perspectives on the Labor Market* (pp. 49–74). New York: Academic Press. Also in: D. Grusky (Ed.) (1994). *Social Stratification: Class, Race and Gender in Sociological Perspective*. Westview Press.

Sørensen, A. B., & Tuma, N. B. (1981). Labor market structures and rates of job shifts. In: D. Treiman (Ed.), *Research in Social Stratification and Mobility* (Vol. 1, pp. 67–97).

Hallinan, M. T., & Sørensen, A. B. (1983). The formation and stability of instructional groups. *American Sociological Review*, *48*(6), 838–851.

Sørensen, A. B. (1983). Conceptual and methodological issues in sociological research on the labor market. *Work and Occupations*, *10*(August), 261–287.

Sørensen, A. B. (1983). Processes of allocation to open and closed positions in social structure. *Zeitschrift für Soziologie*, *12* (July), 203–224. Also in: J. Berger & M. Zelditch, Jr. (Eds) (1990), *Sociological Theories in Progress* (Vol. III, pp. 256–287). New York: Sage.

Hogan, D. P., Featherman, D. L., & Sørensen, A. B. (1984). Entry into adulthood: Profiles of young men in the 1950s. In: P. Baltes & O. G. Brim (Eds), *Life-Span Development and Behavior* (Vol. 6, pp. 160–203). New York: Academic Press.

McLanahan, S. S., & Sørensen, A. B. (1984). Life events and psychological well-being: A reexamination of theoretical and methodological issues. *Social Science Research*, *13*, 111–128.

Sørensen, A. B. (1984). The organizational differentiation of students in schools. In: H. Oosthoek & P. v. den Eeden (Eds), *Multilevel Aspects in the Educational Process* (pp. 25–43). London: Gordon & Breach.

Sørensen, A. B. (1984). Interpreting time dependency in career processes. In: A. Diekman & P. Mitter (Eds), *Progress in Stochastic Modeling of Social Processes* (pp. 89–122). New York: Academic Press.

Sørensen, A. B., & Hallinan, M. T. (1984). Race effects on the assignment to ability groups. In: L. C. Wilkinson, P. Peterson & M. Hallinan (Eds), *The Social Context of Instruction* (pp. 85–103). New York: Academic Press.

Glass, J., McLanahan, S. S., & Sørensen, A. B. (1985). The effects of selection bias in studies of the consequences of divorce. In: G. Elder (Ed.), *Life Course Dynamics* (pp. 267–281). Ithaca, NY: Cornell University Press.

Hallinan, M. T., & Sørensen, A. B. (1985). Class size, ability group size, and student achievement. *American Journal of Education*, *94*(1), 71–89.

Hallinan, M. T., & Sørensen, A. B. (1985). Ability grouping and student friendships. *American Educational Research Journal*, *22*(4), 485–499.

McLanahan, S. S., & Sørensen, A. B. (1985). Life events and psychological well-being over the life course. In: G. Elder (Ed.), *Life Course Dynamics* (pp. 217–238). Ithaca, NY: Cornell University Press.

Sørensen, A. B., & Hallinan, M. T. (1985). Student diversity and instructional grouping. In: A. Kerckhoff (Ed.), *Research in the Sociology of Education and Socialization* (Vol. 5, pp. 59–81). New York: JAI Press.

Hallinan, M. T., & Sørensen, A. B. (1986). Ability grouping: Two conceptual formulations. *Sociological Quarterly*, *27*(1), 1–14.

Sørensen, A. B. (1986). Theory and methodology in social stratification. In: U. Himmelstrand (Ed.), *The Sociology of Structure and Action* (pp. 69–95). New York: Sage.

Sørensen, A. B. (1986). Social structure and mechanisms of life course processes. In: A. B. Sørensen, F. Weinert & L. Sherrod (Eds), *Human Development: Multidisciplinary Perspectives* (pp. 177–198). Hillsdale, NJ: Lawrence Erlbaum.

Sørensen, A. B. (1986). Progress in studying change. A review essay on social dynamics: Models and methods by Nancy B. Tuma and Michael T. Hannan. *American Journal of Sociology*, *92*(3), 691–695.

Sørensen, A. B., & Hallinan, M. T. (1986). Effects of ability grouping on growth in academic achievement. *American Educational Research Journal*, *23*(4), 519–542.

Sørensen, A., & Sørensen, A. B. (1986). An event history analysis of the process of entry into first marriage. In: D. I. Kertzer (Ed.), *Family Relations in Life Course Perspectives* (pp. 53–72). New York: JAI Press.

Hallinan, M. T., & Sørensen, A. B. (1987). Ability grouping and sex differences in mathematics achievement. *Sociology of Education*, *60*(2), 63–72.

Sørensen, A. B. (1987). The organizational differentiation of students in schools as an opportunity structure. In: M. T. Hallinan (Ed.), *The Social Organization of Schools: New Conceptualizations of the Learning Process* (pp. 103–130). New York: Plenum Press.

Sørensen, A. B. (1987). Employment relations and employment processes. In: P. J. Pedersen & R. Lund (Eds), *Unemployment: Theory, Policy and Structure* (pp. 103–130). New York: Walter de Gruyter & Co.

Sørensen, A., & Sørensen, A. B. (1987). Social change and the life course. In: L. Kjølsrød, A. Ringen, K. Skrede & M. Vaa (Eds), *Applied Research and Structural Change in Modern Society* (pp. 93–111). Oslo: INAS.

Sørensen, A. B. (1989). Old age, retirement and inheritance. In: D. Kertzer & K. W. Schaie (Eds), *Social Structure and Aging: Comparative Perspectives on Age Structuring in Modern Societies* (pp. 197–213). Hillsdale, NJ: Lawrence Earlbaum.

Sørensen, A. B. (1989). Schools and the distribution of opportunities. In: K. Namboodiri & R. G. Corwan (Eds), *Research in the Sociology of Education and Socialization* (Vol. 8, pp. 3–25). New York: JAI Press.

Sørensen, A. B., & Blossfeld, H.-P. (1989). Socioeconomic opportunities in Germany in the post-war period. In: A. Kalleberg (Ed.), *Research in Social Stratification and Mobility* (Vol. 8, pp. 85–106). New York: JAI Press.

Palloni, A., & Sørensen, A. B. (1990). Methods for the analysis of event history data: A didactic overview. In: P. B. Baltes, D. L. Featherman & R. M. Lerner (Eds), *Life-Span Development and Behavior* (Vol. 10, pp. 291–323). Hillsdale, NJ: Lawrence Earlbaum.

Song, H. K., & Sørensen, A. B. (1990). State and economic segmentation: An analysis of effects of export promotion strategy on wage differentials in Korea's manufacturing industries. *Korean Journal of Population and Development*, *19*(1), 1–26.

Sørensen, A. B. (1990). Employment sector and unemployment processes. In: K. U. Mayer & N. B. Tuma (Eds), *Applications of Event History Analysis to Life Course Research* (pp. 96–112). Madison, WI: University of Wisconsin Press.

Sørensen, A. B. (1990). Wissenschaftliche werdegänge und akademische arbeitsmärkte. In: P. H. Hofschneider & K. U. Mayer (Eds), *Generationsdynamik und Innovation in der Grundlagenforschung* (pp. 75–101). München: Max-Planck-Gesellschaft.

Sørensen, A. B. (1990). Throwing the sociologists out? A reply to Smith. *American Sociological Review*, *55*(6), 842–845.

Sørensen, A. B. (1991). On the usefulness of class analysis in research on social mobility and socioeconomic inequality. *Acta Sociologica*, *34*(2), 71–88.

Sørensen, A. B. (1991). Merton and methodology: A review essay. *Contemporary Sociology*, *20*(2), 516–519.

Sørensen, A. B. (1991). Academic careers and academic labor markets. In: H. A. Becker (Ed.), *Life Histories and Generations* (Vol. I, pp. 59–88). Utrecht: ISOR.

Sørensen, A. B. (1992). Retirement, individual performance and labor market structures. In: W. J. A. van den Heuvel, R. Illsley, A. Jamieson & C. P. M. Knipscheer (Eds), *Opportunities and Challenges in an Ageing Society* (pp. 73–89). Amsterdam: North Holland.

Sørensen, A. B. (1992). Aktionsforskning om og i arbejdslivet. *Tidsskrift for Samfunnsforskning*, *33*(3), 213–230.

Sørensen, A. B. (1993). Comparative perspectives on gatekeeping in academia. In: W. R. Heinz (Ed.), *Status Passages, Institutions and Gatekeeping* (pp. 61–82). Weinheim: Deutscher Studien Verlag.

Sørensen, A. B. (1994). Concluding essay: Class, status and power. In: D. Grusky (Ed.), *Social Stratification: Class, Race and Gender in Sociological Perspective* (pp. 229–241). Westview Press.

Sørensen, A. B. (1994). Firms, wages and incentives. In: N. J. Smelser & R. Swedberg (Eds), *Handbook of Economic Sociology* (pp. 504–528). Princeton University Press.

Sørensen, A. B., & Spilerman, S. (1994). The intellectual contributions of James S. Coleman. In: A. B. Sørensen & S. Spilerman (Eds), *Social Theory and Social Policy: Essays in Honor of James S. Coleman* (pp. 3–10). Westport, CT: Praeger Publishers.

Sørensen, A. B. (1995). Evaluering som middel til organisationslæring (Evaluation and organizational learning). *UNIPED: Tidsskrift for Universitetslærere*, *17*(2–3), 35–44.

Sørensen, A. B. (1996). Educational opportunities and school effects. In: J. Clark (Ed.), *James S. Coleman* (pp. 207–226). London, UK: Falmer Press.

Sørensen, A. B. (1996). The structural basis of social inequality. *American Journal of Sociology*, *101*(5), 1333–1365.

Sørensen, A. B. (1996). Research on inequality and inequality of opportunity. In: T. Eriksson, P. F. Hjort, J. E. Kolberg, S. Stjernø & A. B. Sørensen (Eds), *Svensk forskning om välfärd* (pp. 89–110).Stockholm, Sweden: Socialvetenskapliga forskningsrådet.

Sørensen, A. B. (1997). Sociology in Scandinavian university systems. In: S. Grønmo & B. Henrichsen (Eds), *Society, University and World Community. Essays for Ørjar Øyen* (pp. 193–211). Oslo, Norway: Scandinavian University Press.

Sørensen, A. B. (1997). Registerforskning: Muligheder og udfordringer. *Samfundsøkonomen*, *4*(July), 43–48.

Sørensen, A. B. (1998). Career trajectories and the older worker. In: K. W. Schaie & C. Schooler (Eds), *Impact of Work on Older Individuals* (pp. 207–234).New York, NY: Springer Publishing Company.

Sørensen, A. B. (1998). Theoretical mechanisms and the empirical study of social processes. In: P. Hedström & R. Swedberg (Eds), *Social Mechanisms* (pp. 238–266). New York: Cambridge University Press.

Sørensen, A. B. (1998). On kings, pietism and rent-seeking in Scandinavian welfare states. *Acta Sociologica*, *41*(4), 363–376. With commentaries by Risto Alpuro, Peter Baldwin, Peter Gundelach, Tore Lindbekk, John. D. Stephens, and Pekka Sulkunen.

Sørensen, A. B. (1998). Response to my critics. *Acta Sociologica, 41*(4), 385–388.

Kang, D. L., & Sørensen, A. B. (1999). Ownership organization and firm performance. *Annual Review of Sociology, 25*, 121–144.

Morgan, S. L., & Sørensen, A. B. (1999). Parental networks, social closure, and mathematics learning: A test of James Coleman's social capital explanation of school effects. *American Sociological Review, 64*(5), 661–681.

Morgan, S. L., & Sørensen, A. B. (1999). Theory, measurement, and specification issues in models of network effects on learning: Reply to William J. Carbonaro and to Maureeen T. Hallinan & Warren N. Kubitschek. *American Sociological Review, 64*(5), 694–700.

Sørensen, A. B. (2000). Toward a sounder basis for class analysis. *American Journal of Sociology, 105*(6), 1523–1558.

Sørensen, A. B. (2000). Employment relations and class structure. In: R. Crompton, F. Devine, M. Savage & J. Scott (Eds), *Renewing Class Analysis*. Blackwell.

Sørensen, A. B., & Morgan, S. L. (2000). School effects: Theoretical and methodological issues. In: M. Hallinan (Ed.), *Handbook of Sociology of Education*. Plenum Publishing Company.

Sørensen, A. B. (2001). Careers, wealth and employment relations. In: I. Berg & A. L. Kalleberg (Eds), *Sourcebook on Labor Markets: Evolving Structures and Processes*. Kluwer/Plenum Press.

BOOK REVIEWS

Review of *Social Stratification and Career Mobility* edited by Karl Ulrich Mayer and Walter Müller. *American Journal of Sociology, 80*(6) (May 1975), 1509.

Review of *Beyond Economic Man* by Harvey Leibenstein (1978, October). *Sociology and Social Research, 63*(1), 237–239.

Review of *Sociological Methodology 1979* edited by Karl F. Schuessler (1979, October). *Contemporary Psychology, 24*(12), 984–985.

Review of *Applied Mathematical Demography*, by Nathan Keyfitz (1981, July). *American Journal of Sociology, 87*(1), 211–212.

Review of *Social Mobility and Social Structure* by Seppo Pontinen (1985, September). *Current Sociology, 14*(5), 617–618.

Review of *Longitudinal Analysis of Labor Market Data* edited by James J. Heckman and Burton Singer (1987, July). *Industrial and Labor Relations Review, 40*(4), 634–636.

Review of *High School Achievement* by James S. Coleman, Sally Kilgore and Thomas Hoffer and *Public and Private Schools* by James S. Coleman and Thomas Hoffer (1988, November). *American Journal of Sociology, 89*(3), 689–692.

Review of *The Constant Flux: A Study of Class Mobility in Industrial Society* by Robert Erikson and John H. Goldthorpe (1992, December). *European Sociological Review, 8*(3), 316–318.

Review of *Diverging Pathways: Social Structure and Career Deflections* by Alan C. Kerckhoff (1994, September). *American Journal of Sociology, 100*(2), 576–578.

Review of *Diversity in the Power Elite: Have Women and Minorities Reached the Top?* By Richard L. Zweigenhaft and G. William Domhoff (1999, March). New Haven, CT: Yale University Press. *American Journal of Sociology, 104*(4), 1576–1577.

Review of *Microfoundations, Method, and Causation: On the Philosophy of the Social Sciences* by Daniel Little (1999, July). New Brunswick, NJ: Transaction Publishers, 1998. *Contemporary Sociology*, *28*(4), 482–483.

Review of *Repositioning Class: Social Inequality in Industrialized Society.* By Marshall, Gordon (1999, July). London, UK: Sage. *The Annals of the American Academy*, *564*, 226.

APPENDIX B: MEMORIES OF AAGE B. SØRENSEN AS A MENTOR

In addition to his scholarly achievements, Aage was a superb teacher and one of sociology's most prolific mentors. In February 2001, Aage was nominated by a group of his former students for an Excellence in Mentoring Award from Harvard University, which he subsequently won. Printed below is an edited excerpt from one of the letters of nomination, which is primarily devoted to the testimonials of many of his more than 40 former Ph.D. students – some of whom were his students while he was at the University of Wisconsin at Madison from 1972 to 1984 and some of whom were his students after he came to Harvard in 1984. Their views were solicited specifically to support his candidacy for the award.

Dear Selection Committee:

Aage Sørensen is a rare scholar. He has a legitimate claim to be the one of the best social stratification researchers in the world and also one of sociology's most prolific mentors. Most scholars are only able to achieve such a dual distinction by forcing their students to work on their own ideas, thus killing two birds with one stone. Aage is completely different in this regard. He thrives on helping students to pursue their own interests, breeding within his students a self-sufficiency that assures their survival as they embark on their own careers.

When Aage arrived in Cambridge to help lead the reconstruction of Harvard's sociology department, he was immediately concerned with the overall welfare of the department's existing graduate students. One of these Harvard students writes:

> I recall when Aage became Chair, he early on met with the grad students and urged us to "get organized." I asked why he would invite mobilization of yet another political constituency that he would have to contend with as Chair (along with some difficult constituencies among the senior faculty). Later, when I became DGS [Director of Graduate Studies] at Cornell, I recalled his advice and the logic behind it, and urged our students to get organized as well. They of course also asked me the same question, and I told them this story and relayed Aage's corporatist reasoning (Michael Macy, Ph.D. 1985, Cornell University).

He took on a set of these students as his own, many of whose dissertation projects were already well underway. This came naturally to Aage, as he enjoyed meeting with students and learning about their own interests:

> He gave me lots of one-on-one time. He found out what I was interested in and wanted to do, then helped me do it (As contrasted with the style of some, which was to try to get you to do what THEY wanted done.) (Arne Kalleberg, Ph.D. 1975, University of North Carolina at Chapel Hill).

> Aage was always supportive of independent thinkers, always ready to debate, but never insisted that he always had to be right. That's what made him a great advisor (Jennifer Glass, Ph.D. 1983, University of Iowa).

> My department had been hostile to my area of study (sociology of sport) after my advisor left Wisconsin. Aage taught a stratification course I took, and he gave me excellent feedback on the term paper. When searching for someone to chair my dissertation committee, Aage agreed (and literally saved my doctoral degree). His questions, advice and easy-going style provided excellent guidance for me and other members of my committee. His demeanor and leadership style were nonthreatening to my department, and his advice and comments were readily accepted. The dissertation writing and defense went so smoothly it was unbelievable – all a product of Aage's mature, professional approach (Susan Greendorfer, Ph.D. 1974, University of Illinois at Urbana-Champaign).

Did he always enjoy these projects? I suspect that he did, but even if he did not, he would have agreed to advise all of them out of a sense of professional obligation. On this topic, Mark Chaves writes:

> A comment Aage once made to me has stuck with me and informed my own practice when grad students ask me to serve on committees for them. I don't remember the context, but I remember Aage saying that it was a faculty person's responsibility to serve on student committees and that one should almost never decline such a request. This stuck with me both as a sign of Aage's commitment to mentoring and as a worthy principle of professional practice. So far, I have followed it, never having turned down a request to serve on a sociology graduate student's M.A., Ph.D., or prelim committee. There have been times I've been tempted to say no, but then I remember Aage's admonition, and I say yes instead. I don't know whether Aage himself always adhered to this rule, but the fact that I have internalized it is probably the most concrete way in which Aage's mentoring has influenced me (Mark Chaves, Ph.D. 1991, University of Arizona).

This sense of duty, coupled with his encouragement and good humor, saved the careers of many students:

> I was discouraged that no faculty seemed interested in gender stratification and new feminist theories about work, and was tired of being poor in graduate school. On the verge of dropping out after four years in grad school, Sara McLanahan (my housemate at the time) introduced me to Aage one summer when he had just gotten back from a two year stint in Norway. I was complaining about no faculty being interested in my work, he was complaining about having no good students to mentor. When I told him I was thinking of quitting, he told me not to be foolish and said he'd be happy to work with me. He pulled some strings so I could work 3/4

> time and afford to eat more than frozen spinach and Noodleroni. I really think that if it hadn't been for Aage, I probably would have quit graduate school and never had a career in sociology (Jennifer Glass, Ph.D. 1983, University of Iowa).

Although the foregoing is sufficient testament to Aage's interest in letting students pursue topics of interest to them, this should not be taken to mean that he is a pushover, or not opinionated. Rather, he brings his own wide-ranging ideas to bear on the interests of his students, and he clearly thrives on claiming to be (and, in the process, often becoming) an expert in everything.

> I found Aage would give you sufficient leeway to pursue your own ideas, then would pose an (the) important question that would cause you to either see your ideas in a new and improved light (or to change them entirely) (John Dencker, Ph.D. 1999, University of Illinois at Urbana-Champaign).

> I think his strength was in the ability to allow you to study your own interests in the ways that you chose and yet give tremendous guidance at needed stages. It combined a hands-off, hands-on approach so well (Donna Eder, Ph.D. 1979, Indiana University).

Aage knew how to motivate his students, and like all good advisors, he recognized that not all students can be motivated in the same way. Because Aage tailored his mentoring tactics to his students' personalities, his students have very different memories of his demeanor. First, there are those who remember Aage as a nice guy:

> The phrase I recall most from him is "Let me see that smile". Even when I felt like work wasn't moving along as well as I would have liked, it did get me to smile (Lucia Benaquisto, Ph.D. 1991, McGill University).

> Aage always was a good listener, and asked probing questions. He was very supportive. He gave a lot of his time to me (Nancy Horak Randall, Ph.D. 1981, Wingate University).

> He was very enthusiastic about my work and that helped my motivation too. I also felt like he treated me as an equal in terms of scholarly ideas, learning from my ideas as I learned from his (Donna Eder, Ph.D. 1979, Indiana University).

> He was supportive without being controlling or suffocating, and critical without undermining self-confidence (Michael Macy, Ph.D. 1985, Cornell University).

Then, there are those who remember Aage as the disciplined taskmaster who doled out the bitter medicine:

> Aage was a merciless slavedriver as my dissertation advisor, a feature of our relationship that I only appreciated years later as I witnessed many a dissertator languishing from lack of attention from their advisors. At one point, Aage was insisting on a chapter a week. Either a new chapter or a revised chapter. Every Tuesday I had to produce one or the other. I finished my degree in record time as a result (Mary Visher, Ph.D. 1984, MPR Associates).

> His mentoring style was to gossip a lot, exchange jokes and then get down to the hard issues of my thesis. It usually didn't require much time on his part because few people are as good as he is at getting down to the key issues and expediting them lean and mean (Gøsta Esping-Andersen, Ph.D. 1978, Department of Political and Social Sciences, University of Pompeu Fabra).

> Aage was always supportive and fun to be around. But what I appreciated most was that he would push REALLY hard, asking all the tough questions (William T. Bielby, Ph.D. 1976, University of California at Santa Barbara).

> Aage worked with "two hands." With one hand he could make me feel like I was God's gift to sociology. With the other, that some argument or other I was making was "silly." His confidence in me boosted my own confidence and that allowed me to work effectively. His "critical" interventions inevitably led me to research strategies I would not have discovered on my own (John Myles, Ph.D. 1976, University of Toronto).

And then, there are those who remember Aage as a gifted sparring partner.

> Aage and I had many, many disagreements, but I never came away from one of our fights feeling anything less than exhilarated. Typically, we exchanged 6 to 8 heated emails, trying to outdo each other's lines of reasoning (sometimes on coauthored papers!). We would eventually find a middle ground and then agree to meet in his office. Making up with him in person was a bit like making up with your parents–slightly uncomfortable but very reassuring. He would often put his hand on my shoulder when I would enter his office, letting me feel like the prodigal son–a bit wayward, possibly too big for my britches, but certainly full of promise and still very much loved (Stephen Morgan, Ph.D. 2000, Cornell University).

While it would be nice to think that this was all strategy on Aage's part, it would be somewhat misleading to claim that it was. The truth is that Aage is extremely emotional and passionate about academic matters, and from time to time he lets it show.

> He invited me in to talk about the first chapter of my dissertation. I entered the room. He asked how I felt and then gave me an envelope. I put it in my bag. No, he said, you've got to read it right now. So I opened the letter. All it said was that I didn't give my best. Then Aage threw the entire first chapter in the garbage can. I was shocked but returned six weeks later with a chapter that is much cited (Jutta Allmendinger, Ph.D. 1989, Nuremberg).

But, he is never inflexible.

> When I was writing the most important chapter in my dissertation, his comment on my chapter seemed not proper. I wrote the chapter again in a very provocative way by taking an extreme position. He wrote me back right away with a very helpful comment, which said that "I may not be consistent with my previous comment . . ." (Kun Lee, Ph.D. 1994, Dongguk University).

These testimonials establish the emotional energy and vigor that Aage brought to his sessions with his students. The results were sometimes quite remarkable:

> If there is one talent that stands out among many, it is his truly amazing capability of unblocking a student and catapulting him or her back on track. I deliberately use the word catapulting because that is what he did. When he advised you it was like providing you with a turbo-engine.

> I remember from my own thesis writing one particular meeting – I doubt it lasted more than 20 minutes – but that meeting saved me months of (useless) work (Gøsta Esping-Andersen, Ph.D. 1978, Department of Political and Social Sciences, University of Pompeu Fabra).

> Aage taught me to think like a researcher. My first dissertation outline consisted of two parts with about 8 chapters on different questions related to the general topic in each. When I went to discuss it with him, he told me all the questions were excellent but that now I had to choose one of them and answer it well. He was right of course (John Myles, Ph.D. 1976, University of Toronto).

He is, nonetheless, willing to provide more than inspiration and provocative debate. He gets into the nitty-gritty details of argument construction and analysis:

> I was most impressed with the day that Aage helped me outline my dissertation chapters. It seemed that he created order out of chaos that day and helped my rambling thinking take a very satisfying shape. I was very motivated after that to carry out the steps that would produce those chapters (Donna Eder, Ph.D. 1979, Indiana University).

> I was always impressed by the fact that Aage always had time to meet with me, talk with me about my research, and always had a solution to the problems I brought him. He was always full of ideas as to how to go about trying to make non-significant results turn into something interesting and significant (Arne Kalleberg, Ph.D. 1975, University of North Carolina at Chapel Hill).

> At least when I was a grad student, he guided and mentored much more closely than just about anyone I knew or know (Rachel Rosenfeld, Ph.D. 1976).

Aage is thus a great motivator, full of emotion and intellectual passion. But, he is also extraordinarily charming and funny. He connects with his students on a personal level that all of us cherish. He simply has style, flair, and good humor:

> Since Aage and I were probably the only two Danish sociologists in the U.S. at the time, and since we came from the same original (and horrible department in Denmark), there was obviously a special bond of complicity between us.... We spent hours (with Mette of course, too) feeling great and exalted by putting down Danish sociology. We also wove together lofty plans and ideas of how one might make Danish sociology great, if only of course, they would listen to us. As it turned out, the Danish government actually appointed Aage to do just that (and he closed down the department!) (Gøsta Esping-Andersen, Ph.D. 1978, Department of Political and Social Sciences, University of Pompeu Fabra).

> He modeled a way of life that I found appealing – making time for leisure as well as work, and also finding many ways to make work fun rather than just pure work (Donna Eder, Ph.D. 1979, Indiana University).

> I'd share memories of the many Madison parties, but we always got so drunk and stoned that no one remembered anything the next day... Surely someone has incriminating photos from those days (William T. Bielby, Ph.D. 1976, University of California at Santa Barbara).

Indeed, one of his most charming personality traits is his Danish accent and his apparent inability to speak without mumbling half of his words. Although the following may not help him win the award, as it does not properly demonstrate just how gifted he is at finding tenure-track jobs for his students, I could not resist including it:

> In my last year, Aage advised me to apply to Arizona. I never did. Given Aage's pronunciation, it came out as a place I'd never heard of and decided it must be an obscure college somewhere (John Myles, Ph.D. 1976, University of Toronto).

Finally, it is important to note that Aage's mentoring extends beyond the completion of the Ph.D.:

> Aage's loyalty and sponsorship continued well into my career. He brought my work to the attention of others, proposed my name to write papers, participate in conferences etc. I returned to Canada after graduate school and I think in part he was working to keep me networked into U.S. sociology. He takes his students' careers very seriously (John Myles, Ph.D. 1976, University of Toronto).

> He advised me a lot over the years on my career . . . He is a hugely generous colleague just as he was a generous advisor (Gøsta Esping-Andersen, Ph.D. 1978, Department of Political and Social Sciences, University of Pompeu Fabra).

> Also, he continues to support his students after they graduate – suggesting them for panels, awards, etc. (Rachel Rosenfeld, Ph.D. 1976).

> He gave advice on many occasions about taking other positions, at Chicago, Washington (Seattle), Yale, Columbia, Northwestern, and University of Oslo. He was very important in the advice he gave, the single most important person I consulted with besides my wife. He must have written letters of reference, but this I don't know, but I know he talked with others about my work. He read drafts of a few papers and gave some comments. He had incisive comments and exquisite judgments on a number of such academic matters. If there was one person I liked to consult, it was Aage (Trond Petersen, Ph.D. 1987, University of California at Berkeley).

For all of these reasons, Aage B. Sørensen is most deserving of a GSC Excellence in Mentoring Award.